D0765529

Perspectives on Tax Reform

Richard E. Wagner
Roger A. Freeman
Charles E. McLure, Jr.
Norman B. Ture
Eric Schiff
foreword by
Thomas F. Johnson

Published in cooperation with the
American Enterprise Institute for
Public Policy Research

The Praeger Special Studies program—
utilizing the most modern and efficient book
production techniques and a selective
worldwide distribution network—makes
available to the academic, government, and
business communities significant, timely
research in U.S. and international economic, social, and political development.

Perspectives on Tax Reform
Death Taxes, Tax Loopholes, and the Value Added Tax

American Enterprise Institute Perspectives—I

Praeger Publishers   New York   Washington   London

PRAEGER SPECIAL STUDIES IN U.S. ECONOMIC, SOCIAL, AND POLITICAL ISSUES

Library of Congress Cataloging in Publication Data

Main entry under title:

Perspectives on tax reform.

(Praeger special studies in U.S. economic, social,
and political issues)
"Published in cooperation with the American
Enterprise Institute for Public Policy Research."
CONTENTS: Wagner, R. E. Death and taxes: some
perspectives on inheritance, inequality, and progressive
taxation. —Freeman, R. A. Tax loopholes: the legend
and the reality. —McLure, C. E., and Ture, N. B. Value
added tax: two views. [etc.]
1. Inheritance and transfer tax—United States—
Addresses, essays, lectures. 2. Income tax—
United States—Addresses, essays, lectures. 3.
Value-added tax—United States—Addresses, essays,
lectures. 4. Value-added tax—Europe—Addresses,
essays, lectures. I. Wagner, Richard E.
HJ2381.P47 1974   336.2'00973   74-1749
ISBN 0-275-09280-1

PRAEGER PUBLISHERS
111 Fourth Avenue, New York, N.Y. 10003, U.S.A.
5, Cromwell Place, London SW7 2JL, England

Published in the United States of America in 1974
by Praeger Publishers, Inc.

Printed in the United States of America

Competition of ideas is fundamental to a free society. Policy makers themselves rarely originate the concepts underlying the laws by which we are governed. They choose among practical options to formulate legislation, governmental directives, regulations, and programs. If there is no testing of ideas by competition, public policy decisions may undermine rather than bolster the foundations of a free society.

The American Enterprise Institute for Public Policy Research strives to foster innovative research, identify and present varying points of view on issues, formulate practical options, and analyze public policy proposals. The studies reprinted in this volume are representative of these efforts.

Monographs, however, are only one form AEI uses to promote competition of ideas. The Institute also sponsors lectures, debates, and panel discussions on issues of topical and enduring interest. The proceedings of these programs are available in video cassettes, audio cassettes, and in printed form.

AEI studies cover a wide range of issues: foreign and domestic, economic and political. They are of two basic types: those which deal with long-term issues and those which deal with current legislative proposals. The latter type of study (the Legislative Analysis series) provides members of Congress and others with a valuable service by summarizing the basic issues involved in proposed legislation as well as the pro and con arguments on the proposal. Other studies evaluate existing government programs and issues which are of enduring concern, such as inflation, defense policy, and, as in the studies presented in this volume, taxes.

Death and Taxes: Some Perspectives on Inheritance, Inequality, and Progressive Taxation, by Richard Wagner, associate professor of economics at the Virginia Polytechnic Institute and State University, Blacksburg, Virginia, is a careful and critical examination of the place of transfer taxation in the American revenue system. Dr. Wagner finds that the prevailing framework of death taxation is replete with inequity and inefficiency. Persons with equal incomes normally pay different amounts of tax; saving is retarded, inhibiting capital formation and economic progress; and, contrary to the conventional wisdom, contributions to private philanthropies are less generous than they would be in the absence of death taxes. Dr. Wagner also notes that these taxes produce insignificant revenue and have virtually no impact as instruments of "social justice." He recommends that separate taxes for wealth transfers be abolished, with such transfers being covered by a radically revised personal income tax.

Tax Loopholes: The Legend and the Reality, by Roger A. Freeman, a senior fellow at the Hoover Institution on War, Revolution and Peace at Stanford University, reviews the exemptions, exclusions, deductions and credits in the federal income tax that cause about half of all personal income in the United States to remain untaxed. It explores the charge that these so-called loopholes mainly benefit the wealthy and enable them to pay far less than their share of the federal income tax. Mr. Freeman shows that most "loopholes" are remedial provisions written into the law not by inadvertence or to favor the wealthy but to improve the equity of the tax structure or to serve other important policy objectives. His analysis of 1970 income tax returns reveals that most of the untaxed income—about $465 billion that year—goes to low- and middle-income taxpayers and that the share of income subject to the federal income tax rises sharply with income. Continued study and refinement of these remedial provisions is essential, the author suggests, but wholesale repeal would be detrimental to the American economy. This study is a joint publication of the American Enterprise Institute and the Hoover Institution on War, Revolution and Peace.

The final selections are devoted to a consideration of the advantages, disadvantages, and actual experiences with the value added tax (VAT). In *Value Added Tax: Two Views*, Charles E. McLure, Jr., professor of economics at Rice University, and Norman B. Ture, an economic consultant in Washington, D.C., offer the reader two sides of the current debate about the nature, burden, and effects of value added taxation. Would a VAT raise prices? Would it be regressive? Is the VAT basically a sales tax, or is it an income tax? Would it improve the U.S. balance of payments significantly? Would capital goods be exempt from the tax? What changes in other parts of the tax system would be necessary or desirable in the event that a VAT were adopted? The two authors disagree on these and other important questions concerning this widely discussed potential addition to the federal government's fiscal arsenal.

While the McLure and Ture selections are basically theoretical—although written in terms the layman can understand — *Value Added Taxation in Europe,* by Eric Schiff, an economic consultant in Washington, D.C., describes and analyzes the actual workings of the VAT in a dozen European countries. What effect has the value added tax had on price levels in the European countries where it has been introduced? What are the relative merits of the value added tax and the retail sales tax? Does European experience provide us with any information about what to expect if a value added tax were instituted in this country? Dr. Schiff's careful examination of these and other questions makes this study a significant contribution to the growing literature on an increasingly important area of tax policy.

The American Enterprise Institute for Public Policy Research, established in 1943, is a publicly supported, nonpartisan research and educational organization. Its purpose is to assist policy makers, scholars, businessmen, the press, and the public by providing objective analysis of national and international issues. Views expressed in the Institute's publications are those of the authors and do not necessarily reflect the views of the staff, officers, or trustees of AEI.

Thomas F. Johnson
Director of Research
American Enterprise Institute for Public
Policy Research
Washington, D.C.

VALUE ADDED TAX: TWO VIEWS
Charles E. McLure, Jr.
Norman B. Ture

LIST OF TABLES AND CHARTS
DEATH AND TAXES

TAX LOOPHOLES

VALUE ADDED TAX: TWO VIEWS

VALUE-ADDED TAXATION IN EUROPE

Chart

DEATH AND TAXES:
SOME PERSPECTIVES ON INHERITANCE, INEQUALITY, AND PROGRESSIVE TAXATION
Richard E. Wagner

ACKNOWLEDGMENTS

My preparation of this monograph has been aided by valuable counsel from several people. While I was preparing the first draft during the spring of 1971, Professor Jacques Melitz, then of Tulane University and now of the French Ministry of Finance, was a continual source of stimulating insight into basic issues concerning the role of inheritance in a free society. My approach to inheritance and the taxation of wealth transfers has been influenced considerably by our many discussions. During the fall of 1972 I received many helpful comments on a later version of this monograph from Martin J. Bailey of the University of Rochester and the U.S. Office of Tax Analysis, James M. Buchanan of Virginia Polytechnic Institute and State University, Harold M. Hochman of the Urban Institute, William A. Niskanen of the University of California, Berkeley, and Jacob A. Stockfish of the Rand Corporation.

The levy of a tax upon the occasion of a person's death has become a hallowed tradition of American fiscal practice. In 1825 Pennsylvania levied an inheritance tax of 2.5 percent on collateral heirs, thereby becoming the first state to tax wealth transferred at death. All states but Nevada now impose some form of tax upon such transfers of wealth. A federal inheritance tax was enacted, and later repealed, in the Stamp Act of 1797; subsequently such a tax was temporarily imposed during the Civil War and again during the Spanish-American War. It was not until the Revenue Act of 1916, however, that death taxation became a permanent fixture in the federal tax arsenal.

The federal government's system of transfer taxation has remained essentially unchanged for a generation. The present rate and bracket structure was adopted in 1941, and the only subsequent change of significance—the marital deduction—was introduced in 1948.

Interest in the performance of our system of transfer taxation has been growing steadily in recent years. During the past decade both the American Law Institute and the Brookings Institution sponsored major studies of our estate and gift taxes. These projects were followed on 5 February 1969 by the Treasury's proposals for substantial reform of our system of transfer taxation. And in a speech before the State Bank Division of the American Bankers Association on 12 October 1970, Wilbur D. Mills, chairman of the House Ways and Means Committee, said that reform of the estate and gift tax system stood high on his committee's agenda. Although recent developments have postponed such consideration, substantial interest nonetheless seems to exist concerning possible revision of Sections 20 and 25 of the Internal Revenue Code of 1954.

This volume explores several issues relating to transfer taxation. I shall try especially to place transfer tax reform into some perspective with regard to the larger issues of taxation and public expenditure. A particular tax institution may be examined within two distinct perspectives, and this monograph examines transfer taxation from both perspectives. One perspective views the prevailing format of separate tax provisions for wealth transfers as given and examines issues of reform within that context. If we 'assume that separate tax provisions for wealth transfers will remain in force, it is important to examine such issues as the choice of a rate structure, the selection of the unit of taxation, the response to trusts, the scope of gift taxation, and the treatment of concurrent taxation by federal and state governments. In a second, contrasting perspective, I consider the entire tax system as variable. Since transfer taxation is but one possible element of a tax system, the primary issue within this perspective is whether transfer taxation should continue as an independent form of taxation, or whether transfers of wealth should be treated as income under a considerably reformed personal income tax.

The analysis will shift intermittently between these two perspectives, at times examining the possible place of transfer taxation within the larger system of taxation, and at other times examining particular aspects of transfer taxation. Chapter 1 describes the essential purposes of a system of taxation and examines the possible scope for transfer taxation within this system. Chapter 2 analyzes the relation between progressive taxation, particularly transfer taxation, and inequality in the distribution of wealth and income. Chapters 3 and 4 examine particular aspects of transfer taxation: Chapter 3 considers some of the primary economic effects and Chapter 4 discusses some important, technical issues. Chapter 5 concludes by summarizing the implications of the preceding analysis for transfer tax reform. (The prevailing structure of transfer taxation is described in an appendix.)

CHAPTER

1

TRANSFER TAXATION
AND THE TAX SYSTEM

Since transfer taxation is but one element of our tax system, its role cannot meaningfully be discussed without first having some idea of the social function of a tax system. A tax system performs two primary functions: it raises revenue to finance the supply of public services and, in conjunction with public expenditures, it transfers wealth among individual citizens.[1] Transfer taxation must be evaluated, therefore, on the basis of its performance in both of these roles.

Transfer Taxation to Raise Revenue

The first of the two primary functions of a system of taxation is to raise revenue to finance the supply of public services. Publicly provided services, like parks, police, and education, differ from privately provided services in that, for the most part, they are not packaged and sold to individual consumers. Rather, such services are made freely available to all, with the services being financed by taxes levied upon the citizenry. A tax, then, is a political substitute for a market price.

The allocative performance of a system of taxation in financing public services depends primarily on how closely the tax institution establishes individual tax prices that approximate the prices that would be established by a private market. If the demand for public

[1] Richard A. Musgrave, *The Theory of Public Finance* (New York: McGraw-Hill, 1959), pp. 3-27. Musgrave lists three functions but recent research has made it questionable whether the third function—to stabilize the economy through variations in taxes and expenditures—can in fact be performed. See, for instance, Milton Friedman and David Meiselman, "The Relative Stability of Monetary Velocity and the Investment Multiplier in the United States, 1897-1958," in Commission on Money and Credit, *Stabilization Policies* (Englewood Cliffs, N. J.: Prentice-Hall, 1963), pp. 165-268.

services should rise proportionately with income, a system of proportional income taxation will approximate the results that would have emerged under a system of market pricing.[2] The selection of a tax institution, then, can clearly exert an important influence on the efficiency with which budgetary choices are made. Whenever services are not packaged and sold to individual consumers, the knowledge provided by market transactions regarding demand and cost is lost. Demand is instead reflected through a budgetary process, in which some tax institutions are more adequate proxies for market pricing than others. Hence it is important to consider the probable relation between the base of a tax and the demand for the service it finances.

A primary virtue of income taxation is that the demand for many public services varies more or less directly with income. Whether a tax system that substitutes perfectly for market pricing would be proportional or progressive, and if progressive, how progressive, depends upon the relation between the change in demand with respect to income and the change in tax liability with respect to income. At a very general level, and with numerous exceptions, however, a system of income taxation is a way of approximating the prices individual citizens would pay for those services if such services were packaged for sale on the market.

Are there reasonable grounds for suggesting that a tax on wealth or net worth could either substitute for income taxation or complement it?[3] If this question is answered "yes," we must then ask whether we can look upon taxation of wealth transferred at death as a convenient substitute for an annual tax on net worth. In principle, of course, a wealth tax is indistinguishable from an income tax, for any income flow can be assigned an equivalent capital value. If an asset yields an annual income of $10,000, and if the rate of return on capital (the interest rate) is 10 percent, the capital value of the asset will be $100,000. An annual tax of 10 percent on the income is then identical to an annual tax of 1 percent on the capital value. Since a capital value is simply a present discounted value of a future income stream, income taxation at t percent would be equivalent to capital taxation at tr percent, where r is the rate of interest. This identity of income and capital taxation suggests that only one of the two bases should be used.

---

[2] For an elaboration of this point and a specification of the necessary caveats, see James M. Buchanan, "Fiscal Institutions and Efficiency in Collective Outlay," *American Economic Review*, Proceedings, vol. 54 (May 1964), pp. 227-35.

[3] For a "yes" answer, see Alan A. Tait, *The Taxation of Personal Wealth* (Urbana, Ill.: University of Illinois Press, 1967), pp. 19-21.

In practice, however, the base of a capital tax differs from that of an income tax. Under the personal income tax, the cost of maintaining physical capital is an expense that is deductible in computing the net taxable income from that asset. Human beings, however, are not allowed to deduct the cost of maintaining their human capital in determining their tax liability. This pair of observations prompts the argument that the income tax discriminates against human capital relative to physical capital, and encourages the suggestion that a net worth tax should be adopted to create an offsetting discrimination against physical capital. If this line of argument were correct, the adoption of a net worth tax to complement the income tax would be a means both for restoring equity between human and nonhuman sources of wealth and for promoting an efficient allocation of resources between human and nonhuman forms of wealth.[4]

An annual net worth tax would require an annual assessment of such personal assets as real estate, consumer durables, stocks, bonds, bank deposits, and cash. The capricious administration of personal property taxes is widely acknowledged, and it is far easier to value real estate than personal property or intangible assets. Thus an annual net worth would involve several times the administrative difficulties of a personal property tax. Faced with these realities of tax administration, a tax levied upon the estate of a decedent may be viewed as a convenient substitute for an annual net worth tax. If wealth accumulation typically begins at age forty and death takes place at seventy, one valuation of wealth upon death would replace thirty during a decedent's life.

---

[4] An "earned" income exemption from the personal income tax could accomplish much the same effect without requiring the development of a new form of tax.

The argument that the personal income tax discriminates against human capital is strongest when individuals must pay for their own investment in human capital. Much investment in human capital is subsidized, of course, which reduces the discrimination against human capital. It is possible, as I illustrate below, for the amount of subsidy to become large enough even to reverse the direction of discrimination. Consider two initial investments of $100,000, one in human capital and one in physical capital. Suppose the annual gross return is $20,000 in both cases, and that annual maintenance costs are $5,000. Let the rate of tax on taxable income be 50 percent. Taxable income from physical capital is $15,000, thus the post-tax rate of return is 7.5 percent. Taxable income on human capital is $20,000, which gives a post-tax rate of return of 5 percent. The impact of "free" education can be illustrated by assuming that the human capital is acquired with a personal outlay of only, say, $50,000. The $5,000 post-tax income from human capital now represents a rate of return to the recipient of 10 percent. Thus the combination of personal income taxation and the heavy subsidization of human capital formation discriminates against physical capital, not human capital.

Given the amount of tax actually extracted from a decedent's estate, a series of annual taxes could always be designed that could have extracted the same present value.[5] If we assume, for arithmetic simplicity, that the interest rate is zero, a death tax of $30,000 would be equivalent to an annual series of thirty net wealth taxes of $1,000 each. Recognition that interest rates are positive complicates the arithmetic without disturbing the principle of equivalence being illustrated. The exact impact depends upon whether we take as a base a $30,000 payment upon death or thirty annual payments of $1,000 during life. If equivalence is defined in terms of a $30,000 payment upon death, the annual taxes would be some amount less than $1,000 such that the actual payments plus accumulated interest sum to $30,000. If equivalence is defined in terms of thirty annual payments of $1,000, the levy upon death would exceed $30,000 by the sum of the accumulated interest earned by the annual payments.

Death taxation may thus serve as a substitute for net worth taxation. The United Kingdom has made substantial use of the estate tax as a source of revenue, and raising revenue is probably the dominant objective of the British estate tax.[6] In 1954, for instance, 15 percent of British deaths resulted in liability for estate taxation.[7] The comparable figure for the United States at that time was one percent. The specific exemption in the United Kingdom is only $7,200, compared with $60,000 in the United States. Although the maximum rates are nearly the same, 80 percent in the United Kingdom and 77 percent in the United States, the highest British rate begins at $2,400,000 while the highest American rate begins at $10,000,000. The British and American estate taxes tend toward the same burden above $10,000,000, but the tax burden on small and medium amounts of wealth is much larger in the United Kingdom than in the United States.

Death taxation once a generation, however, is a poor substitute for wealth taxation once a year. An annual net worth tax would take as its base approximately the entire stock of nonhuman wealth in

---

[5] Tibor Barna, "The Burden of Death Duties in Terms of an Annual Tax," *Review of Economic Studies*, vol. 9 (November 1941), pp. 28-39. Nicholas Kaldor, "The Income Burden of Capital Taxes," *Review of Economic Studies*, vol. 9 (Summer 1942), pp. 138-57. A. C. Pigou, *A Study in Public Finance*, 3rd ed. (London: Macmillan and Co., 1942), pp. 138-46.

[6] "The main object of the tax [the British estate tax] has always been the raising of revenue. . . ." G. S. A. Wheatcroft, "The Anti-Avoidance Provisions of the Law of Estate Duty in the United Kingdom," *National Tax Journal*, vol. 10 (March 1957), p. 48.

[7] Ibid.

the economy. But only a small share of the nation's stock of wealth will ever change hands through death. The preponderance of personally owned wealth is consumed before death. Much wealth, for instance, represents savings made during the middle years of life which will be consumed by the owners during their retirement. If people followed perfectly such a life cycle pattern of saving, they would spend their last cent the instant before death, and die penniless. Under this extreme set of circumstances, none of the economy's capital stock would change hands upon death and death taxation could not substitute at all for net worth taxation. Since people do pass wealth at death, though only a fraction of what they once possessed, death taxation can be looked upon as a substitute for net worth taxation, though a relatively poor one.[8] Since death taxation is a poor substitute for net worth taxation, it cannot be viewed as a reasonable institution for financing the supply of public services.

Transfer Taxation to Redistribute Income

A second function of a system of taxation is to alter the distribution of wealth and income among individual citizens. A shift from a proportional income tax to a progressive income tax of equal yield alters the structure of tax payments made by the citizenry, increasing the payments made by those in the upper income ranges and reducing those made in the lower ranges. Since transfer taxation cannot be viewed primarily as an instrument for financing the supply of public services, it should perhaps be viewed primarily as an instrument for altering the distribution of wealth and income. The limited revenue yield,[9] the high level of the specific exemption, and the steeply progressive rate schedules all suggest that our system of transfer taxation is designed primarily to penalize the ownership of large amounts of wealth per se. To the extent that transfer taxation succeeds in preventing the accumulation of large fortunes, moreover, the revenue

---

[8] Local property taxation is a far closer approximation to a net worth tax on nonhuman wealth.

[9] Estimated federal estate and gift taxation collections for fiscal 1972 were $5.3 billion, of which $1.5 billion was nonrecurring revenue due to a one-shot speed up on the timing of tax collections. The sustainable revenue yield of $3.8 billion is less than 2 percent of estimated federal budget receipts. See *Budget of the United States Government, 1972* (Washington: U.S. Government Printing Office, 1971), pp. 73-74. State governments collected about $900 million from their death and gift taxes in fiscal 1968, which also is less than 2 percent of their total revenue. See *Facts and Figures on Government Finance*, 15th ed. (New York: Tax Foundation, Inc., 1969), p. 175.

yield from transfer taxation will fall. This conflict between the revenue and the "social" objectives of transfer taxation is analogous to the conflict between a protective tariff and a revenue tariff: A perfectly protective tariff will yield no revenue, and a tariff that generates the maximum revenue will yield little protection.[10]

Acceptance of transfer taxation to accomplish "social" objectives is doubtless aided by the widely held attitude that the acquisition of wealth by inheritance is less laudatory than the acquisition of wealth by personal effort.[11] The belief is strong, moreover, though it is not supported by the available evidence, as we shall see in Chapter 2, that wealth begets wealth and poverty begets poverty. It is often alleged that a tendency toward cumulative inequality characterizes a free enterprise economy, with rich people coming from wealthy families and people from poor families caught in a vicious cycle of poverty. Since inherited wealth is viewed by many as both a significant source of inequality and, more significantly, as tending to produce a cumulative inequality in the distribution of wealth, transfer taxation has perhaps understandably been supported as an instrument to help mitigate these tendencies.

Since transfer taxes fall upon prosperous decedents and their successors, albeit unequally among such persons, transfer taxation can be regarded as a crude means of taxing large fortunes. A policy designed to promote the negative objective of penalizing the ownership of large wealth should not be equated, however, with a policy designed to promote the positive objective of greater equality of opportunity in trying to gain wealth. The total value of personally owned wealth in the United States exceeds $2 trillion, so transfer taxes transfer annually only about 0.2 percent of the amount of wealth held by individuals. Moreover, the tax collections contribute to the general support of the government budget, only a small share of which contributes directly to promoting greater equality of opportunity. Since transfer taxation penalizes the ownership of large amounts of wealth, in a purely arithmetical sense a relative advantage is given to those who do not own large amounts of wealth. But the penalty is small and the benefits are diffused among the populace, so the con-

[10] Vasco N. P. Fortuna, "The Sociometric Theory and the Estate Duty," *Public Finance*, vol. 6, no. 3 (1951), pp. 267-71, shows clearly the inherent conflict between the revenue and the social objectives of death taxation. Fortuna specifically notes that if the social objective were fully attained, death tax revenues would fall to zero. (Fortuna, incidentally, argues that estate taxation should be used wholly to reduce inequality in the distribution of wealth.)

[11] Alan A. Tait, "The Taxation of Wealth at Death: A New Proposal," *Scottish Journal of Political Economy*, vol. 9 (February 1962), p. 40.

tribution of transfer taxation to the positive goal of equality of opportunity is negligible. Like many criminal sanctions, transfer taxation might appropriately be regarded as penalizing one segment of the population without significantly assisting the remainder. Transfer taxation, then, should not be viewed as an instrument for promoting some equalization of opportunity by preventing tendencies toward cumulative inequality.

From one perspective, then, it hardly seems sensible to have transfer taxation as an element of a tax system, for there are more appropriate instruments available both for financing the supply of public services and for transferring income among individual citizens. At several points in this volume, especially in Chapter 5, I shall inquire as to what form of tax system would perform more effectively than a system containing separate transfer taxes.

From another perspective tax institutions take on lives of their own, and modification of a tax while maintaining the basic structural framework is far more likely than the replacement of prevailing tax institutions. Since our transfer tax institutions are far more likely to be modified than to be repealed, much of the remainder of this volume—especially Chapters 3 and 4—is devoted to examining issues regarding reform of prevailing transfer tax institutions. Since mild reform is far more likely than radical transformation, I give considerable attention to issues of reform. Yet radical transformation seems likely to be superior, and the politically infeasible ideas of today become the political agenda of tomorrow, so I also devote considerable attention to issues relating to such radical transformation.

2

TRANSFER TAXATION, PROGRESSIVITY, AND THE CONCENTRATION OF WEALTH

It seems clear that transfer taxation exists primarily to penalize the accumulation of large amounts of wealth. And, as a matter of arithmetic, the penalty must reduce somewhat the inequality in the distribution of wealth. Transfer taxation, however, cannot be viewed seriously as an instrument to reduce inequality or to promote greater equality of economic opportunity, for other tax instruments would perform far more effectively in this respect. Transfer taxation penalizes some of the wealthy without significantly assisting the nonwealthy, and in some respects may even penalize the nonwealthy as well.

A Static Perspective on Inequality

Few topics seem capable of stirring emotions so violently as the inequality in the distribution of income and wealth. The basic facts concerning inequality ostensibly are quite simple. The lowest fifth of families in terms of income earn just over 5 percent of the income earned by all families, and the second-lowest fifth of families earn just over 12 percent. The highest fifth of families, by contrast, earn about 42 percent and the second-highest fifth earn nearly 24 percent.

It is widely recognized, however, that figures on the distribution of income overstate the extent of inequality, for such figures result from merging sets of individuals that should be kept separate while interpreting the figures. The relation between age and income is but one example, and can serve to illustrate the issues involved in interpreting the figures. A person's lifetime income profile typically starts low, rises until it peaks during the middle years, then falls off during the retirement years. Consider a world in which all people have identical lifetime income profiles. Figures on the distribution of income will show substantial inequality, with the exact amount depending upon the relative numbers of people in each age class and the rate at which income rises and falls over a person's life cycle. Yet the community should properly be regarded as one of perfect equality in the distribution of income, as all persons will earn equal incomes over their lifetimes.

It is also widely recognized that nonpecuniary differences among occupations will cause the statistics on the distribution of income to overstate the extent of inequality. Other things equal, if people prefer to live in less populous rather than more populous areas at equal wage rates, they will live in more populous areas only if they are compensated by a higher wage. Such factors as this also produce inequality in the distribution of money income, but this inequality in monetary forms of income is necessary to offset an opposing inequality in nonmonetary forms of income. Much inequality in the distribution of income is precisely of this nature. Generally, the higher the educational requirements for entering an occupation, the higher the annual income in that occupation. But at least part of this higher annual income is necessary merely to offset the higher costs of entering that occupation, both the monetary costs of education and the income that could have been earned during the years of schooling. Once again, statistics on the inequality of incomes exaggerate the actual amount of inequality.

Moreover, figures on the inequality of incomes by themselves provide no basis for judging the performance of an economy. Without some notion of an optimal or most preferred degree of inequality, there is no basis for saying that more equality or less equality is desirable. While admonitions to increase the degree of progressivity in our tax system are pervasive, and have been stimulated by the resurgence of populist rhetoric, advocates of such measures rarely specify the point at which such measures would cease—in other words, the desired degree of inequality.

Perhaps the most prominent attempt to specify an optimal degree of inequality is Abba P. Lerner's argument that the optimal degree of inequality is zero.[1] Ignoring possible disincentive effects of complete equalization, perhaps the most damaging argument against

---

[1] Abba P. Lerner, *The Economics of Control* (New York: Macmillan Co., 1944), pp. 26-32. For more recent efforts, see Ray C. Fair, "The Optimal Distribution of Income," *Quarterly Journal of Economics*, vol. 85 (November 1971), pp. 551-79; and Lester C. Thurow, "The Income Distribution as a Pure Public Good," *Quarterly Journal of Economics*, vol. 85 (May 1971), pp. 327-36.

perfect equality as an ideal is that it is an ideal under which few people would want to live. With rare exception, people prefer to take a chance at earning an above-average income even though this implies they may end up with a below-average income. For instance, in an experiment I performed at Tulane University between 1968 and 1972, nearly 400 students were faced with the necessity of choosing among alternative distributions of income.[2] While three students indicated they preferred an equal distribution of income, the remainder preferred to participate under conditions where the distribution of income was unequal. A few preferred extreme degrees of inequality and a few preferred only slight inequality, but most preferred distributions of income that approximated the prevailing distribution of income in the United States. The most preferred distribution of income was characterized by a guaranteed minimum reward of about one-third the average reward, and above this minimum base the amount of inequality roughly resembled the current distribution of income. This evidence would seem to suggest that, aside from the very bottom of the income scale, there is probably little wrong with the prevailing distribution of income. Or perhaps it merely suggests that the distribution of income is not really the object of concern after all.

A Dynamic Perspective on Inequality [3]

The statistical form of the distribution of income may have considerably less importance than the rate of mobility within the distribution, especially among generations. To illustrate, consider three individuals with incomes of $12,000, $8,000, and $4,000. Let us posit that the shape of this distribution will remain unchanged as time passes. One extreme possibility is that a child will come to occupy the same income position as his parents. Thus, children of parents with $12,000 will always have $12,000, and so forth. The other extreme possibility is that a child's income position will be wholly

---

[2] I determined the total number of points to be awarded on any single exam, the total number of exams for the semester, and the relation between total points and the course grade. The relation between points and grade was set such that the mean point value would yield a C+ grade, which was approximately the mean grade for the entire university. Each student faced the task of indicating his preferred distribution of the total points for an examination among the individual exams: that is, they had to specify the number of points to be given to the exam that I ranked first, second, and so on.

[3] For an elaboration on many of the points raised in this section, and also in the remainder of this chapter, see Richard E. Wagner, *The Public Economy* (Chicago: Markham Publishing Co., 1973), pp. 155-65.

Table 1
MEDIAN INCOME OF FATHERS AND SONS
BY FATHER'S OCCUPATIONAL CLASS, 1960

Father's Occupation	Father's Median Income	Son's Median Income
Managers, officials, and proprietors	$6,664	$5,747
Professional, technical, and kindred	6,619	5,737
Craftsmen, foremen, and kindred	5,240	5,195
Sales	4,937	5,608
Clerical and kindred	4,785	5,504
Operatives and kindred	4,299	4,834
Service, including private household	3,310	4,833
Laborers, except farm and mine	2,948	4,686
Farmers and farm managers	2,169	4,234
Farm laborers and foremen	1,066	4,021

Source: Lowell E. Gallaway, "On the Importance of 'Picking One's Parents'," *Quarterly Review of Economics and Business*, vol. 6 (Summer 1966), p. 12.

unrelated to his parents' income position. Thus, children of parents with $12,000 will have an equal chance of earning $12,000, $8,000, or $4,000. In either of these two extreme cases, however, the degree of inequality in the distribution of income will be identical. Although the distribution of income is identical in these two extreme cases, these cases would hardly be considered identical. This suggests that the focus of concern is not the amount of inequality in the distribution of income, but the rate of mobility within the income scale. If one-half the population received $5,000 and one-half received $10,000, the distribution of income would be considerably more equal than the current distribution. Yet without mobility among the two income positions, about one-half the populace would probably reject the prevailing social order.

A substantial amount of mobility seems to exist within the American distribution of income and wealth. In his study of income mobility over time, Lowell E. Gallaway found that 77 percent of the difference between the average income in the United States in 1960 and the median income of the lowest income class was eradicated within one generation.[4] Table 1 shows that the occupational classification with the lowest income in 1960 was "farm laborers and foremen," which had a median income of $1,066. The median income of sons whose fathers belonged to this occupational class, however,

---

[4] Lowell E. Gallaway, "On the Importance of 'Picking One's Parents'," *Quarterly Review of Economics and Business*, vol. 6 (Summer 1966), pp. 7-15.

Table 2

MEAN I.Q. OF PARENT AND CHILD BY PARENT'S OCCUPATIONAL CLASS

Parent's Class	Mean I.Q.	
	Parent	Child
Higher professional	139.7	120.8
Lower professional	130.6	114.7
Clerical	115.9	107.8
Semi-skilled	97.8	98.9
Unskilled	84.9	92.6
Average	100.0	100.0

Source: James E. Meade, *Efficiency, Equality, and the Ownership of Property* (London: Allen & Unwin, 1964), p. 50.

was $4,021. Thus, 77 percent of the gap between their fathers' incomes and the average incomes of all fathers of $4,907 was eliminated by mobility within the income distribution. The opposite effect occurred at the top of the occupational scale. The median income of "managers, officials, and proprietors" in 1960 was $6,664. But the median income of sons from this class was only $5,747. Table 1 shows clearly that sons from the upper classes tend to earn above-average income while sons from the lower classes tend to earn below-average incomes. But Table 1 also shows that the income of sons from the upper classes tends to fall toward the average income while the income of sons from the lower classes tends to rise toward the average income.

The evidence indicates that individual incomes have a tendency to regress toward the mean. While people in the upper income class are likely to find their relative position worsening over time, people in the lower income classes are likely to find their relative income position improving. This tendency for income to regress toward the mean seems attributable to two factors. On the one hand, random elements pervade all economic activities, so luck has much to do with one's economic fortunes.[5] On the other hand, biological inheritance, primarily intelligence, places constraints upon the options that one is likely to be able to exploit.[6]

---

[5] Recall that ancient piece of Hebrew wisdom: "Speed does not win the race nor strength the battle. Bread does not belong to the wise, nor wealth to the intelligent, nor success to the skillful; time and chance govern all." Eccles. 9:11 (New English Bible).

[6] Biological inheritance may itself be viewed as a matter of luck, as the outcome of a genetical poker game.

It is well established that intelligence regresses toward the mean. While children of parents with above-average IQs will tend to have above-average IQs, their IQs will tend to be less than those of their parents. Similarly, children of parents with below-average IQs will tend to have below-average IQs, but their IQs will also tend to exceed those of their parents. Table 2 illustrates this regression toward the mean for six occupational classes. While the mean IQ of parents in the higher professional class was 139.7, the mean IQ of their children was only 120.8. And while the mean IQ of parents in the unskilled class was 84.9, the mean IQ of their children was 92.6. From generation to generation, there is mobility within the intelligence scale, even though the inequality in the distribution of intelligence remains constant. Thus, to the extent that high intelligence produces high income, biological inheritance will produce an intergenerational regression toward the mean income.

Luck also plays a strong role in the distribution of income from year to year. One's personal efforts by themselves play only a modest role in determining one's income. True, one may be able to increase his income by working longer hours or by undertaking special training, though even these opportunities must have somehow availed themselves in the first place. But perhaps the most significant changes in the income prospects facing people stem from changes in circumstances that are largely beyond their control. The value of a college education was oversold in the aftermath of the post-Sputnik hysteria, and the preponderance of college graduates now find it difficult to find jobs commensurate with their expectations, due largely to changes in external circumstances.

Any decision by an entrepreneur to create a new product or by an individual to train himself for a certain occupation is in part a gamble. In all cases an expected rate of return may be computed based on current circumstances. But future conditions will almost certainly differ from present conditions, and some people will gain by the discrepancy and some will lose. For example, people who decided a decade or two ago to become areospace engineers faced bright income prospects that unforeseeably have since turned bleak. Or consider an industrial worker working for a firm that experiences a strong increase in demand for its output, and as a result of the additional labor that is hired, finds himself promoted to foreman. Such an improvement in income prospects is also wholly a matter of chance.

Some people will have a run of good luck in that they invest in areas that will undergo unforeseeable increases in the relative demands

20

for their output. Others will have a run of bad luck in that they invest in areas that will suffer relative decreases in demand. There is a considerable, largely unappreciated, amount of random variation in the distribution of income. The contemporary mythology that the wealthy get wealthier and the poor get poorer is truly a myth. If anything, the wealthy get poorer and the poor get wealthier.

A person with a relatively high income is likely to be one who has benefitted, among other things, from a run of good luck. Similarly, a person with a relatively low income is likely to be one who has suffered a run of bad luck. But luck tends to even out over time. A person may flip a coin ten times and receive all heads. But if he continues playing, tails will appear. Persons with large incomes and wealth will often find their run of good luck turning sour if they continue playing. It is not at all uncommon for relatively wealthy persons to lose their fortunes and even file for bankruptcy, indicating the equalizing power of luck. Similarly, the person who has been dealt a series of bad hands in a poker game will get some good hands if he continues playing. Income and wealth positions are continuously changing. There is no such thing as a cumulative inequality of income and wealth. In fact, the opposite may be descriptively more accurate, as regression toward the mean seems to characterize the distribution of income and wealth. Wealth may grow, but it can also decay, and the greater the wealth, the more compelling the forces of decay.

Inequality and Confiscatory Taxation

Assertions about the cumulative inequality of wealth are usually derived from a line of argument based upon the arithmetic of compound interest. And the arithmetic of growth at compound interest is truly inexorable. If a capital sum grows at 5 percent compounded annually for thirty years, the terminal value will be 4.32 times the initial value. Under these circumstances, it would take an average rate of tax on estates of 77 percent to prevent the accumulation of wealth from generation to generation. Five percent per year is a very modest rate of return once one allows for inflation. Yet if $1,000 had been invested 200 years ago at 5 percent compounded annually, the present capital value would be $17,298,000. If $1,000 had been invested 200 years ago at 10 percent, which is about the average return on common stock, the present capital value would be $189,670,000,000. If wealth grew under these conditions, any ten families that had $1,000 each 200 years ago would together now own practically all of our stock of privately owned wealth (about $2 trillion).

Although reasoning about wealth based upon compound interest is tempting because of its simplicity, it is also contradicted by the evidence. Fortunes do not accumulate at the average rate of return of the economy. Rather some birth and death process is operating. Fortunes may grow for a while, but either incompetence or bad luck will ensure their eventual death. A highly competent person will tend to be plagued by biology with less competent heirs. Moreover, a run of bad luck eventually will strike even the most competent person.[7]

The problem of "the gambler's ruin" is perhaps the most fruitful way of examining the distribution of wealth over time. In its simplest form, the problem of the gambler's ruin states that the probability that a gambler will lose his fortune varies inversely with the size of his fortune relative to that of his opposition. If the gambler, whose fortune is X, and his opposition, whose fortune is Y, face equal likelihoods of winning, the probability that the gambler will eventually lose his entire fortune is $1 - X/(X+Y)$. If the gambler and his opposition are equally rich, 0.5 is the probability of the gambler's eventual ruin.[8]

Especially relevant is the case of the infinitely rich adversary. As the wealth of the adversary increases relative to that of the gambler, the probability of the gambler's eventual ruin approaches certainty. In an economic system, the individual is playing against everyone else, so the individual trying to amass wealth is in the position of a gambler playing against an infinitely wealthy adversary. Although the gambler may encounter lengthy strings of good luck, he will eventually encounter a string of bad luck that will dissipate his fortune.

Of even greater interest than the probability that any given fortune will become exhausted is the expected length of time it will take to exhaust the fortune. It is relatively uninteresting by itself to argue that any fortune will become ruined, for it might take 50 years or it might take 500 years. The expected length of time it will take for the gambler to become ruined is of critical importance, if only 50 years the result may be a happy one, but 500 years may be intolerably slow.

---

[7] On these points see George J. Stigler, *The Theory of Price*, 3rd ed. (New York: Macmillan Co., 1966), pp. 307-09.

[8] The problem of the gambler's ruin is surveyed in William Feller, *An Introduction to Probability Theory and its Applications*, vol. 1, 2nd ed. (New York: John Wiley and Sons, Inc., 1957), pp. 311-13.

Table 3

PROBABILITY OF AND EXPECTED DURATION BEFORE GAMBLER'S RUIN

Probability of:		Initial Fortunes of:		Probability of Gambler's Ruin	Expected Number of Plays Until Ruin
Gambler's winning (p)	Gambler's losing (q)	Gambler (X)	Opposition (Y)	(P_r)	(D_r)
0.5	0.5	10	90	0.9	900
0.4	0.6	10	90	1.0*	50*
0.33	0.67	10	90	1.0*	30*
0.5	0.5	10	990	0.99	9900
0.4	0.6	10	990	1.0*	50*
0.33	0.67	10	990	1.0*	30*

* These values are extremely close approximations. The exact entry for P_r in the second row is 0.999999. Similarly, the exact value for D_r in the second row is 49.999999.

The entries of Table 3 show for a two-person game the probability of ruin and the expected duration of play for several values of p, q, X, and Y. The general outlines of the table are unmistakably clear.[9] Even when he has a 0.5 chance of winning, the gambler's chance of ruin is 0.9 when he has 10 percent of the total wealth, and rises to 0.99 when his share of the wealth falls to 1 percent. When the probability of the gambler's winning falls below 0.5, the probability of eventual ruin is practically certain, even when he initially possesses 10 percent of the wealth. The expected duration of play is highly sensitive to the probability that the gambler will win. When the gambler initially has 10 percent of the wealth, the expected duration of play before ruin is 900 trials. The expected duration falls to 50 when the probability of winning falls to 0.4 and falls to 30 when the probability of success falls to 0.33.

We can now examine the role that confiscatory rates of taxation play in the process of the accumulation and dissipation of wealth over time. An entrepreneur makes investments in alternatives whose

---

[9] Let p denote the probability that the gambler wins and q the possibility that he loses. If $p = q$, the probability that the gambler will become ruined is:

$$P_r = 1 - X/(X+Y). \text{ If } p \neq q, P_r = \frac{(q/p)^{(X+Y)} - (q/p)^X}{(q/p)^{(X+Y)} - 1}.$$

If $p = q$, the expected duration before ruin will be:

$$D_r = XY. \text{ If } p \neq q, D_r = \frac{X}{q-p} - \frac{X+Y}{q-p} \cdot \frac{1 - (q/p)^X}{1 - (q/p)^{(X+Y)}}.$$

23

future payoffs are uncertain. Sometimes he will win; sometimes he will lose (that is, the adversary will win); sometimes nobody will win (in other words, the entrepreneur will break even). Other things equal, the more progressive the rate of tax on winnings, the less willing an entrepreneur will be to take risks. The greater the rate of progressivity, the higher the excess tax on gains vis-à-vis losses. Under a proportional income tax, for instance, an income of $100,000 one year and zero the next will pay the same tax as annual incomes of $50,000 for two years. Under progressive taxation, however, the tax on $100,000 will be more than twice as large as the tax on $50,000.

Whereas an individual might be willing to make an investment with a probability of success on only, for example, 0.40 under proportional taxation, he might require a probability of success of, for example, 0.45 under progressive taxation. And the higher the rate of tax on winnings, the more favorable the odds must be before an entrepreneur will take the gamble. And the more favorable the odds to the gambler, the longer the expected duration of play before his ruin. If mobility within the distribution of income and wealth is considered more important than the shape of the distribution itself, high rates of tax become distinctly counterproductive in that they reduce the rate of personal mobility.

In the absence of inflation, government bonds would be a riskless investment. And if investments were truly riskless, the arithmetic of compound interest would exert itself. The higher the rate of tax on the accumulation of wealth, the more numerous will be the number of people who settle for lower, more certain returns. Fortunes are much less likely to erode under such circumstances. And the fortunes that do erode will erode at slower rates. On the one hand, high tax rates will encourage safe investments, which reduce the probability of ruin and lengthen the duration of time before ruin. On the other hand, by reducing the rate of mobility among wealth positions, high rates of tax also reduce the ability of newcomers to enter the high wealth brackets. On both grounds, then, high rates of tax encourage and promote the retention of large amounts of wealth in the hands of those who already have the wealth.[10]

High rates of taxation on incomes and estates produce results that are clearly inconsistent with expressed desires to make it

---

[10] It is noteworthy in the postwar period of confiscatory taxation that capital gains have been the primary route by which new private wealth has been amassed. Earnings taken in this form, of course, are subject to lower tax rates. Rather than being looked upon as a loophole, however, the capital gains provision should be looked upon as a second-best provision in our tax system, with considerably lower tax rates being first-best.

possible for all individuals to have reasonable opportunities to become wealthy. Present policies protect holders of previously accumulated wealth, both from themselves and from the competition of others who might otherwise amass new wealth. While such policies may penalize some holders of large wealth, they do not make any positive contribution to increasing the opportunity of all citizens to participate in the effort to accumulate wealth if they choose. The distinction between a tax system designed to penalize the wealthy and a tax system designed to assist the nonwealthy is critical, and is a theme to which we shall return in Chapter 5.

3

ECONOMIC EFFECTS OF
TRANSFER TAXATION

It is often claimed that transfer taxation discourages saving and encourages contributing to philanthropic institutions. I shall examine these claims, and then consider how transfer taxation promotes fiscal illusion, thereby injecting an element of irrationality into our fiscal affairs.[1]

The Amount of Saving

It is often suggested that transfer taxation impinges on saving more strongly than other forms of taxation. We may view people who hold wealth upon entering the later years of their lives as choosing the amount of wealth they want to consume themselves and the amount they want to transfer to heirs. An increase in the rate of estate tax increases the price of providing for one's heirs relative to the price of providing for oneself. Since, following the first law of demand, the quantity of bequests purchased will fall as the price of bequests rises, an increase in estate tax rates should reduce the amount of wealth devoted to one's heirs relative to the amount devoted to oneself. Thus the estate tax would encourage dissaving by wealth holders, for dissaving is a means of avoiding estate tax. And transfer taxation, if it diminishes saving more strongly than other forms of taxation, will retard our rate of economic growth more severely than other forms of taxation.[2]

---

[1] The seminal work on fiscal illusion is Amilcare Puviani, *Die Illusionen in der öffentlichen Finanzwirtschaft*, trans. Marianne Hartmann and Felix Rexhausen (Berlin: Duncker & Humblot, 1960). For a brief English-language survey, see James M. Buchanan, *Public Finance in Democratic Process* (Chapel Hill: University of North Carolina Press, 1967), pp. 126-43.

[2] The effect of death taxation upon saving and economic growth is discussed in C. Lowell Harriss, "Revising Estate Taxation," *Tax Review*, vol. 32 (April 1971), pp. 15-16.

If rates of estate tax are set at 100 percent, the inducement to dissaving seems unambiguous. Under fully confiscatory taxation it is impossible to transfer wealth to heirs, so the individual is faced with a choice of leaving it to the state or consuming it himself.[3] Since the state is generally regarded with little affection, as attested by the paucity of bequests it receives, we should expect personal wealth to be consumed before death rather than be left for the state. We might expect that risk aversion combined with an inability to predict with certainty one's time of death would mean that some personal wealth would remain upon death. But we should also expect a greatly expanded use of annuities under such circumstances, which would virtually eliminate such remaining wealth.[4] When the rate of tax is 100 percent, there seems to be little question that estate taxation induces dissaving. And it seems but a simple extension of the argument to derive the same conclusion for intermediate cases: As the tax rate falls below 100 percent, saving would increase but would still be less than it would be in the absence of the estate tax.

We must be wary, however, of such facile use of interpolative reasoning. Saving for bequests has two dimensions, the amount transferred to successors and the amount transferred to government, and it is the sum of the two that is relevant for our analysis of saving. Although an increase in tax rate reduces the amount of wealth transferred to successors, it also increases the government's claim per unit of wealth. Suppose the estate tax rate is 50 percent, which means that a testator must pay a price of $1 for the right to transfer $1 to an heir. Thus the testator must save $2 of his wealth in order to transfer $1. Would a reduction in the tax rate to, say, 25 percent yield an increase, decrease, or no change in the amount of saving? The reduction in tax rate reduces the price of transferring wealth to heirs. With a 25 percent tax, a testator can transfer $1 to an heir by paying a price of only $0.32.

To the extent that saving is motivated by a demand for bequests, the impact of estate taxation upon saving will depend upon the testator's elasticity of demand for bequests. If the demand for bequests is inelastic, a reduction in tax rate (in other words, price of bequests) will reduce saving (that is, the amount spent purchasing bequests). Consider a reduction in tax rate from 50 percent to 25 percent, and assume that the elasticity of demand for bequests is zero. If $1 were transferred from a total saving of $2 with a 50 per-

---

[3] Unless transfers to nongovernmental institutions are exempt from tax.

[4] See, for instance, Gordon Tullock, "Inheritance Justified," *Journal of Law and Economics*, vol. 14 (October 1971), pp. 465-74.

cent tax rate, $1 will be transferred from a total saving of only $1.32 when the tax rate is reduced to 25 percent. If the demand for bequests is unit elastic, a change in tax rate will leave total saving unchanged. Hence, if $1 were transferred from a total saving of $2 with a tax rate of 50 percent, $1.50 will be transferred from a total saving of $2 when the tax rate is reduced to 25 percent. If the demand for bequests is elastic, a reduction in tax rate will increase total saving. If $1 were transferred from a total saving of $2 with a tax rate of 50 percent, something more than $2 will be saved and something more than $1.50 will be transferred when the tax rate is reduced to 25 percent, with the precise extent of increased saving dependent upon the actual elasticity of demand for bequests.

The preceding analysis suggests that the effect of the estate tax on saving is ambiguous. An increase in the rate of tax will increase saving by testators with inelastic demands for bequests, while the increase will reduce saving by testators with elastic demands. Despite this ambiguity, some general tendencies may be described. As a general proposition, the demand curve for any product becomes increasingly elastic as its price rises; even the most inelastic of demand curves must become elastic at some sufficiently high price. Where the marginal rate of tax is relatively low—on testators with relatively modest estates—the demand for bequests is likely to be relatively inelastic. Within this region, then, the estate tax is likely to increase the total amount of saving, though decreasing the amount of private saving. Where the marginal rate of tax is relatively high, by contrast, the demand for bequests is likely to be relatively elastic. In this case, which describes the situation faced by testators with relatively large amounts of wealth, the estate tax is likely to reduce the total amount of saving. While most testators face relatively low rates of tax, the highly skewed distribution of wealth suggests that the bulk of estates will be transferred by testators who face relatively high rates of tax. Hence, most wealth is likely to be transferred by testators who have relatively elastic demands for bequests, which indicates a strong likelihood that estate taxation reduces the amount of saving.

Contributions to Philanthropic Institutions

Analysis of the impact of estate taxation upon the volume of contributions to philanthropic institutions is similar to analysis of the impact of estate taxation upon saving. Given his decision about the amount of wealth to bequeath, we may view a testator as choosing to distribute his wealth between persons and institutions. In the

United States, gifts and bequests to a large number of charitable, educational, religious, and scientific institutions are exempt from tax.[5] Thus the estate tax is applicable to transfers made to persons but not to institutions. Because of this difference in tax treatment, it is commonly claimed that this exemption feature stimulates transfers to such eligible institutions as charities, churches, hospitals, and schools.[6] If this assertion is correct, the charitable deduction can be viewed as a way of subsidizing various nonprofit organizations.

However, it seems very likely that an increase in the rate of tax on estates will reduce bequests to charitable institutions by more than it will reduce bequests to persons. And since the preceding section of this chapter showed that an increase in the rate of estate tax will quite likely reduce total saving, the net result is that estate taxation will probably diminish contributions to philanthropic institutions. As with the case of saving, the analysis hinges upon relative elasticities of demand, in this case between bequests to persons and bequests to institutions.

It seems reasonable that most testators will place first priority on providing for their family rather than placing it on providing for institutions. Thus, generally, the family will be taken care of first, with others sharing the remainder of the estate with the government. The available evidence supports this presumption about testator behavior. The Treasury's special tabulations of estate tax returns for 1957 and 1959 show that charitable bequests were less than 4 percent of gross estates of less than $900,000, while noncharitable bequests were about 76 percent and taxes about 20 percent. Among estates exceeding $10 million, on the other hand, charitable bequests were about 30 percent, and noncharitable bequests and taxes about 35 percent each.[7]

As the average size of estates rise, bequests to institutions increase relative to bequests to persons. Such evidence as this suggests that testators look after their families first, with institutions receiving second consideration. Testators thus have relatively inelastic demands to transfer wealth to persons, and relatively elastic demands to transfer wealth to institutions. An increase in the rate of estate tax is an increase in the price of leaving wealth to individuals,

[5] Internal Revenue Code of 1954, Section 2055.

[6] See, for instance, Werner Z. Hirsch, *The Economics of State and Local Government* (New York: McGraw-Hill, 1970), p. 66; and Carl S. Shoup, *Public Finance* (Chicago: Aldine Publishing Co., 1969), p. 380.

[7] Robert Anthoine, "Testamentary Trusts," in Carl S. Shoup, *Federal Estate and Gift Taxes* (Washington: The Brookings Institution, 1966), p. 155.

so we should expect less wealth to be left. However, since the demand for bequests to persons is inelastic, the amount spent in making such transfers of wealth will increase. Since the total size of the estate is fixed, the residual amount of wealth left for charitable institutions will be reduced by an increase in tax rates.

The issue can be illustrated by a simple example. Assume a decedent during his lifetime decided to leave a target level of wealth to his family giving the remainder to charitable institutions. Suppose his target level of giving to persons is $300,000, and further suppose he would leave an estate of $1 million if the rate of tax were 33 percent. If the rate of tax is 33 percent, it will cost $150,000 to leave $300,000 for the family, and a residual of $550,000 will be left for charity. If the rate of tax is raised to 50 percent, the cost of leaving $300,000 for the family will rise to $300,000 which will reduce the residual left for charity to $400,000, assuming the total estate remains $1 million. To the extent that the increased tax rate reduces total saving, the residual transferred to philanthropic institutions will decline still further. An assumption of a target level of bequests to family members, of course, is an assumption of zero elasticity of demand, and was made only to simplify the arithmetical illustration. In the more general case of less than complete inelasticity, the rise in tax rate from 33 percent to 50 percent will reduce the amount transferred to the family to less than $300,000. Yet the amount of bequest plus the concomitant tax liability would still exceed $450,000, which would still leave less than $550,000 for charitable requests, again assuming that the increased tax rate did not reduce the total estate. If the increased tax rate reduces the total estate, the amount transferred as charitable bequests will decline even further. Therefore, the estate tax would seem to discourage, not encourage, bequests to charitable institutions.

Philanthropic institutions often compete directly with government in providing public-type goods. Private schools and universities compete with public institutions in educating the populace. Religious institutions and government compete in articulating cultural norms and common concerns, as well as in the undertaking of certain charitable activities. Private foundations compete with government agencies in sponsoring scientific research. By diminishing contributions to private philanthropic institutions, estate taxation promotes governmental monopoly over such areas. Yet concern for the maintenance of basic liberties, the preservation of minority preferences and points of view, and effectiveness in providing services all suggest that competition among institutions providing related services is preferable to monopoly.[8]

Rationality in Fiscal Choice

In a market economy firms compete among themselves for buyers, and it is generally acknowledged that the efficacy of market competition varies directly with the degree of awareness about alternatives possessed by the participants. Likewise, in a democracy politicians compete for voter support, and the efficacy of political competition will also vary directly with the awareness of the alternatives possessed by the citizenry. With respect to taxation, political competition will perform more effectively as voters perceive more accurately the tax costs of public services. There are several features about transfer taxation, however, that blur the clarity of taxpayer perceptions of cost.

It is widely acknowledged that inflation is a tax, as the reduction in the value of the dollar corresponds to the inflation-financed expenditures of the government.[9] But under progressive tax rates, inflation also increases the burden of income and transfer taxes by increasing the real rate of tax levied on income and wealth transfers. The federal estate tax initially became effective on 9 September 1916. At that time the range of coverage was small and the progression in tax rates was slight. After a $50,000 specific exemption, the rates ranged from one percent on the first $50,000 of taxable estate to 10 percent on the net taxable estate over $5 million. Table 4, which indicates briefly the historical development of the federal estate tax, documents the continual broadening and extension of the federal estate tax, particularly once we recognize that inflation has increased prices about 350 percent from their 1916 level.

Compared with 1916, for instance, the specific exemption has only been increased from $50,000 to $60,000. Yet merely to offset the erosion of purchasing power through inflation would now require a specific exemption of $175,000. The minimum rate of tax has increased from 1 to 3 percent, and the size of estate subject to the minimum rate has fallen from $50,000 in 1916 to $5,000 at present. Yet if we allow for inflation, the lowest rate bracket would now

---

[8] See William A. Niskanen, *Bureaucracy and Representative Government* (Chicago: Aldine Publishing Co., 1971), for discussion of many facets of these issues of competition and monopoly.

[9] Under fractional reserve banking, part of the tax is collected by the banking system rather than by the government.

Table 4
DEVELOPMENT OF FEDERAL ESTATE TAXATION

Internal Revenue Code of:	Specific Exemption ($ thousands)	Rate	Minimum On Taxable Estate Under: ($ thousands)	Rate	Maximum On Taxable Estate Over: ($ thousands)
1916	$ 50	1 %	$ 50	10%	$ 5,000
1917	50	1.5	50	15	5,000
1918	50	1	50	25	10,000
1924	50	1	50	25	10,000
1926	100	1	50	20	10,000
1932	50	1	10	45	10,000
1934	50	1	10	60	10,000
1935	40	2	10	70	50,000
1941	40	3	5	77	10,000
1942	60	3	5	77	10,000

Source: *Facts and Figures on Government Finance*, 15th ed. (New York: Tax Foundation, Inc., 1969), p. 112.

have to begin at $175,000 to maintain coverage comparable to that of 1916. Whereas the rate of tax on the lowest bracket has increased by 300 percent since 1916, it has increased by 770 percent in the highest rate bracket. Inflationary effects, however, have been partially offset, for the amount at which the maximum rate takes effect has been raised from $5 million to $10 million. A complete allowance for inflation, however, would require that the $10 million be increased to $17.5 million. As it stands now, estates that were valued at less than $3 million in 1916, and are still worth $3 million in terms of real purchasing power, would now be valued at $10 million due to nothing more than inflationary erosions in the value of money.[10]

In the absence of inflation, tax rates would have had to have been raised more sharply and coverage broadened more extensively to accomplish what was accomplished automatically through inflation. Yet it makes a difference whether taxes are increased through conscious modification of tax rates or through automatic adjustment resulting from inflation. Empirical evidence shows that people tend to take an unchanged rate and bracket structure rather than an

[10] The real tax rates of the gift tax have been increased in similar fashion by inflation, though the amounts are less because the present gift tax dates from the Revenue Act of 1932, and the price level has increased by only about 250 percent since then.

unchanged real rate of tax as evidence of an unchanged fiscal environment.[11] People are quite aware of conscious modification of tax rates, but are relatively unconscious of increases in tax rates that occur automatically through inflation. For evidence of this point, one need merely witness the strenuous discussion about the tax surcharge proposal of a few years ago, and compare that with the total failure to recognize that, *under progressive taxation, inflation imposes a similar surcharge each year.*[12]

Taxpayer perceptions about the real cost of public services also depend upon the structure of the tax system. Other things equal, cost in a tax system in which all revenues are raised by a single tax will be felt more strongly by taxpayers than one in which revenues are raised by numerous small taxes. Even though all taxpayers may bear the same tax burden whether they are subject to one larger tax or to ten smaller ones, they will tend to feel that public services are less costly when financed by the set of smaller taxes.[13] A tax provides a signal to the taxpayer at the moment of payment that he is losing income. People also forget, however, so perceptions about the tax become dulled with the passage of time between moments of payment. The clarity of the signal itself varies directly with its strength, so one larger tax will be forgotten less rapidly than ten smaller ones. Thus a taxpayer will tend to be more acutely aware of the real cost of public services when they are financed by one larger tax than by several smaller ones.

Estate and gift tax collections account for less than 3 percent of total federal tax collections. Such a relatively small tax can only contribute to fiscal illusion, thereby promoting some irrationality in the process of democratic fiscal choice. As a general principle of fiscal organization, fiscal choice will become more rational as the proliferation of tax bases is curtailed. This principle suggests that tax revenues ought to be collected from a single base, or at least ought not to rely upon numerous small bases. Estate and gift taxes violate this elementary principle of fiscal rationality.[14]

---

[11] Richard E. Wagner, *The Fiscal Organization of American Federalism* (Chicago: Markham Publishing Co., 1971), pp. 85-88.

[12] Three means exist for correcting the fiscal illusion created by inflation: restore price level stability, adopt proportional rates of tax, or define the bracket structure in real terms so that it is itself adjusted in response to changes in the price level.

[13] For a related discussion, though in a slightly different context, see Wagner, *Fiscal Organization*, pp. 52-54.

[14] For a more extensive examination of these issues concerning the proliferation of tax bases, see Richard E. Wagner, *The Public Economy* (Chicago: Markham Publishing Co., 1973), pp. 227-32.

4

TECHNICAL ISSUES CONCERNING
TRANSFER TAXATION

In this chapter I shall consider five issues that are relatively more technical and more specific than those examined in Chapters 2 and 3: (1) whether transfer taxes should be of the estate or the inheritance form, (2) defining the unit upon which to base tax liability, (3) reducing tax avoidance through the creation of trusts, (4) difficulties associated with the liquidation of closely held businesses, and (5) strains created by the simultaneous taxation of transfers by forty-nine states and the federal government.

Taxation Upon Whom: Transferor or Transferee?

Assuming that a transfer of wealth from A to B and C gives rise to a tax liability, we can ask whether the tax should be levied upon A or upon B and C. This distinction defines the two contrasting forms of death taxation. If the tax is based upon the amount of wealth transferred by A, the transferor, we have the estate form of death taxation. If it is based upon the amount of wealth received by B and C, the transferees, we have the inheritance form of death taxation.

Taxation of the transferor—a unified transfer tax. In its 1969 proposals for tax reform, the Treasury recommended that the estate and gift taxes be combined into a unified tax on transfers. A single rate, bracket, and exemption schedule would apply to all transfers of wealth made by any transferor. The value of a donor's gifts would be cumulated over his lifetime as is done now, but the value of the estate would be added to the value of gifts to determine the total amount of taxable transfers.

Since gift tax rates are set at 75 percent of estate tax rates, it is commonly felt that transfers made by gifts receive more favorable treatment than transfers made by bequest. Supporters of a unified transfer tax contend that the lower rate of tax on gifts violates the principle of horizontal equity. Between two people who transfer the same amount of wealth to successors, the one who makes the more intensive use of gifts will pay less tax, and presumably thus be able to transfer a greater amount of wealth net of tax to his successors. Consider, as an illustration, two transferors, each with wealth of $1,244,275 to be transferred. If the wealth is transferred by bequest, the tax bill will be $420,967.25, which yields a net transfer of $823,306.75—ignoring for computational ease such complicating factors as exemptions. If the wealth is transferred by gift, by contrast, the tax bill will be only $244,275, which enables the donor to make a net transfer of $1,000,000. Thus among two people with equal wealth, the one who makes more extensive use of gifts will be able to transfer a greater amount of his wealth to successors.

It is doubtful, however, whether the lower tax rates on gifts should be considered a loophole, for relatively few donors find the lower rates a sufficient inducement to prefer gifts to bequests. Only those individuals with relatively strong preferences for maximizing the amount of wealth transferred to others will find a strong advantage in making gifts. In the absence of such preferences to maximize the amount of wealth transferred to successors, the prevailing rate differential between gifts and bequests does not seem significantly to subsidize inter vivos gifts.[1]

The case for an integrated transfer tax rests on two primary assumptions. First, that the amount of wealth transferred by the transferor is the appropriate base for taxation. This assumption is not widely held, except on a pragmatic basis. The preponderance of opinion seems to be that the amount of wealth received by the transferee is the more appropriate base for taxation. Yet while granting the conceptual superiority of taxation based upon the transferee, many acquiesce in taxation based on the transferor because it is administratively more convenient. Second, given the appropriateness of basing tax liability upon the size of the transferor's transfers, the assumption is made that better results are forthcoming under

---

[1] For careful analyses of these issues, see Harold M. Hochman and Cotton M. Lindsay, "Taxation, Interest, and the Timing of Inter-Generation Wealth Transfers," National Tax Journal, vol. 20 (June 1967), pp. 219-26; and Eli Schwartz and J. Richard Aronson, "The Preference for Accumulation vs. Spending: Gift and Estate Taxation and the Timing of Wealth Transfers," National Tax Journal, vol. 22 (September 1969), pp. 390-98.

a unified transfer tax. This assumption encapsulates the belief that a person who transfers $1 million during his life and $1 million upon his death should pay the same amount of tax as one who transfers $2 million upon his death, and that both should pay the same tax as one who transfers $2 million during his life. This argument might seem reasonable if interest rates were zero, but it seems unreasonable when interest rates are positive. Compare a transfer of $2 million during life with one of $2 million upon death ten years later. Since the tax payment is made ten years earlier in the case of the inter vivos gift than with the bequest, the tax payment on the gift exceeds the tax payment on the bequest because the interest that could have been earned had the tax not been paid was foregone over that ten-year period. If equal transfers of wealth are to be assigned the same present value of tax liability regardless of the timing of transfer, inter vivos gifts must be taxed at a lower rate than transfers upon death.

Taxation of the transferee—an accessions tax. Whereas liability for an estate tax depends on the size of the decedent's estate, liability for an inheritance tax depends on the amounts received by the heirs to the estate. An accessions tax is a unified tax on transfers, with liability based on the amounts received by transferees rather than the amounts given by transferors. An accessions tax, then, is a combination of inheritance tax plus gift tax on the donee. The base of an accessions tax would thus be an individual's total lifetime acquisitions through gifts and inheritances.

The primary rationale for accessions taxation is that the amount an individual receives is a better indicator of tax liability than the amount an individual gives. What matters is not the size of the decedent's estate, but the distribution of the estate among the heirs. With accessions taxation, an estate of $1 million that was left to a sole heir would pay a larger tax on its distribution than one that was distributed equally among ten heirs. Moreover, an estate of $10 million that was distributed equally among ten heirs would carry the same tax obligation as an estate of $1 million left to a single heir.

A subsidiary argument advanced in support of accessions taxation is that such a form of taxation will encourage a wider sharing of an estate because this is a means of reducing the tax levied upon the devolution of the estate. Large fortunes are thus less likely to be passed on from generation to generation under inheritance taxation than under estate taxation. This subsidiary argument, however, does not by itself support inheritance taxation because the same results can be attained under the estate form of taxation. All that would be necessary would be to establish a minimum exemption per bequest. If up to, say, $100,000 per legatee could be deducted from gross estate, inducement to wider sharing of estates would be given within the framework of estate taxation.

Although considerable feeling exists that it is preferable to base the tax on the amount received instead of on the amount transferred, inheritance taxation is subject to somewhat greater administrative cost than estate taxation. With an estate tax a single value is placed on the estate and the tax is determined. With an inheritance tax, however, a valuation must be placed on the share of each individual heir, and such valuation of individual shares is sometimes more difficult than valuation of the total estate. It is easier, for instance, to place a single value on all household effects than to first apportion the effects among separate heirs and then value each share. In most cases, of course, no significant differences in administrative cost will exist. But it can never be more costly to value an estate than to value separate inheritances, and there will occur occasions in which it is less costly to value the estate than the several inheritances.

Administrative issues aside, however, the primary argument given for an accessions tax over a unified transfer tax is that the size of an inheritance is a better index for basing tax obligations than the size of the estate from which the inheritance devolved.[2] As with the unified transfer tax, the case for an accessions tax rests on the assumption that the rate of interest is zero. Recognition that interest rates are positive creates a different perspective, and the impact on an accessions tax is the reverse of its impact on a unified transfer tax. With a unified transfer tax, equality of present values of tax liability requires a lower rate of tax on gifts than on bequests. With an accessions tax, by contrast, equality of present values of tax liability requires a higher rate of tax on gifts than on inheritances. Since the present value of a gift exceeds the present value of the same size inheritance received, for example, ten years later, the inheritance will be taxed more heavily than the gift if both transfers are subject to the same amount of tax. Therefore, equality of the present value of tax liability regardless of the timing of transfer requires that inheritances be taxed less heavily than gifts.

---

[2] Many people also feel that inheritance taxation is preferable because tax rates can be varied according to consanguinity. See, for instance, Dan T. Smith, *Federal Tax Reform* (New York: McGraw-Hill, 1961), p. 298. But an estate tax can achieve the same effect by allowing a per-legatee deduction that would vary according to consanguinity. Thus, for example, $200,000 could be deductible for transfers to sons and daughters, while only $100,000 could be deductible for transfers to nephews and nieces.

The Unit of Taxation

If a husband dies and is survived by his wife, should a tax be levied upon the husband's estate? The Internal Revenue Code of 1954 says "yes"; the Treasury's 1969 proposals for reform said "no." One's choice of the appropriate unit upon which to base tax liability depends primarily upon one's attitude toward the attribution of ownership. In some legal frameworks property is vested in the family unit rather than in the separate members of the family. Under such circumstances there can be no institution of inheritance, as the surviving members of the family unit cannot inherit what already belongs in common to the family unit.[3] Our legal framework recognizes and assigns individual ownership of property, so a decedent's property devolves upon someone else through succession—an institution that came into being only as societies came to recognize individual rather than family ownership of property.[4]

The federal estate tax recognizes individual rather than family ownership of property, though the 50 percent marital deduction represents a partial recognition of family ownership. Prior to the Revenue Act of 1942, deaths occurring in community property states were taxed less heavily than deaths occurring in common law states, for in community property states one-half of the husband's property acquired after marriage would be attributed to the wife, while in common law states all such property would be attributed to the husband. The Revenue Act of 1942 eliminated this differential treatment by treating deaths in community property states as if they occurred in common law states. The Revenue Act of 1948 maintained the equality of treatment, but did it by extending community property rights to deaths occurring in common law states by allowing a 50 percent marital deduction on noncommunity property.

Even with the 50 percent marital deduction, two families of identical wealth can bear different tax liabilities, depending upon

---

[3] See, for instance, Shultz's description of the Hindu joint-family system in which there is no inheritance because property is owned in common by the family and is acquired by survivorship rather than by succession. William J. Shultz, *The Taxation of Inheritance* (Boston: Houghton-Mifflin, 1926), p. 33.

[4] Eugene F. Scoles and Edward C. Halbach, Jr., *Problems and Materials on Decedent's Estates and Trusts* (Boston: Little, Brown & Co., 1965), p. 5. Moreover, the particular rules of inheritance used by a society will reflect its attitudes toward the nature of the family and its individual members. A patriarchal society will emphasize succession through the male line, for instance, whereas a matriarchal society will emphasize succession through the female line. See George W. Paton, *A Textbook of Jurisprudence*, 3rd ed. (Oxford: Oxford University Press, 1964), p. 493.

whether the richer or poorer spouse dies first. Take the case of a noncommunity property state in which the husband's wealth is $1,000,000 and the wife's is zero. If the husband predeceases the wife, the marital deduction can be taken by the wife, which would reduce the husband's gross estate to $500,000. If the wife dies first, however, no marital deduction can be taken, so the gross estate upon the husband's death would be $1,000,000. Thus the base splitting permitted by the marital deduction can be exploited only if the wealthier spouse dies first. The order of death can make a substantial difference in tax liability: The tax on a taxable estate of $1,000,000 is $325,700, while the total tax on two taxable estates of $500,000 each is $291,400.

The Treasury's 1969 proposals for transfer tax reform, by suggesting that the 50 percent limit on the marital deduction be removed, went a considerable distance toward recognizing the family as the unit of taxation. Ownership would still be attributed to individual members of the family, and a tax liability would potentially be created upon the death of any member of the family. But the family would have available the option of making tax-free transfers between husband and wife.[5]

Full marital exemption now commands wide support, for it is unreasonable to treat the surviving members of a family as receiving a capital gain when one member dies. Since the family is usually considered the basic unit of ownership de facto, even though not de jure, the surviving members of the family do not acquire additional nonhuman capital by virtue of one member's death. Furthermore, the family has suffered a reduction in the stock of human capital available to it. The death of the father sharply reduces the income available to support the family; the death of the mother sharply

---

[5] U.S. Treasury Department, *Tax Reform Studies and Proposals*, vol. 5 (Washington: U.S. Government Printing Office, February 1969), pp. 357-60. Circumstances are conceivable under which tax liability will be greater with a 100 percent marital deduction than with a 50 percent deduction. Consider the case of a husband who dies and leaves $1,000,000 to his wife, who in turn dies within two years. Further assume the wife consumed only the income from her inheritance. Under 100 percent marital deduction, no tax is levied upon the husband's death, while $325,700 is levied upon the wife's death, assuming for arithmetic convenience that the entire estate was taxable. Under 50 percent marital deduction, by contrast, a tax of $145,700 is levied upon the husband's $500,000 and a tax of $271,791 is levied upon the wife's $854,300. Since the wife died within two years of the husband, however, her estate will be credited with 100 percent of her husband's estate tax payment under the provision for quick succession relief. Thus the net tax on the wife's estate is $126,091, producing a total tax of $271,791 on the devolution of the estate, which is $53,909 less tax than with 100 percent marital deduction.

increases the cost of maintaining the family because many of the services provided free by the mother must now be purchased. By treating the family (husband, wife, and dependent children) as the unit of taxation, a tax would be levied as property devolved from the family unit. No tax liability would result from the death of one member of the family so long as there was a surviving member.[6] Such a change would bring the unit upon which tax liability is based into consistency with prevailing attitudes about the appropriate unit of ownership of property. A transfer tax should be levied, if one is to be levied at all, only if there is a clear capital gain to the recipient— and this requires adoption of the family as the unit of taxation.

Generation-Skipping Trusts [7]

The amount of tax levied upon the devolution of an estate will depend upon the form by which the estate is transferred. Consider two different ways of transferring the same estate from father to son to grandson. In the first case let the father transfer $1 million to his son, who lives on the interest income and transfers the remainder to the grandson. The father's estate pays a tax of $325,700 (assuming again for convenience that all figures are taxable amounts), leaving $674,300 to the son. The son lives off the interest from the estate, and transfers the principal amount to the grandson. A tax of $206,705 is levied upon the son's estate, which leaves $467,595 for the grandson. Thus the total tax bill on the devolution of the estate from the father to the grandson via the son is $532,405.

In the second case let the father transfer the $1 million in trust to the grandson, giving the son a life tenancy in the income from the estate. The father's estate again pays a tax of $325,700, which leaves $674,300 in trust for the grandson. Again the son lives off the income from $674,300, but since he does not have title to the property, no tax is levied upon his death. The grandson now receives $674,300, so the generation-skipping trust has reduced the tax liability on the devolution of the estate by $206,705. Yet the two cases are identical in all essential respects.

---

[6] For an early treatment of succession defined in terms of the family unit, see Harold M. Groves and Wallace I. Edwards, "A New Model for an Integrated Transfer Tax," *National Tax Journal*, vol 4 (December 1953), pp. 353-60. For a more recent statement, see Joseph A. Pechman, *Federal Tax Policy* (Washington: The Brookings Institution, 1966), 183-87.

[7] For an extensive survey of trusts and their relation to estate taxation, see Gerald R. Jantscher, *Trusts and Estate Taxation* (Washington: The Brookings Institution, 1967).

Generation-skipping trusts are a modern, though limited, version of primogeniture. Under primogeniture, the eldest son received a life tenancy in the estate, which in turn was passed on to his son, and this pattern of succession continued until either the nation or the family died out. For the most part, generation-skipping trusts are limited only by the rule against perpetuities, which says that interest designated in the trust must vest not later than 21 years after the death of the last person alive at the time of the creation of the trust.[8]

By making the tax liability depend merely on the form of transfer, trusts generate horizontal inequity. By creating a life tenancy rather than bequeathing the corpus, trusts retard the dissipation of large holdings of wealth, reduce risk-taking, and retard the rate of capital mobility. On all these grounds, generation-skipping trusts have undesirable consequences. Yet trusts do serve important functions, so the task is to tax trusts more effectively, not to preclude their use, although more effective taxation will certainly curtail their use. To maintain a sense of perspective, however, we should note that the magnitudes involved are relatively small. Using Internal Revenue Service special tabulations for millionaire decedents, Robert Anthoine found that about 11 percent of gross transfers skipped one generation and about 3 percent skipped more than one generation.[9] Although trusts clearly raise issues about horizontal equity and allocative efficiency, it is also important to recognize that generation-skipping trusts represent a relative trickle in the overall devolution of estates, rather than a flood.

The salient way of taxing trusts is to levy an estate tax upon the death of the life tenant, with the remainder distributed to the remaindermen. Consider as an example a father who leaves a post-tax estate of $1 million in trust to his four grandchildren, with his two sons as life tenants. The sons share the trust income equally, and upon the death of the last surviving son the estate passes out of trust to be divided equally among the grandsons. If the sons should die simultaneously, an estate tax would be levied upon the $1 million corpus, with the remainder distributed equally among the grandsons. Or if one son dies before the other, an estate tax would be levied upon $500,000 of the corpus. Upon the death of the surviving son, a tax would be levied upon the remaining corpus.

Two major objections have been brought against proposals to tax the corpus upon the death of the life tenant. One is largely

---

[8] Foundations, which are also a form of primogeniture, are not covered by the rule against perpetuities.

[9] Robert Anthoine, "Testamentary Trusts," pp. 162-63.

imaginary and one is quite real. On the imaginary level, many claim that it is unfair to levy a full estate tax upon the expiry of the life tenant because the life tenant has not had control over the corpus of the trust.[10] Actually, the life tenant often has considerable opportunity to invade the corpus. Moreover, a policy of levying an estate tax upon the death of the life tenant will itself produce subsequent changes in the pattern of bequests, and judgments of equity must be based on this probable alternative pattern rather than on the prevailing pattern. Taxing the corpus upon the death of the life tenant reduces the relative advantage of leaving estates in trust. Since the advantage of using trusts would be lessened, more bequests would be made outright. Thus taxation upon death of the life tenant would itself reduce the magnitude of the problem by reducing the use of trusts as an instrument for making bequests.

A quite real difficulty in taxing the expiration of life estates lies in the creation of discretionary trusts. Under a discretionary trust, the shares of the various life tenants are not specified in advance, but are left to the discretion of the trustee, although he and the decedent may have in fact agreed upon a specific sharing scheme. If four life tenants share the income from a $1 million discretionary trust, the death of one tenant does not produce an unambiguous increase in the share available to the others. Since the tenants are not assigned individual shares in the estate, it is impossible to specify the increase in the share available to the remaining tenants that results from the death of one tenant. By contrast, if the trust were equally shared among the life tenants, the death of one tenant would increase by $250,000 the amount available to the others. Perhaps the most appealing way of overcoming this problem is to use Gerald Jantscher's look-back approach, under which, roughly, a share of the trust is imputed to a life tenant in the same proportion that the tenant's income from the trust, over some specified period, was to the total income from the trust, over that same period.[11]

---

[10] See, for instance, Pechman, *Federal Tax Policy*, pp. 191-95.

[11] Jantscher, *Trusts and Estate Taxation*, pp. 172-90. There are other ways available for taxing generation-skipping trusts. The Treasury's proposals for reform suggested that a substitute tax be placed on the corpus of generation-skipping trusts, with the tax rate set at some fraction of the testator's estate tax rate. It would also be possible to tax trusts by treating the trustee as the owner of the corpus. Thus when the final life tenant died and the estate passed out of trust, the corpus would be treated as if it passed from one owner (the trustee) to another (the remaindermen). There are many alternative forms for trust taxation, none of which will be perfect, but some of which might be preferable to prevailing institutions.

Liquidity Problems of Closely Held Businesses

The liquidation of assets to pay estate tax sometimes creates special difficulties when the assets are not readily marketable, which is often true with closely held businesses. Considerable evidence suggests that the need to liquidate the assets of closely held businesses to pay estate tax encourages mergers of such businesses with larger corporations. Chelcie Bosland, for instance, estimated that in 63 percent of mergers of closely owned businesses over the period 1955-1959, estate tax considerations played a significant factor in the decision to merge.[12] Two separate motivations seem to lie behind the desire to merge closely owned businesses. On the one hand, there is a fear that the estate will have insufficient liquidity to pay the tax, and merger is a source of liquidity. On the other hand, the amount of tax liability to be assessed is itself uncertain because it depends upon an arbitrary valuation of the business by the Internal Revenue Service, so this uncertainty also creates a demand for liquidity.[13]

Estate tax law permits the executor of an estate to request that liquidation be allowed to take place over a period of up to ten years. This provision would seem to mitigate the problems of liquidation and the mergers produced thereby. The provision for deferred liquidation has had little impact, however, because it is not available unless the executor assumes personal responsibility for all future tax payments, regardless of what should happen to the value of the estate's assets in the interim. Thus the need to liquidate closely owned businesses in order to pay estate tax remains a serious problem. By suggesting that the personal liability for deferred taxes be removed from the executor by giving the government a security interest in the assets for which deferred payment is sought, the Treasury's 1969 proposals for reform took a significant step toward alleviating this problem.[14]

---

[12] Chelcie C. Bosland, "Has Estate Taxation Induced Recent Mergers?" *National Tax Journal*, vol. 16 (June 1963), pp. 159-68. For earlier assessments that reach the same conclusions, see Harold M. Somers, "Estate Taxes and Business Mergers," *Journal of Finance*, vol. 13 (May 1958), pp. 201-10; and Wilbur A. Steger, "The Taxation of Unrealized Capital Gains and Losses: A Statistical Study," *National Tax Journal*, vol. 10 (September 1957), pp. 266-81.

[13] Tax liability also depends upon random fluctuations in stock prices. Since stock prices are sometimes subject to considerable fluctuation over short periods of time, estates composed of identical holdings of stock may carry significantly different valuations because of a few days difference in the time of death. See C. Lowell Harriss, "Stock Prices, Death Tax Revenues, and Tax Equity," *Journal of Finance*, vol. 5 (September 1950), pp. 257-69.

[14] U.S. Treasury, *Tax Reform Studies and Proposals*, pp. 401-08.

Closely related to this liquidity problem is the avoidance of capital gains tax on assets that are held until death. While unrealized capital gains are taxed as part of the decedent's estate, they escape liability for income tax and the successor is allowed to revalue the assets at their present market value. In its 1969 proposals for reform, the Treasury recommended that appreciated capital gains on assets transferred upon death be subject to ordinary capital gains taxation.[15] The application of capital gains taxation to assets transferred upon death may counteract some of the "lock-in" effect of unrealized capital gains, thereby increasing the rate of capital mobility in the economy. A policy of taxing unrealized capital gains upon death, however, will aggravate the liquidity problems of closely held businesses, as the tax liability would be increased significantly in relation to the available liquidity.[16] The choice among alternative approaches to capital gains taxation is especially difficult to resolve because all of the alternatives represent the horns of a dilemma. In his careful examination of the available alternatives, Harold Somers concluded that two primary alternatives exist: (1) tax capital gains upon death, or (2) exempt capital gains during life.[17] That neither can be considered ideal attests to the depth of the dilemma.

Federal-State Concurrent Taxation

In addition to the federal estate and gift taxes, forty-nine states levy inheritance or estate taxes and twelve levy gift taxes. Considerable complexity is sometimes created in tax compliance as a result. A person who maintains a part-time residence in a second state may be claimed as a resident by both states for death tax purposes. Or shares of corporation stock may be taxed both by the state in which the decedent was domiciled and the state in which the corporation is chartered. Such possibilities for overlapping taxation place a cost

---

[15] Ibid., pp. 28-29. For an estimation that full taxation of unrealized capital gains would have increased tax revenues in 1967 by $1.9 billion, see Peter Eilbott, "The Revenue Gain From Taxation of Decedent's Unrealized Capital Gains," *National Tax Journal*, vol. 22 (December 1969), pp. 506-15.

[16] On the average, about one-half of unrealized capital gains are held in either real estate or shares of ownership in unincorporated enterprises. Moreover, the relative holdings of these asset classes fall as wealth rises. A policy of taxing unrealized capital gains upon death would thus impinge more forcefully upon the liquidity position of estates in the middle wealth ranges than in the higher wealth ranges.

[17] Harold M. Somers, "Taxation of Capital Gains at Death," in Paul L. Kleinsorge, ed., *Public Finance and Welfare* (Eugene: University of Oregon Press, 1966), pp. 135-55.

on individuals by inducing them to conduct their affairs so as to avoid such double taxation.

Many people feel that the diversity in state death tax laws introduces excessive complexity into tax compliance. This has led to the suggestion that greater uniformity among the states is a desirable objective of federal policy on death taxation. The simplest way of attaining this objective is to have federal preemption of death taxation.[18] Instead of federal preemption, some people suggest that the federal credit for state death tax payments be used more strenuously to promote greater uniformity among states.[19]

The federal credit for state death taxes initially appeared with the Revenue Act of 1924, and was set at a rate of 25 percent. The rate of credit was increased to 80 percent with the enactment of the Revenue Act of 1926. With the passage of the Revenue Act of 1932, which increased federal estate tax rates considerably, the rate of credit was maintained at 80 percent, but only 80 percent of what would have been estate tax liability under the Revenue Act of 1926. This peculiar subterfuge continued until the Revenue Act of 1954 brought the credit into conformity with prevailing practice; the amounts of credit were not changed, but the computation was based upon prevailing death tax schedules rather than upon what would have taken place under 1926 schedules.

The federal credit for state death tax payments could be modified to encourage greater uniformity in state death taxation. To this end the Advisory Commission on Intergovernmental Relations (ACIR) recommended a three-part reform of the federal credit.[20] First, it recommended a two bracket credit: A credit of 80 percent would be allowed on the first $250,000 of taxable estate and 20 percent on the remainder. Second, the ACIR recommended that the credit be given only for the estate-type of death tax. Third, it recommended that the states be required to practice revenue maintenance for the following five years by certifying that its own death tax collections were not reduced to offset the additional credit.

The credit device could be used even more strenuously to encourage uniformity than the proposal to give credit only for

---

[18] See, for example, Shoup, *Federal Estate and Gift Taxes*, pp. 84-85.

[19] See the report of the Advisory Commission on Intergovernmental Relations, *Coordination of State and Federal Inheritance, Estate, and Gift Taxes* (Washington: U.S. Government Printing Office, 1961); and James A. Maxwell's discussion of it, "A New Proposal for Coordination of Death Taxation," *National Tax Journal*, vol. 14 (December 1961), pp. 382-87.

[20] Advisory Commission on Intergovernmental Relations, *Coordination of State and Federal Inheritance, Estate, and Gift Taxes*, pp. 16-21.

estate-type taxes. More detailed specification of the format of the estate tax would be possible. The base of the state's tax that would be eligible for credit could be specified. The most complete instance of federally imposed uniformity would result from a tax supplement, under which a state simply makes its death tax collections some percentage of the decedent's federal tax liability by a supplement of the federal estate tax. In this way the federal government would exercise considerable control over the form of state death taxation, and such control might serve as the first step toward federal preemption of death taxation.[21]

Support for federal preemption of the death tax field is based upon a desire to eradicate instances of overlapping taxation by two or more states. Some who take this position suggest the federal government share with the states the revenues they preempt, while others do not. In either event this consideration is an incidental matter, for the case for federal preemption seems flimsy. In the first place, double taxation is the exception, not the rule. So federal preemption is a steep price to pay for avoiding a few cases of double taxation. Most cases of double taxation can be handled adequately through the legal system. At one time the Supreme Court had specified a relatively simple set of standards to govern state death taxation: realty and tangible property would be taxed in the state of location and intangible property would be taxed in the state of domicile.[22] By refusing to assign single domiciliary for tax purposes, the Court has since backed away from this principle, thereby contributing to the increased complexity of state death taxation over the past thirty years. At the same time, however, it seems clear that legal modifications can contribute to simplicity in state death taxation. And, moreover, even should the law permit double taxation, it is not clear that serious problems are created so long as prospective decedents are aware of the law. For instance, since the problems that may arise with multiple domiciliary are well known, prospective decedents have the opportunity to arrange their affairs to avoid double taxation.

People in general seem to have a strong fixation with hierarchical orderings. With respect to taxation, it quite naturally seems neater

---

[21] Maxwell, "Proposal for Coordination of Death Taxation," suggested that it would be desirable to use the federal credit to promote greater uniformity among the states as a first step toward attaining the ultimate goal of complete federal jurisdiction over transfer taxation.

[22] William J. Shultz and C. Lowell Harriss, *American Public Finance*, 8th ed. (Englewood Cliffs, N.J.: Prentice-Hall, 1965), pp. 377-78.

to have one set of tax provisions than fifty-one. But this is a line of argument that is true for anything, whether it be tax laws, brands of cereal, styles of clothing, or news stories. However, uniformity in tax institutions, as uniformity elsewhere, is purchased at a price. And the price of federal preemption seems quite steep, especially since the alleged benefits are small and the problems can be handled in other ways.[23]

---

[23] For a good description of credits, supplements, and intergovernmental agreements as alternative ways of securing greater uniformity in state death taxation, see William H. Sager, "Practicability of Uniform Death and Gift Tax Laws," *National Tax Journal*, vol. 10 (December 1957), pp. 361-69.

5

**A FRAMEWORK FOR
FISCAL REFORM**

In this chapter I want to examine some fundamental, long-run issues concerning reform in the taxation of wealth transfers. I shall do this by comparing the incorporation of transfers into the personal income tax with the maintenance of separate provisions for taxing transfers of wealth.

Incorporating Transfers into the Personal Income Tax

Section 102 of the Internal Revenue Code of 1954 specifically excludes from the definition of income any wealth received by gift or inheritance. However, personal income is commonly defined as the maximum amount of real consumption over some period of time that could be undertaken without reducing the real value of capital. In other words, personal income is equal to consumption during the year plus wealth at the end of the year minus wealth at the beginning of the year.[1] Consistent application of this definition of income suggests that inheritances or gifts are income to the recipient. If a person with an annual income of $20,000 and a beginning wealth of $100,000 has an ending wealth of $600,000 due to the inheritance of $500,000, his income for the year would be $520,000.[2] Elementary principles of consistency would seem to make a strong case for

---

[1] See Henry C. Simons, *Personal Income Taxation* (Chicago: University of Chicago Press, 1938), p. 50.

[2] That is, $520,000 = $20,000 + $600,000 − $100,000.

abandoning separate taxes on wealth transfers and treating inheritances and gifts as income under the personal income tax.[3]

If gifts are considered income to the donee and if inheritances are considered income to the legatee, the question arises as to whether such transfers should be considered as a loss of income to the transferor. While the usual presumption is that such transfers should not be deductible from the income of the transferor, there are strong reasons for suggesting that such transfers should be deductible. Consider a donee whose beginning wealth was $50,000, whose consumption during the year was $15,000, and whose ending wealth was $100,000, with the increased wealth reflecting a gift of $50,000. His income for the year is clearly $65,000. Further suppose the donor's beginning wealth was $200,000, his consumption during the year was $40,000, and his ending wealth was $150,000, with the reduced wealth reflecting his gift of $50,000. Using Henry Simons' definition of income, the donor's income is −$10,000. Consistent application of this definition of income suggests that while gifts should be counted as income to the donee, they ought to be counted as losses of income to the donor.[4] As a matter of administrative convenience, however, it would probably be simpler to ignore gifts completely unless they occur within some minimal period of time before the donor's death, in which case gifts would be treated as inheritances.

The principles regarding gifts from the standpoint of the donor and the donee are also applicable to bequests from the standpoint of the legator and the legatee. Consider a legator whose initial wealth was $200,000, whose consumption before his death was $20,000, and whose wealth at the end of the year was zero—reflecting the devolution of his estate to legatees. A consistent application of the definition of income would suggest that the legator's income for that year was −$180,000. Since negative incomes are not recognized by the personal income tax, his income for the year for tax purposes

---

[3] The classic presentation of this position was developed by Simons. See Simons, *Personal Income Taxation*, pp. 125-47. The Income Tax Act of 1894, by the way, proposed to incorporate gifts and inheritances into the definition of personal income.

[4] This was not Simons' position, however, for he did not want to permit transferors to reduce their income by transferring wealth. For his reasoning, see Ibid., pp. 56-58 and 134-40. The provisions of the personal income tax that allow deductions for transfers to philanthropic institutions are compatible with this line of reasoning, though the current practice of allowing deduction for transfers to institutions but not to persons is perhaps an unfortunate practice in an increasingly impersonal society.

should be zero, whereas it would be $20,000 under prevailing practices.

A logical and consistent application of the generally preferred definition of income suggests that gifts and inheritances should be treated as income to the transferees and treated as losses of income to the transferors. Separate provisions for the taxation of wealth transfers are incompatible with a consistent application of the definition of income. Moreover, the treatment of transfers as income and the elimination of special provisions for transfer taxation is more in accord with the functions of a tax system which were examined in Chapter 1. This is so both for financing the supply of public services and for transferring income. Considerations of horizontal equity in the assignment of tax liability to finance the supply of general-benefit public services reinforce the view that separate transfer taxation is unwarranted. Taxation based on either the size of an estate or the size of an inheritance will often result in people with equal incomes paying unequal taxes, due merely to differences among persons in the source of their income.

However, if gifts and inheritances are to be treated as income to the recipient, it becomes exceedingly important to develop expanded provisions for averaging income, at least so long as income is taxed at progressive rates. If income were taxed at proportional rates, there would be no reason for averaging because persons with fluctuating incomes would pay the same tax as persons with constant incomes. But with progressive taxation in the absence of averaging, a person with a fluctuating income would pay a greater tax than a person with a constant income, even though the present values of both income streams were identical. In the absence of averaging, a married person filing a joint return who had a taxable income of $10,000 for four years and $60,000 for one year—the additional $50,000 representing an inheritance—would pay a total tax of $29,580 on the total taxable income of $100,000. By contrast, a married person filing a joint return who had a taxable income of $20,000 per year for five years would pay a total tax of $21,900 on his $100,000 of taxable income. Hence, ignoring for computational simplicity possible differences in present values as between the two persons, the person with the fluctuating income would pay $7,680 more tax on the same income over the five-year period than the person with the constant income. Moderate averaging has been part of the personal income tax since the Revenue Act of 1964. However, if gifts and inheritances should be treated as income under the personal income tax, substantial fluctuations in personal income would become much more prevalent due to the irregular receipts of gifts and inheritances. Therefore, equity in taxation would require that the period for averaging income be extended beyond five years.

Maintaining Separate Provisions for Transfer Taxation

While some support probably exists for treating gifts and inheritances as income, Joseph A. Pechman is probably correct in stating that "tax theorists almost unanimously agree that estate and gift taxation should play a larger role in the revenue system." [5] For instance, during the 1965 Brookings conference on estate and gift taxation, little support was found for incorporating gifts and inheritances into the personal income tax. [6] Yet gifts and inheritances are income. Since income is widely regarded as the most appropriate source of general revenue, it is difficult to comprehend the strong endorsement given to estate and gift taxation as separate institutions.

The maintenance of separate provisions for the taxation of wealth transfers must be supported by some argument to the effect that the source of a person's wealth is a legitimate object upon which to base differences in tax treatment among individuals. It is sometimes suggested that "earned" wealth is more legitimate than inherited wealth, [7] though it is never said just how being born with great athletic ability, a glib tongue, a pleasing singing voice, good looks, high intellect, or a charismatic presence on television can be said to be "earned." Such a suggestion concerning the inferiority of inherited wealth leads to proposals for special taxation of wealth transfers. Using the jargon of modern welfare economics, if some people are envious of those who inherit wealth while no one is envious of those who "earn" their wealth, Pareto-optimality requires that this envy be assuaged via inheritance taxation. [8]

While the sanctification of envy via taxation may be argued by using the vocabulary of welfare economics, such tautological usage

[5] Pechman, *Federal Tax Policy*, p. 200.

[6] Shoup, *Federal Estate and Gift Taxes*, p. 200. Nonetheless, the 1966 report of the Carter Commission on comprehensive tax reform in Canada recommended that gifts and inheritances be taxed as income to the recipients. See "Taxation of Income," *Report of the Royal Commission on Taxation*, vol. 3 (Ottawa: Queen's Printer, 1966), pp. 465-519.

[7] See, for example, Lester C. Thurow, *The Impact of Taxes on the American Economy* (New York: Praeger Publishers, Inc., 1971), pp. 157-58.

[8] Such an argument for using taxation to assuage envy appears in E. J. Mishan, "A Survey of Welfare Economics," *The Economic Journal*, vol. 70 (June 1960), pp. 197-256.

illustrates only the sterility of modern welfare economics. To discuss inheritance with such an analytical framework is to evade most of the issues worth discussing, for the "conclusions" reached by such analysis are implied by the initial premises. Moreover, the acceptance of such modes of analysis precludes any analysis of the properties of a social order operating under different institutions with respect to inheritance. It is far more productive to focus an analysis of inheritance on the comparative properties of social orders operating with and without inheritance. When John Stuart Mill observed that the maintenance of a free society requires "liberty of tastes and pursuits . . . without impediment from our fellow-creatures, so long as what we do does not harm them, even though they should *think* our conduct foolish, perverse, or wrong,"[9] he implicitly established a much richer agenda concerning the institution of inheritance than can ever be established by using the analytical modes of welfare economics. As Mill saw it, the legitimization of envy was inconsistent with the maintenance of a free society; merely to be emotionally affronted by someone cannot be legitimate grounds for legislation if a free society is to survive. While Mills' prognosis may be incorrect on this point, and while there are numerous questions concerning the concrete implication of his dictum, the important point is that an altogether different agenda is established for examining such social institutions as inheritance, an agenda against which the impoverishment of modern welfare economics is starkly exposed.

The issue concerning the social function of inheritance revolves around an analysis of two alternative social orders, one operating with inheritance and one operating without. If inheritance were abolished, some envy would perhaps be assuaged. But there are also several positive features of a social order in which inheritance is sanctioned that would be destroyed if inheritance were abolished.

The abolition of inheritance would reduce saving, and hence capital formation and economic progress, as was described in Chapter 3. As a consequence of this impact, some subtle changes would take place in our society, changes that would occur slowly but with considerable force in the long run. Without inheritance, characteristics compatible with the accumulation of wealth would have less survival value in our society relative to such characteristics as pleasing superiors, scoring well on examinations, and appearing personable in public. Hence over time we should expect to find a reduction in those characteristics that are compatible with accumulating wealth.

---

[9] "On Liberty," in his *Utilitarianism, Liberty, and Representative Government*, Everyman's Library, No. 482 (London: Dent, 1910 [1859]), p. 75 (my italics).

Yet in a free enterprise economy, those who become relatively wealthy are to a considerable extent those who have been relatively more successful in producing services valued highly by other people; the more a person is able to provide services to others that are highly valued by the recipients, the wealthier the provider will become. The characteristic of providing valuable services to others has higher survival value in a social order that permits inheritance than in one that does not, and it would seem quite important to promote the survival of this characteristic rather than to promote its extinction.[10]

Furthermore, the institution of inheritance makes possible the establishment of private sources of wealth. Therefore, inheritance makes it possible for private wealth to compete with public wealth in undertaking a variety of artistic, cultural, educational, philanthropic, and scientific activities. Without competition from private wealth, government would exercise a monopoly over such areas of life. Yet the maintenance of diversity so that minority views may survive and possess a chance of becoming majority views seems a necessary ingredient of a free society. Inheritance promotes such diversity by preventing monopoly control over the financing of such spheres of life.

Moreover, transfers of wealth reflect an interdependence of utility functions between transferor and transferee.[11] That a legator could have purchased an annuity and left no estate, but chose to leave the estate instead, reflects the existence of an affective bond among generations. Gifts reflect such affective bonds perhaps even more strongly. What is the impact of taxing an essentially benevolent activity? One might indeed wish to tax activities that reflect hate, but why activities that reflect love? Currently, little is understood as to how social institutions, by generating selective information through experience, induce changes in preferences. Yet social institutions clearly have such an impact. It seems not at all unreasonable to suspect that one impact of the abolition of inheritance would be to diminish intergenerational bonds, with potentially far-reaching consequences for the character of the social order.

Leaving aside possible changes in preferences, the abolition of inheritance will generate a demand for substitute institutions, thereby creating some excess burden from the resulting adaptations. Inheri-

---

[10] For a seminal examination of the way in which an institutional framework promotes the survival of certain characteristics and not of others, see Armen A. Alchian, "Uncertainty, Evolution, and Economic Theory," *Journal of Political Economy*, vol. 58 (June 1950), pp. 211-21.

[11] For a careful exposition of utility interdependence, see Harold M. Hochman and James D. Rodgers, "Pareto Optimal Redistribution," *American Economic Review*, vol. 59 (September 1969), pp. 542-57.

tance results because transferors have a demand for making transfers of wealth. The prohibition of inheritance does not diminish this demand, but rather establishes a disequilibrium situation in much the same manner as, for example, rent ceilings. If the inheritance of wealth were precluded, adaptations would take place to generate other forms of inheritance in much the same manner as selling furniture to tenants and reduced maintenance of premises is an adaptation to rent ceilings. One possible adaptation to the abolition of inheritance would be an increased inheritance of occupational positions, much as is now practiced by a few labor unions. If such inherited positions were combined with an expanded use of employment tenure, social mobility would be retarded and the social order would come to be based relatively more on caste or status.[12]

There seems little doubt that much support for separate provisions for transfer taxation is due to a genuine concern for assisting those who have been left out of the mainstream of the American economy. Yet there is a fundamental difference between a tax policy designed to penalize the relatively fortunate and a tax policy designed to assist the relatively unfortunate. While high marginal rates of tax may penalize the wealthy, they do not significantly assist the nonwealthy to become wealthier.

Attempts to penalize the fortunate via high marginal rates of tax distort the allocation of resources in several directions, creating a substantial excess burden. High marginal rates of tax reduce the willingness of investors to undertake risky investments, which decreases the rate of mobility of individuals within the distribution of income. Consequently, the wealthy are more likely to stay wealthy and the poor are less likely to become wealthy. Moreover, nominally high rates of estate taxation promote a considerable investment in estate planning to avoid tax. Not only are revenues collected by government, but also considerable investment is made in estate planning, and the investment in the latter is the deadweight loss associated with collecting the former. Taxes are collected on monetary transactions, and the higher the rate of tax the stronger the incentive to substitute in-kind transactions for monetary transactions. Moreover, the higher the rate of tax, the greater the return from investing in seeking privileged tax treatment relative to the return from investing in socially productive activities. Billions of dollars are spent annually in trying to evade taxes, avoid taxes, seek out nontaxable forms of income, and secure privileged tax treatment. The amount of

---

[12] See, for instance, Friedrich A. Hayek, *The Constitution of Liberty* (Chicago: University of Chicago Press, 1959), p. 91.

this excess burden, which is largely generated by the highly progressive structure of nominal rates of tax, could itself promote a substantial war on poverty.

There seems little question but that a genuine consensus exists to the effect that the primary distributional concern of our fiscal system should be to assist the unfortunate, not to penalize the fortunate. A game in which people have a chance to win above average incomes necessarily requires that they may win below average incomes. But the primary topic of concern is not the inequality of rewards, but that the game is fair and that the lowest returns attain some minimum level. Fair treatment ex ante, however, is compatible with unequal returns ex post. A tax system designed to promote equality of opportunity rather than to penalize the wealthy would differ considerably from our present system. Progression in tax rates would be reduced substantially, if not eliminated altogether. The highly progressive portions of our tax system raise little revenue and are counterproductive in important respects, for they are incapable of providing greater opportunity to disadvantaged citizens to earn higher incomes and to amass greater wealth. Below some minimal level of income, a strong case exists for implementing some such program for income maintenance as a wage subsidy or a negative income tax. Such a combination of treating wealth transfers as income, taxing income at proportionate rates, and providing for income maintenance, seems far more capable of making a positive contribution to the equalization of opportunity than the prevailing punitive system of highly progressive nominal rates of tax on wealth transfers and income.

Since an analysis of our system of transfer taxation must be informed by a knowledge of the salient features of the system, the essential features of this system are described in this appendix. Since I want only to present the broad outlines of our transfer tax system, I necessarily ignore or oversimplify many of the complexities of tax administration.

Federal Estate Taxation

A decedent's estate tax liability is determined by following a four-step procedure. First, the value of the *gross estate* is estimated. Second, various exemptions and deductions are subtracted to determine the value of the *taxable estate*. Third, the *gross estate tax* is computed from the tax rate schedule shown in Table A-1. Fourth, the *net estate tax payable* is calculated by subtracting from the gross estate tax certain credits against the tax.

Gross estate.[1] The estimation of a decedent's gross estate is simple in principle but complex in practice. The valuation of real estate for local property taxation is fraught with well-known complexities, and the problems of assessing the gross estate are similar to those of assessing local real estate, except that real estate is only a small portion of the property covered by the estate tax. The gross estate of a decedent is estimated by making an inventory valuation of all the decedent's property, real and personal, tangible and intangible. As Table A-2 shows, corporate stock, real estate, and cash comprised

---

[1] The definition and valuation of gross estate is covered in Sections 2031-2044 of the Internal Revenue Code of 1954.

57

Table A-1
FEDERAL ESTATE TAX SCHEDULE

Taxable Estate			Gross Estate Tax	
At least:	but	less than:	Base plus percent of excess over:	
$ 0	$	5,000	3%	$ 0
5,000		10,000	$ 150 + 7%	5,000
10,000		20,000	500 + 11%	10,000
20,000		30,000	1,600 + 14%	20,000
30,000		40,000	3,000 + 18%	30,000
40,000		50,000	4,800 + 22%	40,000
50,000		60,000	7,000 + 25%	50,000
60,000		100,000	9,500 + 28%	60,000
100,000		250,000	20,700 + 30%	100,000
250,000		500,000	65,000 + 32%	250,000
500,000		750,000	145,700 + 35%	500,000
750,000		1,000,000	233,200 + 37%	750,000
1,000,000		1,250,000	325,700 + 39%	1,000,000
1,250,000		1,500,000	423,200 + 42%	1,250,000
1,500,000		2,000,000	528,200 + 45%	1,500,000
2,000,000		2,500,000	753,200 + 49%	2,000,000
2,500,000		3,000,000	998,200 + 53%	2,500,000
3,000,000		3,500,000	1,263,200 + 56%	3,000,000
3,500,000		4,000,000	1,543,200 + 59%	3,500,000
4,000,000		5,000,000	1,838,200 + 63%	4,000,000
5,000,000		6,000,000	2,468,200 + 67%	5,000,000
6,000,000		7,000,000	3,138,200 + 70%	6,000,000
7,000,000		8,000,000	3,838,200 + 73%	7,000,000
8,000,000		10,000,000	4,568,200 + 76%	8,000,000
10,000,000 and over			6,088,200 + 77%	10,000,000

Source: Internal Revenue Code of 1954, Section 2001.

over 60 percent of gross estates in 1965. Although the gross estate is normally valued as of the date of death, the executor may elect to have the estate valued as of either the date of sale of property in the estate or one year after the decedent's death.

Taxable estate.[2] Several deductions and exemptions are subtracted from the gross estate to determine the taxable estate. Every estate is allowed to take a specific exemption of $60,000. Deductions are allowed for funeral expenses and the expenses of administering the estate, as well as for the decedent's unpaid debts and taxes. Bequests to approved, tax-exempt, charitable, educational, or religious institutions are also deductible from the gross estate. If the decedent is

[2] The deductions and exemptions from the gross estate that yield the taxable estate are covered in Sections 2051-2056 of the Internal Revenue Code of 1954.

Table A-2

GROSS ESTATE, DEDUCTIONS, AND ESTATE TAX, 1965

($ in millions)

Gross estate:		
Corporate stock	$ 9,215	
Real estate	4,275	
Cash	2,612	
Bonds	1,491	
Trust and remainder interests	1,345	
Life insurance	1,112	
Notes and mortgages	720	
Noncorporate business assets	549	
Household goods and other assets	344	
Annuities	95	
Total gross estate		$21,757
Deductions:		
Specific exemption	$5,339	
Marital deduction	4,090	
Charitable bequests	1,309	
Debts	1,112	
Administrative expenses	795	
Funeral expenses	150	$12,795
Less: lifetime transfers		198
Total deductions		$12,598
Taxable estate:		$ 9,160
Gross estate tax:		$ 2,755
Less credits		
State death taxes	$ 280	
Foreign, gift, and prior estate taxes	61	
Total credits		$ 341
Net estate tax payable:		$ 2,412

Source: Internal Revenue Service, *Statistics of Income—1965, Fiduciary, Gift, and Estate Tax Returns* (Washington: U.S. Government Printing Office, 1967), p. 58.

survived by a spouse, a marital deduction of up to 50 percent of noncommunity property in the adjusted gross estate (which is the gross estate less deductions for expenses and debts) may be taken. An adjusted gross estate of $120,000, for instance, could be reduced to $60,000 by taking the full marital deduction. When the specific exemption is then applied, the taxable estate becomes zero.

Table A-2 shows that deductions totaled nearly $13 billion in 1965, which was about 60 percent of the gross estate value. The

Table A-3
FEDERAL CREDIT FOR STATE DEATH TAXES

Taxable Estate			Amount of Credit	
At least:	but	less than:	Base plus percent of excess over:	
$ 40,000	$	90,000	0.8% $	40,000
90,000		140,000	$ 400 + 1.6%	90,000
140,000		240,000	1,200 + 2.4%	140,000
240,000		440,000	3,600 + 3.2%	240,000
440,000		640,000	10,000 + 4.0%	440,000
640,000		840,000	18,000 + 4.8%	640,000
840,000		1,040,000	27,600 + 5.6%	840,000
1,040,000		1,540,000	38,800 + 6.4%	1,040,000
1,540,000		2,040,000	70,800 + 7.2%	1,540,000
2,040,000		2,540,000	106,800 + 8.0%	2,040,000
2,540,000		3,040,000	146,800 + 8.8%	2,540,000
3,040,000		3,540,000	190,800 + 9.6%	3,040,000
3,540,000		4,040,000	238,800 + 10.4%	3,540,000
4,040,000		5,040,000	290,800 + 11.2%	4,040,000
5,040,000		6,040,000	402,800 + 12.0%	5,040,000
6,040,000		7,040,000	522,800 + 12.8%	6,040,000
7,040,000		8,040,000	650,800 + 13.6%	7,040,000
8,040,000		9,040,000	786,800 + 14.4%	8,040,000
9,040,000		10,040,000	930,800 + 15.2%	9,040,000
10,040,000 and over			1,082,800 + 16.0%	10,040,000

Source: Internal Revenue Code of 1954, Section 2011.

specific exemption and the marital deduction accounted for over $5 billion and $4 billion, respectively. Expenses and debts accounted for just over $2 billion, and charitable bequests just over $1 billion.

Gross estate tax. Once the decedent's taxable estate is determined, the gross estate tax is determined as indicated by the tax rate schedule shown in Table A-1. The total amount of gross estate tax for 1965 was $2.7 billion, which was more than 30 percent of the value of taxable estates and was nearly 13 percent of the value of gross estates.

Net estate tax payable. Several credits are allowed against gross ˙ estate tax. The total value of such credits exceeded $0.3 billion for 1965, which reduced the net estate tax payable to $2.4 billion.

The most significant credit is the one allowed for state death tax payments, the rate schedule for which is shown in Table A-3.[3] Table A-1 shows that the gross estate tax on a taxable estate of

---

[3] The credits against gross estate tax are covered in Sections 2011-2016 of the Internal Revenue Code of 1954.

$1,000,000 is $325,700. Table A-3 shows that if a state levies a tax upon either the estate or its distribution, the amount of state death tax payments up to a maximum of $36,500 can be credited against gross estate tax. For instance, if the state levied death taxes of exactly $36,500, the net estate tax payable to the federal government would be reduced to $289,140.

Several less significant credits also exist. Credits may be allowed for death taxes paid to a foreign country. Credit is allowed for gift taxes paid by the decedent if the property upon which the gift tax was paid is subsequently included in the decedent's estate. Finally, credit is sometimes given for previous estate tax payments under what is referred to as the provision for quick succession relief. Suppose the husband predeceases the wife by, for example, one year. Without a provision for quick succession relief, the estate is taxed once upon the husband's death and again upon the wife's death. Quick succession relief softens the force of this double taxation of an estate. If the wife dies within two years of the husband, the wife's estate is given credit for 100 percent of her husband's estate tax payment. If the wife's death occurs within the third or fourth year following her husband's death, the credit is 80 percent of the husband's tax payment, and the credit continues to decline at 20 percent increments at each two-year interval until it vanishes once the wife survives the husband by ten years.

Federal Gift Taxation [4]

The federal gift tax is viewed as a complement to the federal estate tax, not as an independent tax. Gift taxation was instituted and is maintained primarily to increase the yield of the estate tax. In the absence of a gift tax, a prospective decedent could escape estate tax liability by transferring wealth before his death. By reducing this incentive to make inter vivos gifts, the gift tax works to increase the amount of wealth being transferred at death and subject to the estate tax.

The complementarity between the estate tax and the gift tax is shown by the nearly identical structures of the two taxes. As Table A-4 shows, the gift tax has the same rate and bracket structure as the estate tax; the only difference is that for each bracket the rate

---

[4] The determination of gift tax liability is covered in Sections 2501-2504 of the Internal Revenue Code of 1954. The definition and valuation of transfers subject to tax are covered in Sections 2511-2517; deductions and exemptions from the tax are covered in Sections 2521-2524.

Table A-4
FEDERAL GIFT TAX SCHEDULE

Taxable Gifts			Gift Tax Liability	
At least:	but	less than:	Base plus percent of excess over:	
$ 0	$	5,000	2¼ % $	0
5,000		10,000	$ 112.50 + 5¼ %	5,000
10,000		20,000	375.00 + 8¼ %	10,000
20,000		30,000	1,200.00 + 10½ %	20,000
30,000		40,000	2,250.00 + 13½ %	30,000
40,000		50,000	3,600.00 + 16½ %	40,000
50,000		60,000	5,250.00 + 18¾ %	50,000
60,000		100,000	7,125.00 + 21 %	60,000
100,000		250,000	15,525.00 + 22½ %	100,000
250,000		500,000	49,275.00 + 24 %	250,000
500,000		750,000	109,275.00 + 26¼ %	500,000
750,000		1,000,000	174,900.00 + 27¾ %	750,000
1,000,000		1,250,000	244,275.00 + 29¼ %	1,000,000
1,250,000		1,500,000	317,400.00 + 31½ %	1,250,000
1,500,000		2,000,000	396,150.00 + 33¾ %	1,500,000
2,000,000		2,500,000	564,900.00 + 36¾ %	2,000,000
2,500,000		3,000,000	748,650.00 + 39¾ %	2,500,000
3,000,000		3,500,000	947,400.00 + 42 %	3,000,000
3,500,000		4,000,000	1,157,400.00 + 44¼ %	3,500,000
4,000,000		5,000,000	1,378,650.00 + 47¼ %	4,000,000
5,000,000		6,000,000	1,851,150.00 + 50¼ %	5,000,000
6,000,000		7,000,000	2,353,650.00 + 52½ %	6,000,000
7,000,000		8,000,000	2,878,650.00 + 54¾ %	7,000,000
8,000,000		10,000,000	3,426,150.00 + 57 %	8,000,000
10,000,000 and over			4,566,150.00 + 57¾ %	10,000,000

Source: Internal Revenue Code of 1954, Section 2502.

of gift tax is set at three-quarters of the rate of estate tax. The gift tax follows the same format for determining tax liability as the estate tax: A valuation is first placed upon the gifts made by the donor, certain exemptions and deductions are then taken to determine the value of taxable gifts, and the gift tax liability is finally computed. Since the gift tax is governed by the same essential principles as the estate tax, we shall describe only those features of the gift tax that are not found in the estate tax.

Liability for gift tax is cumulative over a donor's lifetime at the rates given in Table A-4. For each year that a donor makes taxable gifts, his tax liability for that year is computed as the difference between his cumulated lifetime tax liability and his previous gift tax payments. To illustrate, consider an individual who as of one year ago had made lifetime taxable gifts of $80,000, upon which his gift tax payments were $11,325. During the current year suppose he makes additional taxable gifts of $40,000. His cumulated value of taxable gifts has risen to $120,000, upon which the gift tax is $20,025. Given his previous payments of $11,325, his additional tax liability for the current year would be $8,700.

The gift tax provides two forms of exemption—a specific lifetime exemption of $30,000 and an annual per donee exemption of $3,000. A donor may give up to $3,000 per year free of tax, with no limit on either the number of years or the number of donees. Gifts, then, enter the tax base only to the extent that a donee receives more than $3,000 in any one year. To illustrate the impact of the annual exemption, consider three donors, each of whom makes gifts of $30,000 during the year and has previously exhausted his $30,000 specific exemption. Let the first make a single gift of $30,000, the second three gifts of $10,000 each, and the third ten gifts of $3,000 each. After subtracting the annual per donee exemption, the value of taxable gifts would be $27,000 for the first donor, $21,000 for the second donor, and zero for the third.

Both the actual tax rates and the annual per donee exemption feature serve to make the effective tax rate on gifts lower than that on estates. The rate of tax on gifts is further lowered relative to that on estates by the exemption of gift tax payments from the base of the gift tax. If a donor makes a taxable gift of $60,000, the donee receives $60,000 and the donor pays a gift tax of $7,125. The total amount of wealth transferred by the donor is $67,125—$60,000 to the donee and $7,125 to the Internal Revenue Service. If the gift tax base was determined in the same manner as the estate tax base, however, the amount of taxable gift would be $67,125. And with this size of taxable gift, the amount of gift tax would be $8,621.25, which would leave only $58,503.75 for the donee.

State Transfer Taxation

All states except Nevada impose death taxes; twelve use estate taxation and thirty-seven use inheritance taxation. Twelve states, moreover, levy a gift tax. Table A-5 shows that considerable variation exists in the rate schedules of the twelve states that practice estate taxation. Ohio provides a specific exemption of only $5,000, while Arizona provides one of $100,000. South Carolina has a nearly proportional tax rate, as the marginal tax rate is 4 percent on the first $40,000 of taxable estate and rises to 6 percent on the value in excess of $100,000. North Dakota, by contrast, has a steeply progressive estate tax, rising from 2 percent on the first $25,000 to 23 percent on the amount of taxable estate in excess of $1,500,000.

Table A-5
STATE ESTATE TAX RATES

State	Marginal Rate Range (on taxable estate)	Minimum Rate Applies To:	Maximum Rate Applies Above:	Specific Exemption
Alabama		Maximum federal credit		$ 60,000
Arizona	0.8%—16%	$50,000	$10,000,000	$100,000
Arkansas		Maximum federal credit		$ 60,000
Florida		Maximum federal credit		$ 60,000
Georgia		Maximum federal credit		$ 60,000
Mississippi	1%—16%	$60,000	$10,000,000	$ 60,000
New York	2%—21%	$50,000	$10,000,000	Variable
North Dakota	2%—23%	$25,000	$ 1,500,000	$ 20,000
Ohio	2%— 7%	$40,000	$ 500,000	$ 5,000
Oklahoma	1%—10%	$10,000	$10,000,000	$ 15,000
South Dakota	4%— 6%	$40,000	$ 100,000	$ 60,000
Utah	3%—10%	$10,000	$ 125,000	$ 10,000

Source: *Facts and Figures on Government Finance*, 15th ed. (New York: Tax Foundation, Inc., 1969), p. 200.

It should be noted that Alabama, Arkansas, Florida, and Georgia all duplicate the exemption and bracket structure of the federal estate tax, with their rates set equal to the maximum federal credit allowed on any given estate. If a decedent in one of these states left an estate of $1,040,000, the state would claim an estate tax of $38,800, which is the full value of the federal credit as shown in Table A-3. Five of the remaining eight states impose pickup taxes to ensure full absorption of the federal credit. Of the three remaining states, the tax liability in two (Mississippi and North Dakota) would clearly exceed the amount of maximum federal credit, leaving only one state (Utah) that may in some instances fail to take full advantage of the federal credit.

Table A-6 shows that considerable variation also exists in the rate schedules of the thirty-seven states that practice inheritance taxation. In New Jersey the rate of tax on transfers to spouse, child, or parent ranges from 1 to 16 percent, while in Delaware it ranges from 1 to 4 percent. The rate of tax on transfers to nonrelatives ranges from 8 to 40 percent in Wisconsin, while in Michigan it ranges from 10 to 15 percent. A similar degree of variation also exists in the size of the specific exemption. Kansas, for instance, permits a specific exemption of $75,000 on transfers to the surviving spouse, while Maryland allows only $150.

Although considerable variety exists in particular rate schedules, the primary features of the inheritance tax are quite similar among the states. All states except Oregon, for instance, vary the rate of tax with consanguinity, with the rate of tax declining as the transferee's relation to the transferor becomes closer. Maine, for instance, taxes transfers to spouse, child, or parent at 2 to 6 percent, transfers to brother or sister at 8 to 12 percent, and transfers to nonrelatives at 12 to 18 percent. All states except Oregon and Maryland, moreover, vary the size of the specific exemption directly with the degree of consanguinity.

Except for Oregon, South Dakota, and West Virginia, states that use an inheritance tax also impose a pickup tax upon the estate in the event the inheritance tax collected from the shares of the estate is too small to absorb the full amount of the federal credit. A federal taxable estate of $240,000, for instance, is allowed a maximum credit of $3,600 for state death tax payments. If a state collects only $2,600 in inheritance taxes from the distribution of the estate, the state would levy a pickup tax of $1,000 against the estate in order to absorb fully the federal credit.

Table A-6
STATE INHERITANCE TAX RATES AND EXEMPTIONS

State	Marginal Rate Range (in percent)			Exemptions ($ thousands)			
	Spouse, Child or Parent	Brother or sister	Other than relative	Spouse	Child or parent	Brother or sister	Other than relative
Alaska	1 - 3.5	3-10-5	5-17.5	$ 10	$ 10	$ 1	None
California	3 -14	6-20	10-24	5	5	2	0.3
Colorado	2 - 8	3-10	10-19	35	10	2	0.5
Connecticut	2 - 8	4-10	8-14	50	10	3	0.5
Delaware	1 - 4	2- 5	5- 8	20	3	1	None
Hawaii	2 - 7.5	3.5- 9	3.5- 9	20	5	0.5	0.5
Idaho	2 -15	4-20	8-20	10	4	1	None
Illinois	2 -14	2-14	10-30	20	20	10	0.1
Indiana	1 -10	5-15	7-20	15	2	0.5	0.1
Iowa	1 - 8	5-10	10-15	40	10	None	None
Kansas	0.5 - 5	3-12.5	10-15	75	15	5	0.2
Kentucky	2 -10	4-16	6-16	10	5	1	0.5
Louisiana	2 - 3	5- 7	5-10	5	5	1	0.5
Maine	2 - 6	8-12	12-18	15	10	0.5	0.5
Maryland	1	7- 5	7- 5	0.15	0.15	0.15	0.15
Massachusetts	1.25-11.25	5-18.75	7.5-18.75	10	10	1	1

State							
Michigan	2 - 8	2- 8	10-15	30	5	5	None
Minnesota	1 - 5-10	6-25	8-30	30	6	1.5	0.5
Missouri	1 - 6	3-18	5-30	20	5	0.5	0.1
Montana	2 - 8	4-16	8-32	20	2	0.5	None
Nebraska	1	1	6-18	10	10	10	0.5
New Hampshire	Exempt	10	10	Unlimited	Unlimited	None	None
New Jersey	1 -16	11-16	15-16	5	5	0.5	0.5
New Mexico	1	5	5	Follows Variable Formula			
North Carolina	1 -12	4-16	8-17	10	2	None	None
Oregon	1 -10	1-10	1-10	None	None	1	0.5
Pennsylvania	6	15	15	1	None	None	None
Rhode Island	2 - 9	3-10	8-15	10	10	5	1
South Dakota	1 - 8	3-12	5-20	15	3	0.5	0.1
Tennessee	1.04- 9.5	6.5-20	6.5-20	Follows Variable Formula			
Texas	1 - 6	3-10	5-20	25	25	10	0.5
Vermont	2 - 6	3- 6	12	15	15	15	None
Virginia	1 - 5	2-10	5-15	5	5	2	1
Washington	1 -10	3-20	10-25	10	10	1	None
West Virginia	3 -13	4-18	10-30	15	5	None	None
Wisconsin	2 -10	2-10	8-40	15	2	0.5	0.1
Wyoming	2	2	6	10	10	10	None

Source: *Facts and Figures on Government Finance,* 15th ed. (New York: Tax Foundation, Inc., 1969), pp. 198-99.

TAX LOOPHOLES:
THE LEGEND AND THE REALITY

Roger A. Freeman

1

WHY HALF OF ALL INCOME
IS NOT TAXED

Introduction

Leadership pronouncements in both houses of Congress during 1972 make it clear that income tax reform will be a major goal of legislative efforts in 1973. Final action, however, may fall far short of announced aims and could be much less significant and extensive than in the Tax Reform Act of 1969. Yet, the importance of the way in which the tax burden is distributed cannot be overrated at a time when governmental revenues—federal, state and local—equal about 40 percent of total personal income. The load should not only be equitable among economic groups and individuals but also have the least harmful effect on economic growth and stability.

All-encompassing as the term "income tax reform" sounds, it has in recent years come to acquire a more specific connotation—namely, a broadening of the federal tax base by repealing or narrowing remedial provisions that now protect large amounts of personal income from taxation, or at least from the full impact of the tax rate schedule. In common terms, reform aims at closing so-called "loopholes" through which it is said much income escapes bearing its proper share of the overall tax burden.

Repeated attempts at reform over the past 15 years have not eliminated the most frequently cited "loopholes." As a result, the chairman of the House Ways and Means Committee, Representative Wilbur Mills, adopted a novel strategy in May 1972: he introduced a bill (H.R. 15230) which called for the repeal, over the next three years, of 54 provisions in existing law that are often referred to as "loopholes." Senate majority

71

leader Mike Mansfield submitted a companion measure (S. 3657) in the Senate. The intent of the bills' sponsors was not to have all or even most of those provisions permanently wiped off the books, but to order them repealed effective in the future—in 1974, 1975 and 1976—so as to force congressional consideration of each provision lest the wholesale repeals go into effect. Representative Mills did not expect Congress to act on tax reform so late in the presidential election year of 1972, but the bills were a gauntlet thrown down to the members of Congress, intended as a warning signal to all interested parties and to the broad public to gird for battle in 1973.

With the Vietnam war, welfare reform and several other major long-contested subjects fading into the background, tax reform could be a principal issue in the 93rd Congress. The deep ideological conflicts and huge economic interests underlying the issue may turn the debate into a divisive and bitterly fought controversy. Whether the drive for federal income tax reform, which became a national force in the mid-1950s and has remained in the forefront of public interest ever since, will bring decisive action in 1973 remains to be seen.

Why tax reform? Taken at face value, the case for federal tax reform by broadening the income tax base is persuasive: the federal income tax now reaches only about half of all personal income as defined in the national income accounts, and even the taxed half is not always subjected to the full impact of the tax rate schedule. Does it make economic sense or promote "equal justice under the law" to levy rates rising from 14 to 70 percent on *half* of all income when just half of this assessment on *all* income—or a flat rate of 10 percent on all personal income, or a 14 percent rate on "adjusted gross income"—would yield about the same amount of revenue to the government? Might it not cause far less distortion, evasion, and complication to levy lower rates on a broader base? Is it wise for the government to continue to dig deep into personal income with a huge sieve that yields only half of what it is supposed to produce? Most of the complexity in the Internal Revenue Code, which over the years has progressed from intricacy to near incomprehensibility, is the result of two factors: (1) the expansion of the code by too many exclusions, exemptions, deductions, and other devices that whittle down "taxable income"; and (2) differential rates imposed on different types or magnitudes of income. While few would expect to see all tax differentials abolished at one blow, the current complication and apparent unfairness of many provisions seem to clamor for radical simplification.

But broadening the base by subjecting much—or most, or all—of the presently nontaxed income to the tax is far more feasible in theory than it turns out to be in the cold light of political reality, when the task is to be tackled in earnest, item by item. Congressional committees—House Ways and Means, Senate Finance, Joint Economic, Joint Internal Revenue Taxation—have conducted tax reform hearings year after year and have gathered tens of thousands of pages of testimony, but these efforts have produced relatively few tangible results. The fact is that the tax code has grown more complicated every time Congress has attempted to improve it—most recently so with the Tax Reform Act of 1969 which is widely, and justifiedly, called the "Lawyers' and Accountants' Full Employment Act of 1969."

The repeal of special provisions that benefit only a small number of taxpayers may produce good and sometimes dramatic publicity but in most cases will yield only small revenue. On the other hand, provisions that account for the big erosions in the tax base tend to affect millions of taxpayers who, when their established privileges seem threatened, rise in wrath—as individuals, as congressional constituencies, as collective economic interests, or through political, state or national organizations—to defend their existing benefits. What some regard as a "loophole" is to others a birthright, an indispensable lifesaver and a means of achieving tax parity with others.

The why of loopholes. Contrary to what is often asserted and widely believed, the remedial provisions in the tax code are seldom there by accident or oversight, let alone as the result of the sinister machinations of special interest lobbyists who either bribed lawmakers or pulled the wool over the eyes of unsuspecting congressmen and the public. The conspiracy theory of tax law is not convincing in view of the legislative history of each of the provisions involved. Virtually all provisions that shield some income from the full impact of the rate schedule—or from any tax—were put there not by inadvertence, or from ignorance, or as a rule for the purpose of giving some favored groups improper advantages or privileges. Most of the tax differentials aim at one or both of these two objectives:

(1) to provide greater equity, horizontal or vertical, among taxpayers and different types and magnitudes of income by taking into

73

account differing circumstances and offering relief for hardships;
(2) to provide incentives to taxpayers to engage in or enlarge activities which are held to be desirable as a matter of public policy. This is done by offering rewards to some and imposing penalties on others.

These two objectives often produce conflicting results when translated into tax policy.

There is a great deal of ambiguity about what constitutes an inequity meriting remedial action and what is desirable public policy calling for governmental or private action. Defenders of special viewpoints or interests almost always present their proposals in the manner of a Western movie: there are the good guys and the bad guys, and nobody can be in doubt as to which is which. But the reality of tax controversies is seldom so black and white; it almost always is a question of differing shades of grey, with more or less reasonable and valid arguments put forth by both sides. The merits or drawbacks of any provision or proposal are rarely if ever as simple as its spokesmen or detractors present them to be.

Perhaps in a very few cases clever manipulators were able to slip a remedial tax provision past an unsuspecting Congress. But such unintended benefits have never remained a secret for very long. If Congress does not favorably respond to the demand of some groups to abolish specified "loopholes," it is not because of a lack of understanding or in deference to secret influences but because the merits of the case are in doubt. Invariably there is another side to the question—problems that the proponents of the particular change do not mention, except in a negative light. If there are not two sides to an issue, then it is really not an issue. When there are no reasons—economic, moral, political or ideological—for objecting to a proposed change, then there is no controversy and the change has a good chance of being accepted.

This does not mean, of course, that all tax provisions as they presently stand necessarily express the informed and balanced judgment of the Congress, or that they are all justifiable and fair. Far from it. But it does mean that when all factors are taken into consideration, the issues are seldom clearcut. Congress must keep the interests of all groups in mind, not only of those with the most effective public relations machinery or organized voting power. It cannot take the claims of one side as the revealed truth without giving a fair hearing to the other side. Time and again Congress finds itself in the position of the judge who, after listening to the plaintiff, nodded to him and said, "You are right." After the defendant had told his story, the judge nodded again and said, "You are right." At that point the clerk of the court approached the bench and whispered in the judge's ear: "But Your Honor, they both can't be right." The judge thought a moment and then nodded to the clerk, "You are right, too."

Neutrality or redistribution? If only material interests were involved, tax conflicts might not be so difficult to resolve. However, frequently the problem centers around deep-seated ideologies, fundamental principles of justice in the distribution of income and wealth, or public policies that do not lend themselves easily to compromise. The principle of "neutrality in taxation," advanced as the epitome of fairness in classic economic thought, has long been honored more in the breach than in observance. While many may think it desirable to leave taxpayers in the same relative position *after* taxes as they were *before*, many others regard such policy as sheer heresy. As a practical matter, neutrality is hardly conceivable given today's political climate and level of taxation. When the tax burden equals no more than 10 to 15 percent of the nation's income as it did in the early part of the twentieth century, a policy of complete neutrality is theoretically, and even politically, feasible. But that is hardly the case when total governmental revenues equal about 40 percent of personal income, as they have for some years in the United States and other industrial nations. Government cannot extract 40 percent of total income and leave all persons in the same *relative* position. Some types of activity cannot sustain such a tax burden without being wiped out—any more than low-income earners could carry such a load and maintain customary living standards.

An even harder division to resolve is the ideological conflict over the government's role in the economy. Some believe that the rewards and punishments of the market are, by and large, merited and fair, and that the highest economic growth is produced by giving market forces the widest possible free rein. To ensure the greatest good for the greatest number of people, then, this faction would wish to leave pre-tax relative positions as undisturbed as possible. But even many advocates of such a free market policy now concede that government may need to provide remedies and relief for those who have fallen by the way-side—whether as a result of impartial forces, the activities of more efficacious groups, or an individual's own fault or contributory negligence. The view has become prevalent that it is government's primary task to remedy the imperfections of market decisions, to alter through the political process the rewards and punishments of the free play of market forces. Some have come to regard government chiefly as a huge machine for redistributing income from those who have more to those who have less, no matter what reasons might underlie an individual's poor economic condition. Some degree of egalitarianism has become part of public policy as a logical result of and concomitant with the one man-one vote principle.

By and large, redistribution of income through progressive taxation and social expenditures has become so generally accepted in the United States and everywhere else that the principle as a rule of public policy is no longer seriously questioned.[1] But it is not at all decided just how far government should go in taking a larger slice from those who produce and earn, and in giving to those who produce less or nothing. How far can government go, for example, without weakening incentives? Should the tax structure be made more progressive than it is, or less? Many, and possibly most, persons and organizations judge a broad-scaled tax proposal by one criterion: does it tend to redistribute more income, or do so more effectively, from those who have more to those who have less? Most arguments over tax issues are shaped, most battle lines are drawn, and most decisions are arrived at by that criterion. All other issues, though they may consume much time and space in the debate, shrink in true significance before the one overriding issue: does the proposal take more from the rich and does it give more to the poor?

The Movement for Income Tax Reform

Though it adopted an income tax much later than most industrial countries, the United States has come to lean on this particular tax as the major source of public revenue far more heavily than other nations. Broad-scaled general consumption taxation, which forms the backbone of government budgets in Europe and most everywhere else, has never gained acceptance in the United States, at least not as a federal tax, though it has been and probably will remain a subject of periodic dis-

---

[1] But the principle as such is at times questioned. Walter J. Blum and Harry Kalven, Jr., *The Uneasy Case for Progressive Taxation* (Chicago: University of Chicago Press, 1953).

cussion. Short of a fiscal emergency, imposition of a major national consumption tax does not now appear very likely in the immediate future. Hence the income tax is economically, socially and politically more important in America than elsewhere—and, incidentally, also more complicated and controversial, if not in principle then in application and structure.

First imposed in 1913 at rates from 1 to 7 percent, principally on only a small number of wealthy persons, the income tax was turned from a class tax into a mass tax during World War I when the levy was extended downward to reach low incomes and its rate scale elevated to between 6 and 77 percent. The 1920s saw a series of reductions in the rate scale to a low of between 0.5 and 24 percent by 1929, a downward trend that was reversed in the 1930s and during World War II when the scale climbed to its highest level ever—from 23 to 94 percent—and the number of taxpayers multiplied tenfold. Tax cuts in the immediate postwar period were quite small and it was not until 1964 that the 14 to 70 percent scale was adopted which is still in effect. Meanwhile, the Internal Revenue Code and regulations grew in size with the addition of a myriad of provisions of unparalleled complexity.

In the years following World War II much attention was directed toward the use of taxes, particularly the income tax, as an instrument of countercyclical fiscal policy. Concern focused on the macroeconomic use of taxation so that tax policy would offer the least obstacle to, and as far as possible would serve to stimulate, steady economic expansion. The Council of Economic Advisers, the Joint Economic Committee of Congress and the President's annual economic report—all created by the Employment Act of 1946—guided the debate toward a goal of maximum employment of the country's manpower and other resources, as well as stimulation of other areas of national growth in which tax policy was to play a significant role. Shortly after the recodification of the Internal Revenue Code in 1954, the Joint Economic Committee conducted what was up to that time probably the country's most comprehensive and intensive tax study: *Federal Tax Policy for Economic Growth and Stability* (1955). Very few of the experts who prepared papers and participated in the panel discussions referred to what became the prime subject of the tax debate in later years—namely, "erosion of the tax base and rate structure." Only limited attention was paid to the subject at the time.

Erosion of the tax base. Interest in this problem increased and gradually, in the second half of the 1950s, turned into a drive for income tax reform by broadening the tax base. At the 1955 annual conference of the National Tax Association, Joseph A. Pechman presented a paper subsequently expanded into an article and published in 1957 under the title, "Erosion of the Individual Income Tax."[2] Mr. Pechman demonstrated that only about 40 percent of *personal* income appeared on federal income tax returns as *taxable* income and estimated that out of personal income of $325 billion in 1956, $189 billion was untaxed:

	Billions
Social insurance and public welfare, wages "in kind," imputed rental on owner-occupied homes, interest on state and local bonds, et cetera	$ 35
Personal exemptions on taxable returns ($600 per head)	77
Excess of personal exemptions and deductions over income on nontaxable returns and "no returns" ..	17
Standard deductions	13
Itemized deductions (mostly state and local taxes, charitable contributions, interest and medical expenses)	21
Unreported income	26
	$189

It is immediately apparent that the bulk of the $198 billion of nontaxed 1956 income was received by persons in the lower income brackets and that only a small percentage of the total redounded to the benefit of wealthy persons. That clearly was and remains the intent of the law.

Mr. Pechman suggested that at least part of the nontaxed income, in all groups, be included in a more comprehensive tax base which would make it possible to reduce tax rates across the board. His appeal caught on rapidly. Within a few years, the concepts of the eroded tax base and untaxed income attained wide public attention, were prominently featured in the media, and finally were placed on the agenda of Congress. As the debate reached the political level, attention shifted sharply from the hundreds of billions of untaxed income—one-half or

[2] See *National Tax Journal,* March 1957. Mr. Pechman, who was then with the Council of Economic Advisers, later joined the Committee for Economic Development and now is with the Brookings Institution.

more of all personal income—to provisions whose impact is far smaller in magnitude but which directly benefit mostly persons in the higher income brackets. This is where the focus of the tax reform movement has remained ever since. It has become not so much a drive to broaden the tax base as to tax the wealthy more heavily.

The House Ways and Means Committee's 1958 hearings on *General Revenue Revision*, extensive as they were (3,600 pages), are part of the "pre-reform" era: they dealt mostly with undue tax impact on certain industries. Soon afterwards though, the committee's new chairman, Representative Wilbur Mills, cleared the decks for a major attack on loopholes, as the drive for tax reform soon came to be known. His oft-quoted article—"Are You a Pet or a Patsy? Our Unfair Tax Laws Coddle Some But Force Others to Pay Through the Nose" [3]—set the pattern for a vigorous study of and campaign for income tax reform. Ways and Means Committee hearings in 1959, to which nearly 200 witnesses were invited (including some of the most prominent American tax experts), aimed at a broadening of the tax base and repeal of special preferences and deductions. They covered virtually every type of income not subject to the full impact of the rate schedule, every type of exclusion, exemption, deduction, credit or preference, and brought forth an infinite variety of ideas and proposals on desired improvements in the income tax. The resulting *Tax Revision Compendium* composed of papers submitted, panel discussions and summaries, still is, more than a dozen years later, the most comprehensive discussion of the major aspects of American income taxation. But contrary to the hopes and expectations of its sponsors this most ambitious effort at tax reform resulted in no legislative action whatsoever in the succeeding four years. It was a splendid academic exercise—and so it remained.

When one of the most knowledgeable and articulate advocates of "loophole closing," Professor Stanley S. Surrey of the Harvard Law School, was appointed assistant secretary of the Treasury for tax policy in 1961, it might have been expected that major proposals for comprehensive tax reform would soon be forthcoming. But although Mr. Surrey devoted much of his considerable energy to the task in the succeeding eight years, very few of his ideas were put into practice. President Kennedy's two tax messages—April 20, 1961, and January 24, 1963—mentioned structural reform and referred to such items as

---

[3] *Life,* November 23, 1959.

tightened capital gains taxation, a floor under itemized deductions and an end to unlimited charitable deductions. But these were minor subjects in messages whose main emphasis was on incentives to stimulate economic growth by tax concessions. "The chief problem confronting our economy in 1963 is its unrealized potential—slow growth, under-investment, unused capacity and persistent unemployment." [4] By far the most important tax proposal adopted was a business investment credit—which some observers have been calling another big loophole ever since its introduction in 1962. In contrast to widespread criticism of the eroding tax base during and subsequent to the 1959 hearings, President Kennedy declared in 1961: "This message recognizes the basic soundness of our tax structure." [5] It is not surprising that only very few minor suggestions among the limited number of structural recommendations survived.

The bill passed by Congress in 1964 was mainly a tax reduction act that freed an additional 1.5 million persons of any tax liability, cut taxes for most other taxpayers (particularly in the lower brackets), and widened rather than narrowed the range and amount of income exempt from taxation. Nor is that surprising: to most taxpayers tax reform means tax relief. This is why the experience of 1964 was repeated in 1969 and in 1971: what had been announced as an attempt at tax reform became basically action to reduce taxes for the great mass of voters in the middle and lower income brackets and to end any liability for millions in the lowest income categories. The tax reform drive promised to offset revenue losses at the bottom of the income scale by substantial tax boosts in the high brackets through repeal, or at least a sharp reduction, of provisions benefiting well-to-do taxpayers. Considering the broad popular appeal and publicity value of such an approach and, above all, the relative size and voting strength of the two constituencies, this seemed to be a well-designed strategy. Resistance to change from the small number of taxpayers at the upper end was to be overcome by approval from larger numbers in the lower brackets.

Estimates of potential revenue gains from tax reform were commonly based on the assumption that the tax changes would not affect the nature and volume of transactions and that, for example, sale of assets, oil exploration programs and bond markets would go on as they had before. Opponents questioned the assumption that operations would

---

[4] *Congressional Record,* January 24, 1963, p. 962.
[5] *Congressional Record,* April 20, 1961, p. 6456.

continue undisturbed and that the promised revenue gains would in fact materialize.

Federal revenue needs soared in the second half of the 1960s, as expenditures jumped from $118 billion in 1965 to $197 billion in 1970 and a huge budgetary deficit loomed ahead (it actuallly totaled $25 billion in fiscal year 1968). To meet this problem, President Johnson, in a message to Congress of August 3, 1967, proposed a $7.4 billion tax boost—not by closing some of the much-discussed loopholes but principally by a temporary across-the-board 10 percent surcharge on the existing tax liabilities of individuals and corporations. Treasury officials had repeatedly emphasized the unused revenue potential of tax reform. Yet now they chose to seek the needed funds by other means. The probable explanation for this reversal is that when the chips were down and the money was badly needed, officials did not rate revenue potential from reform as high—in a realistic evaluation—as they had in some of the other pronouncements on the need for broadening the tax base and tax reform. Congress seemed to agree, too: it imposed a 10 percent surtax but did not touch tax reform.

Though there was no presidential or congressional action on tax reform for about five years following the passage of the Revenue Act of 1964, intensive work continued in the Treasury under the direction of Assistant Secretary for Tax Policy Stanley S. Surrey. Under a con gressional mandate to the President to submit tax reform proposals before the end of 1968, a major staff report with recommendations was prepared. But President Johnson decided not to transmit the proposals to Congress and they were made public only at the request of Congress sometime later, after the new administration had taken office. But, like its predecessor, the Nixon administration did not make the Treasury staff proposals on loophole-closing its own.

The Barr bomb. Two days before leaving office, Secretary of the Treasury Joseph Barr—who served in that capacity for the 31-day interim between Henry Fowler's resignation and David M. Kennedy's assumption of office—delivered a blow that reverberated for a long time and made the tax reform drive a major political force in 1969. On January 17, Secretary Barr issued a stern warning to the Joint Economic Committee of Congress: the country was facing a taxpayers' revolt, not because taxes were so high, but because rich people were not paying their fair share; 155 taxpayers with an adjusted gross income of

$200,000 or more had paid no income tax in 1967, among them 21 persons with an income of $1 million or more. Mr. Barr's statement— delivered without an explanation of why or how recipients of huge gross incomes could escape paying taxes—was prominently featured in news media throughout the country and aroused public sentiment to a high pitch. The result was a situation not too different from the tax-payers' revolt that he had predicted. Some members of Congress who had viewed tax reform with detachment early in the session came back from Easter recess with a mandate from their constituents and a personal determination to "make the rich pay."

On February 18, 1969, about a month before President Nixon submitted 16 minor tax reform proposals (with an insignificant revenue effect) to the Congress, the House Ways and Means Committee began tax reform hearings on such subjects as tax-exempt charitable founda-tions, capital gains, interest on state and local bonds, and depletion allowances. With the new impetus, the committee extended its purview and the House passed a huge tax bill on August 8. The Senate acted even faster and the President signed the measure on December 30, 1969. The 225-page bill, the biggest and most complex addition to the Internal Revenue Code ever, made hundreds of changes in the tax law.

Tax reform in 1969 and 1971. The Tax Reform Act of 1969 was the first genuine attempt to come to grips with the type of tax reform that had been advocated for about 15 years. But in terms of the announced goals of the loophole-closing drive, it was at best a very cautious first step that did not go very far and avoided the "tough" issues. Among other things, the act reduced the gas and oil depletion allowance from 27.5 to 22 percent, tightened the availability of the 25 percent capital gains tax, established a minimum tax on income with limited tax prefer-ences (LTP) and imposed a 4-percent tax on the net investment income of tax-exempt foundations. But all of this was dwarfed by the tax re-ductions the act granted: an increase in the personal exemption to $750, an increase in the standard deduction to 15 percent with a maximum of $2,000 (from 10 percent and $1,000), a reduction from 70 to 50 per-cent in the top rate on *earned* income and a maximum tax for single persons that cannot exceed 120 percent of what they would pay if they were married. In the aggregate, the tax liability of returns in the lowest income bracket was cut by 70 percent (i.e., to less than one-third), that of returns in the highest bracket raised by 7 percent. More than 9 million persons were dropped from the tax rolls altogether.

Though it was announced as an attempt to broaden the tax base, the Tax Reform Act of 1969 increased the percentage of personal income that is *not* reached by the federal income tax by 2 percentage points—from 48.2 percent in 1969 to 50.2 in 1970. Two years later, in December 1971, another revenue bill was enacted that consisted almost exclusively of tax cuts. It not only accelerated some of the relief provided for in the 1969 act but also added numerous other remedial provisions. The 1971 measure permitted credit for political contributions for the first time, greatly liberalized child care deductions, introduced a job development investment credit and reintroduced the 7 percent investment credit. Revenue losses from the 1969 and 1971 acts have contributed substantially to recent budgetary deficits. The unified budget deficit ran between $23 and $25 billion in the fiscal years 1971 and 1972, and may be this high again in 1973. Deficits give all signs of becoming a permanent feature of our fiscal system.

Tax "expenditures"? Spokesmen for the tax reform drive meanwhile continued to point out that huge amounts were being lost each year to the Treasury through tax concessions. Assistant Treasury Secretary Stanley S. Surrey developed the concept of *tax expenditures*—government expenditures made through the tax system—and continued to promote this concept after he left office in January 1969. Most of the tax deductions, exclusions, exemptions, and credits, Surrey theorized, are the equivalent of public expenditures for the benefited purposes, and they ought to be treated as such and subjected to the same type of annual review by the Congress and the executive branch as other expenditures. Ways and Means Committee Chairman Wilbur Mills referred to such tax concessions as "a form of backdoor spending." Surrey subsequently prepared an estimated "Tax Expenditure Budget" which placed the total between $42 and $45 billion for fiscal year 1968.[6] In 1972 he estimated that the federal government would spend from $55 to $60 billion a year through tax breaks.[7]

More recently, tax concessions have been called *tax subsidies* and

---

[6] *Annual Report of the Secretary of the Treasury on the State of the Finances,* for the Fiscal Year ended June 30, 1968 (Washington, D.C.: U.S. Government Printing Office, 1969), pp. 326-40.
[7] *Wall Street Journal,* April 12, 1972.

have been included in studies of federal subsidy programs. The staff of the Joint Economic Committee of Congress estimated the gross budgetary cost of major federal tax subsidies in fiscal year 1971 at $35.8 billion.[8] At the committee's hearings held in January 1972, Joseph A. Pechman and Benjamin A. Okner of the Brookings Institution estimated that a comprehensive income tax would yield $180 billion in 1972—about $77 billion more than the estimated $103 billion yield under current law.[9] Such a 75 percent increase in the aggregate income tax receipts would more than triple the tax liability of persons in the lowest brackets (under $5,000) and nearly double the tax of those in the top brackets ($500,000 and up).

Assistant Secretary of the Treasury for Economic Policy Murray Weidenbaum testified on June 2, 1970, before the Joint Economic Committee's Subcommittee on Economy in Government, that tax aids—a term he preferred to tax expenditures—totaled more than $44 billion in fiscal year 1969. This estimate was brought up to date by Under Secretary of the Treasury Edwin S. Cohen appearing before the Joint Economic Committee on July 21, 1972. Cohen warned that many of the estimates were merely tentative, that each provision was computed independently of any other, that therefore an addition of the separate estimates might not produce meaningful figures and that no consideration was given to the likely impact of such tax changes on investment patterns and activity. With these caveats, he put the total for special tax provisions in calendar year 1971 at $51.7 billion in revenue, of which $41.8 billion came under individual income tax and $9.9 billion under corporate profits tax. Major individual income tax items in Cohen's estimate included:

	Billions
Untaxed part of capital gains	$5.6
Deductions for:	
Home mortgages and property taxes	5.1
Other state and local nonbusiness taxes	5.6
Charitable contributions	3.2

[8] U.S. Congress, Joint Economic Committee, *The Economics of Federal Subsidy Programs,* a staff study (Washington, D.C.: U. S. Government Printing Office, January 1972), p. 31.
[9] U.S. Congress, Joint Economic Committee, *The Economics of Federal Subsidy Programs,* Hearings before the Subcommittee on Priorities and Economy in Government (Washington, D.C.: U.S. Government Printing Office, January 1972), p. 71.

	Billions
Interest on consumer debt	1.8
Excluded pension contributions	3.7
Interest on municipal bonds	.8
Excess of percentage over cost depletion	.2
Exclusion of social security, unemployment compensation, welfare, et cetera	4.7

Estimates of the cost of special provisions—whether they be called tax expenditures, tax subsidies, tax aids, loopholes, or whatever—vary widely because they are based on value judgments rooted in political philosophy. Each author has a different concept of what items should be included in the list and how much revenue could be derived from their repeal; each excludes some major items of nontaxed income accruing to persons in the middle and lower brackets. All agree, however, that the Treasury's loss from these provisions is huge. At a time when large annual budget deficits pose grave inflationary risks, thought might be given to narrowing future deficits by closing or tightening some of the "tax loopholes."

More revenue from tax reform? Recent projections of the federal budget outlook paint a gloomy picture. A group of Brookings Institution economists led by Charles L. Schultze predicted, on the basis of the President's budget for fiscal year 1973, continued huge deficits through 1975 and a possible balanced budget (assuming full employment conditions) by 1977.[10] When Congress subsequently passed a 20 percent social security increase (instead of the 5 percent recommended by the President) and voted other spending increases, the Brookings authors revised their estimates upwards. An article by Alice M. Rivlin, "Dear Voter: Your taxes are going up (no matter who wins on Tuesday)," and a speech by Charles Schultze predicted large deficits through 1976 with a possible excess of revenue in the years after fiscal 1978.[11] This latter forecast was based on the assumption that receipts would grow faster than expenditures, an assumption that receives little encouragement from the record of recent years. The authors cited the massive pressures for new and expanded programs—forces that might prevail and, if they did so, would make illusory any prediction about receipts

[10] Charles L. Schultze et al., *Setting National Priorities: The 1973 Budget* (Washington, D.C.: The Brookings Institution, 1972).

[11] See, respectively, *New York Times Magazine*, November 5, 1972, and *Congressional Record*, October 16, 1972, pp. E 8743–8747.

growing more rapidly than expenditures. About the same time, the American Enterprise Institute's long-range budget project, comprised of David J. Ott and several associates, predicted similar results: unless taxes are boosted, large-scale deficits are to be expected until 1977 (even under full employment conditions) and thus at best a modest surplus cannot materialize until 1978 or after.[12]

Could those expected deficits be met through tax reform? Joseph A. Pechman and Benjamin A. Okner discussed the possibility of having Congress close several loopholes and came up with a modest additional annual yield ranging from $3.1 to $10.2 billion.[13] In other words, even strong proponents of tax reform are not optimistic about the actual revenue potential involved.

To be sure, the subject of tax reform came up repeatedly in the 1972 congressional session and during the presidential campaign. One of the major proposals for reform (S. 3378)—introduced in March 1972 by 12 senators including Senators McGovern, Humphrey, Muskie, Kennedy and Nelson—was designed "to raise needed revenue" estimated at $16 billion. The bill called for 55 changes, such as taxing unrealized capital gains at death (with later provisions to tax as ordinary income), reducing percentage depletion on oil from 22 to 15 percent, inducing state and local governments to issue taxable bonds, repealing accelerated real estate depreciation, and repealing $100 dividend exclusion. In the House, H.R. 13877, sponsored by 59 members, aimed to raise an additional $7.25 billion by similar but less far-reaching changes. The most drastic proposals were the Mills-Mansfield bills mentioned above (H.R. 15230 and S. 3657 introduced in May 1972) which called for the repeal of 54 major tax provisions in installments of 18 each in January 1974, 1975 and 1976.

It came as no surprise when tax reform was injected into the presidential campaign in the form of an appeal to tax high income people more severely. In a New York speech on August 29, Senator McGovern announced that as President he "would seek a fair-share tax reform to raise approximately $22 billion in additional revenues by 1975," mostly from the high tax brackets while persons with middle or

---

[12] David J. Ott et al., *Nixon, McGovern and the Federal Budget* (Washington, D.C.: American Enterprise Institute, 1972).

[13] "Alternative Sources of Federal Revenue," in Schultze et al., *Setting National Priorities,* p. 433.

lower incomes would pay less.[14] A subsequent statement spelled out his proposals in further detail, proposals that paralleled in many respects those contained in the above-mentioned bills. As it turned out, however, tax reform played no significant role in the 1972 presidential campaign. President Nixon had said in his September 1971 request for tax legislation that he would send tax reform proposals to Congress in 1972. But in February 1972, Secretary of the Treasury John Connally had suggested that a presidential campaign year was not a good time to consider tax reform, an issue that should be studied in a cooler and less passionate atmosphere. The President indicated subsequently that his tax reform goals would be spelled out in a special message early in 1973.

Current prospects are that presidential proposals will be forthcoming in the spring of 1973 and will be subjected to extensive congressional hearings. These proposals are not likely to go as far as some of the suggestions made by Democratic party spokesmen in 1972—or by leading advocates of tax reform—and may not involve major revenue gains. If large additional revenues are needed for budgetary purposes in 1973 and in subsequent years, as it now appears, Congress will most likely vote a broad increase in income taxes, such as a surtax, rather than repeal so-called tax loopholes.

The fiscal battle will probably be fought out over income taxes because they dominate the federal tax picture. In recent years, individual and corporate income taxes have produced between 60 and 65 percent of *all* revenues in the unified budget. But this budget includes revenues earmarked for social insurance, highway and other trust funds and therefore not available for general fiscal purposes. If trust fund revenues are excluded (as they were in the administrative budget which was replaced by the unified budget in 1969), income taxes supply about 85 percent of federal revenues. According to Census Bureau definitions and statistics, income taxes have accounted for 80 to 85 percent of all federal tax revenues for the past two decades—with two-thirds to three-quarters of the receipts coming from the individual income tax, the remainder from the corporate profits tax. This shows a far heavier reliance on in-

---

[14] "From McGovern: A New Blueprint for Taxes, Welfare," *U.S. News & World Report,* September 11, 1972; "McGovern's Tax Plan: 22 Billions More by 1975," *U.S. News & World Report,* October 2, 1972; John F. Burby, "Complex McGovern Economics Plan Dissolves in Campaign Heat," *National Journal,* September 16, 1972.

come taxation than in other countries. In fact, the United States is the only industrial nation that does not levy a broad-based consumption tax as a major source of national revenue. It is because of this lopsidedness in our federal tax system that the imposition of a consumption tax, such as a value-added tax, has repeatedly been proposed. But there is a major objection to such a tax: in contrast to the individual income tax, it does *not* redistribute income from the rich to the poor and may well be regressive with respect to income. This argument is a powerful political factor that raises considerable doubt as to whether a national consumption tax can soon be adopted in the United States except in a dire fiscal emergency or in an atmosphere different from that prevailing today.

This leaves four other possible solutions to the budgetary problem in the next few years. Congress could control expenditure growth more effectively than it has shown an inclination to do. But, according to some recent studies, this is not very likely to happen. Congress could, on the other hand, let the large annual deficits that have prevailed in fiscal years 1971, 1972 and 1973 continue into the future, permitting them to become a fixture of the federal fiscal system through the 1970s. To restrain the resulting inflationary pressures, it might then be found necessary to tighten, and extend indefinitely, wage-price and other economic controls instead of gradually relaxing and finally repealing them. A third possibility would be to boost income taxes by raising rates or imposing a surtax to produce the needed revenue, as was done in 1968. Fourth, and least likely, Congress could subject some of the major now-protected forms of personal income to the full impact of the tax rate schedule in a move toward developing a comprehensive tax base (CTB).

Theoretically, tax reform could be enacted on its own, so as to produce additional revenue, rather than be coupled with a tax cut. However, a review of the record of recent decades casts considerable doubt on the revenue potential of tax reform. No matter how tax reform has started out, it has always wound up as tax reduction. But, then, history never quite repeats itself. While the emphasis and force of the tax reform drive are likely to remain on the elusive and controversial concept of equity, there is at least a possibility, slim as it may be, that reform could also help to narrow the huge budgetary deficits that have characterized the past few years. This obviously would call for courageous and disciplined action on the part of Congress.

Do the Rich Pay No Income Taxes?

The tax reform movement gained its greatest strength in 1969 when the issue moved to the front pages of the metropolitan dailies and held the center stage of national attention. Public demand for congressional action reached a crescendo as never before, or after. By the end of the year, feverish action of the tax-writing committees and of both houses of Congress had produced the most extensive and far-reaching tax changes ever. But in terms of its declared objectives, the tax reform drive achieved so little in the Tax Reform Act of 1969 that it may be said that "the mountains labored and brought forth a tiny mouse."

A tempest over taxes. As has been noted, the single event that sparked the tax reform drive in 1969, a veritable bombshell, was Joseph Barr's statement before the Joint Economic Committee just two days before relinquishing the office of secretary of the Treasury. Barr said:

> We face now the possibility of a taxpayer revolt if we do not soon make major reforms in our income taxes. The revolt will come not from the poor but from the tens of millions of middle-class families and individuals with incomes of $7,000 to $20,000, whose tax payments now generally are based on the full ordinary rates and who pay over half of our individual income taxes.

> The middle classes are likely to revolt against income taxes not because of the level or amount of the taxes they must pay but because certain provisions of the tax laws unfairly lighten the burdens of others who can afford to pay. People are concerned and indeed angered about the high-income recipients who pay little or no Federal income taxes. For example, the extreme cases are 155 tax returns in 1967 with adjusted gross incomes above $200,000 on which no Federal income taxes were paid, including 21 with incomes above $1,000,000.[15]

Barr's charges were played up by the media and kept the pot boiling for many months:

> As an unprecedented amount of mail seconding Barr poured into the Treasury and Congress, it finally seemed the long-lost cause of tax reform was an idea whose time had come. House Ways and Means Committee Chairman Wilbur

---

[15] Statement of Joseph W. Barr, January 17, 1969, in *The 1969 Economic Report of the President,* Hearings before the Joint Economic Committee (Washington, D.C.: U.S. Government Printing Office, 1969), p. 46.

Mills scheduled exhaustive hearings to prepare legislative proposals, and the new Nixon administration seemed ready to make tax reform one of its domestic priorities. (*Life*, April 4, 1969)

The plain fact was that middle-income Americans, faced with the biggest peacetime tax bite in memory, were expressing their discontent in an ever-swelling volume of angry mail inundating Capitol Hill. What particularly galled the taxpayers was a system that was hitting them harder than ever while permitting a wealthy few to escape with relatively little tax or even none at all. (*Newsweek*, February 17, 1969)

Mr. Nixon, in the weeks before he sent his tax-reform message to Congress, was receiving reports from all around the country that public anger about taxes had become the hottest political topic in the U.S., topping such things as Vietnam, crime, and the cost of living (*U.S. News & World Report*, May 5, 1969)

In sum, today's taxes tend to broaden the gulf between rich and poor, landlord and tenant, worker and entrepreneur. What upsets Americans most is the feeling they are being cheated. . . . (*Time*, April 4, 1969)

. . . the House Ways and Means Committee will begin hearings on a long list of proposals not only to shut off the escape routes used by the rich and crafty but to make the rules apply more equitably to all. . . .
But the biggest inequity remains the perfectly legal way the rich and super-rich shortage the IRS with financial razzle-dazzle. . . . The rich can wipe out a large part or even all of their tax liability by using one of several forms of personal deductions allowed by the code. (*Newsweek,* February 24, 1969)

It is understandable that such a sensational story—the very rich escape income taxes—emanating from the secretary of the Treasury (if only in office for 31 days) would create a national sensation. For whatever reason, Barr did not disclose the methods or specific code provisions that enabled those high-income earners to avoid any tax liability, although he must have known what they were or could easily have found out. By adding mystery, further attention was drawn to the alleged injustices of the tax system and the matter was left open for wild speculation and for pointed accusations not only against the individuals involved, but against all rich people as tax evaders—and, of course,

Table 1

SHARES OF THE FEDERAL INDIVIDUAL INCOME TAX
By MAJOR INCOME BRACKETS, 1970

Adjusted Gross Income Bracket	Share of Adjusted Gross Income	Share of Tax Liability
Under $7,000	19.5%	10.5%
$7,000 to $19,999	59.2	54.0
$20,000 and over	21.3	35.5
	100.0%	100.0%

Source: Internal Revenue Service, *Statistics of Income, 1970, Individual Income Tax Returns* (Preliminary), 1972; hereafter cited as IRS, *Statistics of Income, 1970.*

against Congress for permitting such a scandal. The fact that the charges were sweeping and the underlying facts obscured enhanced the inflammatory nature of the attack. It was not until a few years later that the Treasury disclosed the results of investigations into high-bracket income tax returns with no tax liability. Treasury Under Secretary Edwin S. Cohen made the facts public in 1972.[16] Some of the factual background is also available from statistical data regularly published by the Internal Revenue Service.

There is no evidence that the middle classes actually bear a disproportionate share of the federal income tax as Barr asserted. In 1970, for instance, they received 59 percent of adjusted gross income and paid 54 percent of the tax (see Table 1). There also may be some doubt about the allegation that the ire of the middle classes (or of the taxpayers in general) is not directed at "the level or amount of taxes they must pay," particularly at a time when the aggregate total of all taxes and governmental revenues equals 41 percent of all personal income in the United States.[17]

---

[16] *Congressional Record,* February 9, 1972, p. H 963; Mr. Cohen's speech on April 29, 1972 (Boston), as well as his testimony before the Joint Economic Committee, July 21, 1972 (with appendixes) and his speech on September 26, 1972 (New York).

[17] Governmental expenditures equaled about 44 percent of personal income in 1971 which suggests that the taxpayer may not have seen the worst yet, if at some time in the future governmental income should be raised to balance outgo. No information has been available on size distribution of personal income since 1964. Therefore, adjusted gross income (AGI) is used as the only available base.

Do the rich go free? For 1970, a total of 15,323 individual income tax returns were filed with an adjusted gross income (AGI) of $200,000 or more; 15,211 of those returns or 99.3 percent were taxable. Combined adjusted gross income on these taxable returns totalled $6.2 billion, taxable income (TI) $4.5 billion, and income tax $2.7 billion. Each taxpayer paid, on the average, a tax of $177,161, equal to 44 percent of his adjusted gross income and 60 percent of his taxable income.

There were 112 returns in the $200,000-and-over adjusted gross income class, with a combined adjusted gross income totalling $47.5 million, that reported *no* tax liability. Since all of the income on these returns was offset by various types of mitigative provisions, the taxpayers in question reported no *taxable* income and therefore paid no tax.

Among the high-bracket returns there were 624 that reported adjusted gross income of $1 million or more. Of these, 621 or 99.5 percent were taxable. Each individual involved paid, on the average, $984,862 in income tax, equal to 46 percent of his adjusted gross income and 65 percent of his taxable income. The aggregate adjusted gross income for this group totalled $1.3 billion, the taxable income $936 million, and the income tax $612 million. This leaves three returns with adjusted gross income of $1 million or more, with a combined adjusted gross income of $10.2 million, that reported no tax liability.

The above figures, of course, are based on pre-audit data. Preliminary reports indicate that many of the returns that were nontaxable as submitted will eventually, as the result of audit review, have to pay some, or even sizeable, income taxes.

In summary, well over 99 percent of all high-income bracket returns for 1970 paid high income taxes. Between 0.5 and 0.7 percent of all returns reported that they had no tax liability—a figure that is likely to be whittled down somewhat by subsequent audits. Out of total adjusted gross income of $6.2 billion in the high bracket ($200,000 adjusted gross income and over), $47 million or 0.8 percent was on returns reported to be nontaxable. That leaves one question: why could 112 tax returns with an adjusted gross income of $200,000 and over—and three returns with an adjusted gross income of $1 million or over—claim no income tax liability. Before going into specifics, a few words must be said about definitions and reporting procedures.

According to the Internal Revenue Code, an individual must include in his reported adjusted gross income "all income from whatever source derived," with specified exceptions. It is the procedures for arriving at adjusted gross income that create some of the confusion about loopholes. In the case of profits from a business or profession, the taxpayer lists his gross receipts on Schedule C and deducts his cost of doing business. He includes his resulting *net* income (or loss) in his adjusted gross income. For example, if he has gross receipts of $100,000 and expenses of $80,000, he includes only $20,000 in his adjusted gross income. But in a different case, for example, that of an investor who is not engaged in a regular business operation, Schedule C is not used and the taxpayer must include all of his *gross* receipts in his adjusted gross income. Suppose that John Brown earns a return of $1 million on $10 million he borrowed and invested; he then reports $1 million adjusted gross income. But if the $10 million he borrowed cost him $800,000 in interest, the *net* income on which he can be taxed is only $200,000. Under existing procedures he deducts the $800,000 interest not *before* reporting his adjusted gross income at $1 million but *afterwards*, as an itemized deduction.[18] He only *appears* to be a millionaire, due to a technicality in the law, but actually he is merely a conduit. If he has other offsets against his $200,000 net profit on this transaction—such as capital losses, loss carryovers, casualty losses, bad debts—or if any number of other factors are involved (for example, transactions in a foreign country that are taxed by that country), he may *under unusual circumstances* wind up with no net tax liability.

Since we are considering here returns that account for only a fraction of one percent of all returns, we are truly dealing with exceptional cases. Moreover, the fact that some returns report adjusted gross income of $1 million or more but owe no income tax does not necessarily indicate deviousness or inequity. To repeat, if interest payable on amounts borrowed for more profitable investment and similar items were deductible *before* computing adjusted gross income rather than *after,* many or most of the high adjusted gross income returns in question would no longer be in the no-tax category. The fact is that, in 1970, interest paid was the principal deduction that accounted for nontaxability on 55 nontaxable high adjusted gross income returns (half the total returns of this type). A minor procedural change would eliminate many returns from the high adjusted gross income nontaxable

---

[18] If, however, the interest he paid *exceeds* his investment income by more than $25,000, it may be disallowed as a deduction, from 1972 on.

statistics without in any way altering the substantive provisions of the income tax.

There are a number of other major reasons why 112 high adjusted gross income returns reported no taxable income for 1970. In seven cases nontaxability was due primarily to foreign tax credits. This means that the income arose from transactions in a foreign country and was taxed there, and that, by statute and sometimes under mutual treaties against double taxation, credit for those tax payments was given in the United States. If such income were taxed by both countries, American citizens would find it virtually impossible to engage in business activities abroad. No business can survive if it is taxed twice at rates up to 70 percent.

Twelve high-bracket individuals paid no federal income tax because their deductions for state and local taxes—mostly state income taxes—exceeded their adjusted gross income. Most of the 12 had had large amounts of nonrecurring income in 1969 on which high state income taxes were payable in 1970 and deductible on 1970 federal income tax returns. Treasury investigation found that, in 11 of the 12 cases, the individuals had paid an average of $1.6 million each in federal income taxes in 1969. The coincidence of high income in 1969 and low income in 1970 produced unusual results of this type in less than one return per 1,000 high adjusted gross income returns.

In another dozen cases, large charitable deductions were the principal reason behind nontaxability for 1970. To be sure, the former "unlimited" charitable deductions (for taxpayers who had paid out at least 90 percent of their income in contributions and income taxes in eight of the preceding ten years) were phased out by the Tax Reform Act of 1969 and replaced by a limitation up to 50 percent of adjusted gross income. But there are a few cases where charitable contributions —when added to deductions such as interest, taxes, medical expenses and casualty losses—equal or exceed adjusted gross income. Those returns are therefore nontaxable.

In 20 cases nontaxability was due to "miscellaneous deductions" (the last item on Schedule A), for example, loss of securities pledged to secure loans, losses on guarantee of loans, payments in settlement of litigation, accounting costs, management, counseling and professional fees, and so forth. These are the kinds of items that an operating business would report on Schedule C and therefore could deduct *prior* to computing adjusted gross income. But individual investors have no way of offsetting such costs against earnings except by the use of itemized deductions *after* adjusted gross income. This could be, and possibly should be, changed by amending the rules. In the meantime, some of those cases will continue to appear in the statistics as high income earners who pay no income tax.

There is other compelling evidence that the 112 tax returns in question are the result of unusual circumstances in a particular year and not of clever manipulations by rich people who regularly manage to escape income taxes: only 12 of the 112 individuals with nontaxable returns for 1970 were also in the nontaxable category in 1966 (when tax returns were studied during consideration of the 1969 Tax Reform Act). In other words, less than one high adjusted gross income tax return in a thousand was nontaxable in both 1966 and 1970.

If we look at all nontaxable returns, not just high income bracket returns, we get a far more comprehensive picture (see Table 2). For 1970, about one tax return in every five was nontaxable. Ninety-seven percent of all these nontaxable returns reported an adjusted gross income of less than $5,000. In fact, over one-half of all income tax returns with an adjusted gross income under $5,000 were nontaxable. Only 1 percent of all tax returns with adjusted gross income of $5,000 or more showed no tax liability. The high incidence of nontaxability in the under $5,000 adjusted gross income bracket is of course no accident. It reflects the intent of Congress to tax low-income persons lightly or not at all. But, by all appearances, it is no less the intent of Congress that, in certain unusual circumstances or combinations of circumstances, *some* returns with an adjusted gross income of $10,000 and over be

Table 2
TAXABLE AND NONTAXABLE INCOME TAX RETURNS, 1970

Adjusted Gross Income Class	Number of All Returns	Number of Nontaxable Returns	Percent of Returns Nontaxable	Percent of All Returns
Total	74,285,982	14,949,114	20.1%	100.0%
Under $5,000	28,302,078	14,482,948	51.2	96.9
$5,000 to under $7,000	9,410,802	321,247	3.4	2.1
$7,000 to under $10,000	12,901,228	105,813	.8	.7
$10,000 and up	23,671,874	39,106	.2	.3

Source: IRS, *Statistics of Income, 1970.*

nontaxable—either to provide equity by adjusting for special burdens or to carry out public policy by providing incentives for certain activities and disincentives for others. As a result, one in every 605 tax returns with an adjusted gross income of $10,000 or over (that is, one-sixth of 1 percent of the total) was nontaxable in 1970.

In conclusion, then, it is a myth that many millionaires and other wealthy persons can and do avoid paying income taxes by escaping through loopholes in the Internal Revenue Code. This claim has been voiced too often, either carelessly or deliberately, and it has succeeded in creating resentment that has led to a "soak the rich" attitude among broad sections of the public and in Congress. The time has come for this myth to be laid to rest. The fact is that many of those taxpayers who submitted returns with a high adjusted gross income did not have a high income. They only *appeared* to have a high income by following the procedural requirements of the income tax form.

This does not mean, of course, that huge amounts of income do not escape taxation or that many taxpayers do not manage in some way or other to avoid bearing their proper share of the overall burden. This problem will be reviewed in the next chapter.

At the outset, the Internal Revenue Code proclaims its intent to tax "all income from whatever source derived." But then it undercuts that sweeping statement by allowing a myriad of exclusions, exemptions, deductions and credits that free about half of all personal income from the impact of the income tax. Over $400 billion remained untaxed in 1970 and the figure was probably in excess of $460 billion for 1972. This makes the federal income tax the tax with the most liberal exemptions—and the narrowest actual base compared with its potential base—in the United States. Sales and property tax exemptions average little more than one-fourth of their overall computed or estimated base.

Table 3

RELATIONSHIP OF PERSONAL INCOME, ADJUSTED GROSS
INCOME AND TAXABLE INCOME ON
FEDERAL INCOME TAX RETURNS, 1950-1970

($ in billions)

Year	Personal Income	Adjusted Gross Income	Taxable Income	AGI as a Percent of PI	Taxable Income as a Percent of	
					AGI	PI
1950	$227.6	$179.9	$ 84.9	79.0%	47.2%	37.4%
1955	310.9	249.4	128.0	80.2	51.3	41.2
1960	401.0	316.6	171.6	78.9	54.2	42.8
1965	538.9	430.7	255.1	79.9	59.2	47.3
1969	750.9	605.6	388.8	80.6	64.2	51.8
1970	806.3	632.0	401.2	78.4	63.5	49.8

Source: IRS, *Statistics of Income, Individual Income Tax Returns,* various years; personal income statistics from the *Economic Report of the President,* January 1973.

Contrary to what is widely believed, the percentage of personal income that is subjected to federal taxation has been gradually increasing over the years, from 37.4 percent in 1950 to a high of 51.8 percent in 1969 (see Table 3). But this progress in making the income tax more comprehensive was not achieved primarily by purposeful tax reform, either by tightening or closing so-called loopholes. Rather, it came about as a result of certain extraneous factors. Growth in incomes and continuous inflation pushed an increasing share of reported income above the personal exemption, which remained steady at $600 from 1948 through 1969; then, personal exemptions were raised for 1970 and again for 1971 and 1972. These higher personal exemptions and other "tax reforms" in the Tax Reform Act of 1969, along with economic trends, helped lower the percentage of personal income subject to the income tax from 51.8 percent in 1969 to 49.8 percent in 1970.

Sources of Untaxed Income

The $405 billion gap between personal income and taxable income in 1970 can be traced to two sources: (1) a $231 billion difference between adjusted gross income and taxable income—a figure that can be derived accurately and in detail from the annual statistics of income tax returns supplied by the Internal Revenue Service; and (2) a $174 billion difference between personal income and adjusted gross income—a figure whose composition can only be estimated. As Table 3 shows, adjusted gross income has remained steady at about 80 percent of personal income over the past 20 years; taxable income as a percentage of adjusted gross income, however, gradually climbed from 47 to 64 percent.

While the difference between personal income and taxable income equals $405 billion, total untaxed income may be estimated at $465 billion because of $60 billion in offsetting items. Major items of untaxed income and offsets are shown in Table 4.

The literature of the tax reform drive usually asserts that most of the "loopholes" were designed for and work to the benefit of the rich, that poor and middle-income taxpayers are taxed on all of their income with no escape possibilities and that most of the income that avoids taxation is to be found in the very high-income brackets. Table 4, however, suggests the opposite: much or most of the untaxed income is in the low- and medium-income brackets.

Table 4

MAJOR ITEMS OF FEDERALLY UNTAXED INCOME, 1970
Reconciliation of Personal Income and Taxable Income
on Federal Income Tax Returns
(estimated)

	$ Billions	% of Total PI
Personal income (PI)	806	100.0
Taxable income reported on federal income tax returns (TI)	401	49.8
Federally untaxed personal income (difference between PI and TI)	405	50.2

	$ Billions	% of Federally Untaxed PI
Tax-free income from social benefits		
Social security, unemployment compensation, public assistance, veterans' benefits, et cetera	72	17.8
Untaxed labor income		
Employer contributions to pension and welfare funds, nontaxable income in kind, nontaxable military pay allowances, et cetera	32	7.9
Imputed income		
Rent on owner-occupied homes, earnings on insurance policies, food and fuel produced and consumed on farms, et cetera	45	11.1
Tax-exempt interest on municipal bonds	2	.5
Nonreported income		
Persons with income below taxable level filing no return, amounts disclosed by audit, evasion	46	11.4
Other nontaxed income		
Property income received by nonindividuals (fiduciaries, nonprofit institutions), excluded business expenses, et cetera	20	4.9
Personal exemptions		
$625 for 195 million persons plus 9 million double for aged and blind	128	31.6
Deductions		
Standard deductions — $32		
Itemized deductions:		
State & local taxes — 32		
Interest paid — 24		
Charitable contributions — 13		
Medical expenses — 10		
Other — 9		
$88	120	29.6
All nontaxed income	$465	114.8

Table 4 (continued)

	$ Billions	% of Total PI
Minus		
Exemptions and deductions in excess of AGI on nontaxable returns:		
Standard deductions	$14	
Itemized deductions	4	
Personal exemptions	21	
	$39	
AGI on those returns	22	−17	−4.2
Taxed income *not* included in personal income as defined in national income accounting:		
Personal contributions for social insurance	$28	
One-half of capital gains	9	
Other	6	−43	−10.6
Difference between PI and TI (as above)		$405	100.0

Source: Derived by author from data in IRS, *Statistics of Income, 1970.*

Tax-free social benefits (such as social security, unemployment compensation and public assistance), untaxed labor income and standard deductions are concentrated in the low brackets. Untaxed income in those categories totals $136 billion. Moreover, one-half of the non-reported income can be attributed to persons with income below taxable levels who file no returns: this must be added for a total of about $160 billion. Personal exemptions and imputed income (imputed rental on owner-occupied homes, et cetera) as well as the remainder of non-reported income are widely, and probably evenly, distributed among taxpayers at all levels and do not gravitate toward the upper income brackets. These benefits total about $200 billion. But even itemized deductions of $88 billion are relatively heavier in the lower brackets (Table 5).

Conclusive evidence on the distribution of the untaxed income by income classes could be obtained by relating personal income to taxable income by income brackets. Unfortunately, however, a breakdown of personal income by income brackets has not been published by the Department of Commerce, nor by anyone else, since 1964 and there

Table 5
ITEMIZED DEDUCTIONS AS A PERCENT OF ADJUSTED GROSS INCOME, 1970

Adjusted Gross Income Bracket	Percent
All returns	19.6
Under $5,000	35.0
$5,000 to under $10,000	23.0
$10,000 to under $15,000	19.1
$15,000 or more	17.4

Source: IRS, *Statistics of Income, 1970.*

Table 6
DIFFERENCE BETWEEN ADJUSTED GROSS INCOME AND TAXABLE INCOME, BY MAJOR INCOME CLASSES, 1970

Adjusted Gross Income Class	Difference between AGI and TI (billions)	Difference as Percent of AGI
All returns	$231	36.5
Under $10,000	114	48.9
$10,000 to $24,999	96	31.1
$25,000 and more	21	22.8

are presently no plans to prepare such statistical information. A detailed comparison between adjusted gross income and taxable income is available from the annual *Statistics of Income* of the Internal Revenue Service and, as Table 6 indicates, it clearly shows that reported untaxed income occurs largely in the lower brackets.

Greater detail by income brackets is shown in Table 7. The figures given there indicate that (1) the major part of the difference between adjusted gross income and taxable income lies in the lower and middle-income brackets—that is, very little is at the top—and (2) effective tax rates on adjusted gross income and on taxable income are steeply progressive. Since most of the difference between personal income and adjusted gross income accrues to persons in the low brackets, the tendency favoring low-income persons is considerably stronger than the table suggests.

The Treasury fiscal staff, under the direction of Assistant Secretary Stanley Surrey, prepared a table in 1968 that incorporated a modified

Table 7

ADJUSTED GROSS INCOME, TAXABLE INCOME AND EFFECTIVE TAX RATES ON FEDERAL INCOME TAX RETURNS, 1970

Adjusted Gross Income Class	Adjusted Gross Income (billions)	Taxable Income (billions)	Difference between AGI and TI (Untaxed Income) as Percent of Adjusted Gross Income	Effective Tax Rate on AGI	Effective Tax Rate on TI
Total	$632.0	$401.0	36.6%	13.8%	20.9%
No AGI	− 2.4	—	—	—	—
Under $5,000	67.6	23.0	66.0	7.7	15.8
$5,000 to under $7,000	56.4	31.1	44.8	9.6	16.8
$7,000 to under $10,000	109.3	65.6	40.0	10.6	17.5
$10,000 to under $15,000	171.9	112.2	34.7	12.0	18.4
$15,000 to under $25,000	136.8	97.6	28.6	14.6	20.4
$25,000 to under $50,000	55.0	42.1	23.5	19.6	25.6
$50,000 to under $100,000	23.1	18.4	20.4	28.9	36.1
$100,000 to under $200,000	8.2	6.4	21.3	37.0	46.9
$200,000 to under $500,000	3.7	2.7	24.9	42.7	56.5
$500,000 to under $1,000,000	1.2	.9	27.9	45.5	62.5
$1,000,000 and more	1.3	.9	29.5	46.5	65.3

Source: IRS, *Statistics of Income, 1970.*

definition of adjusted gross income. However, only a few selected items—one-half of long-term capital gains, exclusions due to percentage depletion and excess of farm losses over farm gains—were added to arrive at "amended adjusted gross income." In other words, the authors included certain untaxed items that they felt ought to be taxable, but did not include most of the large items currently excluded from adjusted gross income. With such selective adjustment, the results are not surprising: effective tax rates for incomes under $20,000 were not affected at all by the "adjustment," but effective rates for the higher brackets were sharply reduced. For incomes of $1,000,000 or more, effective rates dropped from 44.3 to 28.4 percent, for incomes between $500,000 and under $1 million from 44.1 to 30.7 percent.[1] Subsequently such statements about effective rates under "amended" adjusted gross income were widely and repeatedly used to show that high income earners are paying very low tax rates and that their taxes ought to be increased.

Joseph A. Pechman and Benjamin A. Okner used a broader concept of "expanded adjusted gross income" to demonstrate the low level of effective income tax rates. They included a much wider range of items than did Surrey, but again it was mainly a question of which untaxed items the authors thought ought to be taxed. Their results suggested that the effective income tax rate rises from 0.5 percent on incomes under $3,000 to a maximum of 32.1 percent on incomes of $1 million and over.[2] While these figures are less lopsided than Surrey's, it is doubtful that such manipulations truly present an impartial picture.

The fact remains that although public discussion of loopholes and untaxed income has almost exclusively focused on the rich in recent years, most of the untaxed income is in the lower and middle brackets. There are good reasons for this. Under a system of taxing according to taxpaying capacity, persons and families at the lower levels will be largely free of taxation because they need most or all of their resources to sustain themselves at an adequate or minimum standard of living.

---

[1] U.S. Treasury Department, *Tax Reform Studies and Proposals,* joint publication of the Committee on Ways and Means of the U.S. House of Representatives and Committee on Finance of the U.S. Senate (Washington, D.C.: U.S. Government Printing Office, 1969), part 1, p. 81.

[2] Joint Economic Committee Hearings, *Economics of Federal Subsidy Programs,* p. 71.

Redistribution of Income

In 1970 about one-fifth of all individual income tax returns were non-taxable—97 percent of them reporting adjusted gross income under $5,000.[3] Since persons at the lowest income levels generally do not file tax returns, we may estimate that at least one-fourth of the American population paid no federal income tax in 1970. Their number is bound to grow since personal exemptions were boosted to $750 for 1972, standard deductions to 15 percent of adjusted gross income (with a $2,000 maximum) and the low-income allowance to $1,300. A single person with an income less than $2,050, or a couple with two children (or a couple both 65 years or over) with an income less than $4,300, will no longer need to file a return. Additional millions of Americans will thus be freed from any tax liability and more billions of income will become tax exempt.

This may be justified on equity grounds. But it brings about a division of the population—between those who pay the taxes and others, equally entitled to vote, who are interested mainly in obtaining higher benefits from government. In some cases of course there is a clear need for such assistance, but there are also those who will make extravagant demands, knowing that others will pay the cost and that they themselves will not be called upon to foot any part of the bill. If such "representation without taxation" assumes large enough proportions, it invites civic irresponsibility and poses a danger to the preservation of responsible free government. It could lead to demagoguery, to exaggerated promises of more "bread and circuses" by reckless politicians. Not without reason did H. L. Mencken define an election as an advance auction of stolen goods.

To be sure, the drive for greater economic equality, toward raising income in the lowest brackets, has long had broad popular support. On the whole, it has been quite successful—not only during the New Deal and World War II, but also in the postwar period. Table 8, which gives the distribution of families by "money income" class for the three years 1950, 1960 and 1970, shows a decrease in the percentage of families in the lower income classes and an increase in the percentage of families in the middle-income classes. In 1950, 68.6 percent of families had a total money income of less than $7,000 (1970 constant dollars); in 1970 only 31.1 percent were in this category. In just 20 years, income

---

[3] See Table 2, p. 25.

Table 8
DISTRIBUTION OF FAMILIES BY MONEY INCOME, SELECTED YEARS, 1950-1970
(in 1970 dollars)

Money Income Class	1950	1960	1970
Total	100.0%	100.0%	100.0%
Under $3,000	22.8	15.6	8.9
$3,000 to $4,999	22.1	14.1	10.4
$5,000 to $6,999	23.7	16.7	11.8
$7,000 to $9,999	18.3	24.7	19.9
$10,000 to $14,999	13.2	19.3	26.8
$15,000 and over	13.2	9.5	22.3
Median income	$5,385	$7,376	$9,867

Note: "Money income," the concept by which the Department of Commerce computes income distribution, uses a broader definition of income than adjusted gross income on tax returns. The figures are derived from the Bureau of the Census annual surveys rather than Internal Revenue statistics. In 1970, money income in the United States totalled $577 billion.

Source: Bureau of the Census, *Income in 1970 of Families and Persons in the United States,* Current Population Series P-60, no. 80, 1971.

patterns shifted so that 46.7 percent of families now receive incomes between $7,000 and $15,000.

The question is how much government should, through its tax and expenditure policies, seek to redistribute income toward the lower brackets. That policy, by its very nature, promotes consumption but exerts a dampening effect on capital formation and industrial expansion. It is well established that a high rate of savings and nonresidential (business) investment is associated with high rates of growth. Conversely, disincentives to savings and investment tend to retard economic growth and job creation. While heavy taxation of the rich and of business generally has a powerful political appeal, it exacts a heavy price in slower economic growth and high unemployment. Still, elective officials *cannot* forget that four out of every five income tax returns for 1970 reported adjusted gross income under $13,000 and 94 percent were under $20,000. On the other hand, only 1.8 percent of all tax returns (or 1.3 million) reported adjusted gross income of $30,000 or more, and a mere one-tenth of one percent (78,000) an income of $100,000 or more. That distribution of voting strength inevitably influences considerations of tax policy.

When specific tax changes are under consideration, lawmakers are conscious that 87 percent of all income tax returns are in the under-$15,000 adjusted gross income category—and in that bracket, wages and salaries account for 90 percent of all income, while the aggregate of capital gains, dividends and business profits represents only 5 percent (figures for 1970). On $100,000-and-over returns, however, dividends, capital gains and profits account for 63 percent of all income, wages and salaries for only 25 percent. Understandably, political arithmetic plays a major role in public pronouncements on tax reform and has an impact on floor votes and final decisions.

Does equity mean equality? Though the debate over tax reform deals extensively with economic policy considerations, the movement's "gut issue" is equity in taxation, or more specifically, redistribution of income to provide greater equality in after-tax income. The basic aim of many backers of the present tax reform drive is to shift more income from those who have more to those who have less. As Henry C. Simons, University of Chicago economist, wrote a third of a century ago: "The case for drastic progression in taxation must be rested on the case against inequality—on the ethical or aesthetic judgment that the prevailing distribution of wealth and income reveals a degree (and/or kind) of inequality which is distinctly evil or unlovely." [4] The case for reducing or eliminating income inequality rests in Simons's words on another ethical precept: "At any rate it may be best to start by denying any justification for prevailing inequality in terms of personal desert." [5] The late University of Wisconsin economist Harold M. Groves expressed it plainly: "Many people regard inequalities of income as a clear case of the tyranny of the strong and fortunate over the weak and poorly endowed." [6]

A recent and widely acclaimed work by John Rawls, *A Theory of Justice,* presents other current trends in egalitarian thought. Rawls asserts that a social order is just and legitimate *only* to the degree that it is directed to the redress of inequality:

> There is no more reason to permit the distribution of income
> and wealth to be settled by the distribution of natural assets
> than by historical and social fortune. . . . No one deserves his

---

[4] Henry C. Simons, *Personal Income Taxation* (Chicago: University of Chicago Press, 1938), p. 18.
[5] Ibid.
[6] Harold M. Groves, *Financing Government* (New York: Henry Holt & Co., 1946), p. 31.

greater natural capacity, nor merits a more favorable starting place in society. . . . All social primary goods—liberty and opportunity, income and wealth, and the bases of self-respect —are to be distributed equally unless an unequal distribution of any or all these goods is to the advantage of the least favored.[7]

Reviewing Rawls's theory, Daniel Bell called the book "the most comprehensive effort in modern philosophy to justify a socialistic ethic" and added: "It is striking that Rawls, like Jencks, does not discuss either 'work' or 'effort'—as if those who had succeeded, in the university, or in business or government, had done so largely by contingent circumstances or fortune or social background."[8] Some feel that the denial of any merit in economic success is based largely on envy and jealousy.[9] In light of such complex questions, some authors have expressed amazement that egalitarian theories have become so widely accepted and that for some people the issue is no longer even considered controversial.[10]

Some regard redistribution of income from the top down as a clear case of tyranny and exploitation of a productive but vote-weak minority by a greedy and vote-strong majority, and feel that rewards for effort are still necessary. University of Chicago law professors Walter J. Blum and Harry Kalven, Jr., have argued: "Whatever we may think in moments of tranquility, we do not live from day to day without the help of the assumption that those around us and we ourselves deserve in some way the praise and blame, the rewards and the punishments, we all dispense and receive."[11] Blum and Kalven referred to the ever-present danger that tax legislation may be turned into (or is) "class legislation

---

[7] As quoted in Daniel Bell, "On Meritocracy and Equality," *The Public Interest,* Fall 1972, pp. 55 and 56.

[8] Ibid., pp. 57 and 58. Christopher Jencks also attributes economic success to luck or fortuitous circumstances and therefore not a matter of personal merit that would justify a reward in the form of higher income or status. "Economic success seems to depend on varieties of luck and on-the-job competence that are only moderately related to family background, schooling, or scores on standards tests." Christopher Jencks et al., *Inequality: A Reassessment of the Effect of Family and Schooling in America* (New York: Basic Books, 1972), p. 8.

[9] Helmut Schoeck, *Envy: A Theory of Social Behavior* (New York: Harcourt, Brace & World, 1970).

[10] For example, see Irving Kristol, "About Equality," in *Commentary,* November 1972.

[11] Blum and Kalven, *The Uneasy Case for Progressive Taxation* (Chicago: University of Chicago Press, 1953), p. 82.

in its most naked form." [12] In fact, former Senator Joseph S. Clark declared that the "tax issue is at heart a class issue" and may be viewed largely in terms of a "class struggle." [13]

The single-minded concentration of much of the tax reform drive of the past 15 years on the elimination of certain "loopholes" that account for a tiny fraction of untaxed personal income—but which largely benefit high-income persons—and the complete disregard of the overwhelming bulk of untaxed income that redounds to recipients in the lower and middle brackets makes the thrust of the movement primarily to alter, through the political process, the rewards and punishments of the free market system. The question is whether the existing bias against effort and success in our society and in our tax system should be made stronger by a type of tax reform that adds to it or whether neutrality is a more desirable goal of tax reform.

In a sophisticated little book entitled *The Ethics of Redistribution,* Bertrand de Jouvenel pointed at the pitfalls and dangers of increasingly shifting income from those who earn it by producing goods or services for the market to those who do not.[14] He pointed out that a steady whittling down of incentives must lead to a decline in productivity, that it must mean the end of many culturally desirable activities, and that it leads to a steady growth in the power of the state. If taxing at the top does not yield enough, a state will proceed to impose ever heavier taxation on everyone above an income floor.

A new direction? Trends in public sentiment are often hard to appraise. In its fall 1969 issue, *The Public Interest* carried an article by Joseph A. Pechman, "The Rich, the Poor and the Taxes They Pay," strongly advocating a type of tax reform that would redistribute income. Three years later (summer 1972), it featured Irving Kristol's article, "Of Populism and Taxes," which warned that the modern populism of income redistribution by taxation may be losing support among a majority of the American people who are disillusioned with its results and perceive its shortcomings: "One can fairly predict that many middle-class reformers will find, to their surprise, that the populace is going to be quick to bite the hand that aims to feed it. The populace doesn't want

---

[12] Ibid., p. 20.

[13] *Congressional Record,* April 5, 1960, p. A 3008.

[14] Bertrand de Jouvenel, *The Ethics of Redistribution* (New York: Cambridge University Press, 1952).

to be fed: it wants more freedom to graze on its own." [15] Whether Irving Kristol assessed the American public's current mentality correctly or not may become apparent during consideration of income tax reform in 1973.

---

[15] Kristol, "Of Populism and Taxes," *The Public Interest,* Summer 1972, p. 7. In a simultaneous article Kristol disagreed with Treasury Secretary Barr's charge that tax inequities were threatening a "tax rebellion": "The 'tax rebellion' of recent years has been provoked mainly by the rapid growth of the welfare state, not by particular inequities in the tax laws—inequities which, though real enough, would not, if abolished, have any significant impact on the workingman's tax burden." Kristol, "About Equality," pp. 44–45.

3

DEDUCTIONS, CAPITAL GAINS
AND OTHER TAX BENEFITS

Capital Gains Taxation

Of all the tax "loopholes" none is cited more often as a glaring example of the tax system's unfairness than taxation of long-term capital gains at half the normal income tax rate. In the words of the First National City Bank of New York: "It is seen by some as a nefarious device by which the rich avoid paying very high rates on top-bracket incomes, the Treasury loses billions in revenues, and the progressivity of the income tax is weakened." [1] Ways and Means Committee Chairman Wilbur Mills said in the spring of 1972: "It is pretty hard to justify treating a capital gain differently from ordinary income. I've never felt there is anything more sacrosanct about the profit from the sales of an asset than from the sweat of your brow." [2] The most effective statement, however, and the most often repeated during the 1972 presidential campaign, was Senator McGovern's: "Money made by money should be taxed at the same rate as money made by men."

This principle, taken at face value, is persuasive and hard to refute. Why should a man who bought common stocks and sold them after six months at a $10,000 profit pay less in taxes than a man who earned $10,000 by his daily toil over a year? A dollar made from stock profits will buy no less than a dollar made in wages—so why should capital gains not be taxed as ordinary income? Moreover, special treatment for capital gains injects many complications into the tax system and often

---

[1] First National City Bank of New York, *Monthly Economic Letter,* October 1972.

[2] *Congressional Record,* March 2, 1972, p. H 1721.

has more influence on investment decisions than other factors. The income tax law could be greatly simplified by abolishing special consideration for capital gains. Last but not least, capital gains are heavily concentrated in the top brackets and provide little benefit to persons on the lower rungs of the income ladder. For 1970, 93 percent of all returns reported *no* net gain from the sale of capital assets. About half of all reported gains was on returns with an adjusted gross income of $30,000 and up (less than 2 percent of all returns), four-fifths on returns with $10,000 or more. Net capital gains accounted for only 5 percent of the adjusted gross income of taxpayers in the income bracket under $10,000, but for nearly half in the $50,000-and-up group. The higher an income is, the larger will be the share derived from capital gains. Therefore, if special treatment of long-term capital gains is in fact a "loophole," it is certainly one whose direct benefits mainly aid the rich.

But many observers disagree that taxation of only half of net long-term capital gains truly constitutes a loophole. They regard it, instead, as an essential device to provide greater equity and prevent grave economic damage. In their view, capital gains are really not income and therefore should not be treated as income for tax purposes—although these gains may represent *some* taxpaying capacity. For this reason, most countries do not tax capital gains as income—some do not tax them at all, others at lower rates than income—and most tax them more lightly than does the United States.

It is technically correct to say that half of long-term capital gains is exempt from taxation, but this is simply a method of taxing them at one-half the rates applicable to regular income. It may therefore be more appropriate to say that long-term capital gains are taxed at lower rates than current income because they are not current income. National economic accounting has always excluded capital gains from measures of income because nothing is added to current output if an investor shifts from one type of investment to another, even though he does it at a higher price than the one at which he had bought the asset. But to an individual a capital gain *may* constitute income—certainly by R. M. Haig's classic definition: "Income is the money value of the net accretion to one's economic power between two points in time." [3] That concept, if accepted, would call for taxing a person's consumption, plus the

---

[3] Robert M. Haig, ed., *The Federal Income Tax* (New York: Columbia University Press, 1921), Chapter 1.

year-to-year change in his net wealth. This, in turn, implies taxing unrealized as well as realized gains, something that is undesirable for a variety of reasons and could be economically destructive.

There are several arguments why even realized gains should not be taxed like ordinary income. Assets held for a number of years, or even for a decade or more, may have increased in price merely because of inflation. Consumer prices have risen 25 percent in the past five years, 40 percent in the past ten, and nearly 100 percent in the last quarter century. To tax such a "gain" would amount to a capital levy, not just a tax on income. Moreover, under a system of progressive tax rates, the bunching in the year of sale of gains that may have accrued over many years could result in an unduly high rate. This problem probably could be solved by an averaging process, just as the inflation factor could be compensated for by an appropriate time adjustment—that is, a rate scale geared to the length of time that the asset had been held. But the basic fact remains that gains from the sale of long-term assets (in contrast to trading gains) do not arise out of current production and are not current income. They merely represent the conversion of an asset from one form into another. Congress has recognized this for homes. It can be argued that there is no reason to treat a "rollover" in other types of investment differently—except the political reason that millions sell their houses for more than they paid for them (or plan or hope to) but only one taxpayer in 14 enjoys other types of capital gains.

As a compromise between the two propositions of taxing long-term capital gains as income and not taxing them at all, Congress resorted to the often applied principle of "splitting the difference" and taxing them at 50 percent of the income tax rate. That compromise seemed to be so widely accepted and to work so well that the principle was extended to activities that only remotely resemble capital gains—coal, oil and iron ore royalties, livestock used for breeding, timber operations, unharvested crops, lump-sum distributions from retirement plans, employee stock options and others. The present system of taxing capital gains at half the normal rate has now been in effect for 30 years and, although certain tightening and other improvements have been made and more may be indicated, this stability suggests a balance of forces that may not be easy to upset.

Capital gains taxed as income? It is widely believed that the income tax law originally taxed capital gains in full at current tax rates and that remedial provisions were not introduced until the Revenue Act of 1921.[4] The fact is, however, that special treatment of capital gains goes back to the Civil War income tax and was part of our present income tax as enacted in 1913.

Subsequent to the first imposition of an income tax in 1862, the commissioner of internal revenue ruled capital gains to be taxable as income. However, Congress countermanded this order by providing in the act of June 30, 1864, that only the profits from the sale of real estate purchased within the year for which the income was estimated were to be taxed, and that the actual losses from the sales of such property might be deducted from the income. Taxation of capital gains was extended (to property transactions within two years, not just a year, of the original purchase) by the act of March 2, 1867. Five years later the Civil War income tax was repealed.

When Congress reimposed an income tax in August 1894, profits from real estate were again to be taxed as income only when the property had been bought within the two preceding years. Soon after, however, the income tax itself was declared to be unconstitutional by the U.S. Supreme Court in the famous case of *Pollock* v. *Farmer's Loan and Trust Company* (157 U.S. 429). After ratification of the Sixteenth Amendment, an income tax was again adopted in 1913. Representative Cordell Hull, who drafted the section of the bill pertaining to capital gains, "evidently intended to exempt capital gains from taxation, but was not absolutely clear on this point." [5] During the floor debate, Hull assured the House that the tax would apply only to purchases and sales of real estate and securities made within the same year.[6] However, the Emergency Revenue Act of September 1916 provided for taxation of capital gains, with asset value as of March 1, 1913, to govern property acquired prior to that date.

---

[4] The Joint Economic Committee staff reported in *The Federal Tax System: Facts and Problems* (Washington, D.C.: U.S. Government Printing Office, 1964), p. 74: "Prior to 1922, capital assets were not explicitly defined in the law. Gains from the sale of all assets were taxable in full as ordinary income both to individuals and to corporations."

[5] Sidney Ratner, *American Taxation* (New York: W. W. Norton Co., 1942), p. 326; J. S. Seidman, *Legislative History of Federal Income Tax Laws* (New York: Prentice-Hall, 1938), pp. 983–1007.

[6] *Congressional Record,* April 26, 1913, p. 513, and May 6, 1913, p. 1257.

Experience with taxing capital gains at regular income tax rates during and after World War I, particularly the resulting "lock-in" effect on investments, led to a movement for change. Secretary of the Treasury Andrew Mellon suggested that it would be sounder taxation policy not to recognize capital gains and losses, arguing that the government probably had lost more revenue by permitting the deduction of capital losses (between 1918 and 1921) than it had realized by including capital gains as income.

Special treatment of capital gains began with the Revenue Act of 1921 which established a maximum rate of 12.5 percent for capital gains—compared with a top income tax rate that was reduced in that act from 73 to 56 percent and in subsequent steps to a low of 24 percent for 1929. Numerous changes were enacted after 1921. Particularly noteworthy is the 1934 scheme of scaling capital gains rates to the length of time that an asset had been held—from 100 percent of the normal rate for assets bought and sold within a year, 80 percent for assets held from one to two years and gradually down to 30 percent for assets held for 10 or more years. The scheme was abandoned four years later because it was held to influence decisions on the length of the holding period. A "sliding scale" of capital gains taxation, geared to the length of the holding period, has an undeniable appeal, however, and such plans are now again under consideration.

Our current method of taxing capital gains was adopted in 1942: 50 percent of assets held for six months or more were subjected to income taxation, with a maximum rate of 25 percent on total gains. In 1963 President Kennedy proposed a reduction in the share of capital gains taxed to 30 percent for holdings of two years or over, but the proposal was not enacted. The 25 percent maximum rate was abolished for gains over $50,000 in 1969, which means that capital gains may be subjected to a rate of up to 35 percent (half of the top income tax rate of 70 percent), and actually even higher because the nontaxed part of capital gains must now be included in the limited tax preferences which are subject to a 10 percent tax from $30,000 on up.

Limited tax preferences (LTPs) may have a greater impact on capital gains taxation than was originally assumed. According to Treasury estimates, the excluded one-half of long-term capital gains may account for more than 80 percent of the total amount of all LTPs, and could exceed 90 percent in 1972. In other words, most of the "minimum tax" on LTPs will be on capital gains. This, on top of the elimination of the "alternative" 25 percent tax rate, may have a disincentive effect on decisions by investors with large unrealized capital gains (and will of course materially boost the tax on those who liquidate their gains). So, at least for some taxpayers, capital gains taxes were effectively raised by the 1969 amendment.

Potential damage to economic growth. For years it has been a prime goal of some tax reformers to subject all capital gains to taxation at normal income tax rates or, at least, come reasonably close to it. The proposal is asserted mainly on equity grounds, but its sponsors also point out that substantial revenue gains—some estimates put them as high as $12 billion a year—may be involved. Most of those estimates, however, assume that a doubling of the tax rate will have no significant impact on transactions or on economic expansion, a proposition that is open to question. Opponents of the proposal argue that the Treasury could even get less revenue because taxpayers might hang on to investments with unrealized profits while liquidating those with losses. In addition, the measure could lead to a slowdown in new investment and in the economic growth rate.

Dan Throop Smith, a tax policy expert who served as deputy to the secretary of the Treasury during the Eisenhower administration, wrote:

> It is hard to imagine any single change in the tax law which would do as much damage to economic development as the full taxation of capital gains, even if the maximum rate were reduced to 50 percent. The risk of loss is so great in so many important areas of investment that anything like a half-and-half sharing with the government would seriously curtail investment. . . . For emphasis it may be repeated that a tax on capital gains is a more serious barrier to investment than the ordinary income tax is to activity because there are no nonpecuniary incentives for investment.[7]

Another observer summarizes the major damages that could result from substantially boosting capital gains taxation as follows:

> First, risk-taking incentives and the supply of essential venture capital would be seriously curtailed.
> Second, investments in modern plant and equipment and in new technologies would diminish.

---

[7] Dan Throop Smith, *Federal Tax Reform* (New York: McGraw-Hill, 1961), p. 146.

And third, the mobility of capital assets—which is crucial to maintaining a dynamic and fluid economy—would be impeded.[8]

For these reasons no industrial nation taxes capital gains as ordinary income and some of the countries with the most rapid economic growth such as Germany and Japan do not tax them at all—in an effort to stimulate capital formation, introduction of new products and methods, and expanded employment.

Some have proposed that long-term capital gains should be exempt from taxation if they constitute merely a "rollover" or a shift from one investment to another. This rule now applies to the sale of a home and subsequent purchase of another residence. Congress realized that no true and taxable gain arises when a person sells his house and buys another one for which he pays at least the same amount. Why should that principle not also be applied to other types of investment? Some have also proposed eased capital gains taxation but these suggestions have not made much progress in the Congress. Others suggest that the tax rate on capital gains should be geared to the length the asset has been held, which was the U.S. practice from 1934 to 1938. Such a plan could and probably should be tried again.

At the present time a short-term gain (held less than six months) is taxed as regular income while a long-term gain (held more than six months) is taxed as a capital gain. It is hard to tell whether this practice is appropriate since there are no hard and fast rules for distinguishing trading gains from investment gains: some more or less arbitrary time period must be established. The question has been raised repeatedly whether the minimum holding time of six months should be lengthened to one year.

Time and again it has been proposed that unrealized capital gains be taxed at the investor's death lest they escape taxation forever. The proposal has never been enacted, partly because it has been a firmly established principle that a gain does not arise until the asset is sold. The more important consideration is the question of liquidity. If unrealized gains were taxable as part of the investor's estate, insufficient cash might be available to pay the tax without a sale. Thus such a tax

---

[8] U.S. Congress, Senate, *Tax Reform Act of 1969,* Hearings before the Committee on Finance (Washington, D.C.: U.S. Government Printing Office, 1969), part 3, p. 1882; testimony by Robert W. Haack, president, New York Stock Exchange.

could force the breakup or liquidation of many family and other enterprises which were unable to raise the necessary cash. If the inheritor were offered the option of assuming the original tax base (purchase price), he could avoid a high tax liability at the same time at which estate taxes (which range up to 77 percent) are also payable. Thereby the forced breakup of the enterprise or investment could be prevented. But the asset might then be solidly frozen in, for years or for generations, because the capital gains tax would become prohibitively high.

The problem would be eased for a period of time by making only the gains accruing after the enactment of the new law subject to tax. But this would produce little revenue gain and would only postpone, not prevent, the described difficulties. In other words, there is no easy way out—contrary to assertions contained in some frequently discussed plans for taxing capital gains more heavily. Consideration of economic consequence and of equity suggests that long-term capital gains be treated differently from income lest serious harm be done.

Mineral Percentage Depletion Allowances

Mineral percentage depletion allowances for individual operators and corporations have long been denounced, to use Senator Thomas J. McIntyre's words, as "the most notorious of the many loopholes now in our tax laws." The senator added that "elimination of the oil depletion allowance is synonymous with tax reform." [9] Senator Paul Douglas, citing his 20-year battle against percentage depletion, called it "the worst abuse of all," [10] and Professor William F. Hellmuth, Jr., who for some time served as deputy assistant secretary of the Treasury for tax policy, told the House Ways and Means Committee that it was "the most glaring and most widely condemned source of erosion in the corporate income tax base." [11]

Oil and gas get a break. Some of the facts are evident: production of oil and gas and of most other minerals from domestic and foreign sources receives certain large tax advantages that are denied to other

---

[9] *Congressional Record,* September 12, 1969, p. S 10490.

[10] *Congressional Record,* May 29, 1968, p. 15741.

[11] U.S. Congress, House of Representatives, Committee on Ways and Means, *Tax Revision Compendium* (Washington, D.C.: U.S. Government Printing Office, 1959), vol. 1, p. 294.

business activities. This has been the case now for well over half a century—with only comparatively minor changes enacted since 1926. Few subjects have been explored, studied, investigated and considered more thoroughly, more extensively, or more frequently by the Congress. At the same time, few public policies have been tried and found so wanting of merit by the news media and by numerous observers, authors and scholars unconnected with the petroleum industry. It is certainly hard to understand or to accept the fact that the owner of an oil or gas well should be able to write off against his profits considerably more than his investment—sometimes several times as much as his actual cost —or why he should be taxed on only half of his net profits. Though the convenience or simplicity of the arrangement compared with prior provisions is obvious, the logic and justification are elusive, to say the least. It is not surprising that percentage depletion allowances and related write-off privileges for exploration and development costs have been the target of bitter attacks from the public and within the Congress year after year for several decades. Yet, such allowances endure, seemingly as solid and rock-like as ever, with only the slight rate reduction enacted in 1969.

When asked about one of the biggest loopholes in our tax laws, Wilbur Mills replied:

> I frankly don't know. Everybody talks about the depletion allowance. But historically the Congress has felt that some degree of preference is necessary if we don't want to be dependent on the production of oil, gas, and other minerals outside the U.S. Some people want to end the preferences altogether, but what would that do to these industries? That's the question. I'd like to see an income tax law where all income is treated alike, regardless of the source. But that's utopia.[12]

Clearly, gas, oil and other mineral producers receive benefits that are not available to other taxpayers. Virtually all other businesses are limited to writing off through depreciation over a period of years only their consumable capital outlays, inadequate as that may be in the face of rapid inflation and the growing intricacy and sophistication—that is, multiplied costs—of plant, equipment and processes. Permissible capital depreciation allowances often result in insufficient fund accumulation for replacement. Percentage depletion, however, means that write-offs

---

[12] *Congressional Record*, March 2, 1972, p. H 1721. Mills, at the time, regarded capital gains as the biggest loophole.

may exceed—often by several times—the actual investment in a particular well, or that only half of the net income will be subjected to normal tax rates. Yet most other business activities have also profited from tax benefits in the Internal Revenue Code: benefits more appropriate to the unique needs, demands for incentives, and problems of the operations in question. This applies to everything from banking to savings and loans and insurance, from farming to cooperatives and real estate, from hemisphere trade to small business and education. Oil and gas do not stand alone—though they do seem to be more favored than others.

Whenever and wherever tax law deviates from absolutely equal treatment for all taxpayers, the true dimension of equity is hard to appraise, if it can be determined at all. This is particularly true in the case of oil allowances, since the stereotype of the wildcatter who became a multimillionaire, or of the giant multinational corporation that controls vast fields and markets, tends to hide from sight the large number of operators, small or large, who barely make a go of it or who fall by the wayside. Facts and supposed facts have been poured out by the millions to shape public sentiments. The protagonists' positions tend to rest more on their political philosophies or economic interests than on factual evaluation and detached analysis. To resolve the question of justice in oil and gas taxation as opposed to other economic activities by recourse to objective and impartial data seems an impossible task because the opposing sides of the issue insist on using their own quite different yardsticks. The spokesmen's briefs read like the description of an elephant by the four blind men from Hindustan. It seems likely that a solution will have to be found in a pragmatic approach that focuses more on the probably economic and other *results* of whatever tax policy is adopted, and less on abstract, elusive concepts of what equity might be.

Mountains of statistics have been offered to show that the oil and gas industries pay extraordinarily low taxes and reap inordinate profits, while statistics emanating from the industry have attempted to demonstrate the opposite. According to some sources the Treasury loses between $1.5 and $4 billion or even more a year in revenues from special tax benefits to extractive industries. The result, allegedly, is a severe misallocation of resources and gross overinvestment in gas and oil. In September 1972, Senator William Proxmire presented statistics from the Securities and Exchange Commission which showed that the 18 largest oil companies, with combined profits of over $10 billion, paid only 6.7

percent of 1970 net income in federal income taxes—down from 8 to 9 percent between 1967 and 1969—although the tax rate for corporate income over $25,000 is 48 percent and the average rate paid by all corporations was 36.7 percent. The senator added:

> If the public cry for tax reform means anything, it means that situations like this cannot continue to exist. When companies earning over $10 billion a year pay only 6.7 percent of their actual net income in Federal income taxes and individuals earning just over $10,000 a year who file a joint return have to pay 32 percent, it is clear that our tax code is not equitable.[13]

Representative John B. Anderson, Senator Clifford P. Hansen and others presented a different picture.[14] They showed that most of the reported profits came from overseas operations that had already been subjected to foreign taxes. Combined U.S. and foreign income taxes absorbed 36.5 percent of worldwide net income (up from 24.2 percent in 1968). Moreover, local and state severance and excise taxes tend to be far heavier on extractive industries than on others, aside from substantial property, sales, income and other taxes. It is impossible to unravel here this "numbers game" of who pays the most—or too little—that has been played for so many years. Industries linked in the public eye with big money and powerful lobbies are usually on the losing end of public sympathy. This may have been a factor in the mineral industries' partial legislative loss in the Tax Reform Act of 1969 when percentage depletion rates were reduced. While a full comparison of the overall tax burden on mineral as opposed to other industries would far exceed the scope of this analysis, it appears most likely from available data that at least oil and gas enterprises pay higher state, local, foreign and U.S. taxes in relation to their volume and profits than does business in general. In 1967, according to a study by the national accounting firm of Price, Waterhouse and Company, the 21 top oil companies paid 64 percent of their adjusted gross income in direct taxes.

The proof of the pudding is of course in the eating. If it were true that the after-tax return on investment in oil and gas were much larger than in manufacturing and other industries, as has been claimed, capital —in its eternal search for higher profits—would undoubtedly flow abundantly into those fields. An overcapacity of the product and expanding

---

[13] *Congressional Record,* September 6, 1972, pp. S 14157–14159.
[14] *Congressional Record,* June 26, 1972, p. E 6477, and September 8, 1972, p. S 14367.

reserves would result in downward price pressures through competition, eventually reducing the return on investment in oil and gas.

There seems to be evidence, however, that investment in oil and gas may not be as lucrative as the public image suggests. Gas and oil production in the United States has been increasingly *less* able to take care of existing and prospective needs. Brownouts and blackouts have often had to be imposed and, according to most forecasts, they are not only a possibility for the years ahead but are almost certain to become more frequent. Natural gas companies, unable to meet demands from current customers, have been refusing to take on new customers, industrial or residential; known gas reserves have been dropping sharply for at least five years. Oil consumption has been growing, made possible by greatly expanding imports—presently about one-fourth of U.S. consumption—with the prospect that American dependence on foreign oil will increase to more than one-half of total demand in the 1980s. In light of these shortages and dependence on foreign oil, if investment in natural gas and oil production were highly profitable—yielding a higher return than other investments—it would seem likely that exploration would be undertaken at an ever-increasing pace, and that production would increase and known reserves accumulate. However, the number of oil and gas wells drilled annually has dropped by one-half since the mid-1950s. Would this have taken place if the investment incentives were as great as claimed?

Outlook for energy. Assistant Secretary of the Interior Hollis M. Dole stated at Stanford University in January 1970 that U.S. reserves of gas and oil are being used up faster than they are being replaced. In the early 1950s well over a barrel and a half of oil was found for each barrel taken out of the ground. Now that ratio has dropped below unity for both gas and oil. Thus the ratio between known reserves and consumption has been declining. Yet the demand for energy continues to grow, doubling every 10 to 14 years. Under current projections oil reserves will decline by more than one-fourth between 1970 and 1980 while oil use will jump 60 percent; gas reserves will shrink about 30 percent, while demand will soar more than 50 percent.[15]

Essential demands cannot and will not be met if present policies and trends continue. The United States will depend increasingly on

---

[15] Tilford Gaines, "Economic Report: The Energy Crisis," Manufacturers Hanover Trust Company, June 1972.

122

imports for its sources of energy, or it will lack the energy it needs to run its industries and meet residential needs. Vastly increased imports could double or triple our negative trade balance, which is now running at a record high level.[16] Moreover, with so much dependence on energy sources beyond U.S. control, the nation's security would also be placed in jeopardy. Three-fourths of the world's known oil reserves lie in the Mideast and Africa, areas that are steadily beset by turmoil and could become inaccessible any time on short notice. Yet, projecting current trends, the United States will depend on the Mideast for half its oil supplies by the mid-1980s or sooner. Imports already make up about one-fourth of U.S. oil needs. This dependence is making the oil exporting countries increasingly aware of their growing bargaining power—a power that potentially could be used to gain a stranglehold on the United States.

Some have recommended a long-term energy strategy of "depleting foreign countries first" while conserving domestic resources for future years. But for American resources to become useful later, their location and extent must be known and that requires a dramatic step-up in the expensive and time-consuming process of exploration and discovery.

All of this means that desirable as it is to give *equal* tax treatment to all industries and all taxpayers, and important as it is that tax equity be real and apparent to all, differential treatment for vital policy reasons may be the lesser of two evils at some times and in some cases. Equity does not always mean equality. Unless Americans are willing to have the government take control of most of the energy-supplying industries, either directly or through subsidy programs—and with them major parts of American industry on a growing scale—there seems to be no alternative to offering sufficient incentives to increased capital flow into gas, oil and some other mineral fields. The United States has become the richest and most powerful country on earth, the most prosperous when measured by the living standards of its citizens, largely because of the ample availability of low-cost energy sources.[17] Energy consumption still is a valid yardstick of economic development and strength. Therefore, the fact that the consumption of energy resources is increasing more rapidly in the United States than the development of new supply has

---

[16] Oil imports alone, at $4 billion a year, account for about two-thirds of our negative trade balance. They could run at $25 billion by 1985.

[17] The United States now accounts for one-third of the world's oil consumption and for over one-half of its natural gas consumption.

123

broad implications. Eventually a solution will have to be sought from energy sources that are available in practically unlimited supply but are currently not technologically nor economically usable, such as solar or nuclear energy and geothermal power. But for a long time ahead oil and natural gas will of necessity remain the principal sources of energy. There is evidence that, underground and offshore, the United States has ample pools of oil and gas and other energy sources—possibly enough for centuries—but they need to be discovered and developed.

Observers have painted the following picture of energy resource development in the coming years.[18] Between 1955 and 1970, American operators spent a total of $68 billion on efforts to find more petroleum, but it would have taken another $50 billion to have met all needs and maintained a realistic reserve. Meeting needs between 1970 and 1985 will require roughly double the effort of the past 15 years: $140 billion. However, current trends suggest that only $85 billion is likely to be invested. There appears to be no chance of financing an effort of the required magnitude under present conditions. Yet, an adequate future energy supply depends largely on the question of whether 25,000 or 100,000 wells are drilled per year. The U.S. needs to discover more oil and natural gas in the next 15 years than has been found throughout its history. The controlling element, the key to whether this will be done, is availability of sufficient venture capital: such investment must be made more attractive—that is, more profitable—*after* taxes.

Concern about treating gas and oil differently from most other industries is justified. But there are other valid reasons for such a policy: minerals are "wasting assets" that are used up as they are brought from the ground. Exploration is an extremely risky and capital intensive venture. While one in every nine holes drilled may yield oil, only one in every 48 exploratory wells among the thousands drilled in the United States each year is commercially profitable. Unless potential *after-tax* rewards are commensurate with the risk—high enough to lure investors from other attractions—sufficient capital will not be forthcoming. In a homogeneous world market product, "equal treatment" will not generate the exploration and discovery of oil and gas reserves that the United States must have, now and in years to come.

Special treatment for mineral exploration was not provided by Congress in response to the demands of, or for the purpose of aiding, in-

---

[18] John G. Winger et al., "Outlook for Energy in the United States to 1985," The Chase Manhattan Bank, June 1972, p. 39 ff.

dustrial giants. It started and was continued as a means of encouraging the discovery and production of more sources of energy and other minerals. When the provisions of the original income tax code of 1913 proved inadequate during World War I, depletion allowances based on "discovery value" were authorized in 1918. Because there is no relationship between investment in a particular well and its productive value, the original depletion allowance was based on the well's value estimated within 30 days of discovery. The intent of Congress was to get more entrepreneurs, particularly small operators, into the game.

But discovery value depletion proved administratively unworkable: estimates within 30 days were difficult to make and too far off the mark most of the time, and court calendars became crowded with pending cases. So, in 1926 Congress decided to relate depletion allowances to a reliably determinable factor: value of the current output. As a compromise between the Senate version of allowing a 30 percent write-off and the House's 25 percent, a 27.5 percent depletion allowance was established—which remained in effect for 43 years. An upper limit of 50 percent of net profits was established that in many cases came to be the controlling factor on less profitable wells. Later on over one hundred other minerals were added to the special treatment list, with depletion rates ranging from 5 to 23 percent.

The 27.5 percent allowance, though arrived at by a somewhat less than scientific method, seemed to fill the bill: it helped supply the country with essential sources of energy, but did not lead to surpluses or unnecessarily large reserves or to excessive profits in the gas and oil industries. Though always an inviting political target, it withstood innumerable attacks from more than four decades until in 1969 Congress decided "that even if percentage depletion rates are viewed as a needed stimulant at the present time, they are higher than is needed to achieve the desired beneficial results on reserves." [19] Depletion allowances for oil and gas were reduced to 22 percent, and for many other minerals accordingly— although no proof was offered that exploration had been excessive or even that known reserves were adequate and growing. Now it appears amply evident that prospects for oil and gas discovery and reserves are

---

[19] U.S. Congress, House of Representatives, Committee on Ways and Means, *Tax Reform Act of 1969*, H.R. 91-413, part 1, p. 137; U.S. Congress, Senate, Committee on Finance, *Tax Reform Act of 1969*, R. 91–552, p. 179: "The Committee agrees with the House that the percentage depletion rate provided for oil and gas wells is higher at the present time than is needed to achieve the desired increase in reserves."

dismal indeed and permit no complacency. If there is misallocation of resources and overinvestment, there seems to be none in the exploration and production of natural gas and oil.

The United States now derives 94 percent of its energy from fossil fuels. As of 1970, gas and oil supplied over three-fourths of the country's energy, coal one-fifth, water power slightly over 3 percent and nuclear energy .3 percent. The use of nuclear energy will undoubtedly expand but various limitations suggest that only 13 percent of national energy needs will be filled by nuclear sources by 1985. Oil and gas are still expected to supply about two-thirds of the nation's energy requirements by 1985 and about 60 percent by the year 2000. In other words, the discovery rate of oil and natural gas reserves will largely determine the adequacy of the U.S. energy supply for the balance of this century and beyond. Generation of nuclear power may grow faster in the 20th century, as may the utilization of solar energy. Oil shale, of which the United States possesses huge quantities, and tar sands have never been used to produce oil because technological and economic problems are far from resolved. While the slight tax encouragement given in the Revenue Act of 1969 was intended to help with these problems, so far it has not led to commercial oil production from oil shale. More substantial incentives may be needed—possibly along with higher prices for competitive products—to make utilization of this potentially huge resource a reality.

Summary. Percentage depletion allowances for oil and natural gas present a dilemma. Equity considerations undoubtedly pose a serious problem. Somehow the fact that certain industries are permitted to write off more on an asset than they have actually invested in it is hard to accept. But if depletion allowances are viewed as a means to an end—an end that is vitally important to this nation and growing more so with each year—then they have proven their value and should be continued in their present or in a modified form. Senator John G. Tower warned in 1971 that "at the present time our exploration investment is minimal and the level of our domestic exploration is at a 28-year low." To provide an adequate stimulant and to help reverse the trend, he proposed an income tax credit "for expenditures made in the exploration and development of new domestic oil and gas reserves." It failed to pass.[20]

---

[20] *Congressional Record,* November 20, 1971, pp. S 19217-23.

In designing better taxation methods for gas, oil and other minerals, emphasis should be placed increasingly, or even exclusively, on encouraging exploration and discovery (so as to multiply *known* reserves), with production and pricing left largely to market forces. Special tax privileges need not be provided for minerals whose discovery and production are not a pressing national need. But there could be, and most likely would be grave consequences for the economy and security of the United States if—as some have repeatedly suggested—depletion allowances for oil, gas and other strategic minerals were further reduced or even eliminated, without offsetting remedial action.

Admittedly, the logic of mineral percentage depletion is elusive and its appropriateness doubtful, to say the least. There is still a need to search for a better way to accomplish the desired ends. Certainly there are abuses that offend our sense of equity in taxation. The justifiable question of why oil and gas (and other minerals) should be granted tax benefits that are not available, at least to an equal extent, to other industries might thus be answered simply: at this point in time, there seems to be no more acceptable method to achieve ends that are essential to the well-being and future of the United States.

Municipal Bond Interest

While arguments over many of the major tax issues are clouded by factual uncertainties, the substantive questions about municipal bonds are, on the whole, clearcut and noncontroversial. It is a case where two principles, both of which are basically sound and widely accepted, conflict with each other. The policy decision hinges on which of the two principles is to be given priority, which should prevail over the other. The two principles are:

1. Persons of equal income and in similar circumstances should incur an equal tax liability. They should not be offered an opportunity to avoid taxation partially or wholly by means of a "shelter" or "loophole."
2. Governments should reciprocally respect each other's actions and immunities. They should not tax each other or each other's instrumentalities ("the power to tax is the power to destroy"), nor adopt policies that may make it more difficult for other governments—at the same level, or a higher or lower level—to carry out their legitimate functions.

127

The present system of exempting interest from state and local securities from federal income taxation certainly violates the first principle: any person with money can invest his entire capital, or a major part of it, in municipal securities and thereby avoid paying taxes on an income that may total millions of dollars each year. Continued existence of such a tax haven for the rich appears at odds with fundamental precepts of tax justice.

But to repeal the tax exemption, as has long been demanded by one side in this debate, would open the door to one government placing burdens on another. Without compensating measures, it would tighten bond markets and substantially raise the interest costs of state and local governments. Some public works projects might have to be cancelled. Governors, mayors and other state and local officials and their national organizations have long been adamant in opposing any attempt to tax interest on their securities, directly or indirectly, and they have been consistently successful in warding off such efforts. They argue that such immunity "is vital for the preservation of our dual sovereignty which characterizes our system of government." [21] Freedom of individuals and of communities and local governments is held to be indivisible. They further argue that considerations that might favor taxing their bonds "are secondary to the preservation of the sovereignty of our states and the integrity of our local governments. This system simply could not survive if the Federal Government destroys the preferential character of municipal debt or exercises control of local policymaking by the selective taxation of certain categories of municipal bonds." [22]

Mutual immunity? Some hold that it would be unconstitutional to tax interest on municipal bonds. When the United States Supreme Court invalidated the 1894 income tax act in the case of *Pollock* v. *Farmers' Loan & Trust Company,* it based its decision in part on the fact that to tax interest on municipal bonds would amount to an infringement on the power of the states to borrow money. Whether this position was overruled by the Sixteenth Amendment ("to lay and collect taxes on incomes,

---

[21] The subject was thoroughly covered at the 1959 and 1969 tax hearings. House Committee on Ways and Means, *Tax Revision Compendium,* vol. 1 (1959), pp. 679–791; U.S. Congress, House of Representatives, Committee on Ways and Means, *Income Tax Revision* (Washington, D.C.: U.S. Government Printing Office, 1959), pp. 339–402; House Ways and Means Committee Hearings, *Tax Reform, 1969,* part 6, pp. 2185–2354 (the quotation appears on p. 2190).

[22] House Ways and Means Committee Hearings, *Tax Reform, 1969,* p. 2190.

from whatever source derived") is controversial. Certainly, the possibility that municipal bond interest would become taxable under the Sixteenth Amendment played a significant role in the adoption and ratification debate. The pending amendment was attacked in 1910 by New York Governor Charles Evans Hughes (later chief justice of the U.S. Supreme Court) and by many others as permitting taxation of state bonds. They held that "from whatever source derived" meant just what it said, namely, that there was no limitation upon the power to tax. Proponents strongly denied this. Senator William E. Borah declared:

> To construe the proposed Amendment so as to enable us to tax the instrumentalities of the state would do violence to the rules laid down by the Supreme Court for a hundred years, wrench the whole Constitution from its harmonious proportions and destroy the object and purpose for which the whole instrument was framed.[23]

Senators Elihu Root, Joseph W. Bailey and others made equally strong statements to the effect that the amendment did not grant the federal government the power to tax interest from municipal securities. The debate on the constitutionality of taxing interest on municipal bonds has been going on ever since, and associations of city officials have cited numerous court decisions in an effort to prove that their securities' freedom from taxation is firmly anchored in the Constitution.[24]

Following the trend of decisions over the years, however, it does not appear likely that if Congress were to impose such a tax, the Supreme Court would again—as it did in 1895, prior to the Sixteenth Amendment—find it to be unconstitutional. There has been no test because the proponents have so far been unable to prevail upon Congress to pass such legislation. In 1969, when the House adopted three measures that seemed to open the door, at least slightly, state and local officials went to work on the Senate and saw to it that the three provisions were eliminated in the final conference bill. These provisions would have authorized and encouraged state and local governments to issue, at their option, taxable bonds with a federal interest subsidy, would have prorated deductions between taxable and nontaxable income and would have included municipal bond interest in the minimum tax provisions. But the influence of governors, mayors, county commission-

---

[23] *Congressional Record,* February 10, 1910, p. 1698.
[24] House Ways and Means Committee Hearings, *Tax Reform, 1969,* p. 2227 ff.

ers and other officials proved to be superior. Thus the tax exemption of municipal bonds remained unchanged and may be as firm as ever.

Only one minor restriction was enacted in 1968 and that involved industrial development bonds, singled out because of the abuse of issuing such bonds to finance private developments. Even there, some argue that state and local governments have a legitimate interest in aiding chronically poor rural (and urban) areas to expand their economic potential by attracting industrial or commercial development. Tax exemption to finance this development has been said to be simply another form of subsidizing job creation.

To be sure, tax exemption is not a free gift from the federal government to the bondholder: tax-exempt bonds pay a substantially lower interest rate than high-grade corporate bonds. At the close of 1972, high-grade municipal bonds (Standard & Poor's) were yielding about 5.0 percent per annum, while corporate bonds with an Aaa rating (Moody's) were yielding 7.0 percent and those with a Baa rating 8.0 percent. In other words, corporations had to pay a 40 percent higher interest rate on Aaa-rated bonds and a 60 percent higher rate on Baa bonds than well-rated municipalities.[25] This may be viewed as another, and comparatively modest, form of federal aid to state and local governments.

Tax exemption has been called a very inefficient form of aid because the tax savings of the bondholders may total substantially more than the interest savings of state and local governments. It might be much less expensive for the federal treasury to pay state and local governments (or bondholders directly) the difference between the rates they pay on tax-exempt bonds and what they would have to pay on taxable bonds. In the end, state and local governments would be financially no worse off than they are now but the Treasury would have a net savings; most important, a major "loophole" for rich investors would be closed and thereby greater tax equity established.

Such an outcome, however, could be slow in materializing. Whereas it would be possible to remove tax exemption from *future* issues of state

---

[25] Federal taxable bonds were simultaneously traded at prices to yield 5.5 to 6.0 percent or between 10 and 20 percent more than tax-free bonds. This expresses the greater security of federal obligations which partially offsets the tax difference. Comparison of municipal with high-grade corporate bonds may more nearly represent the taxable versus tax-exempt differential.

and local governments, it is hardly conceivable that Congress would do so retroactively, that is, for bonds already sold at lower rates on the promise that their interest would be tax-exempt. Such action would be regarded as a breach of faith that could have trouble surviving in the courts. If only future issues were to be taxable, the changeover would be slow and the revenue effects would become substantial only after the passage of many years.

Tax exemption of bonds has long been a reciprocal practice between federal and state-local governments. It would certainly be improper for the federal government to rescind the tax exemption of municipal bond interest without paying an interest subsidy to state and local governments. Were the federal government to take such a unilateral action, the states would probably attempt to tax the interest of federal bonds, even though they are now prevented from doing so by statute and court decision. If this denial were set aside and the states were to tax federal bond interest, interest rates on new federal securities would rise, at a large cost to the Treasury. Most of the federal debt is short term, while the maturities on state and local securities run, on the average, two to three times longer. Moreover, the federal debt is about two times higher than total state and local debt and federal interest costs are almost four times higher than such state-local costs. Thus there might in the end be a net loss accruing to the U.S. Treasury.

A boon for the wealthy? The high income taxpayer gains the biggest benefit from nontaxation of municipal bond interest. At current interest rates of 5 percent for tax-exempt and 7 percent-plus for corporate bonds, a taxpayer with a marginal rate of 30 percent (taxable income: single $14,000, joint return $20,000) gets a greater after-tax return on 5 percent tax-exempt bonds than on 7 percent taxable bonds. The higher his tax bracket (up to the federal maximum of 70 percent), the better off he is from an income standpoint with tax-exempt securities. This in itself is contrary to generally accepted principles of tax justice. It puts the decision of whether or not to pay an income tax entirely in the hands of the investor and introduces a regressive feature into the system—namely, the higher the investor's income, the greater the benefit he may reap from investing in municipals.

With the financial advantages so evident, particularly for the rich, one would expect municipal bonds to be eagerly sought after by investors. It would stand to reason that wealthy individuals would put much or most of their capital into such bonds. But strangely, this is not the case. If, in fact, tax-exempt bonds were in great demand, their market prices would be high and their interest rates correspondingly low, leaving a large rate differential between taxable and tax-exempt bonds. But it is precisely the low demand for tax-exempt bonds that keeps their interest rates up and reduces the differential. The tax-exempt feature may, indeed, result in more benefits for the bondholder than for the issuing government.

In the 1960s and early 1970s, tax-exempt bonds accounted, on the average, for about one-fourth of all new bonds sold in the market. Their volume was smaller than that of federal bonds and of corporate bonds as well. This is an open market and tax-exempt bonds are available to any buyer who wants them. If demand were strong from investors aiming to take advantage of the "loophole," the interest differential with respect to other bonds would be high, rather than so low as to raise the question of efficiency. Municipals account for only a small share of the investment market. As of 1972 about $170 billion in state and local bonds were outstanding, up from $24 billion in 1950. Alternative investments included: $800 billion in federal and corporate bonds, $300 billion in mutual savings banks and savings and loan associations, $250 billion in time deposits in commercial banks, $400 billion in mortgages, and $250 billion (market value) in stocks traded on registered exchanges. The returns on all of these other assets, which total in excess of $2 trillion, are taxable. State and local bonds offer the only available tax-exempt investment opportunity. Nevertheless, demand for municipal bonds is so small that the break-even point (where after-tax yield on taxable securities equals the yield on tax-exempt ones) is somewhat below a 30 percent marginal income tax rate, given current market prices.

In other words, investors considering the relative advantages and disadvantages of alternative investments do not rate municipal bonds as highly as the sharp critics of this "loophole" usually suggest. The ownership of state and local bonds, by type of investor (individuals, financial institutions, et cetera) or by income bracket is unknown. But a 1966 study by Professor Benjamin Okner for the Michigan Survey Research Center suggested that wealthy persons do not tend to invest heavily in municipals and that few of them hold a substantial or major share of their assets in tax-exempt bonds.[26] In fact, only between one-quarter and one-third of the outstanding tax-exempt bonds are held by individuals, and ownership is not concentrated at the top of the income pyramid. If tax exemption of state and local bonds is indeed a loophole, most investors do not treat it as such or seize on it as an opportunity to minimize their taxes.

In summary, then, opponents of tax exemption of municipal bond interest present a good case for repeal on equity grounds. No one, and least of all a wealthy person, should be enabled by law to escape income taxes. Even if the lower interest rate that municipals pay is regarded as a payment *in lieu* of taxes, the inequity is only reduced, not eliminated. Fairness requires that all types of income be treated alike.

The equity argument loses some of its force, however, since it is evident that wealthy persons have not taken advantage of this escape from taxation to the extent that might be assumed and is widely believed. Moreover, if municipals are taxed, the prospective revenue gains to the U.S. Treasury are not likely to be great: taxes would probably be applied only to future issues, subsidies would be required to compensate states, municipalities, school districts, et cetera, and present holders of municipals are not necessarily concentrated in the upper tax brackets. Moreover, if the immunity of federal securities is ever waived, the states would probably start to tax interest on federal bonds, which would in turn raise the interest cost on those securities. In this event, there could even be a net loss to the Treasury for quite a few years.

So far, state and local governments have strongly opposed change in this area, but recently there have been indications that they would support optional taxable bonds in return for an interest subsidy.[27] A case can be made for not weakening the access of state and local governments to money markets and for letting them handle their own affairs instead of paying them subsidies with conditions attached. Mutual immunity from taxation among governments and noninterference are long established principles that should be disturbed only for compelling reasons. Whether the reasons are compelling enough in this case is in question.

---

[26] Benjamin Okner, *Income Distribution and the Federal Income Tax,* Michigan Government Studies No. 47, Institute of Public Administration (Ann Arbor: University of Michigan, 1966), Appendix A.
[27] See *Proposed Alternatives to Tax-Exempt State and Local Bonds,* Legislative Analysis No. 3 (Washington, D.C.: American Enterprise Institute, 1973).

Personal Deductions

Personal deductions are the second-largest "loophole"—or diminution of income for tax purposes—in our tax system. Only personal exemptions loom larger. For the majority of taxpayers, computing deductions is probably the most time-consuming part of preparing tax returns. Deductions greatly complicate the computing of taxable income, which increases the workload both of the average individual and of the Internal Revenue Service. They are also probably among the most firmly entrenched and, when under attack, most fiercely defended features of our income tax.

In 1970 deductions totalled $120 billion, nearly one-fifth of adjusted gross income. Of this amount, $32 billion was in standard deductions and $88 billion in itemized deductions (see Table 9). In the preceding ten years, the number of returns with itemized deductions rose from 24 to 35 million—from 39 to 48 percent of all returns. The dollar amount of itemized deductions increased 150 percent while adjusted gross income increased only 100 percent.

Deductions in perspective. Although the Internal Revenue Code uses the "gross income" concept for the personal income of individuals—as

Table 9
PERSONAL DEDUCTIONS, 1960 AND 1970
($ in millions)

	1960	1970	Percent Increase
Standard deductions	$13,002	$32,370	149.0
Itemized deductions			
State and local taxes	10,526	32,045	204.4
Interest paid	8,416	23,895	183.9
Charitable contributions	6,750	12,918	91.4
Medical expenses	5,219	10,588	102.9
Other	4,402	8,742	98.6
Total itemized deductions	$35,313	$88,188	+149.7
Total personal deductions	$48,315	$120,558	+149.5

Source: IRS, *Statistics of Income, 1960* and *1970;* figures for standard deductions in 1960 from IRS, *Statistics of Income, Supplemental Report—State and Metropolitan Area Data for Individual Income Tax Returns, 1959, 1960,* and *1961.*

contrasted to business income which is net—it has allowed certain deductions from its inception in 1913. Speaking to a tax symposium in 1957, Dan Throop Smith, then deputy to the secretary of the Treasury and the principal author of the Internal Revenue Code of 1954 (under which we still operate) declared: "Most, if not all, of the allowed deductions are intended to increase the fairness of the tax." [28] Subsequently he wrote: "All of the deductions allowed in computing the taxable income of individuals are designed to give relief to the taxpayers benefiting from them and thereby make the law fairer." [29] C. Harry Kahn of Rutgers University, author of the standard work on the subject, defined two purposes for tax deductions, to provide greater equity and to promote desirable activities. [30]

(1) *Deductions to provide greater equity.* All exemptions and most existing deductions fall into this category. Their purpose is to refine the definition of income so as to come closer to a "net income" concept that expresses true tax-paying capacity. Therefore, deductions reduce the tax base by taking into consideration special burdens borne by the particular taxpayer. For example, of two men with identical gross incomes, one may have more dependents, heavier medical expenses, unusual casualty losses, or greater state and local tax liabilities. So, he is less able to pay federal income tax than the other. Exemptions and deductions are intended to "differentiate between taxpayers whose incomes, though apparently equal, are of different sizes in some relevant sense." [31] They aim to provide greater horizontal equity.

(2) *Deductions to promote desirable activities.* Tax law provides financial incentives to engage in or support activities that are regarded as in the public interest. Some of these activities are of the type that would have to be undertaken and financed by government if they were not provided by voluntary action. The services of hospitals, schools, libraries, museums are in this category. Congress may find that it is less costly to the taxpayer if government offers individuals or organizations

[28] "General Policy Problems of Tax Differentials" in *Income Tax Differentials, Symposium* by the Tax Institute (Princeton: Tax Institute, 1958), p. 6. Smith is now a senior research fellow at the Hoover Institution.

[29] Smith, *Federal Tax Reform,* p. 90.

[30] C. Harry Kahn, "Personal Deductions in the Individual Income Tax," in House Committee on Ways and Means, *Tax Revision Compendium,* vol. 1, p. 392ff.; House Committee on Ways and Means, *Income Tax Revision,* pp. 165–68.

[31] C. Harry Kahn, *Personal Deductions in the Federal Income Tax,* National Bureau of Economic Research (Princeton: Princeton University Press, 1960), p. 174.

an incentive to devote their own funds for such purposes rather than having to underwrite the entire cost through taxes. More important, Congress may prefer that certain activities be carried out under private auspices, partially or fully, rather than under direct governmental control or as a governmental monopoly. Greater diversity is often desirable so as to permit the widest range of individual freedom, consistent with the obligations and purposes of government.

Some deductions are allowed for activities that could not be carried on by government. This applies particularly to donations to churches and other religious institutions and organizations. Government could not, under the "no establishment" clause, expend tax-collected funds for such activities. But it is equally clear that government may encourage —and materially aid—such purposes indirectly. In the *Walz* decision, the Supreme Court was emphatic in stating that though government may not spend public funds for religious purposes, it may indirectly aid them by foregoing the collection of taxes that it would otherwise impose.[32]

Deductions—who benefits? It has often been asserted, and is widely believed, that personal deductions offer a tax haven for the rich while giving little relief to persons of lesser means. But the facts indicate otherwise. As was shown above, for 1970, itemized deductions equaled 35 percent of adjusted gross income in the under-$5,000 bracket on *all* returns and gradually declined to 17 percent in the $15,000 and over bracket (see Table 5). If only *taxable* returns are considered, the comparable bracket is $1,000 to under $5,000 and the comparable figure is 27.5 percent (see Table 10). Only in the $100,000-and-up bracket does the deduction percentage go up, mostly because charitable donations are concentrated in the highest income fields. Table 10 shows, by major income classes, the average deduction per taxable return using itemized deductions and itemized deductions as a percent of adjusted gross income.

The extent and growth of personal deductions have been the object of much criticism as major factors in the erosion of the tax base. Numerous suggestions have been advanced over the years to restrict or cut them back sharply or to disallow most or all of them. Such a broadening of the tax base, it is argued, would make it possible to lower tax

---

[32] *Walz* v. *Tax Commission,* 397 U.S. 664 (1970).

Table 10

ITEMIZED DEDUCTIONS ON TAXABLE FEDERAL INCOME TAX RETURNS, BY INCOME CLASS, 1970

Size of Adjusted Gross Income	Adjusted Gross Income	Itemized Deductions	State & Local Taxes	Interest	Charitable Contributions	Medical Expenses	Other Deductions
	Average amounts per return using the type of deduction						
$1,000 to under $5,000	$ 3,908	$ 1,288	$ 377	$ 377	$ 208	$ 467	$ 172
$5,000 to under $7,000	6,028	1,445	448	413	222	389	195
$7,000 to under $10,000	8,547	1,831	605	607	260	355	222
$10,000 to under $15,000	12,302	2,345	859	783	313	334	253
$15,000 to under $25,000	18,435	3,155	1,276	1,022	453	334	337
$25,000 to under $50,000	32,686	5,379	2,311	1,684	866	463	663
$50,000 to under $100,000	65,997	10,948	4,584	3,379	2,189	678	1,498
$100,000 or more	186,050	41,092	13,171	12,000	13,653	1,143	5,726
All taxable returns	13,009	2,471	920	803	386	355	291
	Itemized deductions as a percent of adjusted gross income						
$1,000 to under $5,000		27.5%	8.4%	4.2%	4.4%	7.4%	3.0%
$5,000 to under $7,000		24.0	7.4	5.3	3.4	5.3	2.6
$7,000 to under $10,000		21.4	7.0	6.0	2.9	3.2	2.2
$10,000 to under $15,000		18.9	7.0	5.7	2.5	2.0	1.8
$15,000 to under $25,000		17.1	6.9	4.9	2.4	1.4	1.5
$25,000 to under $50,000		16.5	7.1	4.2	2.6	1.0	1.5
$50,000 to under $100,000		16.6	6.9	4.0	3.3	0.7	1.7
$100,000 or more		22.1	7.1	4.8	7.3	0.4	2.5
All taxable returns		19.0	7.0	5.2	2.8	2.1	1.8

Source: IRS, *Statistics of Income, 1970.*

137

rates while maintaining the overall yield. But it appears that too many people and too many large economic groups have—or believe they have—a vested interest in certain deductions to permit the drive for cutbacks to get very far. Experience, repeated many times, shows that demands to repeal or restrict established remedial provisions have a chance to succeed—or be seriously considered—only if they benefit small, vote-weak groups that offer easy targets. If a large segment or a majority of taxpayers find the provision useful and apply it on their tax return year after year, which is the case for personal deductions, attempts at reform are stillborn.

On several occasions it has been proposed to establish a floor under itemized deductions. If the purpose of deductions is to give due consideration to special burdens borne by some taxpayers and to compensate for extraordinary expenses that diminish an individual's tax-paying capacity, there is little justification for permitting the deduction of *all* expenditures in a category. All or most taxpayers pay certain amounts of state and local taxes, sustain casualty losses, defray medical bills or make contributions to some worthy cause. Why not permit deduction only if such outlays exceed a certain amount or a specified percentage of income—that is, go beyond a level normally expected for the average taxpayer? The floor concept is now applicable to medical expenses (3 percent of adjusted gross income for total medical expenses, 1 percent for drugs) and to casualty losses (in excess of $100). It would make good sense to extend it to all or most deduction categories. However, whenever proposals to do so have been considered in the House Ways and Means Committee, they have been decisively defeated due to overwhelming opposition from many sides. It is always more popular to liberalize personal deductions than to tighten them and most of the changes since 1913 have been in that direction.

Deductions versus credits. Some feel that the deduction method is a proper way to adjust income for special burdens. For example, to deduct a casualty loss (exceeding $100) from income may be regarded as a refinement of the income concept because such a loss diminishes an individual's taxpaying capacity. But in most cases, because of the combined effect of deductions and the progressivity of our tax schedule, it is doubtful whether deductions are a proper method of adjustment. When a taxpayer in the highest bracket pays $1,000 in interest, for state income taxes or local property taxes, as a contribution to his

138

church or charity, or for medical bills, he can offset $700 of this payment in his federal tax liability so that the *net* cost to him is only $300. But if a man in the lowest bracket expends $1,000 for the same purposes, he reduces his tax liability by only $140 so that the *net* cost to him amounts to $860. That is simply the result of progressive tax rates. Yet, somehow, such an "upside-down subsidy" seems unfair. Moreover, it misses the purpose of giving relief where it is needed the most.

State and local tax systems have long been criticized for being regressive, often more severely than the facts justify. Actually it is mostly the deductibility of state and local taxes on the federal income tax return that makes them highly regressive. Itemized deductions often reduce the progressivity of the income tax. Since a rich man's tax rate is so high, the deductions he may make for medical bills, interest paid or casualty losses are worth more to him than similar deductions are to the poor man. Itemized deductions may be a larger proportion of the adjusted gross income of the poor man and still worth less to him because his tax rate is lower. Donations for educational and charitable purposes are highly concentrated in the top income brackets because they cost so little *after taxes.*

These shortcomings of the deduction method could be corrected by changing to a tax credit system. Under that system, a taxpayer would deduct a uniform percentage of his outlay from his tax liability, not from his tax base. The net cost of $1,000 in state taxes or medical bills or contributions would then be the same for the rich man and for the poor.

Although the use of tax credits has been discussed at various times over the years, Congress has never seriously considered it. Despite drawbacks in the system, the deduction method seems firmly implanted. In order to understand why, it is important to analyze some of the major types of deductions and exemptions in greater detail. Some of them, such as deductions for state and local taxes, interest paid and casualty losses, have been in use from the inception of federal income tax. Others, such as deductions for contributions, medical expenses, child care and several other purposes, were added later.

Deductions for State and Local Taxes

The main justification for allowing a taxpayer to deduct his state and local taxes is that to do otherwise would be to levy a tax on a tax.

To be sure, most states do just that. Only 15 states (three of them with limitations) permit taxpayers to subtract for state income tax purposes their (much larger) federal income tax; the others levy a state income tax on gross (pre-tax) income. The federal practice of allowing deduction of income taxes and most other state and local taxes appears fair because those amounts are, as far as the taxpayer is concerned, merely transitory—they represent fictitious income that is not available to him and that does not increase his taxpaying capacity.[33] If the principle of deductibility were carried to its logical conclusion at the federal level, the federal income tax should be a deductible item for federal income taxes in the year paid. This was in fact part of the 1913 law, but it was repealed after three years because it reduced the progressive nature of the tax. Even deductions, as presently permitted, make the tax system somewhat less progressive, and for that reason suggestions have been made to disallow them. Deductions for taxes, it is held, are a form of subsidy to state and local governments and therefore a tax expenditure. Would it not be preferable to aid or promote desirable activities by direct appropriations instead of giving general fiscal assistance to state and local governments by deductions for taxpayers? This viewpoint, however, never gained much ground in Congress.

Establishment of a tax credit in place of a deduction for state and local taxes does not enjoy widespread support. Some would allow a credit only for state income taxes—not because they are particularly burdensome and justify special relief for the taxpayer, but in order to force the six states that do not now levy an income tax to adopt one and to offer an incentive to the other states to lean more heavily on income taxes by boosting rates. Others have suggested that tax credits be allowed for the residential property tax, which is widely felt to be the most burdensome tax. The present system of permitting deductions for property taxes discriminates against renters who pay for their landlord's property taxes in their rents but get no tax benefits. The suggested "carrythrough" or comparable benefit for renters would be designed to equal the value of property deductions—or, if tax credits were to be authorized, of credits). Renters account for nearly one-third of the population and, on the average or as a group, are economically weaker than homeowners.

---

[33] Taxes on tobacco products, alcoholic beverages, admissions, were deductible prior to 1964, as were auto licenses and driver registration fees.

Others, however, feel that public policy should encourage home ownership in the interests of a stable citizenry and that therefore property tax deductions for homeowners—but not for renters—are justified. Moreover, it is argued that rent includes the tenant's share of property taxes collected from the landlord. In any event, at a time when complaints about the burdens of home ownership (due in part to high mortgage interest and property taxes) have reached a new crescendo, Congress is not likely to increase that burden by withdrawing some of the homeowner tax benefits.

Interest Paid

The original reason for allowing interest to be deducted from income may have been the fact that much borrowing is done for business and investment purposes, that is, to earn income. Hence this cost should be deducted from income. It is technically difficult, however, to distinguish personal interest from such a business interest. A home may be mortgaged to obtain capital to acquire securities or to start or expand a business. With the huge expansion of home ownership in the past 60 years, a large part of the interest paid deduction is due to mortgage interest. Interest on a home mortgage is a personal expense—as residential property taxes are—for consumption of living space. The renter gets no deduction although his rent undoubtedly includes interest on the capital invested.

Just as in the case of residential property taxes, the sentiment in favor of home ownership is strong and is likely to prevent action that would diminish the interest deduction. While many renters regard the interest and tax deductions as inequitable, there is another solution for apartment dwellers: the purchase of cooperative or condominium apartments, which seem to combine some of the tax benefits of home ownership with the convenience of apartment living.

Medical Expenses

Medical and dental deductions were authorized by Congress in 1942 when, to meet the fiscal demands of World War II, the income tax was turned into a mass tax and the number of returns jumped from 7 million in 1939 to 36 million in 1942. By that time the income tax had been in force for 30 years and tax policy had become much more sophisticated than it had been in earlier times. In authorizing the deduction Congress aimed at the hardship element of medical expenses and intended to aid mainly low-income groups. Contemporary reports had indicated that medical outlays of American families averaged slightly over 4 percent of income and that medical bills of that magnitude could be regarded as part of the ordinary cost of living. Therefore, only medical expenses in excess of 5 percent of income were allowed as a deduction for tax purposes. This was reduced to 3 percent in the 1954 Revenue Act, with a separate 1 percent floor for prescription drug expenses. To encourage medical insurance coverage, one-half of such insurance premiums were subsequently exempted from the 3 percent floor. Possibly an even stronger incentive might be advisable to encourage catastrophic medical coverage. On the whole, medical expenses are probably the least controversial deductions. No significant changes should be expected unless national health insurance with universal coverage were to be enacted.

Charitable Contributions

Deductions for donations are of an entirely different nature than all other deductions. They do not aim to compensate for hardships or special burdens that impinge upon the taxpayer, factors wholly or partially beyond his control. Gifts to organizations for religious, educational, medical, welfare, public (governmental), scientific and similar purposes are voluntary and within the donor's discretion.

Congress authorized charitable deductions in 1917 to encourage philanthropy at a time when, during World War I, tax rates were boosted from 7 percent (1913-1915) and 15 percent (1916) to 67 percent in 1917 and finally to 77 percent in 1918. The deduction was limited to 15 percent of income from 1917 to 1952, then raised to 20 percent with an additional 10 percent for contributions to regular educational institutions, hospitals and churches authorized by the Revenue Code of 1954. In 1969 Congress provided, as a general rule, that the limit would be 50 percent of adjusted gross income. But only very few taxpayers donate anywhere near their permissible limit. Itemized deductions for contributions have run at a remarkably steady ratio of 2 percent of *all* adjusted gross income, and close to 3 percent of income on returns with itemized deductions. The latter varied in 1970 only within the narrow range of 2.4 percent to 3.4 percent in the average of tax brackets from $5,000 to $100,000. Only the top bracket, $100,000 income and over, reported contributions as high as 7.2 percent of income.

In other words, boosting the deduction limit from 30 to 50 percent of income meant nothing to most taxpayers and amounted to pushing on a string. It was probably meant to soften the phasing out of the much criticized unlimited charitable deduction, which was previously permitted under certain conditions and affected about 100 taxpayers, most of whom had an income of $1 million or more. If it were desirable to increase incentives for donations and to encourage large numbers of taxpayers in middle and lower brackets to raise their contributions or to contribute to all—a shift from deductions to tax credits would be the way to do it.

Charitable deductions have long been under severe attack as "tax expenditures" made without the proper direction and control of public authorities. Government, it is said, has delegated to private persons the power to spend, according to their own inclinations, preferences or whims, funds that rightly belong to the public treasury. It has enabled individuals to make allocations inconsistent with national priorities. Such private control over public funds should be ended. In its place, the financial needs of the organizations now eligible to receive deductible charitable gifts should be evaluated by public officials and met through budget appropriations, as are the demands of other functions and services.

These views are strongly opposed by those who feel that government has already expanded too much in recent decades and taken on too many vital decisions that properly belong in the hands of individuals. Such centralization of power in the national government, it is said, undermines personal liberty, home rule and local autonomy and should be diminished, not increased.

Many or most of the nonpublic institutions that are now eligible for charitable donations—such as schools, colleges, hospitals, welfare, scientific and research organizations—could operate under government auspices and with direct appropriations. Whether they *should* become part of the state structure or remain under private control with indirect governmental aid is a question of political philosophy on which the battle lines are tightly drawn. Repeal of the charitable deductions provision, or its amendment to severely limit or reduce donations, would end much if not most of the voluntary activity in the United States.

There is one major area in which government could not substitute appropriations for deduction allowances: religion. Under the First Amendment, as interpreted by the U.S. Supreme Court in a chain of decisions, government cannot expend public funds for religious purposes or organizations. Diminution of voluntary giving to churches and related purposes, as a result of a loss of the tax deduction privilege, could deal a mortal blow to much of organized religion in this country. Yet the American tradition has always held that religious activity merits, and needs, benevolent treatment by public authority. There is a long string of testimony on this question—reaching as far back as "Ye Olde Deluder Satan" law of the Massachusetts Bay Colony in 1647 and the Northwest Ordinance of 1787. The latter asserted: "Religion, morality and knowledge being necessary to good government and the happiness of mankind, schools and the means of education shall forever be encouraged." Several Supreme Court decisions within the past half century have touched on this issue, especially the *Pierce* (1925), *Zorach* (1952) and *Walz* (1970) decisions.[34] In the *Walz* case the Court said in regard to tax exemptions benefiting churches: "Few concepts are more deeply embedded in the fabric of our national life, beginning with pre-revolutionary colonial times, than for the government to exercise at the very least this kind of benevolent neutrality toward churches and religious exercises generally. . . ." [35]

The "no establishment of religion" clause has been a complicating factor in proposals for direct aid to educational institutions—many of which are church-connected—and it has caused attention to shift to indirect aid through tax benefits. Deductions for tuition would not offer sufficient help to low-income families but tax credits could. Tuition tax credit plans for higher education passed the U.S. Senate on three occasions but never got by the House Ways and Means Committee. However, a bill authorizing tuition tax credits in nonpublic elementary and secondary schools (H. R. 16141), was approved by that committee late in 1972 and is expected to be considered again in 1973.

Donations of property other than cash have been the subject of intense controversy, particularly for educational institutions. When deductions are being computed, the value of donated property is easy to determine in the case of easily marketable securities but is less certain

---

[34] *Pierce* v. *Society of Sisters,* 268 U.S. 510 (1925); *Zorach* v. *Clauson,* 343 U.S. 306 (1951); *Walz* v. *Tax Commission,* 397 U.S. 664 (1970).
[35] 397 U.S. 676.

for other types of property, particularly for pieces of art and archival material. These donations may be, and at times are, grossly overvalued. Such abuses, however, can be prevented only by strict case-by-case review and enforcement.

Prior to the Tax Reform Act of 1969, the donor generally did not have to pay a capital gains tax for the difference between his acquisition cost (which in some cases is very low) and the current market value which he uses as a deduction. This made some gifts very profitable. However, the act of 1969 reduced the allowable deduction for certain types of contributions—for example, gifts of tangible personal property, such as a work of art, whose use is not related to the purpose or function of the recipient organization. The reduction for an individual contributor is 50 percent of the amount of the appreciation that would have been a long-term capital gain if the property had been sold. In the case of such a gift by a corporation, the reduction is 62.5 percent of the appreciation. But the tax break still remains for many contributions of appreciated property whose sale would result in long-term capital gains to the donor—for example, appreciated stock held for more than six months and donated to a publicly supported institution. Under the new law, appreciation cannot be counted for deduction purposes in the case of gifts of short-term securities.

In the long run, the basic policy position on the tax treatment of charitable contributions hinges—as it does for so many tax policy questions—on the viewer's political philosophy. Those who believe that, in today's world, government must play an increasing role and should extend the scope and intensity of its decision making are likely to be critical of or opposed to tax benefits for charitable donations. Those with a strong belief in widening the range of voluntary action and individual decision making—and in the right of the income earner to his earnings—favor encouraging private action through tax benefits for donations.

4

Personal Exemptions and Standard Deductions

Except for taxpayers in the very high income brackets, much or most of the progressivity in the federal income tax derives not from the rate scales, despite their conspicuous progression from 14 to 70 percent, but from personal exemptions and standard deductions. These particular allowances provide the major tax relief for low and middle income persons. Totalling an estimated $160 billion in 1970—almost double the sum of all itemized deductions—standard deductions and personal exemptions accounted for 40 percent of the difference between personal income and taxable income (see Table 4). They are, technically, the biggest single tax "loophole." With a substantial increase in those allowances for 1972, the amount of income that remains untaxed because of personal exemptions and standard deductions is now certain to be far higher.

Personal exemptions: purposes and effects. The purpose of the personal exemption is to free from taxation the irreducible amount which an individual needs for minimum existence costs and which therefore does not constitute taxable capacity.[1] It is obviously impossible to specify a fixed amount that is proper and fair for both a farmworker family in rural Mississippi and a professional family maintaining a very different living standard in a metropolitan center. Nor does it seem politically

---

[1] The argument is persuasive that amounts needed and spent for mere subsistence are not available for taxation purposes. But by the same logic, for example, federal income tax withheld from wages or paid does not constitute taxable capacity. Yet it is included in the federal tax base.

feasible to vary the personal exemption according to geographical, social or economic circumstances. Only for blind or aged persons were the emotional issues involved strong enough to allow a doubling of the personal exemption.

The decision on a nationally uniform personal exemption, therefore, has to be somewhat arbitrary; the amount that will be grossly inadequate under some circumstances may be ample under others. However, because of the graduated tax rates, the monetary value of the current $750 exemption varies from $105 in the lowest income bracket to $525 in the highest. A tax credit would provide more even benefits than an exemption, at all income levels, and several states have adopted such a system. But on a nationwide basis the credit method would raise the question of differential requirements more strongly.

The $3,000 exemption that the 1913 income tax law allowed the individual taxpayer ($4,000 for couples) was reduced to $1,000 in World War I and to a low of $500 in World War II. It was raised to $600 in 1948 and remained there for 21 years until the Tax Reform Act of 1969 boosted personal exemptions by steps, to $750 as of 1972. By historical comparison, the present $750 exemption is quite low. Since 1942, when the exemption was lowered to $500 to meet World War II fiscal needs, consumer prices have risen by 130 percent, wages and income by well over 300 percent, and the exemption by only 50 percent. On a maintained "price" basis the exemption should now be about $1,150, on a "wage" basis close to $2,000. This has not been done and cannot be done for a simple reason: boosts in the personal exemption are the most expensive type of revision in the income tax. With 204 million exemptions claimed in 1970, the cost of a $100 raise in the amount allowed per person reduces revenue by well over $4 billion. An increase to a level that is economically comparable to the one that prevailed in 1942 could wipe out one-third to one-half of all income tax collections. This brings home two facts: the federal income tax burden is now much more severe than it was during World War II and present yields can be obtained only if the tax base is kept broad (that is, the exemption relatively low) because there is not enough income at higher levels to make up for a substantial raise in the exemption.

Standard deductions: purposes and effects. Standard deductions were introduced in 1944 not to provide for greater equity—they did not then and still do not—but for reasons of administrative simplification. When the number of tax returns multiplied about six times in World War II and the income tax became more of a mass tax, it was necessary to reduce its complexity for the vast majority of taxpayers who were not used to dealing with the intricacies of income tax returns. It was also necessary to ease the burden of audits and enforcement. In 1944 when taxpayers were first allowed to deduct 10 percent of their adjusted gross income (up to a maximum of $1,000) in lieu of itemizing deductions, 82 percent of them availed themselves of this opportunity. But as the amounts eligible and reported for tax deductions multiplied after World War II, itemizing became increasingly popular until by 1960, 40 percent of all returns and by 1970, 48 percent showed itemized deductions. Obviously, the simplification value of standard deductions had been grossly reduced as a growing number of taxpayers—now more income-tax wise than their parents were in 1944—found it worthwhile to shift to itemizing.

The Tax Reform Act of 1969 lifted standard deductions in steps to 15 percent of adjusted gross income (with a $2,000 maximum) by 1972. This is expected to cause 70 to 75 percent of all taxpayers, as many as 11 million in all, to shift to standard deductions. The increased use of standard deductions may not necessarily ease tax calculations for millions of taxpayers who in preparing their returns will still want to add their deductible items to make certain that they will do as well or better with the standard deduction. But it will ease the workload for the Internal Revenue Service computers and auditors.

Whether these changes will make the income tax fairer is another question. A major purpose of itemized deductions is to grant relief for such special burdens as heavy medical expenses, casualty losses and taxes. More generous standard deductions inevitably reduce that type of relief. They will also weaken the incentive for charitable contributions. It could be that many persons who used to donate regularly, because the gifts were deductible, may now claim the standard deductions and refrain from philanthropic giving. That could hurt many meritorious activities, a potent argument against raising standard deductions even higher, as has been suggested by some. At this point it is likely that the 1969 changes, which became fully effective in 1972, will be given a tryout for some years until their results can be studied.

At the time of the passage of the Economic Opportunity Act of 1964 (the war on poverty), Congress noted that many persons and families whom the poverty yardsticks classified as poor nevertheless incurred income tax liabilities. It did not seem to make sense to devise extensive financial support schemes for such persons—and then to tax them. Congress authorized a minimum standard deduction of $300 for a taxpayer and $100 for each dependent which freed about 1.5 million people of any income tax liability. By the end of the 1960s, however, due to continued inflation and higher poverty yardsticks, millions of persons below the official poverty level had to pay income taxes. In the Tax Reform Act of 1969 Congress boosted the low-income allowance gradually to $1,300 per taxpayer in 1972. This relieved more than 5 million persons from any income tax liability, and reduced the tax of over 7 million others. While it may seem a matter of equity to free growing numbers of low-income persons from the burdens of taxation, it also increases the incidence of "representation without taxation." It multiplies the number of citizens who vote but bear no responsibility for paying for enlarged governmental services and benefits. As was pointed out above, this poses a danger to the preservation of *responsible* free government.

Split Income versus the Single Taxpayer

From inception it was the intent of the income tax law that taxpayer units with the same income should pay the same tax. For the past quarter century, however, the law has made a sharp distinction between taxpayers who are single and those who are married. Through the use of a joint return and the application of a different rate schedule, a married couple incurs a much lower tax liability on the same income than a single person. From 1948 on, when the "split income" provision was first enacted, single persons paid up to 42 percent more than married persons with equal income. When Congress in the Tax Reform Act of 1969 limited the singles' tax disadvantage to 20 percent, a reverse situation emerged, unintentionally, for some upper-middle income couples and it still exists: if the income of the two spouses is approximately equal they may incur a tax liability that is up to 19 percent higher than it would be if they were not married and each reported his own income. In other words, as the law stands, it imposes upon most unmarried taxpayers a penalty for being single but levies on *some* married taxpayers a penalty for being married. That does not make much sense, and it violates the principle that the tax law should be neutral.

150

Single persons and their organizations have long been loudly protesting to Congress against this discrimination in the tax law. Within the past three years certain married persons have been complaining with at least equal vigor that they are being fined for being married. Both groups have a good point. But there does not seem to be a simple solution that is perfectly fair to all parties under all circumstances. The present law is the result of a compromise, but whether it is the fairest compromise possible is a matter on which opinions differ. After holding hearings in the spring of 1972, the Ways and Means Committee decided to leave matters as they are. This, of course, satisfied neither side.

For 35 years, from 1913 to 1947, the law contained only one tax rate schedule to which all taxpayers were subjected, whether single or married. Two developments brought a change in 1948. A 1942 law permitted a divorced man to deduct alimony from his income for tax purposes, and it taxed that alimony to the recipient wife. That appeared fair enough, but the result was a reduction in the combined income tax of couples who underwent divorce. For example, under the progressive rate scale, two persons with $10,000 and $6,000 in income, respectively, pay a lower tax than one person with a $16,000 income. To some lawmakers and others that seemed like a reward for divorce and thereby a penalty on marriage.

But what led to congressional action was the problem caused by the existence of community property laws in eight states from California to Louisiana. These laws, which derived from Spanish and French law rather than from English common law, gave each spouse a vested claim to one-half of each other's earnings. This means that in those states the husband and the wife could (and still can) each report for federal tax purposes one-half of their combined (community) income. In the remaining states no such "income splitting" was possible prior to 1948. In a common law state, a husband with a taxable income of $44,000 (and his wife earning nothing) had to report and pay tax on $44,000; in a community property state, under otherwise identical circumstances, he and his wife could each report an income of $22,000 which meant a substantially lower tax liability. The Internal Revenue Service objected to such income splitting by residents of community property states but was overruled by the U.S. Supreme Court which held that the husband could not be taxed on the one-half of his earnings that, under the laws of his state of residence, belonged to his wife.

151

The unfairness of a federal income tax imposed at higher rates in some states than in others was obvious. Nor is it surprising that a growing number of common law states became concerned over the fact that many of their residents paid heavier taxes than the residents of community property states. Some states began to convert from common law to community property law. But this was an extremely complicated process which caused innumerable legal problems and threatened to tie up legislatures and courts for many years.

Congress finally relented. In 1948 it authorized joint tax returns that were subject to a rate schedule designed to produce the same result as if each of the spouses had earned and reported half of their combined income. This restored federal tax uniformity throughout the United States. But it made the unmarried status very expensive, taxwise, for a person in the middle and upper-middle income brackets. An individual could reduce his or her income tax liability very substantially just by getting married. A single person had to pay, between 1948 and 1969, up to 42 percent more in income tax than a married couple with the same income. In 1951 Congress added another category of taxpayer, unmarried heads of household, on which it conferred about half the advantage of a joint return. But this status was and is available only to persons having dependents, not to singles living alone or with other singles.

Single persons were at a substantial disadvantage from 1948 on and continued to petition their representatives in Congress for redress. But being a distinct minority, their influence was limited. In 1970, 42.4 million joint returns were submitted, suggesting 85 million potential voters, whereas only 25.7 million returns were filed by single persons.[2] In 1969 single persons were able to convince Congress that they were being unfairly punished: their tax disadvantage was cut in half, that is, reduced to a maximum of 20 percent over married persons. That may seem a reasonable compromise but, as was indicated above, there are complications, and now both sides are complaining about inequities. Single persons claim there is no reason why they should pay a 20 percent higher income tax than they would if they were married. Working couples with approximately equal incomes in upper-middle income

[2] There also were 2.4 million separate returns of married persons (many of them from community property states or in status of separation prior to a divorce decree becoming final) and 3.6 million unmarried heads of households.

brackets believe that they should not have to pay up to 19 percent more in taxes than if they were unmarried.

Table 11 compares the tax liability at selected income levels for single persons and for married couples with only one earner. The one earner situation applied to 55 percent of joint returns in 1970. On another 25 percent of joint returns, one spouse earned 70 percent or more of the combined incomes—which still gives some advantage to couples filing joint returns.

On only 11 percent of all joint returns did one spouse earn between 31 and 40 percent of combined earnings and on only 10 percent between 41 and 50 percent. It is married persons in the latter group—where earnings are approximately equal—who are at a disadvantage compared to single persons. As Table 12 shows, there is no difference at low-income levels, and only a relatively small one at medium-low and top levels, but two persons with medium-high *equal* income pay a tax that is as much as 19 percent lower if they are single than if they are married. This has been called a "tax on marriage," a "detriment to matrimony" and "savings from living in sin." It is unjust and highly undesirable as a matter of public policy.

To be sure, only a small number of taxpayers—couples in upper-middle income brackets with each spouse having approximately the same income—is at a substantial tax disadvantage because of being married. Nevertheless, the law has created an awkward situation and

---

Table 11

FEDERAL INCOME TAX LIABILITY AT SELECTED INCOME LEVELS
ON SINGLE RETURNS AND ON JOINT RETURNS
WITH ONE EARNER, 1972

Taxable Income (after exemptions & deductions)	Tax Liability		Singles' Tax Higher Than Joint	
	Single returns	Joint returns	Dollars	Percent
$ 8,000	$ 1,590	$ 1,380	+ $ 210	+ 15.2
14,000	3,210	2,760	+ 450	+ 16.3
20,000	5,230	4,380	+ 850	+ 19.4
32,000	10,290	8,660	+ 1,630	+ 18.8
44,000	16,590	14,060	+ 2,530	+ 18.0
100,000	53,090	45,180	+ 7,910	+ 17.5

Source: Computed by author from the relevant provisions of the Internal Revenue Code.

Table 12

FEDERAL INCOME TAX LIABILITY AT SELECTED INCOME LEVELS ON SINGLE RETURNS AND ON JOINT RETURNS, WITH SPOUSES' EARNINGS EQUAL, 1972

Taxable Income (after exemptions & deductions)	Tax Liability			Joint Higher Than Two Single Returns	
	Single return	Two single returns	Joint return (at double income level)	Dollars	Percent
$ 4,000 (joint $ 8,000)	$ 690	$ 1,380	$ 1,380	+ $ 0	+ —
8,000 (joint 16,000)	1,590	3,180	3,260	+ 80	+ 2.5
14,000 (joint 28,000)	3,210	6,420	7,100	+ 680	+ 11.0
20,000 (joint 40,000)	5,230	10,460	12,140	+ 1,680	+ 16.1
32,000 (joint 64,000)	10,290	20,580	24,420	+ 3,840	+ 18.7
44,000 (joint 88,000)	16,590	33,180	37,980	+ 4,800	+ 14.5
100,000 (joint 200,000)	53,090	106,180	110,980	+ 4,800	+ 4.5

Source: Ibid.

154

proposals have been made to correct it. One bill sponsored by Senator Charles Mathias proposes that no couple should incur a higher tax liability than it would if the two spouses were not married.[3]

Simultaneously, a strong drive is underway to reduce or eliminate the remaining disadvantage of single persons. An amendment by Senator Robert Packwood would abolish the tax rate scales for single returns and heads of households and restore conditions very similar to those existing prior to 1948—one tax rate schedule applying to all taxpayers whether married or single. However, to avoid an inequity between residents of community property states and common law states, this proposal would use a different rate schedule applicable only to married persons filing single returns (which would mostly be residents of community property states).[4] The Packwood amendment lost 41 to 55 in 1971 but, on resubmission, was passed by the Senate (by voice vote) in 1972.[5] It was dropped when the bill (on the debt limit, H.R. 16810) went to conference with the House.

The question of the tax disadvantages of single persons—or of married persons under certain circumstances—remains unresolved and will probably continue to plague the tax-writing committees of Congress. On the one side, it is argued that conferring certain tax benefits on married status is an acceptable way to promote family stability and ease the added costs occasioned by family living.[6] Established tax deductions for mortgage interest and residential property taxes, it is said, are justified as deliberate aid to home ownership and family status. Public policy in favor of the family should be expressed through a split income tax rate schedule as well as through the allowance of deductions. On the other side, singles' organizations hold that no person should be penalized for being unmarried, whether by choice or by necessity, and that the tax law should treat all persons alike, regardless of their family status. The reversal in the vote on the Packwood amendment between 1971 and 1972 seems to suggest a shift in congressional sentiment in favor of the singles' viewpoint.

---

[3] S. 3629, *Congressional Record,* May 18, 1972, p. S 8078.

[4] Similar bills were introduced by Senator Ribicoff, Conn. (S. 869), Rep. Koch, N.Y. (H.R. 850, H.R. 14193) in the 92nd Congress, co-sponsored by over 100 other members.

[5] *Congressional Record,* October 13, 1972, p. S 18100.

[6] Others however, suggest that there are substantial economies in family living versus single living (two can live more cheaply together than separately).

The Internal Revenue Code is full of enough exemptions, exclusions, deductions and credits to make a mockery of the view that it should tax all income from whatever source derived. It is no secret that huge amounts of income escape bearing their share of the federal income tax burden. But not too many people realize that that tax now reaches only about *half* of all personal income in the United States; the other half remains untaxed. This makes the federal income tax by far the "leakiest" of U.S. taxes—the one with the smallest actual base compared with its potential. In contrast, exemptions from sales and property taxes generally amount to no more than one-fourth to one-third of their respective bases.

An estimated $465 billion of personal income remained federally untaxed in 1970 and the total may have exceeded $500 billion in 1972. Why does the tax law allow half of all personal income to go free? Surely this could not have come about by mere accident or oversight. According to repeated and widely believed charges, special interest lobbyists have either bribed or fooled congressmen into writing huge loopholes into the tax code, into establishing tax shelters so that wealthy persons can avoid paying their share of taxes or even paying any taxes at all. But the conspiracy theory of tax policy is refuted by the record. No public laws are subject to more painstaking and detailed congressional study, to more extensive open hearings, to more thorough debate, year after year, than the tax laws. With but few exceptions, remedial tax provisions were put in the law not out of inadvertence, ignorance or, as a rule, a desire to give favored groups improper advantages or privileges. On the contrary, most remedial provisions aim to provide greater equity

157

among various economic groups and individuals or to offer incentives for activities that are held to be desirable as a matter of public policy. If Congress retains provisions that have been long assailed as loopholes by some groups, it does so not from lack of knowledge or in response to sinister influences but because its majority believes, after due consideration, that the provisions have merit. In recent years, whenever Congress has considered proposals for tax reform, it has usually widened more loopholes than it has tightened and has wound up with an increase in the nontaxable portion of income—and an even more complicated tax law.

On its face, it would make great sense to switch to a comprehensive tax base, to tax *all* income at half the present rates rather than *half* of it at rates that are twice as high. A flat rate of 10 percent on all personal income would yield about as much revenue as the present 14 to 70 percent rate schedule produces on half of personal income. Moreover, most of the complications in the tax law that make compliance a severe burden on taxpayers and administrators result from remedial provisions (and limitations thereon) and from differential rates and treatment. The income tax could be quite simple and easy to comply with if it were levied at a flat 10 percent on all income—or even on a graduated schedule—provided there were no deductions, exemptions, exclusions or credits. But such simplification runs into big roadblocks.

A telling example of the difficulties confronting framers of tax law is the issue of the married versus the single taxpayer. Single persons used to have to pay up to 42 percent higher taxes than married persons with the same income. In 1969 Congress reduced the singles' disadvantage to 20 percent. But now, as an unintended consequence, there are certain circumstances in which some married couples must pay up to 19 percent more than they would if they were single (whether living together or not). And every possible solution to this dilemma is highly controversial, fought by one side to the issue or by both.

As a result of the 1969 change, there are now four different rate schedules in the law—and many unhappy taxpayers. The best answer might yet be to revert to only one rate schedule for all taxpayers, married or single (as was the case until 1948), and—in order to take care of the special situation posed by the eight community property states—require all married persons filing single returns to use a special scale. Needless to say, even this solution would not make everybody happy. But it would be more equitable than the present system.

Two persons or two families with the same income do not necessarily have the same taxpaying capacity—if their other circumstances or burdens differ widely. Nor are all types of income-producing activities able to bear the same burden in as diversified and internationally dependent an economy as ours. The law must take an infinite variety of conditions and situations into account. Most students of taxation acknowledge that there must be some differentiation, some remedial provisions, and that the idea of taxing *all* income alike, though appealing, is impractical. Realistically, the question is not whether there should be loopholes but which loopholes and for whose benefit.

The most frequent assertion in the drive to close tax loopholes—or for a more comprehensive tax base—is the claim that most existing loopholes benefit the very rich while the great majority of taxpayers in the middle-income ranges, whose income tax is withheld from their wages, have no tax shelters and are forced to bear the full brunt of the income tax. Allegedly many millionaires pay no income tax and others very little. This is the charge that transformed the campaign for loophole-closing into a tax reform movement.

But the charge does not stand the test of critical analysis. Most of the $465 billion of personal income that was untaxed in 1970 redounded to persons in lower and middle-income brackets. Only a small percentage of it was accounted for by the more frequently cited loopholes that benefit directly persons at high income levels.

The biggest "loopholes" are the personal exemption (raised from $600 in 1969 to $750 in 1972) and the standard deduction (raised from 10 percent with a $1,000 maximum in 1969 to 15 percent with a $2,000 maximum in 1972). In 1970 these two loopholes exempted about $160 billion of income from taxation. Tax-free income from social benefits (social security, welfare, veterans' benefits, et cetera) and labor income (for example, employer pension contributions) totalled another $104 billion. Itemized deductions—for state and local taxes, interest paid, medical expenses, charitable contributions, et cetera—amounted to $88 billion. Analysis shows that the percentage of income that is subject to the federal income tax rises sharply with income and that it is highest at top income levels.

Recent tax legislation, particularly the Tax Reform Act of 1969, has freed millions of persons in the lower income brackets of any tax liability, and sharply reduced the taxes of millions more. The resulting situation may serve a good social purpose but it also raises the danger of increased "representation without taxation"—of growing numbers of citizens that benefit from government programs but do not have to foot any visible part of the bill. Voters in this group are likely to clamor for or support ever rising government spending at other people's expense.

The oft-cited tax provisions on capital gains, mineral percentage depletion, municipal bond interest, and so forth, account for only a small amount of lost revenue. More importantly, they were enacted and are retained not for the purpose of benefiting the rich but to prevent serious harm to the American economy. Taxing capital gains as if they were regular income, making no allowance for the special circumstances of mineral discovery and production, tightening up on depreciation, repealing the investment credit—such measures could have grave consequences for economic growth, employment, and the balance of payments.

Steady vigilance and periodical tightening up is necessary to prevent abuses and to block new ways of "getting around the law." But such review is different from wholesale repeal or diminution of needed tax mitigation.

As it is, the American tax structure—it would be ironic to call it a system—is strongly biased in favor of consumption and against capital formation and investment. The American people are paying a price for it. The United States leans more heavily on progressive income taxes than other countries, deals more harshly with capital gains and depreciation than most European nations and is unique in not levying a broad consumption tax as a major producer of national government revenue.

The underlying conflict in the tax reform debate is probably not so much one of economic theory as of ideological preference for greater income equality. Some view government largely as a huge machine for redistributing income from those who have more to those who have less. Others believe that free market forces are the most effective means of stimulating economic expansion, from which in the end all or most segments of society will benefit. It comes down to the old question of whether it is better to fight over how to slice the pie—or bake a bigger pie.

If the battle over tax reform in the past ten to fifteen years is any guide, it appears that there is no grand solution, no simple way to improve the tax system by closing the most often criticized "loopholes." This has been suggested time and again, in vain. The present distribution of tax burdens and benefits appears to reflect, by and large, the balance of power and economic interests among the American people as represented in the Congress. The repeated defeat of plans to close all "loopholes for the rich" while leaving intact other remedial provisions that account for most of the presently untaxed income suggests the existence of a broad consensus and an understanding of the grave damage that precipitate action might cause.

To be sure, there are many shortcomings in the tax law that need study and improvement, with a view to moving in the direction of a more comprehensive tax base. But the answer is far more complicated than most spokesmen for loophole-closing claim. That huge budget deficits can be met and enlarged federal spending financed through the closing of loopholes is not a possibility but a mirage. The realistic and practicable way of ending budgetary deficits is through tighter control of expenditures than we have so far seen.

VALUE ADDED TAX: TWO VIEWS
Charles E. McLure, Jr.
Norman B. Ture

THE TAX ON VALUE ADDED: PROS AND CONS

Charles E. McClure, Jr.

Summary and Conclusions

When it was rumored in early 1972 that President Nixon might propose a federal value added tax (VAT), interest in this form of taxation spread from the tax specialist to the congressman, newsman, and layman. Yet altogether too little material was available for the interested nonspecialist since most of the existing literature about the VAT had been written by experts in taxation for their fellow experts. This essay is intended to fill this gap by explaining what the value added tax is, how it operates, and the chief economic effects (and therefore advantages and disadvantages) of substituting revenues from a newly enacted VAT for part of the revenues from existing taxes.

A conscious attempt has been made to present the analysis in terms comprehensible to the educated layman—something always difficult to achieve for an inherently complex and technical matter. Because that effort may have fallen short of the mark and because some readers may simply not want to know as much about the value added tax as is presented in the body of the essay, the most important points are summarized in the next few pages. Footnotes in the summary refer to relevant portions of the text itself.

The term "tax on value added" is at once quite descriptive and highly misleading. It describes well the way in which the tax is collected. Each firm pays a tax on the increase in the value of goods that occurs because of the firm's productive activities; hence the term "tax on value added."[1] If the tax is levied on all firms in the productive process, including retailers, it will be collected upon the total value of the final product. Thus in its pure form the tax is essentially equivalent to a general single-stage sales tax levied at the retail level.[2] In this sense the value added tax is not a tax on some new and different tax base; it is simply a different way of collecting a general tax on consumption.

Because the VAT is intended to be a tax on all domestic consumption, it is necessary to make what are called border tax adjustments (BTA) on goods entering international trade. In other words, in order that exports not be burdened by the domestic tax on consumption, it is necessary to rebate any VAT previously collected on exports. Similarly, in order that imports bear the same tax as domestic consumption goods, it is necessary to apply the tax to them. These border tax adjustments are among the most famous characteristics of the VAT. (It is worthwhile to note that under a retail sales tax border tax adjustments are unnecessary; exports would have incurred no tax, and imports, like domestic products, would be taxed at the retail level.)[3]

Because it would ideally be levied at a uniform rate on all items of consumption, the VAT is said to be neutral. It does not distort economic decisions among products or methods of production. In this sense it is similar to the personal income and social security payroll taxes and quite different from the corporation income and property taxes. The corporation income tax, for which the VAT has most commonly been proposed as a substitute, is distinctly nonneutral. It discriminates against the products of the corporate sector, against the use of the corporate form of business organization, against the use of equity (share) financing in the corporate sector, and against the use of capital (as opposed to land and labor) in the corporate sector. Thus, partial replacement of the corporation income tax with a truly general tax on value added (one with few exemptions and a uniform rate)

---

[1] In actuality, in all nations now using the tax the firm incurs a tax liability equal to the tax rate applied to the value of its sales, but receives credit for taxes it has paid on its purchased inputs. As discussed further in section 2C of the essay, this *credit method* of taxation yields essentially the same results as applying the tax rate directly to value added.

[2] These statements are strictly true only for the consumption type VAT, the variant most likely to be adopted in the United States. See section 2B for a description of the income and consumption variants of the VAT.

[3] See section 2E for a detailed discussion of border tax adjustments.

would represent a distinct gain in neutrality, provided it were accompanied by increased taxation of retained earnings.[4]

A similar, if less dramatic, increase in neutrality would result from using revenues from a general VAT to replace part of the revenues from local school property taxes, the scheme President Nixon has proposed for consideration. The property tax, as it now operates, distorts intra-urban choices of industrial location and retards the renewal of decaying central cities. Partial replacement of the property tax on improvements with a neutral VAT would reduce these distortions.

Only a truly general VAT would be completely neutral. If the tax contained important exemptions or if it were applied to different products at different rates, its inherent neutrality would be lost. For this reason exemptions should be kept to a minimum and a single rate should be applied to all products. Nevertheless, it is virtually certain that an American VAT would contain important exemptions. For one thing, it is very difficult to tax housing and the output of financial institutions under the VAT. If only these and several other difficult-to-tax items were exempted, the tax base would fall to about 80 percent of personal consumption expenditures. Moreover, several items of expenditure might be thought worthy of exemption as a matter of social policy. Examples are medicine and medical expenses, public education and research expenditures, and religious and welfare activities. Exemptions of this type might reduce the tax base further, to only about two-thirds of personal consumption expenditures. Finally, such things as household utilities and food for home preparation might be exempted in order to lessen the regressivity of the tax. If so, the tax base would fall to less than one-half of personal consumption expenditures.[5] Exemptions of this size would, of course, render the VAT far from the neutral fiscal device that it is in its pure form. One of the most important ways to forestall the erosion of the tax base and maintain neutrality would be to offset the regressivity of the VAT through refundable credits against the income tax or a negative income tax, rather than through the exemption of necessities. This is discussed further below.

---

[4] Simple elimination of a part of the corporation income tax would partially free retained earnings from taxation. Retained earnings could be taxed via increased capital gains taxation or the integration of the two income taxes (attributing all corporate profits to shareholders and including them in personal income tax returns); see section 4B.

[5] See section 3 for a more detailed description of the potential erosion of the ideally neutral tax base.

Assessment of most of the effects of replacing part of the corporation income tax with a levy on value added hinges crucially upon one of the most controversial issues in economics, the incidence of the corporation income tax.[6] Traditional economic theory states that the corporation income tax cannot be shifted to consumers in the form of higher product prices or to labor (or suppliers) in the form of lower wages (or input prices); rather, it must be borne by shareholders in the form of reduced earnings. Other theoretical analyses and certain controversial empirical studies report quite different results, namely, that the corporation income tax can be and is shifted. Thus the best that can be done is to make conditional statements. *If* the corporation tax is shifted to consumers, it probably has about the same effects in the aggregate as the VAT or any other general consumption tax. *If* it is not shifted, but is borne by shareholders, the result is quite different. In what follows we summarize the likely results of replacing part of the corporation income tax with a VAT under both sets of assumptions about shifting.

If the corporation tax is not shifted, the rate of saving and investment in the economy would probably rise markedly if the VAT were substituted for the corporation tax. Presumably this change would raise the rate of growth in the United States. But if the corporation tax is shifted, probably little impact on the rates of saving, investment, and growth would occur. If the VAT were substituted for the personal income tax, social security payroll tax, or property tax, the impact on these rates would probably also be small.

Evidence from the 1968 income tax surcharge suggests that temporary changes in income tax rates are not strong tools of discretionary counter-cyclical policy. The same conclusion probably would hold for the payroll tax. Thus the VAT might be a more useful tool of discretionary fiscal policy than any of these direct taxes, since temporary changes in it would be likely to cause consumers to accelerate or postpone purchases of durable goods at just the right times. Of course, we do not expect the property tax to be varied as a tool of stabilization policy. So far as contribution to the built-in stability of the economy is concerned, it seems unlikely that the various taxes differ significantly.

---

[6] See section 4A for a brief discussion of the incidence of the corporation income tax. The remainder of section 4 considers in detail the implications for neutrality, growth, stabilization, and the balance of payments of substituting a VAT for the corporation income tax. Distributional effects of the substitution are left for section 5. Each of these effects is discussed for the substitution of VAT for the personal income and payroll taxes in section 6 and for the substitution for the property tax in section 7.

Perhaps the most important way in which the VAT would differ from the income taxes is in its incidence. The VAT, being a tax on consumption, would almost certainly be markedly regressive since consumption as a percentage of income falls as income rises. On the other hand, the personal and corporate income taxes are progressive (if the corporate tax is not shifted; if the corporate tax is shifted, it too is regressive). Thus substitution of VAT for part of either of these taxes is felt by many observers to be grossly inequitable. They would oppose substitution for the personal tax and would favor substitution for the corporate tax only if the change were accompanied by heavier taxation of capital gains and relief for low-income families. This relief ideally would take the form of a refundable income tax credit or a negative income tax, but some would accept exemption of necessities such as food from the tax base. Such exemptions would, as noted above, be a distinctly inferior form of relief because they would destroy the neutrality of the VAT, one of the chief advantages of the tax in its pure form.

Perhaps the most widely advertised of the supposed advantages of an American switch to the VAT is an expected improvement in the balance of payments. In its simplest form this argument is probably fallacious; it simply states that, because border tax adjustments are allowed for the VAT, exports would increase and imports would fall. The problem with this view is that the BTA are seen as import taxes and export subsidies, without recognizing that, as noted above, they would be needed to assure that the American tax is applied to all domestic consumption and that exports occur free of the tax. The fallacy in the argument is easily seen if we try to apply the same reasoning to the economically equivalent retail sales tax; hardly anyone would argue that imposition of that tax would, per se, improve the balance of trade. Only if the prices of goods failed to reflect fully either the retail tax or the VAT would the tax itself improve the payments position. Theoretical reasoning suggests that the VAT probably would raise prices by the amount of the tax, so there seems to be little reason for hope of balance of payments improvement on that score.

The real possibility of a switch to VAT improving the balance of payments arises, instead, from the assumption that the corporation income tax is shifted. Traditional theory holds that the corporation tax is borne by shareholders, and thus has no effect on prices. Reduction of the tax would therefore not affect prices, and the switch to VAT would improve the balance of trade only if prices failed to rise by the amount of the newly imposed tax. On the other hand, if the

169

corporation income tax is currently shifted to consumers, it resembles a sales tax except that no BTA is allowed for it. Thus the switch to VAT would have no effect on domestic prices (so long as the corporation tax is "unshifted" when reduced) but imports would be subject to the compensating import duty under the VAT and the tax rebated on exports. This result should, of course, improve the balance of payments.

What can we conclude about the effect of the switch on domestic prices and the balance of payments? Unfortunately, the answer is that we cannot conclude anything very firmly because we do not know whether or not the corporation income tax is shifted. But on balance it seems likely that domestic prices would rise by about the amount of the tax and that the balance of payments probably would not improve significantly if VAT were substituted for part of the corporation income tax. This conclusion is almost certainly accurate if the VAT were substituted instead for part of the personal income, payroll, or property tax.

Arguments with regard to neutrality, equity, stability, growth, and the balance of payments have been summarized here. It is reasonable to ask how the various effects should be weighed since they do not all point together toward one single optimum direction for tax policy. The answer is clear: primary attention should be devoted to the implications for neutrality and equity. There are other tools, though imperfect ones, for the achievement of economic growth, stability, and an improved balance of payments; but neutrality in the tax system and equity in the distribution of tax burdens among households cannot very well be handled except through structural tax policy.[7]

If this reasoning is accepted, several conclusions stand out. First, if the corporation income tax is shifted to consumers, VAT should be substituted for it. Neutrality would be improved, with no substantial change in the equity of the tax system. But if the corporation income tax is not shifted, the trade-off between neutrality and equity must be faced squarely. The VAT is more neutral than the corporation tax, but it is also regressive. Of course, if the tax haven in the form of retained earnings, which would be created by reduction of the corporation tax, were closed, both neutrality and equity would be furthered. But it is virtually certain that relief from the regressivity of the VAT would need to be provided for low-income families. In the interest of maintaining neutrality, this relief should be provided

---

[7] This argument is presented in more detail in section 9.

directly through refundable credits or a negative income tax rather than through exemption of necessities from the VAT.

The choice between the VAT and the property tax is similar to that between the VAT and a shifted corporation tax. Neutrality would probably be increased while the overall incidence of the tax system probably would not change much. But housing might very well be exempt from the VAT, whereas it is currently taxed quite heavily under the property tax. The substitution of VAT for part of the personal income tax, on the other hand, would seem to make little sense. It would move the tax system toward regressivity and improve neutrality very little. Substitution for the payroll tax might be more or less a matter of indifference. Neutrality would be similar under both taxes, as would the aggregate distribution of burdens. But the VAT would bear more heavily on consumers, as a group, relative to workers, as a group.

Since administration of the VAT seems to be more involved than administration of the economically equivalent retail sales tax, it might reasonably be asked why there is so much interest in a federal VAT in preference to a federal retail sales tax. The answer is partly a matter of historical accident. France has used a form of value added tax since 1954, and since 1967 a dozen European countries have adopted, or have made arrangements to adopt, a VAT. The mystique of a tax used increasingly in Europe and largely unknown in the United States and the belief in some quarters that the U.S. balance of payments would be improved by adoption of a value added tax probably go a long way in explaining U.S. interest in the tax. The merit of these arguments for VAT deserves brief attention.

The European countries adopted value added taxes for reasons that are largely irrelevant to the United States. First, in many instances the VAT replaced what are known as cascade-type turnover taxes. These taxes apply to the entire value of a firm's sales at every trans- action rather than to value added, and discriminate severely between products and methods of production, whereas a VAT is neutral with regard to both products and methods of production.[8] Second, the border tax adjustments that can be made precisely for the VAT can be made only roughly for cascade taxes. Third, and perhaps most important in European decisions to switch to value added taxation, the members of the European Common Market desired to harmonize their systems of indirect (consumption) taxation, something that could be achieved relatively easily under a VAT, but not under a regime of

---

[8] See section 2A for a more complete description of cascade taxes and their faults.

cascade taxation. Finally, because of the way it is administered, the VAT has self-enforcing features not shared by the cascade tax and many others.

None of these reasons for the European adoption of value added taxation is compelling in the United States. The United States, having no defective indirect tax such as the European cascade tax, need not impose a VAT to replace such a tax. And it is generally assumed that the level of taxpayer compliance in the United States is much higher than in Europe, and high enough to make the self-enforcement features of the VAT relatively unimportant. Finally, we have argued above that the switch to VAT probably would not improve the U.S. balance of payments very much, and that a switch to a retail sales tax would probably have roughly the same effect in any case. There are good reasons for preferring a value added tax to a retail tax, if either is to be adopted (and good reasons for preferences to run the other direction, as well), but neither the European precedent nor the balance of payments argument is among them.[9] Thus if some form of general sales tax is to be adopted, the VAT should not be chosen over the retail sales tax without a careful comparison of the relative administrative advantages of the two taxes.

1. Introduction

During the last ten years an increasingly popular topic in the world of fiscal affairs has been whether or not the United States should adopt a tax on value added (VAT).[10] The discussion began in earnest at about the time the Neumark committee recommended that all countries of the European Common Market should adopt a value added tax, and it intensified as that recommendation was implemented.[11] It

---

[9] See section 2F for a presentation of arguments on both sides of this issue.

[10] I defer to the judgment of readers of an earlier draft of this essay in using the abbreviation "VAT," rather than "TVA." I base my personal preference for the latter usage upon the grammatical superiority of "tax on value added," over "value added tax" and the prior use of TVA by the French—long before the United States seriously considered using the tax. Fortunately the French language does not readily admit such grammatical monstrosities as "value added tax."

[11] "Report of the Fiscal and Financial Committee (Neumark Report)," *The EEC Reports on Tax Harmonization*, International Bureau of Fiscal Documentation, Amsterdam, 1963. Thus far only the initial stages of the recommended changes have been completed. That is, all the countries of the EEC except Italy have adopted a VAT. The further stages of adoption of uniform rates and the origin principle with regard to trade internal to the EEC (see section 2E below) have yet to be implemented.

reached a crescendo recently when President Nixon suggested that the United States consider levying a federal VAT in order to lighten the burden of the property tax in the financing of education.

It seems accurate to say that support for an American VAT has been based in part upon a mystique derived jointly from the novelty of the idea and the fact that the Europeans are placing increasing reliance upon the tax and in part upon the improvement in the U.S. balance of payments that some persons thought the tax would produce, especially if it were substituted for part of the corporation income tax. In some quarters the neutrality of the VAT has been touted, as has its potential contribution to the rate of economic growth in the U.S.[12]

Critics of the VAT have decried the bandwagon effect that the VAT's mystique has seemed to create and have doubted that the balance-of-payments effects would be nearly as large as its supporters think. Moreover, they have argued that equilibrium in the balance of payments and a higher rate of economic growth could be achieved without such a radical change in tax policy. And while they have been willing to admit the neutrality of the VAT, if it were not riddled by exemptions, they have opposed imposing a regressive federal tax on consumption in the absence of income tax reform and low-income relief. It would be especially inequitable, some have argued, to substitute the regressive VAT for the progressive corporation income tax. Finally, even if the case were granted that the U.S. should have a broad based federal tax on consumption, many have claimed that the more familiar retail sales tax would be preferable to the economically equivalent tax on value added.[13]

The purpose of this study is to present the arguments on both sides of the VAT question in a balanced and objective manner, so that the reader can decide for himself whether or not the U.S. should adopt a tax on value added. It proceeds by explaining in the next section

---

[12] In addition, the state of Michigan for a while had a quite imperfect variant of a tax on value added, the business activities tax (by coincidence, BAT). For two quite different assessments of the experience under this tax, see James A. Papke, "Michigan's Value-Added Tax after Seven Years," *National Tax Journal*, December 1960, pp. 350-63 and Clara K. Sullivan, *The Tax on Value Added* (New York: Columbia University Press, 1965), pp. 298-311.

[13] For a recent exchange on the merits and demerits of the VAT, see Stanley S. Surrey, "Value Added Tax: The Case For," and Dan Throop Smith, ". . . The Case Against," *Harvard Business Review*, December 1970, pp. 77-94. The present author has also examined the issues in "The Economic Effects of Taxing Value Added," mimeographed, 1970. His own views are expressed in testimony given before the Joint Economic Committee on March 21, 1972 and in the concluding section of this essay.

how the VAT is administered, important technical questions of the definition of the tax base for a general VAT applied without exemptions, and how the tax differs from a general retail sales tax in its administration. Section 3 examines the tax base as it would probably be in reality, i.e., given the seemingly irresistible tendency for any ideal tax base to be eroded by tax preferences and exemptions.

Whereas sections 2 and 3 discuss essentially the VAT itself (the comparison with the economically equivalent retail sales tax in section 2 being made primarily to clarify the operation of the VAT and to establish whether or not it is administratively preferable to a retail sales tax), the remainder of the study compares the VAT with other, quite different, taxes. In particular, section 4 compares the VAT and the corporation income tax with regard to neutrality, the effect on the rate of economic growth, use as macroeconomic stabilizers, and the impact on the U.S. balance of payments, while section 5 compares the incidence or distributional implications of the two taxes. The study, like most of the discussion in the last decade, concentrates on the comparison of these two taxes. For the sake of completeness the same comparison with the payroll and the personal incomes taxes is made in section 6.

Section 7 examines briefly the Nixon suggestion that a federal VAT might be substituted for the local property tax as a means of financing education. The analysis is done in the same terms as that of substituting VAT for the corporation income tax. But the Nixon proposal involves serious questions of fiscal relations between levels of government. Thus any meaningful analysis must go beyond these simple comparisons. Section 8 summarizes briefly European experience with the VAT, especially with regard to rate structure, coverage of the tax, and the impact on the price level of the introduction of the value added tax. The final section brings together the main points of the study, describes what the author believes is the proper framework for considering a tax on value added, and summarizes the author's views on the policy issues raised in this essay.

2. The Tax Base: Theory [14]

Though it is not strictly true, as is explained further in this and the next section, value added taxation can conveniently be envisaged as a means for collecting a general tax on consumer goods (and services)

---

[14] For a detailed exposition of the administration of value added taxes, see Carl S. Shoup, *Public Finance* (Chicago: Aldine Publishing Co., Inc., 1969), pp. 250-64.

174

as they pass through the stages of the production process, rather than entirely on the final sale to consumers, as under a retail sales tax. An example will make this clear. Assume that production involves three stages (A, B, and C) and that in a given taxable period production and transactions are as shown in Table 1 below. Firms at stage B buy inputs from those at stage A and sell their output to firms at stage C, which in turn sell only to ultimate consumers.[15]

Table 1
THREE-STAGE EXAMPLE OF 10 PERCENT VALUE ADDED TAX

| | Stage of Production | | | |
	A	B	C	Total
1. Sales	$300	$700	$1,000	$2,000
2. Purchased inputs	—	300	700	1,000
3. Value added (1 − 2)	300	400	300	1,000
4. Tax on value added (10% of 3)	30	40	30	100
5. Retail sales tax (10% of C1)	—	—	100	100

Under a 10 percent retail sales tax, $100 in revenue would be obtained on the $1,000 of sales made to consumers at stage C, as indicated. The same amount of revenue would be collected under the value added tax, but in an administratively different way. Each firm would be taxed at the 10 percent rate on its contribution to the value of the final product, or value added, which can be measured by the difference between its sales and its purchases of inputs. Thus firms at the three stages would pay VAT of $30, $40, and $30, respectively, on their value added of $300, $400, and $300. The total of VAT payments would, of course, equal the $100 collected directly on sales to consumers under the retail sales tax. The advantages and disadvantages of collecting the tax in this way, rather than simply at the retail level, are discussed in section 2F below, after further explanation of the operational details of the tax.

A. Cascade Taxes and VAT Compared. It may be worthwhile at this point to digress momentarily to examine the difference between the value added tax and the gross turnover, or cascade, taxes being replaced by the VAT in Europe. Table 2 will help clarify the distinc-

[15] No distinction is made at this point between inputs of intermediate goods and capital goods. For a detailed discussion of the difference in treatment accorded them, see section 2B below.

Table 2
**THREE-INDUSTRY COMPARISON OF 10 PERCENT VAT AND
5 PERCENT GROSS TURNOVER TAX**

| | Stage of Production | | | |
	A	B	C	Total
Industry I (from Table 1)				
Sales	$300	$700	$1,000	$2,000
Purchased inputs	—	300	700	1,000
Value added	300	400	300	1,000
Value added tax	30	40	30	100
Retail sales tax	—	—	100	100
Gross turnover tax	15	35	50	100
Industry II				
Sales	—	—	1,000	1,000
Purchased inputs	—	—	—	—
Value added	—	—	1,000	1,000
Value added tax	—	—	100	100
Retail sales tax	—	—	100	100
Gross turnover tax	—	—	50	50
Industry III				
Sales	800	900	1,000	2,700
Purchased inputs	—	800	900	1,700
Value added	800	100	100	1,000
Value added tax	80	10	10	100
Retail sales tax	—	—	100	100
Gross turnover tax	40	45	50	135

tion between the VAT, a tax on net accretions of value, and the tax
on gross sales. It shows the turnover tax liabilities that would be
incurred by three hypothetical industries, each producing $1,000 of
value added, if a cascade type tax were levied on gross sales at a rate
of 5 percent. Industry I is repeated from Table 1 to give us a bench-
mark for comparison. Industry II is completely integrated, so that
there is only one stage in the productive process. Finally, industry III
has three stages, like industry I, but the split of value added by stages
is quite different.

Because gross sales in industry I total $2,000, the 5 percent turn-
over tax on gross sales yields the same revenue as the 10 percent tax
on value added, $100.[16] But the sales of the vertically integrated

---

[16] This example is inaccurate in one respect. The tax at any stage would be
incorporated in the price of the taxed good. Thus the tax at the next stage would
be applied to the gross price, including taxes paid at earlier stages. This aspect of
taxing previous taxes is much less important than the multiple taxation of value
added as it moves through the production process.

industry II are entirely to ultimate consumers, so that gross sales equal the value added of $1,000. Thus in this industry the 5 percent turnover tax yields but half the revenue of the 10 percent tax on value added. Whereas either the VAT or the retail sales tax would impose the same percentage tax burden on the products of the two industries, the turnover tax discriminates in favor of vertically integrated industries (and production processes).

Industry III has the same number of stages as industry I. But because value added occurs earlier in the production process and is subjected to the turnover tax repeatedly as it moves through later stages, total sales of the industry are greater than for industry I. Thus, in total, the industry bears a $135 tax burden rather than the $100 burden on industry I. As a rule the turnover tax discriminates against industries whose value added occurs early in the production process.

It was because of the distortions created in the domestic economies by this nonneutral tax (plus the difficulties in calculating border tax adjustments, mentioned in footnote 27 of this section) that the Neumark Report recommended that the cascade type turnover taxes be replaced by the nondistorting tax on value added.[17] Because of the discrimination inherent in it, the cascade type turnover tax is a decidedly inferior form of taxation.

B. Income and Consumption Type VAT. The above example of computing the tax base under a value added tax ignored the question of how capital goods should be treated in the computation. For convenience we simply assumed implicitly that there were no capital goods. To make the example more realistic and more informative, we now consider explicitly the tax treatment of capital goods.

The two alternatives that are relevant in the present discussion are the income and consumption varieties of VAT.[18] Under the consumption variety, purchases of capital goods, as well as intermediate goods, are offset immediately against gross sales in computing taxable value added. Thus, there is no need to distinguish between the two types of business purchases, and the example in Table 1 is directly applicable.

Under the income type VAT, only depreciation on capital goods (as well as purchases of intermediate goods), rather than the entire

---

[17] For a further discussion of neutrality and tax-induced distortions, see section 4 below.

[18] See Shoup, *Public Finance*, pp. 251-53 for a description of the gross product and wage type value added taxes.

purchase price in the period of acquisition, can be offset against sales. Thus capital goods must be distinguished from intermediate goods, and depreciation schedules for tax purposes must be established for the former. Table 3 gives an example of the calculation of value added under the income type VAT, and compares it with the calculation under the consumption variety.

Table 3
COMPARISON OF INCOME AND CONSUMPTION TYPE TAXES ON VALUE ADDED

	Stage of Production			Total
	A	B	C	Economy
1. Sales	$300	$700	$1,000	$2,000
a. Intermediate goods	300	500	—	800
b. Capital goods	—	200	—	200
c. Consumer goods	—	—	1,000	1,000
2. Purchased inputs				
a. Intermediate goods	—	300	500	800
b. Capital goods	—	—	200	200
3. Capital stock				
a. Initial (assumed)	800	1,000	1,200	3,000
b. Purchases of capital goods (2b)	—	—	200	200
c. Depreciation (.05 × (3a + 3b))	40	50	70	160
d. End of period (3a + 3b − 3c)	760	950	1,330	3,040
e. Net investment (3d − 3a)	− 40	− 50	130	40
4. Value added				
a. Income base (1 − 2a − 3c)	260	350	430	1,040
b. Consumption base (1 − 2a − 2b)	300	400	300	1,000
5. Factor payments plus net profits				
a. Wages	160	220	300	680
b. Rent	40	30	20	90
c. Interest	30	50	60	140
d. Net profit	30	50	50	130
e. Total	260	350	430	1,040

Because purchases of both intermediate goods and capital goods are offset immediately against sales under the consumption type VAT, the net tax base equals sales of final products to ultimate consumers, or consumption. Thus it is equal to the base of an ideal retail sales tax, that is, of a single-stage sales tax applied only to sales to final consumers.

On the other hand, the tax base under the income type VAT equals income, rather than consumption, since for capital goods only depreciation is allowed as an offset against sales. This distinction can be seen in Table 3 by noting that value added under the income type VAT equals the sum of factor payments and net profits. For this reason a value added tax of the income variety is equivalent to a flat rate personal income tax with no exemptions or deductions. Of course, the base of the income type VAT exceeds that of the consumption type by the amount of net investment. Because the base for a VAT would be income or consumption, and not some new or different tax base, it is proper to think of the value added tax as an administrative device for collecting a tax on one of these bases rather than as a wholly new tax.

In most of what follows, especially in sections 4 to 7, attention focuses upon the consumption type tax because it is the most likely to be adopted in the United States. This likelihood is attributable to several factors. First, the consumption type VAT is used in Europe, and pressure to use it here would be strong. Second, the treatment of capital goods is far simpler than under the income type tax, which would require depreciation schedules and accounting. Finally, an additional tax on income could far more easily be implemented directly, by adding several points to the personal income tax rates, rather than by imposing an income type tax on value added.

C. Calculating Tax Liabilities. Section B above described in general terms the calculation of value added under the income and consumption varieties of value added tax. It may be useful, however, to describe in greater detail several alternative accounting techniques for computing tax liabilities. This detail will enable us to understand better the administrative advantages and disadvantages of the VAT, relative to the retail sales tax, which are discussed in section 2F.

The two most straightforward methods of calculating tax liabilities under the VAT are variants of what can be called the deduction method. Under the first, the subtraction method, the statutory tax rate is applied directly to the firm's value added, which in turn is calculated by subtracting purchased inputs from sales. Under the consumption type VAT, immediate deduction is made for purchases of both intermediate and capital goods, whereas under the income variety deduction for capital goods is allowed only as the assets depreciate. Thus, Table 4 shows the tax liabilities that would result from a 10 percent tax and the transactions and production indicated in Table 3. Total tax liabilities under the consumption type tax would

Table 4

COMPARISON OF THREE METHODS OF CALCULATING
LIABILITIES UNDER VALUE ADDED TAXATION

	Stage of Production			Total Economy
	A	B	C	
1. Subtraction method:				
a. Value added (from Table.3)				
1. Consumption base	$300	$400	$ 300	$1,000
2. Income base	260	350	430	1,040
b. Tax liability at 10% rate				
1. Consumption base	30	40	30	100
2. Income base	26	35	43	104
2. Credit method:				
a. Sales (from Table 3)	300	700	1,000	2,000
b. Purchases (from Table 3)				
1. Intermediate goods	—	300	500	800
2. Capital goods	—	—	200	200
c. Depreciation (from Table 3)	40	50	70	160
d. Gross tax liability on sales, at 10% rate	30	70	100	200
e. Tax on purchases and depreciation at 10% rate				
1. Consumption base (10% of b1+b2)	—	30	70	100
2. Income base (10% of b1+c)	4	35	57	96
f. Net tax liability				
1. Consumption base (d−e1)	30	40	30	100
2. Income base (d−e2)	26	35	43	104
3. Addition method:				
a. Sum of factor payments and profits (from Table 3)	260	350	430	1,040
b. Tax liability at 10% rate (income base only)	26	35	43	104

be 10 percent of sales to consumers, while under the income type tax they would be 10 percent of income; in either case the tax would be collected as the goods moved through the production process.

Under the second variant of the deduction method the firm calculates its gross tax liability by applying the statutory rate to its total sales. It then deducts from the result the amount of tax it has paid on its purchases in order to calculate its net tax liability. Because credit is allowed for the taxes previously paid on inputs, this method of calculating tax liability is known as the credit method. Of course, under the income type VAT, credit can be taken for taxes paid on capital goods only as the assets depreciate, whereas under the consumption type tax, credit is allowed for the total tax immediately. Table 4 also shows calculations of tax liabilities under the credit method. Liabilities are, of course, the same as those calculated under the subtraction method for each of the two types of VAT.

The second basic method of computing tax liabilities under the VAT, the addition method, takes a different approach. It recognizes that value added under the income concept equals the sum of factor payments and profits. Thus under the addition method the statutory rate is applied directly to value added, as under the subtraction method. But value added is calculated by adding together factor payments and profits. By its very nature the addition method is suitable only for the implementation of the income type VAT, and only the calculation for that type of tax is shown in Table 4.[19] Liabilities are, of course, the same as under the subtraction and credit methods.

One of the reasons for the popularity of the credit method VAT in Europe is the automatic production of documents that can be used in enforcment of the tax both up and down the line in the productive process. A firm's need to have proof of purchases or of tax payments made on purchases (under the subtraction and tax credit approaches, respectively) creates demands for receipts which provide information to the revenue agents about sales of the firm's suppliers. Or, viewed from the other end, receipts issued by a supplier contain information useful in the validation of the purchasing firm's claims of purchases made or taxes paid.[20] Information gained in this way is also potentially useful in enforcment of income and other taxes. These self-enforcing features may, however, be fairly unimportant in the U.S., where the level of taxpayer compliance is generally agreed to be higher than in Europe.

The administrative appeal of the addition method, which it shares with the subtraction method, is that most of the records it requires are internal to the firm. But whereas the firm's interest in understating sales and overstating purchases is countered by the opposite pressures of its customers and suppliers under the subtraction or tax credit approaches, under the addition method the desires of the firm and

---

[19] Theoretically a consumption type VAT could be implemented under the addition method, but only if profits were reduced by the amount of net investment.

[20] The subtraction method, described as the "accounts method" in National Economic Development Office, *Value Added Tax* (London: Her Majesty's Stationery Office, 1971), pp. 55-56, would be based upon firms' accounts rather than simply upon invoices. But the accounts would probably need to be substantially different from those now kept and firms would be put in an adversary position vis-à-vis their suppliers and customers, unlike the situation under the addition method.

those of the recipients of the factor payments it makes are likely to be in accord. That is, both benefit from the understatement of factor payments, if there is an income tax as well as a VAT. Moreover, there is little secondary benefit in the form of increased knowledge useful in income tax collection in this case.

The addition method is also markedly inferior to the subtraction and credit methods for other reasons to be noted below. This is especially true if American interest were to focus primarily upon the consumption type VAT, which was suggested before as likely. The choice between the subtraction and credit methods is less clear, as is demonstrated below. But on balance the credit method, which is universally used in Europe, seems preferable. It is primarily in terms of a credit method VAT that the discussion of sections 3 to 7 is framed.

D. Differential Rates. Although one of the advantages usually claimed for the VAT is the neutrality inherent in a uniform ad valorem rate, as noted below, there may be occasions in which rate differentials are either desirable or inevitable. Examples of desirable differentials would be final products or certain stages of production chosen for preferential tax treatment. Less desirable but inevitable differentials include cases in which, for political or administrative reasons, certain stages or products cannot easily be subjected to the otherwise general rate of tax and cases in which tax rates are altered temporarily for macroeconomic reasons. The implications of the various methods of calculating the tax under these conditions are spelled out here.

Differentials desired. If it is desired as a matter of social policy to tax certain *final products* at higher or lower rates than the generally prevailing rate, the goal can be achieved conveniently only under the tax credit method. A general and important characteristic of this approach is that only the rate applied at the last stage in the production-distribution process matters, since credit is received by the firm at this stage for all taxes it has paid on purchases. Thus if it were desired to exempt food for equity reasons or to encourage housing construction as a matter of national policy, exemptions from the VAT could be allowed for these items at the final stage. Credits (or refunds) would eliminate any burden imposed by the taxes previously paid on inputs into the exempt product at earlier stages. (Notice that only to the extent that it built houses would the construction industry be favored.)

Under both the subtraction and addition methods the tax rate prevailing at each stage is applied literally to the value added at that stage. Exemption or differential taxation of the final stage would therefore be of little consequence for products with relatively little value added at that stage, unless rebates could be provided for taxes previously incorporated in the prices of inputs. Thus differential taxation of final products would be difficult to achieve, and an unsuccessful attempt to achieve it by taxing only the final stage differentially would favor products, production processes, and firms with relatively large (or small, depending on the differential) fractions of value added occurring at the last stage. In short, differential treatment of final goods requires the tax credit approach.

On the other hand, if a given productive *activity* (for example, agriculture) is to be favored as a matter of public policy, the tax credit approach is conceptually inferior to the other two means of calculating tax liabilities. Precisely because the rate at the last stage is the only one that matters under this approach, the rates levied at previous stages are irrelevant and it is impossible to treat different activities differently.[21]

Conversely, either the addition or subtraction method theoretically provides differential treatment of activities quite easily. As noted above, both methods apply the tax rate for each stage directly to value added at that stage. As a practical matter, however, it would be difficult to apply differential rates to the various outputs of a given multiproduct firm under the subtraction method.[22] Thus the tax credit method allows differential taxation of products, but not of activities, and the other two approaches allow activities, but not products, to be taxed differentially.

---

[21] This is not quite true since credits can be granted for taxes "as if" paid, as has been done in Holland and Ireland; see "VAT in Europe," *The Economist*, March 25, 1972, p. 65. But such schemes are difficult to administer. Note in addition that there is considerable difference between a stage being exempted from the tax on value added and a stage being kept in the VAT system but taxed at a zero rate; the comments in the text apply only in the latter case. Complete exemption from the VAT system would amount to being treated like the household sector and could work a hardship on the firms involved. Thus, suppose that in the example in Table 4 the sales of firms at stage B were exempt from the 10 percent VAT. The stage B firms would pay the tax of $30 on purchases, but being outside the VAT system could claim no credit for those taxes. On the other hand, firms at stage C would pay the full $100 VAT on its sales, but have no credit, since its purchases had not been taxed. The net result of this break in the chain of tax credits is overtaxation equal to the tax paid on sales before the exempt stage, or $30 in this example.

[22] An arbitrary allocation of purchases to sales would be necessary, as it would not be practical to deduct purchases from the sales to which they relate strictly as inputs; see National Economic Development Office, *Value Added Tax*, pp. 15-18, for a short discussion of the points covered in this and the previous footnote.

Differentials not desired. Whereas some products and activities may be the object of consciously differential taxation, others may be taxed differentially solely as a matter of accident or administrative or political necessity, or because macroeconomic conditions require temporary changes in tax rates. By assumption, such differential taxation of products is unintended and undesirable.

Suppose, first, that because of the large number of firms involved it is decided not to extend the VAT to the retail level. The tax would discriminate against industries and processes in which value added occurs early and favor backward integration by retailers (but only if this would not subject the retail price to taxation). But there would be no particular differences in the distortions caused by the three methods of calculating tax liability. Under each approach all value added up to the retail stage would be subject to taxation. Similar comments apply if a particular final product could not be subjected to the VAT for some reason.

If it were some other stage (or activity) at which administrative difficulties or political pressures forced differential rates (or no tax), the situation would be different. Under the addition or subtraction method the value added at the hard-to-tax stage would be taxed relatively lightly, but collections at other stages would not be affected. Thus the favorable treatment of one stage would carry through to the end in the form of a reduced tax burden on goods passing through that stage. On the other hand, under the tax credit approach any difficulties of collection would theoretically be made up in subsequent stages. The differentially lower rates would be reflected in lower credits for taxes paid on purchases. Thus this kind of undesired differential would be more easily overcome if the tax credit approach were employed, so long as at least one taxable stage follows the differentially taxed stage. The more important risk is that complete exemption of one stage from the VAT would result in a break in the chain of credits, so that goods passing through that stage would actually be overtaxed by the amount of taxes collected before the break.[23]

---

[23] See footnote 21 above. A further unintended discrimination may result from variations in tax rates resulting from discretionary manipulation of the VAT rate for stabilization purposes. As suggested previously, under both the addition and subtraction methods the tax rate applied to value added occurring during a given period would be subjected to the tax rate prevailing then. Under the tax credit approach all value added would be subjected to the rate prevailing at the time of final sale. Which approach would be preferable from a stability viewpoint is a largely unexplored question.

E. **Border Tax Adjustments.** Thus far little has been said of the way value added taxation affects international trade or of border tax adjustments, perhaps (whether rightly or wrongly) the most famous aspect of the administration of the tax. This section examines this important administrative question. How the VAT would affect international trade is the subject of section 4E.

Commodity taxes on products entering international trade can be levied on either of two bases. If the product is taxed where produced, and not where consumed, the tax is an origin-principle tax, or a tax on production. If, on the other hand, the product is taxed where it is consumed, but not where it is produced, we have a destination-principle tax, or a tax on consumption. A retail sales tax is an almost perfect example of a destination-principle tax.[24] Goods (and ideally services) are taxed at their point of sale to ultimate consumers, whether they are produced domestically or imported. Thus the tax is levied only upon consumption, or at the point of destination. On the other hand, a tax on value added levied without border tax adjustments (described below) would be levied on production, or in the nation of origin. For example, referring to Table 1, suppose that the production at stage A took place in one country and that the production at stages B and C took place after importation into another country. Value added on production of $300 occurs in the first country and on production of $700 in the second. Thus each nation could levy its own tax on the production occurring within its borders if it followed the origin principle.[25]

But what if we wished to tax commodities under the VAT where consumed, and only there? In that case we would need to exempt exports from tax and rebate any tax already paid on them, so that they would enter world trade unencumbered by taxes levied in their nation(s) of origin. Similarly, it would be necessary to levy a tax on imports to equalize tax burdens vis-à-vis domestically produced goods. The exemption from, and rebate of, taxes on exports and the com-

---

[24] Conceptually, the retail sales tax is a perfect example. In fact, retail sales taxes are often levied on capital and intermediate goods, and thus included in the price of exports. Moreover, many consumer durables bought in low-tax states by residents of high-tax states to minimize taxes are subjected to the retail sales tax in the state where they are purchased and not to use taxes in the state of residence of the consumers.

[25] Given the virtual certainty that the origin principle would not be considered seriously in the United States, there is no purpose in going into detail in its administration. We might note, however, that it is probably best implemented using the addition or subtraction methods for an income type VAT. An origin-principle tax using the credit method is practically impossible. For a further discussion, see Shoup, *Public Finance*, pp. 262-64.

pensating import duty levied to convert an otherwise origin-principle VAT to a destination-principle are called border tax adjustments (BTA).

An example based upon Table 1 will help to clarify the function and operation of border tax adjustments. Assume as before that stage A occurs in one country and stages B and C occur in another. Then we would want the goods to leave the first country free of tax and to be taxed upon entry into the second, in order that taxation would be based on the country of destination. Tax-free exportation is easily achieved in this one stage example; simply exempting exports from the VAT would suffice. If, however (and contrary to the example), the tax had already been paid at an earlier stage, it would be necessary to rebate it. This is easily achieved under the credit method. The exporter would claim credit for any taxes paid on inputs, including those used to produce exports, against his liability for taxes on domestic sales. (Export sales would be exempt.) Or, if his total credit for taxes paid on inputs exceeded his gross tax liability on domestic sales, he would receive a refund of the credit from the treasury.[26] He would pay the tax on purchases, but be allowed credit or refund for his tax payments, so that on balance exports would occur tax-free. The subtraction method would operate in a similar way. Inputs would be subtracted from domestic sales and the VAT paid on the difference. If that figure were negative, a refund would be due. On the other hand, it would be difficult to administer border tax adjustments under the addition method.

Equalizing the tax burden between imports and domestically produced goods can be achieved simply by taxing the goods at the point of importation, under any of the three methods of calculating tax liabilities. But under the credit method it is not even necessary to tax imports directly, except when they are made by ultimate consumers. So long as the goods pass through at least one taxed transaction after being imported the value added occurring before importation will be taxed. Since there would be no credit for previously paid taxes, the firm making the first taxed sale subsequent to importation would be liable for the tax on the entire value of the goods. In fact, any understatement of value at the time of import would be corrected on subsequent sale under the credit method. Theoretically the same result could be effected under the subtraction

---

[26] All the European countries refund excess credits immediately to the extent that they arise from exports. On the other hand, France applies a "buffer rule" to credits arising from other sources. Under this rule excess credits resulting from investment can only be accumulated and applied to subsequent tax liabilities.

method, but administration would, in reality, probably be much more difficult. Finally, under the addition method any value that was not taxed at import would escape completely, due to the mechanics of the method. Again, the credit method seems administratively superior to the addition and subtraction methods.

It is worth returning briefly to the cascade type turnover tax considered in section 2A above. Suppose that the goods produced in the three industries considered in the example of Table 3 were exported at stage C, instead of being sold to consumers. Ideally the exports would occur tax-free under the destination principle, as noted above. And for industry II tax-free export would be achieved simply by exempting exports from the turnover tax. But for industries in which some value added had occurred at earlier stages, export rebates would be virtually impossible to implement accurately, especially if goods had passed through several stages. This is easily seen by noting that (besides the direct exemption of exports from the tax) rebate of taxes would need to be made at different rates on the value of input purchases in industries I and III. In industry I rebate of $50 of taxes on purchases of $700, or a rate of about 7 percent, would be required, whereas in industry III purchases of $900 would have been taxed a total of $85, or almost 9½ percent. There is no way that rebates could be given automatically and accurately, as under the VAT. Rebates would of necessity be based on averages, which means that discrimination would occur between industries, methods of production, and firms. This is one of the primary disadvantages of the cascade tax.

The situation is, of course, the same on the import side. Ideally, imports would be taxed at the same ad valorem rate as domestic goods at the same stage of production. But we see from Table 3 that by stage C domestic output in the three industries is being taxed in total at rates varying from 5 to 13.5 percent. There is no one rate at which to tax imports.[27]

It is worth repeating at this point that unlike the cascade type turnover tax, the retail sales tax (in its pure form) achieves destination-principle taxation of internationally traded goods automatically.

[27] Because of the necessity of using averages, border tax adjustments were not exact under the turnover taxes, as they are under the VAT, and it was generally agreed that Germany, in particular, undercompensated under the old cascade tax. Thus in shifting to the VAT and its perfect equalization, Germany gained a trade advantage, though it was doing something that was perfectly legitimate under the rules of the General Agreement on Tariffs and Trade (GATT). To avoid adverse effects on international monetary stability, Germany initially allowed BTA at only half the rate of the domestic VAT, moving to full BTA at the time of the subsequent revaluation of the mark.

Exports occur tax-free since all sales besides domestic sales to ultimate consumers are exempt. Similarly, imports and domestically produced goods are treated identically since the tax is applied at a given rate to all sales to consumers, regardless of the nation of origin of the taxed commodity. That this is true is especially important since the existence of border tax adjustments under the VAT has drawn so much attention. Those border tax adjustments are necessary solely to provide under the VAT the destination-principle taxation that occurs naturally under the retail sales tax. A VAT with border tax adjustments therefore constitutes no more of a trade advantage than would a retail sales tax since in their pure forms the two taxes are economically equivalent.

F. VAT vs. Retail Sales Tax. Although in theory the VAT and the retail sales tax are economically equivalent, in actuality the two taxes are likely to be different for administrative reasons, quite aside from differences in their tax bases that result from policy decisions. These differences, and the resulting administrative advantages and disadvantages, are reviewed in this section. For the sake of holding the discussion to manageable proportions, the retail sales tax is compared only to the consumption type VAT imposed under the credit method, the most likely candidate for adoption in the United States.[28]

Probably the primary advantage of the value added tax relative to the retail sales tax (RST) involves the treatment of services and capital goods. Under a consumption type VAT, credit is allowed for taxes on all inputs, whether of capital, services, or intermediate goods. Thus only consumer goods and services are taxed under the VAT.[29]

Under the RST the solution is not so simple. Since some goods (and services) can be employed either as productive inputs or as

---

[28] This discussion draws heavily upon Carl S. Shoup, "Experience with Value-Added Tax in Denmark, and Prospects in Sweden," *Finanzarchiv*, March 1969, pp. 236-52 and "Factors Bearing on an Assumed Choice between a Federal Retail Sales Tax and a Federal Value-Added Tax," mimeographed, 1970; and John F. Due, "The Case for Use of the Retail Form of Sales Tax in Preference to the Value Added Tax," mimeographed, 1970. Among minor problems not discussed here are the larger number of firms reached by the VAT, the self-policing features of the VAT, the VAT's unfamiliarity in the U.S., the increased book-keeping burden on small firms under the VAT, etc. These are all self-explanatory and need only be mentioned here.

[29] There is, of course, a problem of credit taken for taxes on goods purchased for business use but converted to consumption by the owner of the business. This problem seems to be more or less comparable for the two taxes, though under VAT a falsified tax return is required if this result is to be achieved. Shoup has emphasized this point in "Experience with the Value-Added Tax in Denmark."

consumer goods, a way must be found to exempt them from tax when purchased for business use. Otherwise discrimination will occur between domestically produced goods, and accurate border tax adjustments will be impossible because of taxes paid on inputs at earlier stages and incorporated in prices. One approach is to exempt from tax the sales of specific items used largely for business purposes. This is clearly unsatisfactory since for many products this kind of distinction is untenable; steam turbines can be exempted from the tax with little danger of an error in the classification, but hammers and shovels cannot be.[30]

A second approach is to exempt all purchases by registered firms on the assumption that purchases by nonregistered customers will be made almost entirely by consumers. The obvious problem is, of course, guaranteeing both that production inputs are largely free of tax and that not too much otherwise taxable output intended for the private use of the firm's owner passes through tax-exempt transactions. Moreover, businessmen object to the necessity of dividing sales into taxable and exempt categories and accounting for them separately. Authorities differ as to the relative effectiveness of the RST and VAT in handling purchases of business firms, including services and capital goods.[31]

It was noted in section 2D that complete exemption of any stage of the productive process (besides the last) from paying a credit-method VAT on its sales could pose problems. The problem is not that the final output would be undertaxed since the tax would be made up at later stages; it is, rather, that being exempt from tax the firms in the exempt sector might not be allowed credit for taxes paid on their purchases. If the chain of credits were broken, the product would be overtaxed rather than undertaxed. To that extent the VAT would differ from the retail sales tax. This problem may be important, for example, for professional services, which often are outside the VAT system. The importance of this source of double

---

[30] A further problem, not inherent in retail sales taxation, is that in actual practice effort is not usually made to exempt all purchases of business firms from the RST. States adopt rules providing exemption only for goods that are to become "component parts" of final products or that are for "direct use" in the production process. If the retail sales tax is to be a consumption tax, exemption should be allowed for *all* purchases by business firms.

[31] See Shoup, "Choice between Retail Sales Tax and Value-Added Tax," and Due, "Case for Retail Sales Tax." Due notes that it should be possible to implement a hybrid tax that, while essentially a retail sales tax, would allow business firms to buy inputs tax-free, subject to audit, or receive credit for taxes paid on inputs.

taxation depends upon the level of tax rates and the importance of purchased inputs.[32]

Finally, the author has argued at length elsewhere that from the standpoint of intergovernmental relations the federal government should adopt a retail sales tax, rather than a credit type VAT, if it is to adopt either.[33] This contention rests upon the ease of piggy-backing state and local levies on a federal retail sales tax and the difficulty of doing so under a federal VAT.[34] It might be objected that federal use of a retail sales tax would be considered an intrusion into a field of taxation heretofore reserved for the exclusive use of state (and more recently local) governments. But this argument is based more on illusion than on reality, even if the shaky argument that general consumption taxation should be left to the states and localities is granted. Retail sales taxes and value added taxes of the consumption type are basically equivalent, as noted above. Thus a federal retail sales tax would involve no more intrusion into the general consumption tax field than would a VAT.

3. The Tax Base: Practice

The above discussion implies that the VAT would apply at uniform rates to all goods and services. If it did, the tax base, at 1970 income levels, would be $615.8 billion, the total of consumption expenditures in that year (see Table 5). Thus a 3 percent levy would yield almost $20 billion and a 5 percent tax would produce over $30 billion of revenue.

In fact, however, the tax base and revenues are likely to be considerably less than that, for a number of reasons. One of the administratively difficult areas of application of a tax on value added involves owner-occupied housing.[35] Ideally, the VAT would be

---

[32] Shoup has noted in "Experience with the Value-Added Tax in Denmark," p. 243, that professionals may be given the option of entering the VAT system.

[33] Charles E. McLure, Jr., "TVA and Fiscal Federalism," *Proceedings of the 1971 Conference of the National Tax Association*, pp. 279-91. This point is also mentioned by Due, "Case for Retail Sales Tax."

[34] The necessity of a uniform definition of taxable sales in all states would be a distinct plus for such a piggyback approach, provided the federal definition were written with care to achieve accurate taxation of only sales to ultimate consumers. Many state retail sales taxes now impose heavy burdens on business inputs, but exempt services. Moreover, piggybacking would probably eliminate the need for use taxes, one of the most troublesome features of existing state retail sales taxes.

[35] Conceptually there is no similar problem with regard to rental housing, which could be handled like any other business venture. However, small amounts of value added tax would need to be collected from a large number of landlords with no other taxable receipts.

applied to sales of new houses and owner occupants would be charged the tax on the gross value of imputed rental income, as though they were renting the housing to themselves. Correspondingly, owners of houses would be allowed credit for taxes paid on houses at the time of their purchase and on repairs, improvements, etc.[36] On balance, owner-occupied housing would be taxed on a consumption basis like rental housing and other goods and services. But this ideal solution involves the imputation of rental income to owner occupants, a problem that for years has stymied proposals to include this element of income in taxable income. There would seem to be little chance that this approach would be implemented. Thus a deduction from the $615.8 billion potential tax base mentioned above is almost certain.

A compromise solution would be to treat owner-occupied housing as a consumption item, rather than as a capital good, and tax it at the time of purchase, with no subsequent tax credit or imputation of rental income. Taxing owner-occupied housing in this way, and rental housing as any other business, would result in a reduction of the tax base by $41.7 billion to $574.1 billion (see Table 5). Certainly this approach would be administratively feasible, and presumably it would be applied to consumer durables such as automobiles and household appliances. But it would discriminate against owner-occupied housing relative to rental housing and other goods and services, and it would favor present homeowners relative to new homeowners.[37] This discrimination would help to offset the favorable income tax treatment of housing that currently exists, but it is unlikely to be politically acceptable, since a 5 percent VAT would add $1,000 directly to the price of a $20,000 home.[38]

Since owner-occupied housing is not likely to be taxed either immediately as a consumer good or over time by imputation, it might not be taxed at all. If not, then rents on rental residences should not be taxed since to tax them would accentuate the preferential treatment accorded owner-occupied housing under the income tax. Complete exemption of housing would serve to offset the high sales tax

---

[36] Since immediate credit for taxes on house purchases would far exceed gross liabilities for taxes on imputed rental income, carry-over of credits or refunds would be necessary, as is true in other instances of large net investment.

[37] A true consumption type VAT would treat tenants and existing and future homeowners equally, by taxing the imputed rental value of all owner-occupied housing at the same rate that would apply to house rents.

[38] For a recent analysis of the income tax advantages of investment in owner-occupied housing, see Henry Aaron, "Income Taxes and Housing," *American Economic Review*, December 1970, pp. 789-806.

equivalents of existing property taxes, and might accord with social priorities in any case.[39] If housing were removed from the tax base entirely, the latter would fall below total personal consumption expenditures by $91.2 billion, to $524.6 billion, at 1970 income levels.

Next, there are other items of consumption that are intrinsically difficult to tax under any consumption tax. Perhaps the most obvious examples are domestic services and expenditures abroad by Americans. Much more important are the services of financial intermediaries, including insurance companies. The difficulties involved in the taxation of financial institutions can be seen in the following quotation from Shoup:

> *Banks, insurance companies, and other financial institutions are exempt* from the Danish value-added tax simply, it is said, because of the difficulty of applying to them the concepts of total sales and taxable purchases. Interest as such is of course not subject to the consumption-type of value-added tax; but "interest" as a payment for services rendered by a bank free of direct charge (e.g. free check books and checking services) is in principle taxable. Such a service would have to be given an imputed value, and divided into that part rendered to business firms and that part rendered to households, so that the tax levied on the service rendered to firms could be taken by those firms as a credit against the tax on their own sales. An approximate solution would be to tax the financial institution on its payroll, and divide this tax between the two groups of customers on some relevant basis, perhaps number of checks handled, but Denmark has been unwilling to attempt this or any other rough substitute. Meanwhile the exclusion of these financial institutions from the value-added tax system has caused some difficulty. The banks have set up a cooperative electronic data processing institute to perform services for the smaller banks, but these services are held taxable, and the small banks get no tax credit, being themselves exempt. The larger banks perform their own EDP services, and pay no tax on that value added.[40]

---

[39] Dick Netzer in *Economics of the Property Tax* (Washington, D. C.: Brookings Institution, 1966), pp. 29-31, 106, estimates that property taxes now represent the equivalent of about a 20-25 percent sales tax on housing.

[40] Shoup, "Experience with the Value-Added Tax in Denmark," p. 245. It should be noted that a problem exists only for services provided directly to households. The value of services provided to the business sector would be included in their value added under the credit method. In fact in this case the more important problem would be overtaxation because of breaking the chain of tax credits, as noted above.

Deduction of the $38.4 billion involved in these three items, plus a number of minor items, after the complete exemption of housing, would reduce the likely tax base (at 1970 levels) to $486.2 billion (see Table 5).[41]

Third, some items included in the total for personal consumption expenditures are likely to be excluded from the tax base as a matter of social policy. It is almost inconceivable that the tax would be applied to private education and research and to religious and welfare activities. Moreover, medical care expenses, funeral expenses, and perhaps legal expenses could very well also be exempt as a matter of social policy.[42] Deductions for these items, totaling $74.4 billion, would reduce the tax base further to $411.8 billion.

Moreover, several kinds of utilities might be exempt from the tax, especially as they are often provided by municipal governments. In addition, taxing them might be thought to add too much to the regressivity of the tax. Examples would be household utilities and purchased local transportation. Deductions for these items are placed at $26.8 billion, leaving a tax base of $385.0 billion at 1970 income

---

[41] It may be worthwhile to explain the construction of Table 5. The first column simply shows the composition of personal consumption expenditures in 1970. Column 2 provides an illustration of the effect of treating owner-occupied housing as a consumer durable item. Since this treatment is unlikely to materialize, this column is included for comparison only. Column 3 shows the effects of eliminating from the tax base housing and other items that for administrative reasons are hard to tax. From the total of consumption expenditures of $615.8 billion given in column 1 the sum of these items, $129.6 billion, is subtracted, leaving $486.2 billion. In the remainder of the columns exemptions that might be made as a matter of social policy, for utilities, and for food are treated analogously. Each of these potential exemptions is subtracted from a tax base already reduced by the amounts shown in previous columns (except column 2). Thus the $100.5 billion for food in column 6 is subtracted from the tax base of $385.0 billion shown in column 5; the latter figure reflects exemption for housing, "socially justified" exemptions, and exemption for utilities.

[42] Organizations in these fields could be kept in the system, but taxed at a zero rate. Thus they would receive credit for any taxes paid on purchases. Similar treatment could be accorded state and local governments. This approach is far superior to attempting to exempt sales to these organizations and governments from the tax. The assumption that nonprofit organizations, governments, and firms in sectors exempted from the VAT would be granted refunds for taxes paid on all purchases may not be totally realistic, but it appears to be a reasonable working hypothesis for the present analysis. It allows us to employ consumption figures from the national income accounts in estimating the tax base. In his testimony before the Joint Economic Committee on March 22, 1972, Norman Ture makes the interesting point that the VAT would not truly be a consumption-based tax unless expenditures on investment in human capital, as well as physical capital, were exempt. This provides a strong rationale for the exemption of much of both educational and medical expenses. (One could carry this reasoning to the ridiculous extreme by applying it to the activities of religious organizations—treating them as *really* long-term investment!)

Table 5
PERSONAL CONSUMPTION EXPENDITURES AND ADJUSTMENTS FOR POTENTIAL EXEMPTIONS FROM BASE, 1970 LEVELS
($ in billions)

| Type of Product | Total Personal Consumption (1) | Exclusion of Imputed Rent and Taxation of Purchase Price of Owner-occupied Homes[a] (2) | Adjustments for Housing Exemption and Other Administrative Exemptions[a] | | | |
| | | | Adjustment for Socially Justified Exemptions | | Adjustment for Exemption of Utilities, etc. | |
			With no other adjustments (3)	No other adjustments (4)	No other adjustments (5)	Adjustment for food (6)
Food and tobacco	$142.9	—	−2.8[b]	—	—	−100.5[l]
Clothing, accessories, and jewelry	62.3	—	−0.2[c]	—	—	—
Personal care	10.1	—	—	—	—	—
Housing	91.2	−41.7	−91.2	—	—	—
Household operations	85.6	—	−4.7[d]	—	−23.7[i]	—
Medical care expenses	47.3	—	—	−47.3	—	—
Personal business	35.5	—	−23.2[e]	−6.0[g]	—	—
Transportation	77.9	—	—	−1.9[h]	−2.1[j]	—
Recreation	39.0	—	—	—	−1.0[k]	—
Public education and research	10.4	—	—	−10.4	—	—

Religious and welfare activities	8.8	—	—	-8.8	—	—
Foreign travel and other, net	4.8	-41.7	-7.5f	—	—	—
Total	615.8	-41.7	-129.6	-74.4	-26.8	-100.5
Previously detailed adjustments	—	—	—	-129.6	-204.0	-230.8
Total adjustments	—	-41.7	-129.6	-204.0	-230.8	-331.3
Tax base after adjustments	—	574.1	486.2	411.8	385.0	284.5
Tax base as percent of total personal consumption expenditures	—	93.2%	79.0%	66.9%	62.5%	46.2%

a Treatment of housing as consumption expenditure included for comparison only. Further calculations assume complete exemption of housing.

b Food furnished government and military employees and food produced and consumed on farms.

c Standard clothing issued to military personnel.

d Domestic service.

e Services furnished without payment by financial institutions, including expense of handling life insurance.

f Foreign travel by U.S. residents and expenditures abroad by U.S. government personnel.

g Legal services and funeral and burial expenses.

h Legitimate theaters and opera, and entertainments of nonprofit institutions; clubs and fraternal organizations except insurance.

i Household utilities (except telephone and telegraph).

j Bridge, tunnel, ferry and road tolls; street and electric railway and local bus.

k Pari-mutuel net receipts.

l Food purchased for off-premise consumption.

Source: Derived from U.S. Department of Commerce, *Survey of Current Business,* July 1971, part 1, tables 2.5 and 7.3.

levels. Finally, the $100.5 billion worth of food purchased for off-premise consumption might very well be exempted, also in an effort to reduce the regressivity of the tax.[43] In such a case the tax base would be but $284.5 billion, or 46 percent of personal consumption expenditures.

Table 5 indicates the size of the tax base under various combinations of exemptions. It is almost certain that in practice the base (at 1970 levels of consumption) would not be much larger than $500 billion, and it might be as small as $300 billion. In the former case a 3 percent tax would yield $15 billion and a 5 percent tax $25 billion. But in the latter case those two rates would provide revenue of only $9 billion and $15 billion. To place these estimates in perspective, we can note that in 1970 the corporation income tax yielded $32.8 billion (national income accounts basis).

4. Economic Effects

In this section we examine the economic effects of substituting a consumption type tax on value added for part of the corporation income tax. In particular, we discuss how this tax substitution would affect the neutrality of the tax system, the rates of saving, investment, and economic growth, the success of efforts to use tax policy to stabilize the economy, and the nation's balance of payments. Effects upon the distribution of income are considered in the next section.

One might reasonably ask why cast the entire discussion of this study in terms of substituting VAT for part of the corporation income tax (or other taxes), especially when the VAT could be considered as a new source of additional revenue. The answer is simple. Most obviously, virtually the entire discussion of VAT up to now has been precisely in terms of a replacement for part of the corporation income tax. But more important, the VAT cannot be considered in a vacuum, even if it is considered as a new source of revenue. There is almost always an alternative tax that could be used instead of the VAT as a source of additional revenue.[44] Thus it makes sense to compare the

---

[43] It is argued below that a superior approach to the alleviation of regressive taxation would be the allowance of refundable credits against personal income taxes of a given amount of value added taxes or a general program of low-income relief. The estimate presented here is made only for completeness, as there is a good chance that food would be exempted.

[44] Of course we might also consider forgoing the added expenditure, financing it through inflation, or using tight monetary policy to choke off enough private spending to prevent inflation in the face of increased federal outlays. Comparison of VAT with these alternatives would take us far beyond the scope of this study.

VAT with alternative taxes that could be imposed or raised. One such alternative form of increased federal financing is an increase in the corporation income tax. Other obvious alternatives, increases in the payroll and personal income taxes, are considered briefly in section 6 below. The possibility of using revenues from a federal tax on value added to replace revenues from the local school property tax is considered even more summarily in section 7. A federal retail sales tax would, of course, have about the same economic and distributional effects as a VAT.

A. **Digression on Incidence.** Almost any careful discussion of substituting a value added tax for the corporation income tax quickly digresses into a discussion of the incidence of the two taxes, since virtually all of the effects of the substitution depend crucially upon that question.[45] (Most obviously, the distributional implications of such a tax substitution depend directly upon the incidence of the taxes, that is, upon who bears their burdens.) Thus in this section we digress momentarily at the beginning of our discussion of the economic and distributional effects of substituting a VAT for part of the corporation income tax (CIT) to consider explicitly the incidence of the two taxes. We cannot hope to settle the issue, but we can lay out the arguments. Then in what follows we can simply describe the implications of the tax substitution under various incidence assumptions, leaving to the reader the choice of the most relevant set of assumptions and implications. Those familiar with the literature on tax incidence can, of course, proceed directly to section 4B.

A consumption type VAT would almost certainly be borne by households roughly in proportion to consumption expenditures, though this view is not universally held.[46] Thus primary interest in

---

[45] For the purpose of the present discussion it is sufficient to think of tax incidence as a matter of how a given tax affects relative prices and of who bears the burden of the tax because of induced price changes. A conceptually "clean" definition of incidence would take us further afield than is justified. For further details on the methodology of incidence analysis, see Charles E. McLure, Jr., "Tax Incidence, Absolute Prices, and Macroeconomic Policy," *Quarterly Journal of Economics*, May 1970, pp. 254-67 and "The Theory of Tax Incidence with Imperfect Factor Mobility," *Finanzarchiv*, 1971, pp. 27-48.

[46] For a convincing argument to this effect, see Richard A. Musgrave, *Theory of Public Finance* (New York: McGraw-Hill Book Co., 1959), chapter 16. For two contrary views, see John F. Due, "Sales Taxes and the Consumer," *American Economic Review*, December 1963, pp. 1078-84, and the testimony by Norman Ture before the Joint Economic Committee on March 22, 1972 and Ture's essay in this volume.

this discussion focuses not upon the incidence of the VAT, but upon the incidence of the corporation income tax, which is far less certain.

Traditional theory holds that any tax on economic profits can only be borne by recipients of profit income, at least in the short run. According to that theory, prices in competitive industries equal the marginal costs of marginal firms that, having no profits, pay no tax. On the other hand, a firm that has a monopoly position in an industry maximizes profits by setting marginal costs equal to marginal revenue. In either case the existence of the profits tax, which affects neither marginal costs nor marginal revenue, has no effect on the determination of price. Thus, the reasoning goes, the tax is reflected in lower profits net of tax.[47]

But there is a multitude of reasons for believing that the corporation income tax is (at least partly) shifted, either to consumers or to labor.[48] First, corporate income for tax purposes includes the return to equity capital, and is not comprised solely of economic profits. Thus part of the tax does constitute an element of costs. Second, important portions of the corporate sector of the U.S. economy fit neither the perfect competition nor the pure monopoly mold, and oligopoly behavior is quite consistent with substantial shifting of the corporation tax. The tax, for example, may act as a signal for firms setting prices in a consciously parallel fashion, whether with or without an established price leader. Moreover, wage settlements with strong unions may result in labor sharing the burden of such a tax. Finally, corporate goals other than short-run profit maximization (e.g. avoidance of antitrust action, constrained sales maximization, or limit-pricing based on long-range profit maximization) may lead to shifting of the tax. Thus one can find strong theoretical support on both sides of the incidence argument.[49]

Unfortunately, empirical work done on this subject over the past decade leaves us very much in the dark. The pioneering work by Krzyzaniak and Musgrave found that the tax is completely shifted in manufacturing, a result not theoretically inconsistent with the oligop-

---

[47] Arnold C. Harberger has argued in "The Incidence of the Corporation Income Tax," *Journal of Political Economy*, June 1962, pp. 215-40, that the tax is borne by all recipients of capital income rather than only owners of corporate shares. This qualification is ignored in this discussion; however, it would not seriously alter any of the conclusions.

[48] For a summary of both the traditional theory and most of the important qualifications to it, see Musgrave, *Theory of Public Finance*, chapter 13.

[49] It is worth noting that businessmen seem almost universally to take for granted that the tax is shifted.

oly structure of much of manufacturing.[50] But this analysis has been subjected to considerable criticism, and it seems best to report only that the jury is still out on the question of the short-run incidence of the corporation income tax.[51]

Finally, it is not even clear whether the short- or long-run incidence of the tax is of more importance for policy purposes. For questions of economic neutrality, economic growth, stabilization policy, and the balance of payments, short-run effects are crucial. But where equity is concerned, it may be more useful to consider the incidence in a long-run context.[52]

Given the uncertainty about the answers to important questions of the incidence of the corporation income tax, it seems best, as noted above, to present the arguments of this and the next section under alternative assumptions. Even then, however, only two extreme views are considered—that the tax is borne by recipients of capital income and that it is shifted to consumers. Neither intermediate positions, such as 50 percent shifting, nor alternative shifting assumptions, such as partial shifting to labor, are considered. Intermediate shifting assumptions lead to intermediate results and need not be considered explicitly. Shifting to labor, while theoretically possible, does not have widespread professional support, and the added complication of including it in the analysis does not seem justified.

B. Allocational Efficiency (Neutrality). One of the chief advantages of the VAT, at least in its ideal form, is its allocational neutrality. Because the tax ideally would apply at equal rates to all goods and services (consumption variety) or to all factors incomes (income

[50] Marian Krzyzaniak and Richard A. Musgrave, *The Shifting of the Corporation Income Tax* (Baltimore: Johns Hopkins Press, 1963). It should be noted that this study offers no conclusions as to the methods or direction of shifting.

[51] Among the best critiques of the work by Krzyzaniak and Musgrave are Richard E. Slitor, "Corporate Tax Incidence: Economic Adjustments to Differentials under a Two-Tier Tax Structure," and Richard Goode, "Rates of Return, Income Shares, and Corporate Tax Incidence," both in Marian Krzyzaniak, ed., *Effects of Corporation Income Tax* (Detroit: Wayne State University Press, 1966), pp. 136-206 and pp. 207-46, respectively; Robert J. Gordon, "The Incidence of the Corporation Income Tax in U.S. Manufacturing, 1925-62," *American Economic Review*, September 1967, pp. 731-58; and John G. Cragg, Arnold C. Harberger, and Peter Mieszkowski, "Empirical Evidence on the Incidence of the Corporation Income Tax," *Journal of Political Economy*, December 1967, pp. 811-21. Replies and rejoinders appear in Krzyzaniak, ed., *Effects of Corporation Income Tax*, pp. 247-61, *American Economic Review*, December 1968, pp. 1358-67, and *Journal of Political Economy*, July-August, 1970, pp. 768-77.

[52] For a penetrating analysis of the proper time frame for the question of tax incidence and distributional equity, see Marian Krzyzaniak, "Differential Incidence of Taxes on Profits and on Factor Incomes," *Finanzarchiv*, 1971, pp. 464-88.

variety), it would distort no decision as to the way consumers spend their incomes or the way goods and services are produced.[53]

This neutrality may be difficult to comprehend in the abstract, but nonneutrality is easily understood when we examine the corporation income tax, even if we ignore the tax preferences in the existing law. Assume for the moment that the corporation income tax is not shifted. In such a case it discriminates against equity financing and in favor of loan finance. Moreover, since the tax is collected only on corporations, it creates a long-run tendency for underutilization of the corporate form of business organization.[54] And since some products can realistically be produced only if the corporate form is used, the tax also discriminates between products. Finally, since the tax is levied only on one type of return to capital, and not on labor, it discourages use of capital-intensive methods of production in the corporate sector. In the long run, capital investment is likely to be misallocated toward the products of the noncorporate sector. Thus the corporation income tax is distinctly nonneutral.[55]

This observation is true even if the tax is shifted to consumers or to workers. If it is shifted to consumers, it is a capricious sales tax on the products of the corporate sector, and diverts consumption choices away from those products.[56] If it is shifted to workers, it also discriminates in the long run against production in the corporate sector.

---

[53] It should be noted that in the strict sense only the consumption type VAT is truly neutral because the income type VAT taxes saving and therefore is not neutral between present and future consumption; see Musgrave, *Theory of Public Finance*, pp. 374-82. This distortion is ignored here, though it is discussed in a different context in sections 6A and 6B.

[54] This effect may, of course, be offset by the congruence of high-marginal tax rates and preferential treatment of long-term capital gains under the personal income tax.

[55] For an attempt to measure the welfare cost resulting from the nonneutrality of a non-shifted corporation income tax, see Arnold C. Harberger, "Efficiency Effects of Taxes on Income from Capital," in Krzyzaniak, ed., *Effects of Corporation Income Tax*, pp. 107-117. Harberger takes account of existing tax preferences in his analysis. A further waste that is difficult to quantify is the excessive expenses incurred in the corporate sector because the federal government shares in all costs as well as all profits.

[56] This nonneutrality is not solely in terms of *final* products of the corporate sector. The distortion occurs to the extent that the value added in the final product passes through the corporate sector. For an attempt to quantify the distortions introduced by the corporation tax by using input-output analysis to take account of the tax reflected in higher input prices, see Henry Aaron, "The Differential Price Effects of a Value-Added Tax," *National Tax Journal*, June 1968, pp. 162-75. This analysis suffers, as Aaron recognizes, from the use of a value added tax of the gross product type, rather than a VAT of the income or consumption variety.

Not surprisingly, the neutrality of the ideal value added tax is one of the strongest arguments in favor of substituting the VAT for part of the notoriously nonneutral corporation income tax.

However, comparing the conceptually pure VAT with the existing corporation income tax is hardly fair or instructive. As was noted in section 3, it is almost certain that any VAT that might be adopted will not apply at uniform rates to all consumption expenditures. Because they are difficult to tax, housing, the services of financial institutions, and household services will almost certainly be treated differently from all other uses of income. Moreover, items such as food, medical care, funeral and legal services, and utilities might be exempted from the tax as a matter of social policy or to prevent it from being overly regressive. Finally, preferential treatment will be accorded to any industry or pressure group politically potent enough to achieve it. The net result is likely to be a combination of tax base and rate structure that differs considerably from the ideal tax applied at a uniform rate to all value added. Estimates in Table 5 suggest that from one-fifth to over half of personal consumption might be excluded from the tax base. Thus it is far from clear that the VAT would, in practice, be much more neutral from an allocative standpoint than the corporation income tax.[57] This consideration suggests that exemptions for administrative reasons and exemptions intended to reduce the regressivity of the VAT should be kept to a minimum, especially since there are other more nearly neutral ways of reducing regressivity at the lower end of the income scale.

Finally, it should be noted that while substituting a VAT for part of the corporation income tax would eliminate the distortions inherent in the latter, it would do so only at the expense of creating an

---

[57] One potential basis for optimism is the possibility that demand for the items likely to be tax-exempt is relatively insensitive to price. If it is, the tax would not seriously distort consumer choices, even though it drove a nonuniform wedge between marginal costs of production and market prices. This is, of course, an empirical question. But it seems unlikely that demand would be price inelastic for as much as 20-50 percent of the entire market basket of consumers. This is especially true where housing and food are concerned. The quantity of housing and food consumption, whatever that may mean, may be more or less invariant to price, but the quality of housing and food consumed almost certainly is not. Thus exemption of these items would probably result in a greater shift toward expenditures on them than would occur under a truly general tax on value added or retail sales tax. Of course if housing were exempted as a matter of public policy, rather than simply for administrative reasons, we could not consistently term the resulting shift to higher housing expenditure the result of price distortion. Presumably the shift would be the objective of the exemption. Only if exemption results solely from administrative difficulties of taxing some items or efforts to lessen regressivity, rather than from a deliberate public policy decision to favor certain activities, can we legitimately say that it distorts choices.

important new distortion. To the extent that the corporation income tax were eliminated, corporate profits would be taxed only if distributed to shareholders. Thus there would be substantial pressures to retain a greater proportion of earnings and thereby convert profits taxable under the personal income tax as ordinary income, if distributed, into preferentially taxed long-term capital gains. This result would have important consequences for the rate of private saving, the incidence of the tax system, and income distribution. But of more relevance to the immediate discussion, it would constitute a substantial nonneutrality in favor of existing high-profit industries and firms and against low-profit and new undertakings. Firms with substantial profits would not need to stand the test of the marketplace in competing for funds. Double taxation of dividends, itself nonneutral, would have been traded for a substantial tax shelter in retained earnings. This result could be avoided most directly by integrating the corporate and personal income taxes, and less directly by increasing the taxation of long-term capital gains. Many opponents, and even some advocates of the VAT, argue that some such measure should accompany partial substitution of a VAT for the corporation income tax.[58]

C. Growth. One point usually made in favor of a consumption type VAT is that it would be more favorable to saving and economic growth than many of the present components of our tax system. Moreover, the argument goes, elimination of the corporation income tax would reduce the penalty this tax now imposes upon innovation, efficiency, and profitability, and thereby encourage investment and economic growth. In examining the validity of these contentions it will be convenient to address separately the two sides of the saving-investment question. It will be assumed in this section, of course, that the corporation tax is not shifted; if the tax were shifted, the tax substitution would have little effect on either saving or investment.

Private saving. There is little doubt that substitution of the VAT for part of an unshifted corporation income tax would increase savings.

---

[58] Integration of the two income taxes involves treating corporate profits as though they were earned by a partnership and allocating them to shareholders, to be included in the individual income tax returns of the latter, rather than imposing a separate income tax on corporations. Thus corporate profits would be taxed to the individual at his own marginal tax rate, whether distributed or retained. For the arguments for and against integration, see Musgrave, *Theory of Public Finance*, pp. 173-75 and Richard Goode, *The Corporation Income Tax* (New York: John Wiley and Sons, 1951). For examples of how complete and partial integration would work, see Joseph A. Pechman, *Federal Tax Policy*, rev. ed. (Washington, D. C.: Brookings Institution, 1971), pp. 140-47.

Approximately five-sixths of increases in net corporate profits flow into retained earnings.[59] Thus a reduction of, say, $10 billion in the corporation income tax would be reflected in an increase in retained earnings of over $8 billion, which would be supplemented by saving out of the increased dividends made possible by the tax reduction. To be offset against this sum would be a reduction in personal saving of something like $500 million resulting from imposition of the VAT. Thus on balance it would appear that an increase in total private saving of roughly $8 billion would be induced by the $10 billion tax substitution.[60]

Federal budget surplus. It is usual to think explicitly of how structural tax policy affects the level of private saving, but much less frequent to ask about the role of tax policy in determining the amount of saving achieved through the federal budget. Since total saving comprises both private saving and the public surplus, it is well to consider both components in our discussion.

Whereas the level of private saving is influenced largely by the *structure* of taxes, the amount of saving effected through budget policy (assuming a given amount of expenditures) depends primarily upon the *level* of taxes. Since in principle the level, as well as the structure, of taxation is a matter for policy determination, we have more latitude in setting fiscal policies to increase the nation's saving rate than merely adjusting the structure of the tax system, say by substituting VAT for part of the corporation income tax. We should be able to increase total saving by increasing taxes and the budget surplus, as well as by using structural tax policy to induce more private saving (assuming the maintenance of full employment).[61]

---

[59] William H. Oakland, "Automatic Stabilization and the Value-Added Tax," in Albert Ando, E. Cary Brown, and Ann F. Friedlaender, eds., *Studies in Economic Stabilization* (Washington, D. C.: Brookings Institution, 1965), pp. 41-60. Oakland's estimate comes from John Lintner, "Distribution of Incomes of Corporations Among Dividends, Retained Earnings, and Taxes," *American Economic Review*, May 1956, pp. 97-113 and John Brittain, "The Tax Structure and Corporate Dividend Policy," *American Economic Review*, May 1964, pp. 272-87.
[60] This estimate ignores the (slight) possibility that stockholders would reduce personal saving because of the increase in their personal wealth resulting from the increase in retained earnings. Moreover, no account is taken of the increased capital gains tax liabilities that would be paid on the higher stock prices due to increased corporate retention of earnings. Finally, it is worth noting that a considerable amount of this increased flow of retained equity capital would be locked in by the desire to avoid capital gains taxes. This probable result emphasizes the need to tighten the taxation of capital gains if VAT is to replace the corporation income tax.
[61] For an excellent statement of this proposition, see Richard A. Musgrave, "Growth with Equity," *American Economic Review*, May 1963, pp. 323-33.

Investment. It seems intuitively clear at first glance that reduction of the corporation income tax would result in more innovation and investment since the tax penalizes success in risk-taking. If this is true, then substitution of the VAT for the corporation tax would increase investment since the VAT is essentially neutral with regard to risk-taking and investment.

However, this view neglects the obverse side of the penalty on success represented by the federal sharing of gains from productive investment. By the same token that the federal government, via the corporation income tax, shares in profits from successful ventures, it assumes part of losses incurred in unsuccessful ventures, so long as adequate allowance is made for offsetting losses against gains from other undertakings or profits realized in other periods. Thus it is not clear on theoretical grounds whether on balance the corporation income tax should be expected to discourage investment and innovation or to encourage them. Theoretical analysis based upon notions of utility maximization and portfolio selection suggests, however, that for a given stock of funds encouragement of risk-taking may be the more likely outcome.[62] If so, investment out of a given flow of corporate saving is likely to be somewhat less under the VAT than under the corporation income tax, contrary to our original intuitive notion. Nonetheless, the far more important factor may be the much larger amounts of retained earnings likely to be generated under the VAT.

This conclusion is suggested strongly by empirical analysis linking investment to the cash flow of corporations. According to one set of estimates, as much as 80-90 percent of the increase in cash flow would eventually find its way directly into increased investment.[63] Thus an increase of as much as $8-9 billion might result from a $10 billion VAT-corporation tax substitution. Though the determinants of investment are the subject of considerable debate, and the effect might not be this great, it seems safe to predict a marked rise in investment. However, and this is worth repeating, such would be the case only if the existing corporation income tax is not shifted.

---

[62] The path-breaking analysis of this problem was by Evsey D. Domar and Richard A. Musgrave, "Proportional Income Taxation and Risk-taking," *Quarterly Journal of Economics*, May 1944, pp. 387-422. It has been given increasing rigor and sophistication in James Tobin, "Liquidity Preference as Behavior Towards Risk," *Review of Economic Studies*, February 1958, pp. 65-87 and Joseph E. Stiglitz, "The Effects of Income, Wealth, and Capital Gains Taxation on Risk Taking," *Quarterly Journal of Economics*, May 1969, pp. 263-83.

[63] See Charles W. Bischoff, "Business Investment in the 1970s: A Comparison of Models," *Brookings Papers on Economic Activity*, 1971(1), pp. 13-58, especially p. 47.

Summary. Substitution of VAT for part of the corporation income tax would increase private savings substantially—perhaps by as much as 80 percent of the amount of the tax change—if the latter tax is not shifted. (If the corporation tax is shifted, little change would result from the tax substitution.) Thus, it should be conducive to a higher rate of economic growth, provided the added saving flows into investment rather than simply acting as a drag on the economy and causing unemployment. The actual outcome depends itself upon budget policy. It seems reasonable to assume, however, that the bulk of the increased cash flow resulting from the tax substitution would flow into investment, raising the efficiency and the rate of growth of the economy.

Of course, budget policy plays a role on both sides of the saving-investment equation. Private saving can be supplemented by an increased budget surplus (or reduced deficit). It might appear that saving from this source would be largely sterile if corporations prefer strongly to invest internal funds rather than to go to capital markets. But budget surpluses and debt reduction could supply funds for residential construction. The nature of the government tax and monetary policies necessary to assure that result deserves further research, but to pursue the question further here would take us too far afield. Rather, we turn now to a more general discussion of the role of the value added and corporation income taxes in economic stabilization.

D. Stabilization. The impact of the hypothesized tax substitution upon efforts to stabilize the economy along a target path of full employment and price stability can be discussed under three subtopics: the initial effect upon the price level, the relative effectiveness of the VAT and the corporation income tax as automatic stabilizers, and the usefulness of variations in the rates of the two taxes as instruments of discretionary fiscal policy.

Initial effect on prices. Prices would probably rise by the amount of the VAT upon its substitution for the corporation income tax.[64] Under traditional shifting assumptions this is surely so; the VAT would raise prices, but the lowering of corporate tax rates would not result in offsetting reductions in prices. Only if, contrary to traditional assumptions, the corporate tax is shifted, would we expect the

---

[64] It is, of course, conceivable that the substitution could result in prices rising by even more than the percentage amount of the value added tax. This would be especially true if the initial price increase resulting from the substitution were to induce wage increases via escalator clauses in collective bargaining agreements. The likely extent of this potential phenomenon is unknown.

substitution not to result in higher prices; one shifted tax would replace another. But even if the corporation tax is shifted, it might not be automatically "unshifted" when reduced.[65] If not, higher prices would almost certainly result from the tax substitution. And even if unshifting in the sense of realignment of relative prices were to occur, it might be in the context of a general rise in prices. Thus it seems reasonable to believe that the tax substitution would result in a rise in the price level.[66]

Automatic stability. The effectiveness of various taxes as automatic stabilizers depends upon how tax revenues respond to cyclical variations in the value of national output and the effects that changes in revenues have upon private demand. Corporate profits, and therefore corporation income tax collections, respond strongly to changes in GNP. On the other hand, consumption fluctuates less than GNP, and so would receipts under a consumption type VAT yielding an equal amount of revenue at full employment.

This result is not enough, however, to guarantee that the corporation income tax would be the more effective built-in stabilizer. If the tax is borne out of profits, its increase during the upswing would restrain the net flow of internal funds and would probably hold back investment.[67] But investment might not respond with equal strength to reduced tax collections in the downswing because of the perception of inadequate investment opportunities. If not, the reduced VAT burden on consumers might be the better stimulus to private spending. Thus it is possible that the corporate tax might be more useful in automatically restraining demand in an upswing, but not much more useful than the VAT in cushioning a fall in demand. Of course, if the corporation tax is shifted, the more volatile corporate tax should be the better stabilizer.[68]

---

[65] It is worth noting that the pioneering work by Krzyzaniak and Musgrave that reports complete shifting also finds less than complete unshifting when the tax is removed; *Shifting of the Corporation Income Tax*, p. 58.

[66] The German experience of little rise in prices is not directly applicable here. In Germany a cascade type turnover tax was replaced, whereas the present discussion concerns replacing part of the corporation income tax. The German precedent would be instructive primarily if forward shifting and unshifting of the corporation income tax were assumed. It is also worth noting that the German substitution was preceded by a massive educational campaign aimed at forestalling price increases.

[67] In making statements of this kind it is necessary to assume that monetary policy and the level of autonomous expenditures would be the same in either case (except as fluctuations in tax receipts took money from the private sector).

[68] A menacing possibility is that a shifted corporation tax might raise prices during an upswing to a level that would not fall in a downswing. Presumably a flat-rate VAT would not have this effect.

Discretionary fiscal policy. There seems to be no reason to prefer either the VAT or the corporation income tax as tools of discretionary fiscal policy on the basis of administrative convenience.[69] Both could be changed quickly and easily. However, both theoretical analysis and empirical evidence from the 1968 surcharge suggest that temporary changes in the VAT would be more effective stabilizers than temporary changes in the corporation income tax of similar size. If corporate investment is based on long-range projections of profitability, it is unlikely to be affected much by temporary changes in corporate tax rates.[70] Moreover, if investment behavior is of the accelerator type, the most effective way to influence this behavior might be through consumer purchases. Only if investment is a fairly simple function of contemporaneous flows of internal funds, is it likely to respond strongly to temporary variations in the corporation income tax rate.

On the other hand, consumption might be affected quite strongly by a temporary change in the VAT rate. Not only would much of the tax be collected from persons with high marginal propensities to spend; perhaps more important, variations in the VAT rate, if known to be temporary, would induce postponement or acceleration of purchases, especially of durables. No similar intertemporal substitution effect characterizes changes in the corporation income tax.[71] Thus it seems that the VAT would rank ahead of the corporation income tax as an instrument of discretionary fiscal policy, if the corporation tax is not shifted. Of course, if instantaneous shifting of the corporation tax occurs, variations in that tax supposedly would be as effective in stabilizing output as would changes in the VAT. It is doubtful, however, that the shifting response is so perfect.

Summary. Substitution of the VAT for part of the (unshifted) corporation income tax would probably raise prices by about the

---

[69] It should be noted, however, that executive authority to change tax rates for countercyclical reasons within predetermined limits and subject to congressional veto, while desirable for the corporation income. tax, would be essential for the VAT. Otherwise anticipatory buying and postponement of purchases of durables during the discussion of rate changes would perversely affect efforts to stabilize the economy.

[70] Robert Eisner, "Fiscal and Monetary Policy Reconsidered," *American Economic Review*, December 1969, pp. 897-905 and "What Went Wrong," *Journal of Political Economy*, May-June 1971, pp. 629-41. For four comments plus a reply by Eisner, see *American Economic Review*, June 1971, pp. 444-61.

[71] The nearest equivalent under the corporation income tax is the variation in the investment tax credit for stabilization purposes since 1966. Being a tax credit based on the spending of funds, it can have strong intertemporal substitution effects.

amount of the tax. But once enacted, the VAT would probably be a more useful tool of discretionary fiscal policy. On the other hand, the corporation income tax would probably be the more effective built-in stabilizer, especially in the upswing.

E. International Aspects. The value added tax first drew significant attention in the United States when it was recognized that border tax adjustments are allowed under the VAT for products entering international trade. If was felt in some quarters that U.S. reliance on the corporation income tax, for which no border tax adjustments are allowed, together with European conversion to value added taxes, placed American producers at a competitive disadvantage in international markets and was therefore deleterious to the U.S. balance of payments.[72] Moreover, the argument went, the United States could improve its balance of payments by substituting a value added tax for part of the corporation income tax.

There are several separate points in this line of argument that are often confused. First, there is a substantial difference between arguing that the U.S. balance-of-payments position could be improved by substituting a VAT for part of the corporation income tax and arguing that U.S. reliance upon the corporate income tax is in some way disadvantageous to U.S. producers in world markets. The validity of the first contention, which is discussed in detail in the paragraph immediately following, depends upon how the imposition of the VAT and the removal of the CIT would affect prices of internationally traded goods. What the second contention involves is not always made clear, but in most statements favoring the VAT it seems to be assumed that the two arguments are essentially equivalent. To the author this seems to be erroneous. He has argued elsewhere that since the relative reliance of European countries and the U.S. upon direct and indirect taxes has not changed appreciably in the implied direction since the early 1950s, it is more sensible to look to inappropriate exchange rates and differential rates of inflation in the various coun-

---

[72] Among the strong statements of this proposition are Richard W. Lindholm, "National Tax Systems and International Balance of Payments," and Milton Leontiades, "The Logic of Border Taxes," *National Tax Journal*, June 1966, pp. 163-72 and 173-83, respectively.

We have discussed in section 2E the implementation of border tax adjustments for a tax on value added and the way BTA converts an origin-principle tax into a destination-principle tax. The important point in the present context is that under the General Agreement on Tariffs and Trade (GATT) border tax adjustments are allowed for indirect taxes, but not for direct taxes. Thus the corporation income tax, being considered a direct tax, cannot be rebated on exports or levied on imports, as can the VAT, an indirect tax.

tries as the cause of imbalance in the international payments position of the U.S. than to blame that imbalance upon the relative tax structures in the U.S. and its trading partners. [73] This position implies, of course, that the December 1971 realignment of exchange rates should tend to silence complaints about the unfair tax treatment of U.S. firms relative to those in other nations, though in fact it is unlikely to do so.

Turning now to the question of whether or not substituting a VAT for part of the corporation income tax would improve the U.S. balance of payments, several points must be made. First, and most fundamentally, the recent changes in exchange rates should, at least in principle, make the entire discussion—which was germane when the question first arose—passé. Since the U.S. was running chronic balance-of-payments deficits in defense of an unrealistic exchange rate, alternatives to devaluation that would improve the balance of trade, and hence the balance of payments, were worth considering. But since exchange rates have been realigned, trying to use tax policy to improve the trade balance still further makes little sense, provided the new exchange rates are equilibrium rates. Only if the dollar is still overvalued and could not be devalued further, might it make sense to try to achieve through tax policy the trade-equilibrating effects of a greater devaluation. But then the overvalued exchange rate, and not the tax structure, should be identified as the culprit in the piece.

Second, whether the tax substitution would in fact improve the balance of trade depends upon how it would affect domestic prices.[74] According to classical incidence assumptions, the VAT (with its compensating import levy) would be reflected in higher prices for all goods in U.S. markets, including imports, but would be rebated on exports, and therefore would leave the general price of exports unchanged. On the other hand, the traditional assumption is that in the short run

---

[73] Charles E. McLure, Jr., "Taxes and the Balance of Payments: Another Alternative Analysis," *National Tax Journal*, March 1968, pp. 57-69. It is noted there that there may be some truth to the contention that U.S. taxation under the corporation income tax is less neutral than European taxation under the VAT, and that this nonneutrality may be worth worrying about. But neutrality is not the stuff that arguments about balance-of-payments positions are made of, and it certainly is not what most advocates of the VAT seem to have had in mind in their discussion of the international aspects of the proposed tax substitution.

[74] This point is similar, but not strictly equivalent, to the question of whether the two taxes are shifted. Tax incidence and shifting depend upon effects upon *relative* prices, while the question at hand is a matter of the effects on absolute prices and price *levels*. Since as a practical matter shifting and unshifting can be expected to occur through changes in absolute prices of taxed products, this distinction is ignored in the text. For more detailed discussions of the issue, see Musgrave, *Theory of Public Finance*, chapter 15 and McLure, "Tax Incidence, Macroeconomic Policy, and Absolute Prices."

the corporation income tax is borne by shareholders, and that its removal would have no impact upon prices. Thus the tax substitution would increase the prices of both imports and U.S. goods by the amount of the tax, and therefore would have no effect upon imports. Similar results apply on the export side. The prices of U.S. exports would be unaffected by the tax substitution, so that no trade improvement would result.

Thus the argument that the tax substitution would improve the U.S. balance of trade involves challenging traditional incidence theory. If, contrary to the traditional assumptions, the corporation income tax is shifted to consumers, removing part of it would lower the prices of U.S. products, provided that the tax is unshifted when it is removed.[75] Combining this effect with the effects of imposing the VAT with its border tax adjustments, discussed above, results in a fall in the price of domestically produced goods relative to both imports in U.S. markets and foreign-produced goods in other countries. Thus imports should fall and exports should increase as a result of the tax substitution, provided the relevant elasticities of demand are large enough.[76] Of course, if the newly imposed VAT were not fully reflected in higher product prices, a trade improvement would result even under traditional assumptions of incidence of the corporation income tax, and if both exceptions to the traditional assumptions occurred, the favorable impact would be even greater. But given the downward inflexibility of wages, it seems unlikely that VAT would not raise prices. Thus it is unlikely that the tax substitution would improve the trade balance unless the corporation income tax is shifted (and would be unshifted when removed). Whether the corporation income tax is in fact shifted remains, as noted above, one of the unsolved riddles of economic analysis.

On balance, it is unlikely that the tax substitution would improve the balance of trade significantly. This is true if traditional incidence theory accurately describes the events that would follow the substitution. And even if the corporation income tax has been shifted,

---

[75] As noted above, the evidence from Krzyzaniak and Musgrave that the corporation tax is shifted does not also support unshifting.

[76] One estimate of the effect of such a substitution, assuming a given set of demand elasticities (imports: 1.0; exports: 2.0) is that a 5.65 percent VAT substituted for the corporation income tax would result in a $5.19 billion improvement in the U.S. balance of trade; see Maurice D. Weinrobe, "Corporate Taxes and the United States Balance of Trade," National Tax Journal, March 1971, pp. 79-86. Weinrobe also provides formulas for the calculation under alternative elasticity assumptions. The present author has also made estimates of balance-of-payments effects of substituting VAT for CIT in "The Economic Effects of Taxing Value Added."

as well it could have been, it probably would not quickly be unshifted. Unshifting might occur only as some prices rose less rapidly in the future than might have otherwise been the case. Thus on either account a substantial improvement in the trade balance seems unlikely.

An additional balance-of-payments effect of uncertain magnitude would result if reduction of the corporation income tax made the U.S. more attractive to investors. In such a case improvement on the capital account would occur. The uncertainty here derives from the complex effects of tax treatment of foreign investment income in various countries. Moreover, in large part the flows involved would represent an adjustment of stocks, and would be difficult to predict, as to both magnitude and duration, especially as they might be swamped by capital flows resulting from the recent devaluation of the dollar. On balance, some net inflow of capital would almost certainly result, but its size would be difficult to estimate.

F. Summary. The results of this section can be summarized briefly. Perhaps the first thing to notice is the unfortunate fact that nearly all conclusions about the economic effects of substituting the VAT for part of the corporation income tax depend upon the incidence of the latter tax, one of the great enigmas of economic analysis. The VAT is a neutral tax, if it is not riddled with exemptions, say to reduce its regressivity. On the other hand, the corporation income tax is distinctly nonneutral, especially if it is not shifted. It distorts choices of means of financing, factor proportions, form of business organization, industry mix, et cetera, besides resulting in double taxation of dividends (if not shifted). Yet if the corporation tax is not shifted, simple replacement of part of it with the VAT would not produce neutrality since the double taxation of dividends would be replaced by the nontaxation of retained earnings. Only integration of the two income taxes or increased taxation of capital gains would prevent introducing this distortion. But if the corporation tax is shifted, simply replacing part of it with a VAT would represent a distinct gain in economic efficiency. It will be seen in the next section that these questions of neutrality and distortion also play a role in the assessment of the distributional implications of the proposed tax substitution.

There can be little doubt that the tax substitution would increase the rate of private saving and investment in the economy, if the corporation tax is not shifted. If the tax is shifted, the tax replacement would not make much difference. Moreover, the VAT might be a better tool of discretionary fiscal policy than the corporation income tax, though it might not be as effective as an automatic stabilizer, again under the assumption that the latter tax is not shifted. If the corporation tax is shifted, it would be the better automatic stabilizer, but for discretionary use the taxes would be comparable. Finally, the tax substitution would probably raise prices initially by about the amount of the tax, the exact result again depending upon the incidence of the corporation tax. If so, not much improvement could be expected in the balance of payments. The possibility that adoption of the VAT would improve the balance of payments has, of course, been one of the chief advantages claimed for the tax.

5. Distributional Equity

Thus far we have considered the administrative advantages and disadvantages of the value added tax and the likely economic effects of substituting the VAT for the corporation income tax. Now we turn to what many observers—particularly critics of the VAT—consider to be the crucial issue in the debate, the distributional implications of the VAT-corporate tax substitution. These, of course, revolve about the incidence of the two taxes, that is, who is burdened by them.

We noted above that a consumption type VAT would almost certainly be borne by individuals in proportion to consumption expenditures, but that the incidence of the corporation income tax is much less clear. Thus the best we can do is to consider the distributional implications of the tax substitution under two alternative assumptions about the incidence of the corporation income tax. As before, we assume alternatively that the tax is borne by shareholders and that it is shifted to consumers.[77]

If the corporation income tax is shifted to consumers, there is little reason on equity grounds not to substitute the VAT for it. In such a case the corporation tax is borne more or less in proportion to consumption in the aggregate, as the VAT would be if enacted. Yet it would be capricious in its incidence, given its nonneutral impact on various industries, (see section 4A above), and it might affect family budgets quite differently, depending upon consumption patterns. In short, if the corporation income tax is merely a tax on consumption, it is an extremely complex and nonneutral one that

---

[77] Backward shifting to labor, besides having little support from professional economists, would not result in a greatly different pattern of incidence than if forward shifting occurs, at least in the aggregate. Both patterns would differ little from the incidence of the VAT. Alternatively, the corporation tax would have about the same incidence as that of the payroll taxes, which are discussed in the next section.

could best be replaced by a relatively simple and neutral tax on value added (or a retail sales tax).

If the corporation income tax is not shifted to consumers, but is borne by shareholders, as traditional theory suggests, the question of replacing it in part with a VAT is more controversial. In this case we would be replacing a tax that contributes significantly to the overall progressivity of the American tax system with a regressive tax on consumption. Moreover, we would, as noted above, be creating a tax shelter in retained earnings. Whether such a step would be desirable depends in part upon society's views of equity in taxation and how the present tax system accords with them. Or, even if such a shift were thought by itself to be undesirable on equity grounds, it might be supportable if it would accomplish other economic objectives. In such a case we would be faced with a question of trade-offs between equity and the achievement of those other objectives.[78]

Some critics of both the nonneutrality of the present corporation income tax and the regressivity of the value added tax have offered an ambitious solution that would incorporate the best of both taxes. This solution would be to integrate the personal and corporation income taxes and make up the revenue lost in integration through a tax on value added.[79] The distortions inherent in the separate taxation of corporation income would be largely eliminated without creating a tax haven in retained earnings. The result would be a nearly neutral combination of (a) an individual income tax that included retained earnings and avoided double taxation of dividends and (b) a general tax on consumption. Such a policy could involve a rate structure that would leave more or less unchanged the overall progressivity of the tax system, or the rate structure could be adjusted to make the tax system more or less progressive, as desired.

A less extreme approach to avoiding creation of a tax shelter in retained earnings and its regressive incidence would be to combine replacement of the corporation tax by the VAT with a substantial tightening of capital gains taxation. In addition, it would be possible to mitigate the regressivity of the VAT at the lower end of the income scale by exempting purchases of basic necessities or providing refundable income tax credits to each family for the VAT on a given volume of purchases of basic consumer goods. Either approach would

---

[78] Krzyzaniak has argued persuasively, "Differential Incidence," that there may even be important conflicts between long- and short-run distributional objectives, in that egalitarian short-run policies may worsen the long-run position of low-income groups by reducing investment and the future capital stock.

[79] For a brief description of integration and references, see section 4B above.

reduce the VAT's regressivity, but from an economic viewpoint the refundable credit would be preferable to the exemption approach. The refundable credit would not distort choices between various items of consumption, whereas exemptions would discriminate in favor of the exempted items. Many critics of the simple replacement of the corporation tax with a VAT consider this dual approach of subjecting capital gains to more nearly full taxation and reducing the VAT burden on low-income consumers the least that should be done to lessen the regressivity of the tax change and make the substitution acceptable.

A more far-reaching approach would go beyond mere integration of the two income taxes. Integration would be supplemented by elimination of tax preferences under the income tax and initiation of low-income relief through something like a negative income tax.[80] Since the loophole closing would affect mainly upper income groups and the negative income tax would raise the disposable incomes of low-income households, the combination would greatly outweigh the regressivity of the VAT. Critics of this plan would object to the elimination of tax preferences or the payment of negative income taxes, or both. As always, equity is a matter of viewpoint and not of economic science.[81]

6. Comparison of VAT with Personal Income and Payroll Taxes

Up to now the economic and distributional effects of the VAT have been compared only with those of a corporation income tax. In this section we quickly make the same comparisons with the two federal

---

[80] The author has advocated this approach in his testimony before the Joint Economic Committee on March 21, 1972. For a further elaboration, see section 9 of this essay.

[81] It is of interest in this context to quote one observer's interpretation of policies accompanying Danish adoption of the VAT: "A modern variant [of the principle of tax neutrality] might be that a taxation reform would have to take into account, i.e., be neutral, as regards the existing 'social balance'. Such a relative neutrality of distribution has been maintained in connection with the introduction of the Danish value-added tax, steps having been taken to counteract its regressive effect by adjusting income tax rates; by introducing personal grants, which are inversely progressive in relation to income; by increasing the existing child grants; and by introducing subsidies granted to reduce the prices of certain dairy products. In this way we have obtained a system of direct and indirect negative taxes the avowed political objective of which is relative neutrality of distribution." From Mogens Eggert Möller, "On the Value-Added Tax in Denmark and the European Economic Community and the Renaissance of Tax Neutrality," *Bulletin for International Fiscal Documentation*, October 1967, p. 433, quoted in Shoup, "Experience with the Value-Added Tax in Denmark," pp. 240-41.

taxes that are more important sources of federal revenue than the corporation income tax, the personal income tax and the social security payroll tax. These comparisons deserve to be made since there is no a priori reason that only substitution for the corporation income tax should be considered. Certainly many opponents of the VAT would feel that if a VAT is inevitable it would be more palatable as a substitute for part of (an increase in) the payroll tax than for part of (an increase in) the corporation tax.[82]

Fortunately, the comparisons can be made quickly since in most cases the substitution would make relatively little difference, and the differences that would result are straightforward. This facility results from the fact that the incidence of these two taxes is itself fairly straightforward and more-or-less accepted, unlike the case with the corporation income tax. Economic theory suggests strongly that both the personal income tax and the payroll tax are borne by the income recipient involved, and there is as yet little empirical evidence to the contrary.[83] Thus in what follows it is assumed that both these taxes are borne by recipients of the taxed personal income or payrolls.[84]

A. Neutrality. Except to the extent that tax preferences in the individual income tax distort economic decisions and income taxation discriminates against saving, replacing part of that tax with a VAT

---

[82] On the other hand, many persons would argue against replacing the payroll tax financing of social security with any other tax, including a value added tax, because of the assumed similarity of social security to private insurance. For a thorough appraisal of the "insurance myth" and the economic effects of the social security taxes, see Joseph A. Pechman, Henry J. Aaron, and Michael K. Taussig, *Social Security: Perspectives for Reform* (Washington, D. C.: Brookings Institution, 1968) and the forthcoming volume by John A. Brittain, *Payroll Taxes for Social Security*, Brookings Institution.

[83] For a theoretical analysis of the situation in the short run, see the present author's "The Theory of Tax Incidence with Imperfect Factor Mobility." For a longer term view, see Krzyzaniak, "Differential Incidence," which also contains references to Krzyzaniak's various other writings on the subject. One empirical analysis of the incidence of payroll taxes, which supports the present author's theoretical presumption of incidence on workers, is John A. Brittain, "The Incidence of Social Security Payroll Taxes," *American Economic Review*, March 1971, pp. 110-25.

[84] It may be necessary to note explicity that both the employee's and employer's shares of payroll taxes are attributed to employees, as theory indicates they should be. To the extent that some or all of either share is passed on to consumers, replacing the payroll tax with a VAT would have no effect, and need not be considered explicitly. Thus the reader can interpret the analysis of the text as being applicable to whatever portion of the tax he believes is borne by labor, instead of by consumers.

would have little effect upon economic neutrality, so long as the latter is not riddled with exemptions; one neutral tax would be replaced with another. Of course, reduction of the existing personal income tax would mean that presently preferentially treated activities would be less favored than now by the tax law. Similarly, imposition of a VAT would favor any industries exempted from it. In this regard, it is worth noting that some important activities that are presently favored would probably continue to be favored, though perhaps not to the same extent. Housing is the most prominent example. Substituting VAT for part of the payroll tax would be neutral, except as exemptions in the former distort choices, since coverage of the latter is now nearing universality.

B. Growth. A tax on value added of the consumption type should be slightly more favorable to saving than the existing income tax for two reasons. First, being a regressive levy (see section 6E below), it takes income away from those most likely to spend it (and not save it), as compared to the income tax. Stated differently, the average of the marginal propensities to consume of those who would bear the burden of the VAT is greater than the average for the income tax. Second, because the VAT exempts saving and the income tax does not, substituting the former for part of the latter would lessen the disincentive against saving. How important these effects are is difficult to assess with any precision, but it seems that the differential impact of the two taxes on saving would be minor. Certainly, it should not be difficult to achieve the same increase in saving through less extreme means.

Similar conclusions hold for the substitution of the VAT for part of the existing payroll taxes, but the differential effects would be even smaller. Capital and labor would be treated equivalently under the VAT, whereas the payroll tax applies only to labor. Thus saving would become less attractive. But the impact flowing from the redistribution of tax burdens and differences in marginal propensities to consume would be quite insignificant. Thus, in total, it seems unlikely that much added saving could be expected from either of the tax substitutions considered in this section.

Similarly, there seems to be little reason to expect any dramatic shifts in risk-taking, innovation, and investment because of these tax substitutions. As with the corporation income tax, the personal income tax results in governmental sharing of both risks and returns, and may either stimulate or retard investment from a given flow of saving. In either case the expected results are not great, and for the payroll tax they are even less. In total, then, it does not seem likely that either potential tax substitution would appreciably affect the rate of economic growth in the United States.

C.   Stability. As in the discussion of section 4D, the effects the postulated tax substitutions would have on the achievement of full employment and price stability can be considered in three stages: the initial and direct effects of the substitution upon the level of prices, the relative effectiveness of the tax alternatives as built-in stabilizers, and the usefulness of the taxes as instruments of discretionary countercyclical policy.

First, it seems likely that removal of either the personal income tax or the payroll tax would have little effect upon prices. On the other hand, the newly imposed VAT would probably be reflected in higher prices. Thus the initial effect of the substitution would probably be an increase in the price level about equal to the rate of the VAT.

The effectiveness of the various taxes as built-in stabilizers depends upon the response of receipts to cyclical deviations from the target path of GNP and the impact these changes in receipts would have upon private spending. VAT receipts would respond less than receipts from the payroll tax and much less than those from the personal income tax. But by the very same token that VAT receipts, being based on consumption, may be relatively insensitive to fluctuations in income, fluctuations in income and payroll tax receipts may induce little change in private spending. In either case, consumption behavior based on permanent income, rather than upon contemporaneous income flows, is the culprit. Private spending may be sufficiently insensitive to near-term alterations in income that none of the three taxes would be a strong built-in stabilizer. Thus there seems to be little reason to prefer one of the taxes over the other on the grounds of contribution to automatic stability.

As a tool of discretionary fiscal policy, the VAT seems to have a slight edge over its two direct tax alternatives. From an administrative standpoint all three could be altered with comparable ease.[85] But the effect of the temporary change in the VAT would probably be considerably stronger, especially if the tax measures were known

---

[85] It would be necessary to allow the President to alter VAT rates within preset limits for countercyclical purposes, as noted in section 4D. Otherwise, anticipatory buying and postponement of buying of consumer durables would create perverse effects while the measure was being debated, since tax rate changes might be fairly large.

to be temporary. Experience with the 1968 income tax surcharge suggests that temporary income tax changes are reflected in altered consumption only gradually and with a considerable lag, on the average. Therefore they must be planned well in advance and tailored closely to stabilization needs.[86] There is no reason to believe that consumption would respond very differently in the short run to a temporary change in the payroll tax.

On the other hand, a temporary change in a tax on consumption, precisely because it is temporary and is geared to consumption, rather than to income, can be a quite effective tool of discretionary fiscal policy. Besides simply reducing private purchasing power, as do changes in the income and payroll taxes, the change in the VAT would create a strong incentive to postpone or speed up purchases in order to make them under the lowest possible tax rate. This intertemporal substitution effect is, of course, missing under the income and payroll taxes, since these taxes apply to the earning of income rather than the spending of it.[87] Thus, the VAT would probably be a better instrument of discretionary stabilization policy than either the income tax or the payroll tax.

In summary, the initial replacement of part of either the personal income tax or the payroll tax with the VAT would almost certainly lead to prices rising by the amount of the tax on value added. The VAT would probably be a more powerful tool of discretionary stabilization policy than either of the direct taxes, but as automatic stabilizers the three taxes would probably not differ much in effectiveness.

D. Balance of Payments. Imposition of a VAT in place of part of the personal income tax or payroll tax would not be likely to affect the balance of payments significantly. Reduction of either direct tax would not affect domestic prices, but imposition of the VAT would

---

[86] One appraisal of the 1968 surcharge is presented in Arthur M. Okun, "The Personal Tax Surcharge and Consumer Demand, 1968-70," *Brookings Papers on Economic Activity*, 1971(1), pp. 167-204. A more pessimistic view is taken in Robert Eisner, "Fiscal and Monetary Policy Reconsidered" and "What Went Wrong." The present author has reviewed fiscal policy during the 1960s in *Fiscal Failure: The Lessons of the Sixties* (Washington, D. C.: American Enterprise Institute, 1972).

[87] This intertemporal substitution effect is discussed in William H. Branson, "The Use of Variable Tax Rates for Stabilization Purposes," mimeographed, 1971. It is proposed there and in McLure, *Fiscal Failure*, pp. 67-71, that attention be given to a variable tax-subsidy arrangement related only to consumer durables (and investment), rather than to all consumption spending, since it is for these large durable items of expenditure that we would expect the intertemporal substitution to be the greatest.

raise them by the amount of the tax. However, the VAT would be rebated on exports and applied to imports, so that exports would occur free of the tax and imports would compete on an equal footing with domestic products (so far as the U.S. VAT goes). Thus little or no improvement would be expected to occur in the trade account because of the tax substitution. There might be some inflow of capital in response to lower personal income tax rates, but it would probably be an insignificant amount. Of course, lower payroll taxes would have virtually no effect on the capital account.

E. Distributional Effects. The most dramatic effects of substitution of a VAT for the personal income tax would be the shift toward regressivity that would occur in the incidence of the U.S. tax system. Though it is riddled with loopholes, the personal income tax is a markedly progressive element of the U.S. tax system, especially over some income ranges. The VAT, on the other hand, being a general tax on consumption, would be a regressive levy. Even if exemptions were allowed for housing, medical expenses, household utilities, and food, as they well might be (see section 3 above), the incidence of the VAT would probably fall short of proportionality. Thus substituting a value added tax for part of the personal income tax would be to substitute a regressive tax for a progressive tax, a result surely unacceptable in many quarters. Just how great the shift toward regressivity would be would depend upon the exemptions in the VAT and the form of the personal income tax reduction. A fully general VAT would be more regressive than one with liberal exemptions for basic necessities, as noted above. Of course, a refundable credit for a fixed amount of VAT paid on basic necessities would be a preferable means of reducing the regressivity of the tax, as noted in section 4B. A uniform percentage reduction of personal income tax liabilities would lessen progressivity more than an equal reduction in all tax rates or a further increase in personal exemptions, et cetera.[88]

The distributional implications of substituting a VAT for part of the payroll tax would not be great, in the aggregate. The VAT

---

[88] It should be noted that none of these methods of reducing the personal income tax would benefit those families presently exempt from the tax. To extend to them, the "tax reduction" would have to take the form of initiation of (or an increase in payments under) a negative income tax. These families would, of course, pay part of the VAT, unless the refundable credit were granted. The distributional implications of raising additional revenue through a VAT and various other taxes is examined in Charles L. Schultze, Edward R. Fried, Alice M. Rivlin, and Nancy H. Teeters, *Setting National Priorities: The 1973 Budget* (Washington, D. C.: The Brookings Institution, 1972), pp. 440-48.

would probably bear slightly more heavily on the lowest income groups than the payroll tax, due primarily to its inclusion of the consumption of low-income persons not taxed heavily by the payroll tax. The most important group in this category is the aged. Thus in one sense the tax substitution, while distributionally roughly neutral in the aggregate, would result in an income transfer from nonworkers to workers, in particular from the aged to the young and middle-aged members of the labor force. In the last respect it would offset in part the transfer from the young to the aged resulting from the social security system.[89]

F.   Summary. The rates of saving, investment and economic growth, the neutrality of the tax system, the automatic stability of the economy, and the balance of payments probably would not be affected much by substituting a tax on value added for part of either the personal income tax or the payroll tax. The VAT should be a somewhat stronger tool of discretionary fiscal policy than either of the others, but its initial substitution for them would raise prices. Replacement of part of the payroll tax with a VAT would not affect the distribution of real income much in the aggregate, but it would result in a transfer from consumers as a group to workers as a group. The most important social aspect of this transfer would be the added burden on the aged living on pensions and social security. If the substitution were for part of the personal income tax, the overall incidence of the federal tax system would move toward regressivity.[90] The extent of the shift would depend upon the exact form of the income tax reduction (equal percentage reduction in liabilities, equal percentage point reductions in rates, increase in exemptions, initiation of a negative income tax, et cetera) and whether steps were taken to reduce the regressivity of the VAT (via exemptions or refundable credits for the VAT that hits basic necessities). If a general VAT were matched with an equal percentage reduction in all personal income tax liabilities, the shift to regressivity would be substantial indeed, and probably the most important effect of the tax substitution.

7.   VAT and the Property Tax

President Nixon has suggested that the United States should consider initiating a federal tax on value added, the revenues from which would

---

[89] See Brittain, *Payroll Taxes for Social Security.*

[90] It should be mentioned that an offset would occur due to the deductibility of state and local taxes in calculating liabilities under the federal income tax. Reduction of rates would reduce the value of these deductions in terms of tax saving.

be used to relieve the burden of the local property tax, presently the primary local source of financing for education. The details of any such proposal are not at all clear at this time. But given the successful attack on property tax financing of education in recent court cases, it seems essential that our study should at least consider in broad outline the effects of substituting revenues from a federal tax on value added for those currently being raised by the local property tax. This section briefly examines these effects, the analysis following the same approach as above. No effort is made to investigate in depth all the many ramifications that adoption of such a proposal would have for the financing of federalism.

A. Neutrality. Like the federal corporation income tax, the portion of the property tax levied on improvements is distinctly nonneutral.[91] It does not necessarily discriminate between industries, as the corporation tax does, but it discriminates between geographic areas.[92] Because of the political fragmentation of the nation at the local level there are literally thousands of taxing jurisdictions, each with its own property tax base and rate. Far from having uniform rates, many of these jurisdictions have been created, and are perpetuated, precisely to provide preferentially low tax treatment of property within their boundaries. And even when differences in taxation have not been the conscious goal of public policy, different property tax bases and revenue requirements and faulty local assessment practices have resulted in uneven taxation. Thus we can expect substantial distortion in the geographic location of economic activity to result from the lack of uniformity of the property tax. This distortion is likely to be greatest within a given metropolitan area since locational choices as between cities are likely to be made on nonfiscal grounds.[93]

One of the most adverse effects of the property tax is the disincentive it imposes upon private efforts to rebuild the decaying central cities of the nation. The result is the hastening of flight to the suburbs and the worsening of urban blight, which in turn renders more difficult the financing of urban public services via the property tax in the central cities.[94]

Finally, and this can be considered under the heading of both income distribution and resource allocation, reliance upon the property

---

[91] The portion levied on land is, of course, neutral since it affects no economic decisions at the margin.

[92] Interindustry distortions may occur, however, depending upon the law and assessment practices in various states.

[93] See Netzer, *Economics of the Property Tax*, especially chapter 5.

[94] Ibid., pp. 83-85.

tax for the financing of education results in vastly differing resources being devoted to a child's education, depending upon where he lives. If there are benefits to society from the education of its children and future citizens, as is usually assumed and as is implicit in public support of education, it seems to make little sense from the viewpoint of resource allocation to provide such divergent levels of education for these children. Moreover, the court cases mentioned earlier have ruled that such divergent levels of support for education within a state are unconstitutional.

Replacement of the portion of the local property tax that is imposed upon improvements with revenues from a tax on value added would eliminate most of these distortions of resource allocation.[95] The VAT would apply at uniform rates across the nation and therefore would not distort locational decisions. Similarly, it would be neutral with regard to decisions of central city renewal. Finally, if revenues from the VAT provided a uniform minimum grant per student, educational differentials would probably be reduced. Even if they were not, students in areas with inadequate property tax bases could be provided education of a satisfactory quality to meet social demands. Thus it seems likely that the proposal would improve resource allocation.[96]

B. Growth, Stability and Balance of Payments. Presumably the replacement of part of the property tax, a tax on capital, with a tax on consumption would raise the rate of growth somewhat, though this consideration should probably not be important in the decision to make the change. Similar comments apply to the built-in stability of tax revenues and the balance of payments. Revenues from a VAT would be somewhat more variable over the cycle than those from a property tax.[97] It seems unlikely that the VAT rate would be varied over the cycle if receipts from it are tied closely to the financing of education. Finally, part of the property tax on improvements may be

---

[95] Because the portion of the property tax levied on land does not cause distortions, as noted above, there is no need (on efficiency grounds) to replace it. Equity considerations are taken up in section C below.

[96] It might be noted that elimination of the property tax on housing and exemption of housing under the VAT would accentuate the existing preferential treatment of owner-occupied housing under the income tax. On the other hand, income tax deduction for property taxes on homes would no longer be so bothersome.

[97] It probably would not be desirable to allow the variation in revenues to be reflected in variations in the amount of funds available for support of education. Stable revenue flows could be achieved in several ways, and need not be discussed here.

shifted to consumers, in which case the proposed tax substitution would result in both a rise in the price level of less than the amount of the VAT and a slight improvement in the balance of payments. None of these effects seems to be very important, however, especially when compared with the implications for neutrality and income distribution.

C. Distribution. It has been estimated that the property tax is markedly regressive over the lowest income brackets, and regressive even at high-income levels if the offset against the federal income tax is taken into account.[98] This regressivity results from the large portion of the tax falling on housing and the portion shifted to consumers.[99] Since the part of the tax levied on land is almost certainly more progressive than that on improvements, there is little doubt that the portion on improvements is itself regressive, and distinctly so at the lowest income levels. Whether the VAT or the property tax (on improvements) is more regressive is not clear, but there is one big difference in the two taxes. The property tax bears especially heavily upon housing, while the VAT would probably exempt it. This consideration is especially important for the aged, who in many states pay large property taxes on their homes but would pay relatively small amounts of VAT.[100]

Finally, we must turn briefly to an issue that until now we have been able to avoid—the distribution of the benefits of public expenditures, in particular those of education. It is possible, if not certain, that education would be financed more generously under a VAT than under continued major reliance upon the property tax. If so, it is worth noting that the regressivity of the VAT would probably be more than offset by the pro-poor distribution of benefits from education. On the other hand, it can be argued that financing the same pro-poor benefits through increased federal income taxation, rather than through a federal sales tax, would be even more advantageous to the poor. Whether the level of financing would be equally high under the VAT and the income tax is an open question.

---

[98] Netzer, *Economics of the Property Tax*, chapter 3.

[99] Of course, if the tax on improvements is borne by capital, rather than by consumers, the result is quite different. For a discussion of this difficult theoretical problem, see Peter M. Mieszkowski, "The Property Tax: An Excise Tax or a Profits Tax?" *Journal of Public Economics*, March 1972, pp. 73-96.

[100] It should be noted that the property tax causes distortions primarily as it affects new construction. Similarly, removing the tax on existing real property would create windfall gains to present owners. It may be preferable to phase out the property tax by not applying it to newly made improvements rather than simply removing it.

D. Summary. It seems that a VAT would be far less distorting than the property tax, and that its incidence by income brackets would not differ too much from that of the property tax. The incidence of both taxes would, however, depend crucially upon the family's market basket, in particular upon its consumption of housing, since the property tax hits housing especially hard and the VAT would probably exempt it. This distinction is particularly important for the aged. Considerations of growth, economic stability, and the balance of payments should probably play a distinctly minor role in the discussion.

Finally, it should be questioned whether a VAT is the proper tax to substitute for property tax financing of education, if a substitution is to be made. There seems to be little reason to prefer the VAT to a retail sales tax. Moreover, some critics of the VAT would support transfer of educational financing to the federal income taxes rather than to either type of general sales tax.

8. The VAT in Europe [101]

Among the questions that naturally arise when one is considering the adoption of a federal tax on value added in the United States are "how is it done in Europe?" and "what have been VAT's effects in Europe?" This section provides a brief and necessarily incomplete answer to these questions.

The first VAT in Europe was adopted by France in 1954. But this tax extended only through the wholesale level, and the French extended the tax to the retail level and to services only on January 1, 1968, the date Germany substituted a value added tax for its notoriously defective cascade type turnover tax. Thus the Danish VAT, adopted as a replacement for a tax levied at wholesale in July 1967, was the first truly general VAT in Europe. Other European nations utilizing this tax are the Netherlands and Sweden (1969), Norway and Luxembourg (1970), and Belgium (1971). Italy, after numerous delays, was scheduled to implement a VAT in mid-1972, the year of Ireland's proposed initial use of the tax, but has been given a further extension until January 1, 1973. Finally, Britain and Austria have also announced proposals to adopt a VAT in 1973.

Only Denmark and Norway have adopted single-rate taxes on value added, though the disadvantages of multiple-rate systems are well known. (Sweden nominally has one rate, but it applies the tax

---

101 This discussion is taken largely from National Economic Development Office, *Value Added Tax*, pp. 31-50, and "VAT in Europe," pp. 64-65.

to a reduced tax base.) Germany, the Netherlands, and Luxembourg have two rates and both France and Belgium have four rates. (See Table 6 for a compilation of existing and proposed rates. (The proliferation of rates is apparently attributable to union resistance to higher rates on essential goods and services than existed under previous tax systems. Not surprisingly, the reduced rates (and exemptions) apply primarily to items that might reasonably be considered necessities: food, housing, transportation, electric utilities and telecommunications, newspapers, and social and medical services. Conversely, differentially high rates apply primarily to luxury items —which in effect means automobiles. In this regard it has been noted that "Possibly by coincidence, the single-rate countries are also those with the most developed social welfare systems, and the most progressive direct tax scales; as a result they least need to attempt income redistribution via high VAT rates on luxuries and low ones on necessities."[102] Finally, the financial sector is usually exempt on the services it provides, though not on its purchases. In a similar vein, those in certain activities can choose whether or not to be in the VAT system, and thus able to take credit for taxes paid on purchases.

It is difficult to generalize about the economic effects of the adoption of the tax on value added in Europe. Effects on the efficiency of resource allocation are not directly observable, and can only be surmised from theoretical arguments and the nature of the pre-existing tax systems. Where the VAT replaced a cascade type turnover tax, as in Germany, Luxembourg, and the Netherlands, the gains in economic efficiency are almost certain to be great. On the other hand, where it replaced a retail sales tax, as in Norway and Sweden, or even a wholesale tax, as in Denmark, the gains are not likely to be so important. Where it replaced a variety of indirect taxes, as in Belgium and France, an intermediate result is likely. Since in no case has the VAT replaced an important direct tax (except in France, where the social security payroll tax was eliminated), the European evidence on this score would be of little relevance to the U.S.

Similar statements can be made about the effect of adoption of a VAT on the rates of saving and investment. First, the effects probably would not be large since the VAT replaced primarily other indirect taxes. Second, the effects would be difficult to isolate, even using sophisticated econometric techniques, since the initiation of the VAT occurred in the context of economic growth. Finally, the rele-

---

[102] "VAT in Europe," p. 64. The passage quoted in footnote 81 of section 5 about the maintenance of relative neutrality of distribution when the VAT was introduced in Denmark supports this view.

Table 6

RATES OF VALUE ADDED TAXES IN EUROPE

	Date of Introduction	Taxes Replaced	Rates (percent)				
			Standard	Lower	Intermediate	Upper
France	1968	Various indirect	23	7.5	17.6	33⅓
Germany	1968	Cascade	11	5.5	—	—
Italy*	1973	Various indirect	?	?	?	?
Belgium	1971	Various indirect	18	6	14	25
Netherlands	1969	Cascade	14	4	—	32**
Luxembourg	1970	Cascade	8	4	—	—
Denmark	1967	Purchase tax	12.5**	—	—	—
Norway	1970	Retail sales tax	20	—	—	—
Sweden	1969	Retail sales tax	17.65	3.53**	10.59**	—
Austria*	1973	Cascade	16	8	—	—
Ireland*	1972	Purchase tax + retail sales tax	16.37	5.26	9.82	30.26
Britain*	1973	Purchase tax	10	0	—	—

*Proposed. **These figures, printed here as in the original table, are in error. No upper rate has been set for the Netherlands; the Danish standard rate should be 15 percent; the Swedish lower and intermediate rates should be 3.09 and 9.89 percent, respectively. See note 12, p. 274.

Source: "VAT In Europe," *The Economist*, March 25, 1974, p. 65. The dates for the Italian and Dutch adoption of VAT have been corrected; Italy was granted an extension until January 1, 1973, after the original table was printed, and the Netherlands adopted VAT in 1969, not 1968, as *The Economist* reported.

vance to the U.S. consideration of a federal VAT is limited, in any event, as noted above.

Probably the single question asked most often about the European taxes on value added is how they affected prices when they were introduced. The answer to this question is crucial for the likely effects on the balance of payments, as well as in its own right. Here the evidence is mixed. Germany was perhaps the most successful in its efforts to prevent a large increase in the price level from accompanying its introduction of the VAT. It is generally agreed that the substitution of the VAT for the German cascade tax had little effect on the price level. France was only slightly less successful in that less than 1.15 percent inflation has been attributed to the VAT. In Luxembourg and the Netherlands the price increases associated with the introduction of the VAT have been estimated at 2.0 percent and 1.5 percent, respectively. These increases occurred in spite of a freeze on prices, as did the 5.8 percent price increase that has been attributed to the Norwegian tax on value added. The worst price increase was that in Denmark—7.9 percent, but this increase was mitigated by a general increase in wages and special relief for low-income persons.[103]

Again, most of this European experience is not directly relevant to an appraisal of the likely effects of the introduction of a federal tax on value added in the United States, since in most cases the VAT replaced indirect, rather than direct, taxes. (The most analogous case is that of Norway, in which a switch from direct to indirect taxation occurred simultaneously with introduction of VAT. In that instance a price increase of almost 6 percent—as compared to a VAT rate of 20 percent—occurred.) Because European experience is not directly relevant to the U.S., it is necessary to rely on theoretical analysis. As was indicated earlier, it is probably safe to say that the impact of the introduction of the VAT itself would be to raise prices by about the percentage amount of the tax. Only if the corporation income tax (or another direct tax) had been shifted forward in the form of higher prices and would be unshifted when reduced, as seems to have been roughly the case for the indirect taxes replaced by the VAT in all the European countries except in Norway and Denmark, could we expect prices not to rise markedly with introduction of a VAT. If the corporation tax is not shifted, or if it would not be unshifted when reduced, prices would probably rise by about the amount of the tax. Similarly, the balance of payments probably would not improve if the corporation tax is not shifted or if it is shifted

---

[103] National Economic Development Office, *Value Added Tax*, pp. 43-45.

but would not be unshifted. Only if the corporation tax operates exactly like an indirect tax could we expect much improvement in the balance of trade from the tax substitution.

9. Concluding Remarks

Most of the discussion to this point has been relatively free of normative judgments, as indeed it should be, in order that the author's views on equity, neutrality, et cetera, and the trade-offs between them would not intrude. An attempt has been made simply to establish the likely economic and distributional implications of various possible tax substitutions, and the areas of substantial uncertainty, without expressing any preferences on how the various implications should be valued. In this final section, a normative framework for weighing the implications of substituting VAT for other taxes and the author's personal views on the policy alternatives outlined in this essay are described.

A. A Normative Framework. Which aspects of the substitution of VAT for various other taxes should count most in determining whether the United States should adopt a tax on value added? To answer this question, it is necessary to analyze what can be done only (or most directly) by tax policy and what can be done in other ways, the idea being that judgments of the desirability of an American VAT should be framed primarily in terms of the former. The discussion of the desirability of a VAT should center on the issues of neutrality and equity. Distortions introduced by a tax such as the existing corporation income tax can hardly be undone, except by replacing the tax with a truly general tax and taxing retained earnings, and to try to offset these distortions in any other way would greatly complicate our economic system. Similarly it would be extremely difficult to offset existing inequities in the distribution of income except via taxes and transfers related to income, and newly imposed taxes working in the opposite direction would only worsen the problem.

On the other hand, one can think of many measures to increase the rate of economic growth, stabilize the economy, and improve the U.S. balance of payments. For example, one can increase the rate of saving in the economy, if that is a factor, by increasing the government surplus (assuming that full employment can be maintained). If lagging innovation and investment pose a problem, they can be subsidized directly. Though it is more difficult to stabilize the

228

economy than to talk about doing it, the basic structure of the tax system should not be dictated by the needs of stability, without regard for the efficiency of resource allocation or the distribution of income. A similar argument applies to improving the balance of payments, as recent events have shown. Something as important as the basic nature of domestic tax policy should not be made to hinge upon the need to protect the international strength of the dollar.

Thus we come to the basic question of whether the gain in neutrality that would result from substituting a VAT for part of the corporate income tax is worth the reduction in progressivity that would result. No answer can be given to this question at a technical level, but several things should be kept in mind in making the choice. First, if the corporation tax is now shifted, there seems to be only one answer: the more neutral VAT should be adopted in place of the equally regressive corporation income tax. Second, the substitution would not result in true neutrality unless taxation of retained earnings were part of the substitution. But (assuming no shifting of the corporation tax) that would also mean that the regressivity of the tax change would not be as great as if a simple substitution were contemplated. Thus the conflict between neutrality and progessivity is not as great as appears at first glance. Third, regressivity at the lower end could be reduced by allowing exemptions for basic consumer goods. But since these exemptions would distort consumption choices a preferable means of reducing regressivity would be to allow a refundable credit for a fixed amount of value added tax payments or to initiate low-income relief directly, say through a negative income tax. Finally, the regressivity of the VAT could be more than overcome while eliminating further distortions by combining with it the integration of the corporate income tax, income tax reform, and low-income relief.

With regard to the choice between the VAT and the personal income tax, the choice itself is a matter of value judgment, but the basis for the choice seems fairly clear. The taxes are probably about equally neutral, so the decision can be made on the basis of equity. There is perhaps even less to choose between the payroll and value added tax. Both are more or less neutral, and their incidence by income brackets may not differ too much. But the payroll tax favors recipients of capital income and retirement income relative to consumers and recipients of labor income.

As regards the proposal of a federal VAT to replace the local property tax as a source of financing education, the issues again are clear. The property tax is distinctly nonneutral, whereas the VAT is, at least in principle, a neutral tax. The primary question on the equity side involves the differentially heavy taxation of housing under the property tax and the likely exemption of housing under the VAT. Moreover, some critics of the VAT would argue that the property tax burden should be relieved by sharing revenues from an increase in the federal income tax, instead of those from a newly imposed federal sales tax.

Finally, it should be noted again that virtually any effect of a tax on value added can be achieved by imposing a tax on retail sales rather than the VAT. In fact, many of the questions of economic effects examined in this essay can more easily be answered in the context of the familiar retail sales tax than in the context of the relatively unfamiliar VAT. That the U.S. should impose a VAT, and not a federal retail sales tax, if it should decide to impose either, should be decided on administrative grounds rather than being taken for granted.

B. Author's Personal View. I have tried to be objective in presenting the pros and cons of the various tax substitutions discussed in the main body of this study, though I have almost certainly fallen somewhat short of complete success. It is, after all, difficult enough to tolerate opinions we cannot share; to play them back accurately and without prejudice is even more demanding.

In this short section I wish to state my own views on the questions discussed in the study, if only because I am often asked what they are. The reader may find this statement of opinion useful, so that he can better detect how my views have infiltrated the allegedly objective presentation of pros and cons. In any case, in this statement I need no longer feel encumbered by the mantle of objectivity.

First, it should be obvious that no simple answer can be given to the question of whether the U.S. should adopt a VAT. As is so often the case in the field of tax policy, the answer depends upon what tax the VAT would replace and the context in which the replacement would occur.

The combination I would prefer would involve integration of the personal and corporate income taxes, closing of loopholes in the newly integrated income tax, and initiation of low-income relief. Such a package would eliminate the distortions created by the existence of a separate corporation income tax, but without removing retained earnings from the tax base. Moreover, it would provide relief at the bottom of the income scale, without introducing exemptions and the distortions they entail. Finally, the added progressivity resulting from income tax reform and low-income relief would make the regressivity of the VAT bearable, especially since the rate structure could be adjusted in the interest of equity.

In the context of a thorough overhaul of the tax system, such as the one described above, the reduction of the property tax on improvements would be attractive. The property tax is a particularly unsatisfactory tax, whose demise would not be widely mourned. I have argued elsewhere that if federal financing were rationalized as suggested above, the property tax could be replaced by general local taxes on sales or income or by shared revenues from a federal VAT, a federal retail sales tax, or the federal income tax.[104]

If one were to stop short of this rather radical tax reform, a VAT might still be acceptable if accompanied by the proper measures. Substitution of the VAT for the corporation tax would probably be acceptable *if* the taxation of capital gains were tightened and relief were provided to low-income families through a refundable credit against their income tax liabilities. Simple substitution without these additional measures would, however, not be acceptable. The tax shelter in retained earnings would be unacceptable on both equity and efficiency grounds. Similarly, imposition of a VAT in place of part of the corporation income tax without low-income relief would be unacceptable on equity grounds, and relief through exemptions, while barely acceptable on equity grounds, would distort choices too much to be acceptable on neutrality grounds.

Substitution of the VAT for the personal income tax or payroll taxes would represent no great gain in neutrality, but by the same token it would be acceptable on efficiency grounds. On the other hand, the equity implications of replacing part of the progressive personal income tax with a regressive VAT are unacceptable. Replacing the payroll taxes with a VAT would be acceptable, though it would not represent a great leap forward in equity.

Next, I would not find the proposal the President has outlined particularly objectionable. Elimination of the property tax on improvements would, I think, be a step forward, and perhaps even a large one. On the other hand, the equity implications do not seem to be too bad since the property tax is itself probably a regressive levy.[105] Moreover, the net effect of substituting the VAT for property tax financing of education might be to equalize the sum of net real income

---

[104] Charles E. McLure, Jr., "Revenue Sharing: Alternative to Rational Fiscal Federalism," *Public Policy*, Summer 1971, pp. 457-78.

[105] But some reduction of the preferential income tax treatment of owner-occupied housing would seem to be in order in this case.

and the value of education (though not as much as if the income tax, rather than the VAT, were substituted), since the proposal should improve education most where it is now the worst. That result, of course, depends crucially upon the formula chosen for sharing the revenue from the VAT. (A flat per student allocation seems to be the most sensible.)

It will have been noted that in this statement no mention has been made of the effects of a VAT on the rate of growth, the stability of the economy, or the balance of payments. This silence reflects the viewpoint, expressed in section 9A, that equity and neutrality should be the key considerations in judging basic changes in the tax structure of a country, with other considerations assuming only minor roles. These other factors are important, and all the implications of adopting a VAT would need to be watched so that policy adjustments could be made for them, but they should not control the decision.

Finally, although the discussion thus far in this statement of personal views has been in terms of a VAT, I personally would prefer (though not strongly) that the federal government adopt a retail sales tax, if it is to adopt either form of general sales tax. The two taxes should be economically equivalent, so that the decision can be made on administrative grounds. I believe that these support a preference for the retail tax, though there is room for considerable disagreement on that score. One thing is clear about the choice, however: it should be based on a far more careful assessment of the two alternatives than has surfaced to date.[106] The choice should not go by default to the VAT because no one bothered to ask the question.

---

[106] Due, "The Case for Retail Sales Tax" and Shoup, "Value-Added Tax in Denmark" are, of course, excellent statements of the issues by experts. But few people indeed are familiar with the points discussed in them.

2

ECONOMICS OF THE
VALUE ADDED TAX
Norman B. Ture

Introduction and Summary

The subject of the value added tax (VAT) has commanded increasing attention in the United States over the past several years, primarily in the academic and business communities. Much of the interest in the tax lies in the possibilities it might afford, by virtue of border tax adjustments, for improving the nation's international trade balance and in its superiority over the income tax as a means of taxing business. Moreover, the fact that the tax is the central revenue raising device in the fiscal harmonization of the European Economic Community and that several other countries in Europe and in Latin America have adopted the tax inevitably raises questions as to whether the United States would not do well to introduce a VAT into its revenue system.

More recently, consideration of the VAT has gained in urgency as a result of the substantial federal deficits in fiscal years 1971-73. The rapid rate of increase in federal spending, combined with forecasts which suggest that present taxes even at full employment will provide less revenues than projected outlays, has impelled a search for new revenue. And in the past year an additional source of urgency is the developing crisis in financing public education that results from recent court decisions challenging the constitutionality of the local property tax funding of public schools. If federal financial aid is to be provided localities to replace property taxes, substantial federal revenue increases in all likelihood will be required. Reducing property taxes, widely characterized as regressive, and bolstering local governments' financial resources for education might well be regarded as appropriate occasions to add a VAT in order to augment the federal inventory of taxes. This possibility, hinted at by the President in his January 1972 State of the Union message and publicly discussed by various administration officials, brought the VAT to the front pages of the nation's newspapers.

To date, unfortunately, most of the discussion in the press and in popular forums has had the tone of an adversary proceeding, convicting the VAT of fiscal crimes before affording it a fair trial. The VAT is generally labeled a national retail sales tax. Bearing the label of a sales tax, it is then characterized as regressive on the assumption that all sales taxes bear more heavily on the poor than on the affluent. Moreover, it is asserted that imposition of the VAT would be inflationary, raising the prices of consumption goods and services across the board. These are, of course, important issues, but they deserve more objective treatment than the *ad hominem* assertions which are so frequently made. A fair appraisal of the tax by the general public is made even more difficult by discussing it as an alternative to local property taxes, thereby confusing the issues pertinent to the VAT with other issues such as the extent to which the federal government should assume responsibility for public school financing and difficult questions as to the incidence of property taxes.

The relevant issues raised by the proposal for a federal VAT concern the correct characterization of the tax, its impact, shifting and incidence, its distribution by income level, and its likely economic effects. These issues should be examined separately from the question of what public expenditures the VAT might finance. In a nutshell, the relevant question is whether a VAT would be a better tax for the federal government to impose than those it now relies upon. Or if federal revenues must be increased, would it be better to raise additional funds by imposing a VAT rather than by increasing the rates or broadening the base of one or more existing taxes?

It is argued in the discussion which follows that the VAT, properly structured, is not a "consumption" tax but a proportional tax on payments for the service of factors of production. The VAT would not raise the general level of prices. Compared with existing federal taxes, it is far more nearly neutral in its effects on consumption and saving and on the mix of labor and capital services used in production. Compared with the income tax, it would lead to a larger stock of capital used with labor in production and would thereby enhance labor's productivity and real earnings. As a corollary, the

U.S. balance of trade would in time show a larger surplus (or smaller deficit) if a VAT rather than income taxes were relied upon to raise any given amount of revenues. The VAT would not be regressive; the distribution of VAT liability by income level would be substantially the same as the distribution of labor and capital income.

On these grounds, this discussion concludes that substituting the VAT for the present income taxation of business would be a major step toward constructive tax reform. Moreover, the substitution should be undertaken irrespective of whether federal fiscal requirements exceed the revenues to be expected from existing taxes. In this event, business income taxes should nevertheless be reduced with the VAT supplying both the revenue foregone plus such additional revenues as may be desired.

1. What Is a Value Added Tax?

To begin with, we should be sure of what the VAT is—that is, what is the base of the tax?

As the name suggests, a VAT is a tax on the value added during the course of a business's operations to the goods or services it sells. In the simplest terms, the amount of value so added is measured by the difference between the dollar amount of the firm's sales and its purchases from other firms. Simple arithmetic shows that this difference is precisely equal to the payments the business makes for the labor and capital services it uses in its operations, i.e., to the sum of its payroll and "profits."

There are varying versions of a VAT, but the one which has engaged our attention and is most widely used elsewhere is the so-called "consumption" version.[1] In this version, a business in calculating its VAT base deducts from its net sales all of its purchases from other businesses—raw materials, semi-finished goods, finished goods for resale, fuel, power, light, office supplies, and the amount of its purchases of capital facilities, e.g., plant, machinery, equipment, store and office furniture and machines, etc. Because it deducts the cost of production facilities in the year in which they are acquired, the business claims no other deduction for depreciation, depletion, or other form of capital consumption allowance. Its tax base, to repeat, is equal to its net sales less all of its purchases from other firms. Simple arithmetic shows that this base is equal to the amount it pays for the labor it hires and its profits, where profits are adjusted

---

[1] I use the term "consumption" merely to conform to popular usage. As I shall show later, the tax is not on consumption.

by adding back any capital consumption allowances and by subtracting any change in inventory and outlays for production facilities.[2]

The national income variant of the tax differs in one major respect. Instead of subtracting the full amount of capital outlays from the base in the year in which these outlays are made, a capital consumption allowance (depreciation and/or depletion) is permitted. In this version the "profit" component of the tax base is very much the same as under the present corporation income tax.

The third principal version of the tax is the so-called gross national product variant, under which no deduction whatever is allowed for capital outlays, either in the year in which these outlays are made or over a period of years in the form of a depreciation or depletion allowance.

Of these three variants of the VAT, only the first, the so-called "consumption" type, should, in my judgment, be given serious consideration. This type of VAT most closely conforms to the criterion of neutrality as between consumption and saving and as between the use of labor and capital services in production.[3] The "national income" version retains the bias of the present income tax against saving and capital, and the "gross national product" version increases that bias manyfold.

In the remainder of this discussion, all references are to the so-called consumption version of the VAT.

2. Exemptions

One of the advantages claimed for the VAT by some of its proponents is that, at least in theory, the tax should apply unexceptionally to all economic entities, in the business sector, the household sector, and in the public sector as well. The theory behind this view is simplicity itself. The base of the tax is the sum of the payments made by an economic entity for the factors of production it uses. In an efficiently operating economy these payments are at least roughly equal to the value of the products those factors of production would supply in their best alternative uses. These payments are therefore a pretty fair measure of the opportunity cost to the economy as a whole of the economic entity's particular use of the factors of production it

---

[2] A number of other adjustments to the income tax measure of profits are also required. Principal among these is to add gross proceeds from the sale of any and all assets and to ignore entirely any gain or loss on the sale of capital assets. In addition, dividends received are not included in the VAT base.

[3] That is to say, imposition of the VAT does not change the relative cost to any individual of consumption and saving nor the relative cost to any producer of using labor or capital production inputs.

employs. And every economic entity using factors of production, and thereby depriving the rest of the economy of their use, imposes that same sort of cost, no matter what its production consists of. Accordingly, there is no basis for exempting any economic unit from the tax.

Moreover, applied without exception, the tax minimizes distortions in the allocation of resources. Since the base of the tax is value added in production, equal to the cost of the productive services used therein, its universal application would not differentially affect production costs among companies, industries, or lines of activity. Hence, the levy would not induce taxpayers to alter proportionately the use of their resources, the exercise of their claims for consumption or saving, or the composition of their market baskets or investment portfolios. Any exemption erodes this neutrality and should, on these grounds, be resisted.

Opponents of the VAT counter by asserting that, as a practical matter, exemptions would be provided and that, as a consequence, the tax would become an administrative nightmare and in the process lose much of its claim to superiority on neutrality grounds. This possibility, of course, should not be ignored. On the other hand, exemptions are not an intrinsic or necessary feature of the tax, and surely the administration and Congress are not required to emasculate a VAT by riddling it with exemptions.

If a VAT is to be adopted with exemptions, these should be severely restricted. Households might be exempt on the ground that total value added in the household sector, hence the VAT liabilities thereupon, is so small as to fall short of the administration and enforcement costs attributable to this sector. It is unlikely that the federal government would impose a VAT on itself, and almost equally unlikely that the tax would be imposed on states and localities.

No other exemptions than these would be warranted. It is often urged that certain categories of production, such as food, clothing, housing, and medicine, should be exempt to overcome the allegedly regressive impact of a VAT. The argument is based on the assumption that the VAT is a sales tax, its burden resting on consumers. But the VAT is, in fact, a tax on payments for factors of production, not a tax on the consumption of commodities and services. As such, there is no more reason to exempt from the VAT the value added in the production of food, say, than there is for exempting from the present payroll taxes the wages paid to labor in the food growing, processing, and distributing industries, or to exempt from income tax the profits of companies engaged in these activities.

With exemptions limited to value added in the government, household, and institutional sectors of the economy, the VAT base in the U.S. in 1971 would have been about $756 billion.[4] The exemption of value added in the production, processing, and distribution of food would have reduced the tax base by about $50 billion; exempting rent on low- and middle-income housing would have eliminated another $30+ billion from the base; and the exemption of medical and other health services and of educational services would have brought the VAT base down by another $39 billion. In other words, the exemptions of these economic activities would have cut the VAT base by roughly $120 billion, a little less than one-sixth, to about $636 billion.

Of course, additional exemptions, however unwarranted on analytical grounds, might be afforded, or as sometimes proposed, the alleged regressiveness of the VAT might be ameliorated by an income tax credit for low-income taxpayers. The VAT's annual revenues, thus, might range from a high of $7.6 billion per percentage point of tax to a low of, say, $6.0 billion. To put these revenue yields in perspective, a 5 to 6 percent VAT would have generated the same revenues as the federal corporation income tax (measured in the national income accounts) in calendar year 1971.

3. Methods of Computing and Collecting

The mechanics of computing and collecting the VAT has commanded much attention in popular discussions of the tax. Indeed, the method used in most countries—the credit or invoice method—seems to be largely responsible for its widespread characterization as a sales tax.

In fact, there are three basic, alternative methods for computing the tax: the addition method, the subtraction method, and the invoice or voucher method. The addition method calls for adding up all the payments made by the business for the production services it uses— its payroll and profits—and subtracting from that amount (1) the change in inventories and (2) capital outlays.[5]

---

[4] This estimate assumes that roughly half of the value added in residential construction that year would have been embodied in rental property. Calculations of the VAT base for 1971 are shown in the technical note. Data are from U.S. Department of Commerce, Bureau of Economic Analysis, *Survey of Current Business*, April 1972.

[5] For this purpose, profit is adjusted by adding back any capital recovery allowances and other special deductions allowed for income tax purposes, and by subtracting certain other receipts included for income tax purposes, e.g., dividends and net gains or losses.

The subtraction method requires the taxpayer to calculate his total net sales and receipts (excluding dividends and gains or losses but including gross proceeds from the sale of capital assets) and to subtract from this total all of his purchases from other businesses, including his capital outlays.

For either the addition or the subtraction method, virtually all of the information required to compute the tax is included on the present income tax forms and supporting records. No new information is called for; no record-keeping other than that now required for ordinary business financial statements is needed. Either quarterly returns (as in the present payment system) or a single, annual return, with supporting records, would provide all the necessary documentation, and the return itself could be completed on a very short form. Complying with any tax is burdensome, but these two methods of computing the VAT involve far less of a chore for the taxpayer and the tax administrator than does the present income tax.

The third method—the invoice method is the one used in virtually all of the countries having a VAT. Under this method the taxpayer applies the VAT rate to the amount of his sales and shows this amount of tax as a separate item on his sales invoice. Every business making purchases from other businesses, therefore, finds the amount of the tax on each such purchase separately stated on the invoice he receives. To compute the amount of tax he pays the government, he adds up all the VAT he has "charged" his customers, subtracts all the VAT his suppliers have "charged" him, and the remainder is his VAT liability.

It is frequently assumed that the invoice method will be proposed for use in the United States. The principal advantage claimed for this method is that it is self-enforcing: to establish the correctness of his own VAT liability each taxpayer would have to show the amount of tax he "paid" in his purchases from other businesses, and he would want to be sure that he "passed on" to his customers the amount of tax owing on his sales, which his customers presumably would insist on seeing separately on their purchase invoices for the same reason. However valid this method may be for other countries, its use is not obligatory in the United States. U.S. taxation is based on significant differences in tradition, custom, history, compliance, and enforcement machinery. The compliance record of U.S. taxpayers is excellent, and there is no reason to believe that it would not continue to be so with respect to the VAT.

If exemptions and/or differential rates were to be provided, compliance would be less burdensome under the invoice than under the subtraction method. Under the invoice method, it is clear, each taxpayer would need only his purchase and sales invoices to determine the amount of tax to remit to the Treasury. Under the subtraction method, however, the taxpayer would have to segregate his purchases by VAT rate in order to determine how much of these purchases were deductible. For example, suppose wheat growers were not required to remit VAT, but the value of the wheat was nevertheless to be included in the VAT base at the next production stage, say the miller. Under the invoice method, the miller would have no VAT on his purchase invoice to deduct from the VAT on his sales invoices; the latter would automatically include the VAT payable on both the wheat growing and milling value added. Under the subtraction method, on the other hand, the miller would have to know that wheat purchases were not deductible. If numerous exemptions or rate differentials were provided, therefore, compliance would be more cumbersome under the subtraction method than under the invoice method. Of course, this argument is as valid in reinforcing the case against exemptions and differential rates as in supporting the invoice rather than the subtraction method.

The invoice method, by requiring a separate notation on each invoice of the amount of VAT ostensibly generated by each sale, conveys and reinforces the incorrect notion that the tax is passed forward in full from one production stage to the next. As we shall see later, what is meant by "passing the tax forward" is by no means clear. Suffice it is say at this point that the VAT required to be shown on any given invoice is not the seller's VAT liability with respect to that sale; as we have seen, his liability is the amount he shows on his invoice *minus* the VAT amount he has "paid" to his suppliers on his purchases. In fact, his VAT liability can be determined only at the end of the taxable period when he takes into account all of his purchases, including capital goods, from other businesses. The invoice method, thus, misrepresents the amount of tax due on the value added by each seller.[6]

If for no reason other than to avoid the impression that the VAT is automatically shifted forward to the final consumer, the invoice

---

[6] One counter argument addressed to this point is that the VAT is not intended to be a tax on the company, measured by the value added in its business, but a tax on the value of the final product, i.e., a retail sales tax collected at each production stage up to and through the final sale. Thus, it is maintained, every business is supposed to "pass the tax forward," acting only as a collection agency. Indeed, it is contended, in this view of the tax the company's profit and loss statement should be completely unaffected by the VAT. In the subsequent discussion we show that irrespective of the accounting procedures prescribed for the VAT, it must in fact affect the real cash flow of virtually every business.

method should not be used for a VAT adopted in the U.S. The subtraction method is just as easy to comply with; indeed, in many cases, it might well be easier, and it much more readily identifies for the taxpayer the elements in his business operations which affect his VAT liability.

A. Border Tax Adjustments. Earlier, it was noted that the VAT is imposed on imports and rebated on exports. Assuming that any VAT adopted by the U.S. would include these border tax adjustments, the mechanics would be relatively simple.

In the case of imports, the VAT would be applied, at the same rate applicable to value added in domestic production, to the full value of the imports as reported to the Customs Bureau as the imports entered customs. In the case of exports, the U.S. exporter would deduct the invoice value of export sales from his total net sales and receipts before deducting his purchases from other businesses in arriving at his taxable value added, assuming the subtraction method is used for computing the tax. Under the invoice method the taxpayer has no VAT liability on his export sales and claims a credit for all of the VAT shown on his purchase invoices.

4. Burden

When we talk about the burden of a tax, we ask who is "worse off" because the tax is imposed. So far as the VAT is concerned, there is a broad consensus that its burden rests on consumers. Presumably, the tax is "passed forward" by the producers and sellers at each production stage until the full amount of the accumulated tax is included in the price of consumer products and services in their final sale. Consumers bear the burden of the tax, so the argument goes, because the prices of the consumption goods and services they buy are higher by virtue of the VAT.

The discussion that follows attempts to demonstrate that this assignment of burden is incorrect. The burden of the VAT is not on the act of consumption, hence not on consumers. Rather, the tax rests, as suggested above, on the costs incurred in production, hence on the incomes gained by the factors of production.

A. Why Call VAT a Consumption Tax? To begin with, let us critically examine the contention that the burden of the VAT rests on consumers, i.e., that the VAT is a consumption tax.

It is far from clear what is intended by characterizing the VAT as a consumption tax. In nontechnical discussions, the "consumption tax" or "retail sales tax" characterization of the VAT appears to derive in large part from the method of assessing the tax used in European countries. Under the so-called invoice or credit method, as described above, each business "charges" its customers a VAT equal to the tax rate times the value of the sale. To determine the amount of VAT it is to remit to the government, each business subtracts the amount of VAT it has been "charged" by its suppliers from the amount of VAT it has "charged" its customers. Superficially, the VAT collected in this way appears to be a sales tax with an offsetting credit for the tax paid on the business's purchases.

This method of computing and collecting the tax, of course, tells us nothing about its burden. As suggested above, the invoice method conveys the impression that every producer-seller passes the tax forward. Suppose this were true. Would it mean that the VAT burdened only consumers and that producers were unaffected by the tax?

It is clear, of course, that the imposition of the VAT does not increase either consumers' or producers' income or wealth; no one has more money because the tax is levied. If every producer-seller were to pass the tax forward, what would consumers, with no more income or wealth than before, do when they observed that the prices of every consumer good and service had been increased by the accumulated amount of VAT? Presumably, they would reduce the physical volume of their purchases of such goods and services. But if they were to do so, then the tax has resulted in a reduction in the physical volume of sales and, unless producers are willing to build inventories endlessly without prospect of increasing sales, in the physical volume of production as well. But if the amount of goods and services produced decreases, so too must employment of the factors of production, unless businesses are willing endlessly to pay for labor and capital services they are not using. And if employment of these production inputs is reduced, so too must be the incomes of those who provide the labor and capital services. But then the burden of the tax is not uniquely on people as consumers; it is borne also by those who contribute to production in the form of a reduction in incomes received for supplying production inputs.

But suppose it is argued that consumers will not reduce the physical amount of their purchases in response to the increase in prices resulting from the imposition of the VAT. With no increase in income or wealth, if people were to buy the same physical quantity of consumer goods and services and pay more for them, then clearly they would have to reduce their saving, and by an amount equal to the VAT "passed forward." This argument, thus, leads to the startling conclusion that this alleged consumption tax actually is a tax solely on saving.

In technical discussions, the consumption tax characterization of the VAT seems to rest on the argument that since purchases of capital goods are deductible from the tax base, the tax bears only on the value added in the production of consumer goods. In the aggregate, the base of the tax—ignoring any exemptions—is asserted to be equal to the value of final sales of consumer goods and services.[7] Hence, it is argued that VAT is merely a cumbersome way of collecting a tax on the retail sales of consumer goods and services.

Assuming that some useful purpose is served by applying distinctive names to various taxes, the label "sales tax" or "consumption tax" is not appropriate for the VAT. On semantic grounds, the base of a sales or excise tax is the value of the sales (or the number of units sold). The base of the VAT, as we have seen, is the difference between the value of sales and the value of purchases from other businesses, which for any taxpayer is equal to the amount of his payments for the labor and capital services he employs.

It might be argued that the VAT is an excise on the firm's production costs. There is merit in this characterization just as there is in labeling virtually any tax an excise on the taxed subject or thing. A payroll tax is an excise on one component of production—the cost of labor services—just as a profits tax is an excise on another component —the cost of capital services. An income tax is an excise on using one's resources to generate income measured in the market, and an estate or gift tax is an excise on certain property transfers. For many analytical purposes, treating every tax as an excise is highly useful, but for purposes of quickly identifying familiar things we find it more useful to apply different names to the various taxes. If for no other reason, naming the VAT a sales or consumption tax is misleading and interferes with an objective and constructive evaluation of the tax.

On analytical grounds, the characterization of the VAT as a consumption tax is simply wrong—not merely a matter of semantic confusion. The VAT does not single out consumption as the object to be taxed. The VAT does not differentially burden consumption

---

[7] The assertion is wrong unless specific exemptions are provided not only for value added originating in the government sector but also for the value added generated in the production of goods in the private sector for sale to governments. See the calculations of the VAT base in the technical note.

compared with saving. The VAT does not tax people in their role as consumers and exempt them as savers-investors. The VAT does not differentially affect the prices of consumption goods and services as compared to production goods and services.

As repeatedly suggested earlier, it is more accurate to characterize the VAT as a tax on the opportunity costs imposed by the taxpayer in his employment of production services. The immediate impact of the VAT is on the business's payroll and "profits"; it is, in short, a combination of a payroll and a profits tax. If some label other than VAT is necessary or desirable, perhaps "consolidated business tax" would be most appropriate.[8]

B. How to Characterize a Tax. It is clear, of course, that every tax reduces the private sector's claims over production resources and their outputs. Every tax, thus, is intended to reduce the taxpayer's spending on something, either his purchases of goods and services for consumption, his purchases of claims to future income, his purchases of real assets which will generate income for him over an extended period, or all of these purchases in some degree or other. The fact that any particular tax results in less spending for consumption than would occur in the absence of the tax does not justify labeling the tax a consumption tax, unless it can be shown that the tax disproportionately reduces consumption outlays relative to other uses of income. In evaluating the consumption tax characterization of the VAT, therefore, the critical question is whether the tax reduces consumption outlays in greater proportion than it reduces savings or capital outlays.

The ultimate effects of any tax depend on its initial impact in changing relative prices and on how people respond to these changes. Since every tax changes the price of something(s) relative to the price of other things, the nature of the adjustments in the economy to the imposition of the tax depends on the character and the extent of the response to this relative price change, i.e., on the price elasticity of the "thing" on which the tax initially impacts. When the shifting process, i.e., the adjustment to the imposition of the tax, has been completed (or substantially so), one may compare the new state of affairs with that which existed before the imposition of the tax and characterize the incidence of the tax in terms of the differences between the two. Thus, if in a post-tax equilibrium, a smaller proportion of private sector claims is used for consumption than in the pre-tax

---

[8] Mr. John Englested, chairman of the board of the O. S. Walker Co., suggested this as a better, more descriptive name for the tax. Only its acronym suffers in comparison with "value added tax."

economy, one could describe the tax as a "consumption" tax. Or, if after the responses to the imposition of the tax were substantially completed, one found that the real income of the "poor" had been reduced in greater proportion than that of the "rich," one might characterize the tax as regressive. Or if one found, in comparing the pre-tax and post-tax equilibrium situations, that there were less capital services in use relative to labor services in production generally, one could characterize the tax as burdening capital.

In truth, it is difficult to make these comparisons in a dynamic economy in which many things are continuously changing and in which the data required to isolate the effect of a tax are most elusive. While it is a relatively simple matter to identify the nature of the change in relative prices associated with the imposition of the tax, to delineate the kinds of adjustments which will occur because of this change in relative prices, and to define the conditions under which no further changes in economic activity will occur, it is extraordinarily difficult to measure these changes. As a practical matter, therefore, most discussions of the shifting and incidence of taxes depend on heuristic analysis. The quality of such analysis depends critically on how accurately the initial price impact of the tax is identified.

With this preface concerning analytical methodology, let us return to the question of the impact and incidence of a VAT. In the following discussion it is shown, first, that the VAT is not a consumption tax but falls in equal proportion on consumption and saving. Secondly, it is demonstrated that the VAT does not differentially affect the prices of consumption goods and services and of capital goods and services.

C. Effects on Consumption and Saving. To begin with, let us imagine an economy without taxes and with efficiently operating markets. Every decision-making individual in the economy allocates his income between current consumption and saving on the basis of his preferences between present consumption and future income. The more of today's income he saves, the larger will be his income tomorrow. The amount of the increase in his future income depends on the "interest" he receives on his saving (the amount of "interest" he receives is determined by his and everyone else's preferences as between present consumption and future income, i.e., the supply of saving, and the productivity of the capital in which savings may be embodied). Given the rate of interest he finds in the market, each individual determines how much of his current income to consume and how much to reserve for increasing future income.

Clearly his (and everyone's) consumption-saving choice is influenced by a host of factors. But given all these influences, the amount he consumes and saves depends on the relative cost of consumption and saving. The cost of consumption, of course, is the amount of future income foregone; similarly, the cost of saving is the amount of consumption and the satisfaction therefrom which the saver must forego. When the individual has allocated his income between consumption and saving optimally, given his preferences, that relative cost is equal to the interest rate he finds in the market.

If the relative cost of savings and consumption is changed, the individual is likely to change the proportion of his income which he saves. Thus, if a tax is to fall neutrally, i.e., with equal proportional impact on consumption and saving, it must not alter their relative cost. A tax which raises the relative cost of saving, then, may be characterized as a tax on saving. Similarly, a tax which raises the relative cost of consumption, hence reduces consumption by a larger proportion than it reduces saving, may be fairly characterized as a consumption tax.

Coming back to our taxless economy, let us assume that it is decided to impose a flat-rate tax on everyone's income, where income for tax purposes is measured as including current saving. Suppose the tax rate is, say, 50 percent. Before the tax was imposed, a person needed $1 of current income either for $1 of current consumption or for an income of $.10 per year in perpetuity (assuming the "interest" rate is 10 percent).[9] With a 50 percent income tax, he needs $2 of current pre-tax income to finance $1 of current consumption, but he needs $4 of pre-tax income for a perpetuity of $.10 after-tax income.[10] Thus, while the income tax at 50 percent has doubled the cost of current consumption, it has quadrupled the cost of saving, i.e., of buying the same amount of future income in this form. Clearly, the tax has reduced the relative cost of consumption or, equivalently, raised the relative cost of saving. Following the suggestion above, the tax should be characterized as a tax on saving (although, to be sure, both consumption and saving will be reduced), since it has increased the cost of saving relative to consumption.

---

[9] The amount he would have to pay for this $.10 per year income is given by the expression for the present value of a perpetuity $A\infty = \dfrac{Y}{r}$, where Y = the annual income and r = the interest rate.

[10] Since the "interest" earned on his saving is also taxable at the 50 percent rate, he needs to save $2, on which his after-tax "interest" will be $.10. To save $2, he needs a pre-tax income of $4.

It is often argued that private saving is insensitive to changes in the rate of interest and that, accordingly, it is little if at all affected by tax provisions which increase its cost relative to the cost of consumption. If this were the case, it would mean that consumption would decline in greater proportion than saving in response to the imposition of an income tax of the sort described above. But surely this is a highly unlikely proposition, for it asserts that when the cost of consumption is *reduced* relative to the cost of saving, *less* rather than more consumption—as a proportion of income—results. (By the same token, if the relative cost of consumption were increased, consumption presumably would increase rather than decline, according to this proposition.)

Now suppose that the tax which is to be imposed on the initially taxless economy allows a deduction for current saving, taxing the "interest" on that saving as it is earned. If the taxpayer spends $1 for current consumption, he needs $2 of current, pre-tax income. But if he wished to forego that $1 of current consumption in order to have a perpetuity of $.10 per year, he needs only $2 in pre-tax current income, not the $4 required in the case of the income tax.[11] In this case the 50 percent tax has increased the cost of current consumption by 100 percent, and it has increased the cost of saving, i.e., of future income, by the same percentage. In other words, the relative cost of saving and of consumption has not been affected by the tax. The tax which allows a deduction for saving from current income, therefore, is neutral as between consumption and saving.

To be sure, both consumption and saving are likely to be reduced by the tax. But if we assume that the taxpayer had optimally allocated his income between consumption and saving, he will not presumably alter that allocation after the tax (which allows the deduction of savings) is imposed, since, as shown, that tax does not alter the relative costs.

A VAT of the so-called (and misnamed) "consumption" variety falls between the two taxes sketched above. As described, the VAT would indeed allow deductions for saving to the extent that saving was embodied in businesses' purchases of production facilities, increases in inventory or other real assets, i.e., elements included in the national income accounts measure of "gross private domestic investment." But other private saving, particularly that embodied in human capital which is erroneously treated as consumption spending, might

---

[11] To have an income of $.10 per year, after tax, he needs $.20 per year pre-tax. Since, by hypothesis, his saving would be deductible for purposes of *this* tax, he needs only $2 of pre-tax current income to pay for the perpetuity.

well remain subject to tax unless specific provision were made for the deduction of such saving. To the extent that the VAT were to apply to factor incomes where these incomes included returns to human capital, for which no deduction had been allowed at the time the saving therein embodied was made, the VAT would not be perfectly neutral as between consumption and saving but would retain some bias against saving. Compared with the present income tax, however, the VAT would represent a major step toward neutrality with respect to consumption-saving choices, and away from the tax bias against saving and capital formation.

D.   Impact on the Cost of Consumption and Capital Goods. One of the popular (and mistaken) allegations about the VAT is that since the taxpayer deducts his purchases of production facilities in arriving at the base of his VAT, the cost of capital services is exempt from the tax. Hence, it is maintained, the VAT rests only on consumption goods, i.e., increases the cost of consumption goods and services but not the cost of capital services.

As I have attempted to show, the VAT is not properly characterized as a consumption tax; it does not increase the cost of consumption relative to saving. Then what, indeed, is the burden of the VAT?

As shown earlier, the direct impact of the VAT is to increase the cost to producers of using production inputs. For any company, the VAT base is equal to its sales less all of its purchases from outsiders, which is the same as the sum of its payroll plus its profits, less its change in inventories and net addition to its production facilities. Clearly, the initial impact of the tax is on the payments made for factors of production employed by the firm, i.e., the payments the firm makes for the services of the labor and capital it employs. Since these payments are also the incomes of those providing the labor and capital services, the VAT is properly viewed as a proportional tax on the income of the factors of production employed by the taxpayer.

The deduction for purchases of the facilities which provide capital services does not remove the cost of these services from the VAT base; rather, it places the taxation of the payments for these services on an equal footing with the taxation of the payments for other production services. On the other hand, failure to allow the deduction of capital outlays, as in the income tax, results in imposition of the tax first on the capitalized value of all the services to be generated by the capital at the time the capital facilities are acquired and subsequently on the payments for these services as they are provided over time. Nondeductibility of capital outlays, thus, results in a compounding of the tax on the payments for capital services and raises the cost of using these services relative to the cost of other production inputs. Permitting the deduction for capital outlays at the time they are made, by the same token, confines the application of the tax to the gross returns for the capital's services as these returns are generated over time. The VAT does not exempt capital from taxation but merely taxes payments for capital services at the same rate as payments for other factors of production. (It is, thus, neutral with respect to the tax burden it imposes on the use of all production inputs.)

To illustrate: in the absence of a tax, a firm wishes to purchase $X of production facilities. It needs to allocate thereto $X of its own income (or $X of outsiders' incomes if the outlay is to be externally financed). To warrant the outlay, the present value of the net returns allocable to the facilities must be at least equal to the price of the facilities, $X. Thus, in equilibrium in efficient markets,

$X = A_r^N Y$, where

A_r^N = the expression of the present value of an annuity of $1 for N years, discounted at r percent; and

Y = the annual income allocable to the facilities, i.e., the amount the facilities must earn if the owner(s) of the company is (are) to provide the $X of saving to the company for the purchase of the facilities. In other words, Y is the annual payment for, or cost of, the capital services provided by $X of capital facilities.

Now suppose a VAT were imposed, allowing a deduction for capital outlays but no depreciation deduction from the annual income attributable to the facilities purchased by these outlays. The gross earnings of the facilities now bear a tax each year $= tY$, and the annual after-tax earnings are $Y - tY = Y(1-t)$, the present value of which is $A_r^N Y(1-t)$. With no change in r, however, an annual income of $Y(1-t)$ will not warrant the outlay of $X for the facilities. The annual pre-tax income of the facilities will have to increase sufficiently so that after paying the tax, Y remains, i.e., $Y_1 = \dfrac{Y}{1-t}$, where Y_1 is the pre-tax amount which the facilities must earn if $X are to be provided for their purchase. For example, if $X = \$1,000$, $Y = \$100$, and $t = 20$ percent, Y_1 must equal $125.

The deductibility of capital outlays under the VAT, therefore, does not exempt capital goods from the tax. On the contrary, VAT increases the cost to the company of using capital services and in the same proportion as it increases the cost of using other production inputs. For example, if before the tax, L man-hours of labor service were employed at an hourly rate of w, these labor services would have to contribute $wL=W$ to the company's revenues. If the same amount of labor services are to be employed at the same hourly rate after the tax is imposed, their pre-tax contribution to revenues will have to increase sufficiently so that the after-tax amount, $W_1(1-t) = W$, where $W_1 =$ the required pre-tax contribution to revenues. In other words, W_1 must $= \dfrac{W}{1-t}$. Thus, the tax increases the cost of using labor services in the same proportion as it increases the cost of using capital services, i.e., by $\dfrac{1}{1-t}$.

E. Effects on the Price Level. One of the fiscal crimes of which the VAT is widely accused is that it raises the price level. Often this charge is based on casual observations rather than analysis. It is frequently contended, for example, that where the VAT was adopted in Europe, the price level promptly rose. An examination of the facts shows no consistent pattern of change in the price level in relation to the rates of the VAT. A closer relationship emerges between changes in the price level and in the stock of money. Looking at the following table, the general conclusion one should reach, it seems to me, is that increases in the money stock, not the introduction of the VAT, account for the increases in the price level.

It is possible that the use of the invoice method by most of the countries which have adopted the VAT contributed to a temporary surge in prices. Since this method instructs the taxpayer separately to show and to add the VAT to his sales invoices, it is plausible that business quite generally did so without adjusting the base sales price at first, until they had had the opportunity to see the effect of these increases on their sales. In time, however, prices must have adjusted so that they generally were about in line with the level which basic monetary, fiscal and market conditions dictated.

Apparently, the conviction that the VAT raises prices is of a piece with the view that it is a tax on consumption and/or a tax that is passed along from production stage to production stage until it comes to rest on the consumer. I have attempted to show earlier that the tax would be neutral with respect to the relative cost of consumption and saving and is not therefore properly characterized

Table 7
MONEY, CONSUMER PRICES, AND THE VAT IN EUROPE

Country	VAT Rate(s) at Date of Adoption	Percentage Change	
		From 4th qtr. preceding adoption of VAT to date of adoption	From date of adoption of VAT to 4th qtr. after adoption
Belgium	6%, 15%, 20%, 25%[a]		
Money		.07	n.a.
Consumer prices		.03	n.a.
Denmark	10%		
Money		.09[b]	.17[c]
Consumer prices		.08[b]	n.a.
Netherlands	4%, 12%[d]		
Money		.10	.08
Consumer prices		.08	.03
Norway	20%		
Money		.05	.05
Consumer prices		.09	.07
Sweden	11.11%		
Money		−.08	.02
Consumer prices		.02	.06
West Germany	5%, 10%[e]		
Money		.02[f]	.10
Consumer prices		.03[f]	.02

[a] Each of the four VAT rates is levied on different, specified items. A basic rate of 18% is levied on items not specifically taxed at one of these rates.
[b] 4th quarter 1966 and 4th quarter 1967; VAT adopted 3rd quarter 1967.
[c] 4th quarter 1967 and 4th quarter 1968; VAT adopted 3rd quarter 1967.
[d] 12% on most items; 4% on food, etc.
[e] 10% on most items; 5% on food and agricultural products, etc.
[f] 4th quarter 1966 and 1st quarter 1968; VAT adopted 1st quarter 1968.
Source: International Monetary Fund, *International Financial Statistics*, vol. XXIV, no. 9, September 1971.

as a consumption tax. But let us consider from another point of view the contention that the tax is passed on and hence raises prices.

The argument that the VAT would raise prices appears to be that since every business, presumably, would pay the tax, each business would pass on the tax it pays to its customers. The raw material producer would pay its tax on the amount of its value added and presumably include that tax in the price it charges the, say, manufacturer which buys those raw materials. The manufacturer, in turn, would deduct from its net sales the full cost, including tax, of its purchases from the raw material producer, and pay the value added tax on the difference. It would, supposedly, add its value added tax to the price of its output when it sells that output to, say, a wholesaler. And so on down to the ultimate consumer.

But could every business pass along to its customers the full amount of its VAT liability? Could the prices of all products and services sold to consumers increase by the full amount of the tax?

All prices could be raised enough to pass the tax along fully only if there were a general inflation just because the VAT was imposed. And this could come about only if our monetary authorities were to increase the money supply sufficiently to allow all prices to rise. Hopefully, the Federal Reserve Board would not follow this course. If the Federal Reserve were to hold to a steady course of money expansion, prices generally could go up only if the amounts of goods and services offered for sale decreased. If the physical volume of sales goes down—or rises more slowly than otherwise—so does the physical volume of production and so does, therefore, the use of the factors of production, labor and capital. But if employment and the use of capital rise more slowly than otherwise, in time, wage rates and profits will rise more slowly than otherwise. And in time, for that very reason, prices generally will be lower than otherwise.

This analysis leaves us with this conclusion: if the money supply grows no faster than it would have in the absence of a VAT, the imposition of a VAT cannot generally and permanently raise prices.

This is not to say that no company or industry would be able to pass the VAT along to its customers in the form of higher prices. As we all know, some prices can be raised with little loss in sales, and these prices would be raised to pass along the VAT. But other prices would come down. The overall result, in time, must be the same price level which would prevail given basic monetary and market determinants.

F. The VAT as a Proportional Income Tax. As we have seen, the deductibility of capital outlays does not exempt the payment for capital services from the VAT; rather, the tax applies at the same rate as on a company's payments for labor services. Thus, if a company were paying $W per unit of labor services (L) and $Y per unit of capital services (K), its VAT liability would be t($WL + $YK). With given market prices of labor and capital services, the VAT obviously increases their cost to the user.

If the company is to continue to use the same amount of these production services and to pay the same market price per unit, it is clear that its total revenues from the sale of the goods or services they produce must increase, i.e., the price of the output must rise. The amount of the required increase per dollar is $\dfrac{t}{1-t}$. Thus if $t = 20\%$, a product that formerly sold for \$1 must now sell for \$1.25.

The question whether the VAT could be fully and directly "passed forward" in higher prices was examined above and it was concluded that the VAT itself could not raise the general level of prices, that such inflation could occur only because of untoward monetary expansion, and that such monetary expansion was not an essential accompaniment of the adoption of a VAT. Let us suppose that the stock of money (or the change therein) is not affected by the introduction of the VAT. Under these circumstances, if the same amount of production services is to be employed, the market price per unit of these services, i.e., their incomes, clearly will have to fall (or at least rise less rapidly than otherwise). If the prices of these production services are sticky downwards, i.e., either do not fall or rise as rapidly as in the absence of the tax, fewer of these production services will be employed. As before, the aggregate income of the suppliers of these services will be reduced.

Next, assume that monetary expansion permits increases in product prices to "pass the tax forward," so that the same amount of production services will be employed at the same market prices as before the tax. Now the increase in the price level with the same market prices of production services means that the *real* incomes of those supplying these services must fall.

The conclusion that the tax must reduce real income, of course, is not unexpected. Every tax must have this effect. A tax which failed to do so simply would not be a tax at all, i.e., it would not affect the total volume of real claims available to the private sector and therefore would not transfer any real claims to the government. What distinguishes the VAT from other taxes, however, is that it falls in equal proportion on all incomes.

G. Is the VAT Regressive? The point has been made repeatedly in the preceding discussion that the VAT is a proportional tax on the incomes of factors of production. The popular view of the tax, on the other hand, is that it is regressive. This assertion apparently is based on the view that the VAT is a tax on consumption and that consumption represents a declining fraction of income as income increases. Hence, the lower the income, the greater the ratio of VAT paid to income. As shown earlier, VAT is not a consumption tax, either in the sense that it is passed on from producer to consumer or in the sense that it increases the cost of consumption relative to saving. In some more sophisticated discussions, the charge that VAT is regressive appears to rest on the assertion that capital is exempt from the tax and that the distribution of capital ownership is skewed toward the rich. However, as shown, capital is not exempt from the VAT, but is taxed on equal terms with other production inputs.

A third basis for the allegation that the VAT is regressive arises in connection with proposals to substitute the VAT for the income tax on corporations. In this case, it is sometimes explicitly conceded by the VAT critic that the VAT is in fact a proportional income tax, but it is maintained that the corporation income tax is progressive in the income-level distribution of its burden. Hence, it is argued, a substitution of the VAT for the corporation income tax represents a switch from a progressive tax to a proportional tax, i.e., a move toward regressivity. This contention clearly rests on the characterization of the corporation income tax as a progressive income tax, a matter which lies beyond the immediate purview of my discussion. Suffice it to say that there is hardly a consensus as to the ultimate incidence of the corporation income tax. Indeed, many VAT critics are persuaded that the corporation income tax is largely "passed forward" to consumers, a conviction which surely must undercut this basis for opposing a substitution of the VAT for the corporation income tax. Until there is a sturdier empirical demonstration than is now available of the impact and incidence of the corporation income tax, one cannot confidently compare this tax with the VAT from the point of view of regressivity.

5.   Capital Formation and Productivity

Just as criticism of the VAT often exceeds the constraints of carefully reasoned analysis, advocacy of the tax is sometimes more enthusiastic than is warranted. This exaggeration is nowhere so clear as in the case of the claims made on behalf of the VAT with respect to private capital formation.

In most instances, the favorable impact of the VAT on investment is attributed to the alleged exemption of capital from the tax. But, as shown above, the VAT does not exempt capital but merely avoids the compounded taxation of capital imposed by an "income" tax.

If we go back to our example of the initially taxless economy, we find that the imposition of the VAT will increase, in equal proportion, the cost of private consumption and of private saving and investment. The amount of both should decline, at least relative to what they would have been in the absence of the tax, and again in equal proportion, other things being equal. Moreover, so too would the amount of private employment of labor services fall and in the same proportion as the reduction in capital services, since, as shown above, the VAT would not alter the relative costs of labor and capital inputs. In sum, the imposition of the VAT should result in a reduction of private sector output, at least relative to what it would have been in the tax-free economy. Of course, this reduction is precisely the objective of taxation, i.e., to increase the cost of private uses of production capability relative to public uses in order to reallocate resources from the private to the public sector. To repeat, a VAT would raise the costs of both consumption and saving, and of both capital services and labor services, in equal proportion.

It is this neutrality of the impact of the VAT which should chiefly commend it as the principal tax in our revenue system. By the same token, it is this neutral impact which is the principal basis for advocating the substitution of the VAT for the present income taxation of business.

Compared with the present corporation income tax, the VAT would indeed impose far less of a tax burden on private capital formation. The corporation income tax is an extremely high-rate, selective excise on the use of equity capital in corporate enterprises. It is, moreover, an incremental burden on saving and investment, since the individual income tax itself is biased against saving and for consumption by virtue of the fact that saving is included in the tax base. Substituting the VAT for the corporation income tax, while retaining the other taxes in the federal, state and local fiscal systems, would not eliminate the anti-capital bias in the total revenue scheme, but it would greatly mitigate the additional differential tax burden on capital imposed by the corporate tax. In this respect, therefore, the substitution would represent a major contribution to constructive tax reform.

Substituting the VAT for the corporation income tax would substantially reduce—though not eliminate—the excess cost of using capital services compared with labor services. Reducing the relative cost of capital services would result in an increase in the amount of such services employed with any amount of labor services. Moreover, with a greater rate of private capital formation, the total stock of capital in the private sector would not only be larger but on the average newer and more technologically advanced as well. As a consequence, assuming the law of diminishing returns has not been repealed, labor's productivity and real earnings would be greater than under the present tax system.

The introduction of the VAT as a means of raising additional revenues, rather than as a substitute for existing business taxes, would increase the cost of capital and labor services. Other things being equal, this policy would retard the increase in employment of both labor and capital inputs. Compared with an increase in the corporation income tax rates in order to raise the same amount of additional revenue, however, the VAT would have a more moderate impact on capital formation.

6. The VAT and the Balance of Payments

Much is made by many VAT advocates of the so-called border tax adjustments which are associated with the VAT, i.e., the imposition of the VAT on imports and the rebate of the tax on exports. Ostensibly, these border tax adjustments would increase the prices of imported goods and reduce the prices of exports. Presumably, this change in relative prices would result in a reduction in imports and an increase in exports, hence an increase in the trade surplus (or reduction in the trade deficit).

Upon closer examination, however, the effects of the border tax adjustments are uncertain. They would depend on a number of factors, including whether the VAT were substituted for existing business income taxes, whether monetary and fiscal policies were set so as to preclude an increase in the general level of prices, and the degree of specialization of U.S. exports and imports. For example, assume that monetary-fiscal policy holds the price level unchanged and that the VAT is introduced as a substitute for the present income tax on business profits. Further assume that substantial amounts of U.S. exports are relatively nonspecialized in the sense that exported goods are also produced for U.S. domestic markets, face close substitutes in international markets, and represent a relatively small fraction of the total of such goods traded in these markets. On these assumptions the tax should result in a prompt improvement in the balance of trade. This improvement would result, on the export side, from the fact that export business would become more profitable because of the general exemption of exports from the value added tax. This increased profitability would induce a shift from domestic to foreign sales by the producers of those goods which are not highly specialized in one or the other market. To the extent that our exports encounter close substitutes and are a relatively small fraction of total sales in the world market, U.S. export producers would have no reason to cut the prices of their exports. Increased volume, not price cuts, therefore would be the route to increased export sales revenue.

On the import side, the tax substitution would result in a relative price advantage for import-competing goods domestically produced. This advantage arises from the fact that import prices would rise by the amount of the value added tax imposed on them as they entered the U.S., while prices of domestically produced goods would remain unchanged. The effect on the total value of imports would depend on the elasticity of U.S. demand for imports with respect to their prices, which in turn would depend on the degree of specialization of imports.

If we assume that both our exports and imports are highly specialized, the substitution of value added for corporate income taxation would require a longer period of time to affect the trade account in our balance of payments. As in the former case, the rebate of the value added tax on exports would increase the profitability of the export business. Unless there were excess capacity in export production, however, there would be no reason to reduce export prices. Increases in export volume would occur only as additional production capacity was built up, a time-consuming process. Much the same would be true on the import side. The imposition of the tax on imports would raise their prices relative to domestically produced goods and afford, thereby, an incentive for some reallocation of production capability to import-competing goods. Again, this reallocation would take time.

Next assume that the VAT is adopted not as a substitute for existing taxes but as a source of additional revenue and that the domestic price level rises by the amount of the tax. On these assumptions the imposition of the VAT on imports would not alter the relative prices of imports and of domestically produced import-competing products, nor would the rebate of the tax on exports result in a reduction of export prices compared with their level prior to the adoption of the VAT. Hence, the border tax adjustments would have no immediate impact on the trade account. However, profit margins on export production would be increased relative to those on domestic sales, and some reallocation of output and production capacity to exports would occur. As before, the speed of this adjustment would depend in large part on the degree of specialization of exports.

While these alternative assumptions do not exhaust the possibilities, they do illustrate the cautions required in establishing the impact on the balance of trade of the VAT with border tax adjustments. It may well be that some VAT advocates attribute too much to these border tax adjustments for the short run, just as some observers and policy makers may have counted too heavily on the near-term benefits for our trade balance of the realignment of exchange rates.

Be that as it may, substitution of the VAT for the corporation income tax should in the long run result in important changes in the balance of payments. In the last analysis, any country's trade balance depends on its real comparative advantage in production, hence on the productivity of its production inputs. The productivity gains associated with replacing the corporation income tax by the VAT, therefore, should contribute to improving the trade balance.

A further effect of the substitution should be seen on capital account. Since the U.S. corporation income tax is a very high-rate excise on equity capital, and since the base of the VAT is far larger, the rate of the VAT required to replace corporation income tax revenues is much lower than the corporate tax rate. The substitution, accordingly, would greatly reduce the effective rate of taxation on the returns to equity capital. It is surely reasonable to expect that the increase in after-tax returns would attract foreign investors and induce U.S. investors to allocate more of their capital to domestic enterprises. This change would be only a one-shot effect but possibly of large magnitude.

7. Concluding Comments

Much of the analysis in this discussion has been framed in the context of the VAT as an alternative to the present income taxes on business. For purposes of elucidating the nature of the VAT and its economic impact, this is a useful and appropriate mode of exposition. Moreover, many of the analytical propositions presented above are unaffected by assuming that the VAT would be adopted not as a substitute for, but in lieu of, an increase in present taxes.

The current discussions of the VAT are in a context of enormous deficits in the federal budget, with little prospect, given the present trends in spending and taxes, for their substantial reduction in the near future. Regrettable as it is in the judgment of many economists, it appears that the VAT is more likely to be proposed as a means of obtaining additional revenues than as a substitute for all or part of existing taxes.

If in fact expenditure growth cannot be curbed or if that growth is desired by a majority of the citizens, then it will be necessary to face up honestly to the desirability of increasing taxes. Our examination of the VAT suggests that, given the other objectives and criteria of public financial policy, it would be better to rely on the VAT for the desired additional revenues than to increase any of the existing taxes in the federal revenue system. If the overall effective rate of taxes on the private sector's income must be increased, the VAT would be the least damaging means of doing so.

Technical Note: Calculation of the VAT Base in 1971

The VAT base is readily derived in alternative calculations from the national income accounts (NIA).[12] Four methods are shown in the tables below. The first begins with gross national product, a measure of the total value added in all sectors of the economy, and adjusts this total for those components of GNP which, it is assumed, would be excluded from the VAT base. The second method begins with the NIA estimates of value added in the private sector of the economy. The third starts with national income, a measure of the total payments for factors of production and adjusts this total (a) to exclude such payments made in the government sector, as well as capital outlays, and (b) to add back capital consumption allowances and existing excises, sales, and other so-called indirect business taxes. The last method consists of value added in consumption goods and services plus that in private sector output sold to federal, state, and local governments, less value added originating in households and institutions.

In all of the calculations, value added originating in the government and household sectors of the economy is excluded. As a corollary to the exclusion of the household sector, one-half of the value added in residential construction is included in the VAT base, on the assumption that one-half of the value of residential construction is accounted for by owner-occupied housing. Since the household sector is assumed to be excluded from the tax, no deduction of outlays by households for residential structures would be allowed. On the

---

[12] Cf. U.S. Department of Commerce, Bureau of Economic Analysis, *Survey of Current Business*, April 1972, pp. 13-15.

other hand, the remaining 50 percent of residential construction is assumed to be rental property, the owners of which would deduct their outlays for property acquisition in computing their VAT liabilities.

$ Billions

VAT Base Derived from Gross National Product, 1971

Gross national product	1,046.8
Plus:	
Imports	65.3
	1,112.1
Minus:	
Exports	65.3
GNP originating in government sector	124.0
GNP originating in households and institutions	35.5
Nonresidential fixed investment	108.7
50% of residential structures	20.3
Change in business inventories	2.2
Value added tax base	756.1

VAT Base Derived from Private Sector GNP, 1971

Private sector GNP	922.7
Plus:	
Imports	65.3
	988.0
Minus:	
Exports	65.3
GNP originating in households and institutions	35.5
Nonresidential fixed investment	108.7
50% of residential structures	20.3
Change in business inventories	2.2
Value added tax base	756.0

VAT Base Derived from National Income, 1971

National income	851.1
Minus:	
National income originating in:	
Government	124.0
Households and institutions	35.5
	691.6

Plus:

Capital consumption allowances	95.2
Indirect business tax and nontax liabilities	102.1
Business transfer payments	4.3
	893.2

Minus:

Nonresidential fixed investment	108.7
50% of residential structures	20.3
Change in business inventories	2.2
Subsidies less current surplus of gov't enterprises	1.0
Statistical discrepancy	4.9
Value added tax base	756.1

VAT Base Derived from Personal Consumption in GNP, 1971

Personal consumption expenditures	662.1

Plus:

Government purchases from private sector	109.0
50% of residential structures	20.3
	791.4

Minus:

GNP originating in households and institutions	35.5
Value added tax base	755.9

**VALUE ADDED TAXATION
IN EUROPE**
Eric Schiff

Proposals to adopt a federal tax on value added (VAT) have been widely discussed in the United States during the last few years, and the issue will probably remain a live one for some time. In the course of the debate, European experiences with VAT—a tax levied on the value added to a good or service at each stage in its production and distribution—have naturally attracted attention. As of July 1973, twelve European countries are operating fairly comprehensive systems of value-added taxation; the United Kingdom was the latest to introduce VAT, effective April 1, 1973.

Certain facts undoubtedly limit the relevance of European experiences for American decisions regarding VAT. There is, first, the relatively short time span during which European experience could develop. As late as July 1, 1967, no European country had a VAT system extending over all stages of commodity production and distribution and covering the majority of services.[1] Secondly, in all European countries that have adopted VAT since that time, the system replaced some other type of general sales tax, whereas in the United States the value-added tax would be the first general sales tax at the national level. On the other hand, some proponents of VAT in this country have suggested it as a partial substitute for the corporate income tax, whereas in Europe, substitution of VAT for direct taxes was not the rule. True, in a few countries, such as Denmark, some reduction in direct taxation (and some increase in transfer payments) took place once the value-added tax began to yield a satisfactory flow of revenue. But only in Norway were a

---

[1] France has had a value-added tax since 1954 (indeed, since 1948, in a very rudimentary form) but before the tax reform of 1968 it covered only mining, manufacturing, and some special cases of wholesale trade.

265

reduction of direct taxes—in this case, on corporate profits—and an expansion of social services explicit parts of the reform plan that provided for the switch to VAT. In the United Kingdom, such a combination was discussed, but rejected.

Despite these limitations, European experiences with the value-added tax are relevant to tax reform plans in this country. Chapter 1 of this essay offers some observations on historical developments that led to the adoption of the system in European countries. Chapter 2 deals with the system of gross turnover tax (GTT) that in many countries was replaced by the value-added tax. Although this system is now history in most of the European countries in which it had long been *the* form of general turnover tax,[2] analysis of it is important for an understanding of the reasons behind the changeover. Besides, not all the effects of the old system became instantly extinct with its abolition. Some of the countries that switched continue to struggle with certain of its aftereffects. These aftereffects require discussion, the more so as they largely explain the difficulties of measuring the price effects of VAT in Europe—the topic of the third section. While others have contrasted the basic properties of the gross turnover tax and of the value-added tax, and thus any new discussion of the corollaries—the great advantages of VAT over GTT—must move over familiar ground, the confrontation here may have news value at least in point of form, for it is presented in algebraic terms. This form of analysis should also be helpful for clarifying the problem of determining VAT tax rates that are equivalent to given GTT rates, in terms of revenue yield or tax burden on the consumer. This is another matter that has lost its policy importance in European countries that have already made the switch. But an understanding of the equivalence problem is essential for an understanding of the decisions on the VAT rates to be applied after the switch.

Price developments in three countries of the European Economic Community (EEC) and in two Scandinavian countries before and after introduction of the value-added tax are examined in Chapter 3. Only those countries are discussed which offer some chance that, on the basis of the information obtained, attempts to isolate the price effects of VAT from simultaneous price effects of other factors might prove successful. Where this was not the case, it seemed better to pass over the country rather than to come up with mere conjectures. This is why Chapter 3 is silent on so important a country as France, whereas little Denmark is discussed at some length.

---

[2] In Switzerland, GTT is still on the statute books.

Wherever adoption of a general sales tax at the national level is under consideration, the value-added tax and the retail sales tax (RST) are nowadays by far the most serious candidates. In the United States, the issue of VAT versus RST has been debated extensively, and the debate will undoubtedly be resumed with new vigor, should the question of a federal general sales tax ever reach the decision-making stage. The fourth and final chapter therefore presents a brief survey of the main arguments that were used in Europe for and against each of the alternatives before the decision fell. Some European judgments on the merits of the decision in the light of subsequent experience are also presented. It seemed useful in this context to cast a side glance at Canada. There, the matter is still undecided, but an eminently authoritative document, the Carter Report, has come out against the decision that was made in Europe.

This essay should be regarded only as a fragmentary attempt to approach some topics that deserve a far more thorough analysis. In fact, the only subject that has been treated systematically in this study is the effect of VAT on prices. Such important matters as the effects of the switch to VAT on the demand for capital goods, or European experiences with border tax adjustments since the switch, are discussed at several places, but not nearly as thoroughly as they deserve. One intricate topic, the effect of the switch to VAT on the liquidity position of business firms, has been bypassed entirely, because the empirical evidence seemed too slender to rely on. For the topics treated, an effort has been made to utilize European source material that, for language or other reasons, is not easily accessible in this country.

Description and analysis of European experiences and trends of thought are the sole purposes of this study. While it is hoped that the study will contribute to American thinking on the VAT question, no attempt has been made to draw from the surveyed European material any direct inferences for American tax policy.

The Recent VAT Sweep in Europe

The rapid adoption of value-added taxation by a number of European countries since 1967 represents an important move in the process of economic integration of Western Europe. The process started with the establishment of the European Economic Community pursuant to the Treaty of Rome (March 25, 1957). The abolition, as from July 1, 1968, of all customs duties and quotas in the trade between EEC member countries was a necessary but not a sufficient step in the movement toward a common market with equality of competitive conditions. It was also necessary to replace with a common system the varying systems of indirect taxes which, apart from other weaknesses, had distorted competitive conditions between the member states. The Neumark Report,[1] which prepared the ground for the decisions of the subsequent years, visualized ultimate acceptance by all EEC countries of all-stage value-added tax systems identical, or nearly identical, in structure as well as in all the important details of tax rates, exemptions, and so on. The report acknowledged that such an all-round harmonization could be achieved only gradually. In particular, it pointed out that some member countries might find it difficult to include retail trade in a value-added tax system. So the report recommended as the next step that all EEC countries replace the gross turnover tax systems, then on the statute books

---

[1] *Report of the Fiscal and Financial Committee* (FFC), Chairman, Professor Fritz Neumark (Frankfurt a.M., 1962). The FFC had been set up by the Commission of the European Economic Community. The report was first released in German; a semi-official English translation was published in 1963 by the International Bureau of Fiscal Documentation in Amsterdam (hereinafter cited as *Neumark Report*).

in all these countries, with systems of value-added tax, if possible with nearly identical tax rates, extending to all stages up to but excluding the retail stage, which was to be subject to a separate supplementary tax.[2]

Two directives dated April 11, 1967, and issued by the Council of Ministers of the six original EEC countries, cleared the path for decisive action. In broad agreement with the recommendations of the Neumark Report, the EEC states were required by these directives to abolish the existing gross turnover tax systems and to introduce comprehensive systems of value-added taxation.[3] Inclusion of the retail stage was stated to be highly desirable, but members that found the inclusion too difficult were permitted to subject this stage to a separate tax, at least for an interim period. Later, the council became more insistent on the inclusion of retail trade in the common VAT structure, and, in fact, all EEC countries (and, for that matter, all other countries that have since adopted VAT) have extended the system to it.

The tax rates were left to the individual member states; to require uniformity of rates *between* countries, as outlined in the Neumark Report, was obviously considered, for the time being, too great an abridgment of national sovereignty. But the council felt keenly the desirability of a high degree of rate uniformity at least *within* each member state. By the second directive, the member states were required to adopt standard rates applicable to the sale of goods as well as to the rendering of services. But they were permitted to set special rates for certain goods and services.[4] The directives also stressed the desirability of introducing as few exemptions as possible. So far the attempt at uniformity has met with only limited success. France and Belgium both have four different VAT rates; Ireland and Italy have three;[5] and rules about exemptions are quite complex in several countries.

Here is the first major lesson of European experience with VAT. The inconvenience of multiple tax rates and complex exemption rules

---

[2] Ibid., pp. 124, 126.

[3] Unlike the recommendations of the FFC, the directives of the council were regarded as binding guidelines for the tax policy of the member states.

[4] *Second Directive*, Article 9, Parts 1 and 2 (pages 9-10 of the French text as published by the French Department of Economics and Finance), April 11, 1967.

[5] An EEC directive of 1969 ruled, however, that as of January 1, 1974, no member country will be permitted to use more than two VAT rates. See Alan A. Tait, *Value-Added Taxation* (New York: McGraw-Hill, 1972), p. 148.

was clear enough.[6] But several European governments felt too strongly about the need for these differentiations to eschew them (or were under too strong popular pressure about it), and used them partly to favor certain lines of industrial production, and partly to offset the regressivity of the VAT system by prescribing lower tax rates for "necessities" and higher ones for "luxuries." Any country that will adopt VAT will have to struggle with this dilemma.

Some Delays—The Special Case of Italy

According to the two 1967 directives, the changeover to VAT in the Common Market was to be accomplished by January 1, 1970. Two EEC countries, Belgium and Italy, failed to meet the deadline. Belgium was permitted by special arrangement to postpone the introduction of the new system until January 1, 1971. Italy's delay stemmed mainly, though not exclusively, from apprehension about the particular difficulties of administering a VAT system extending to retail trade. Although the EEC council had become increasingly insistent on this point, the Italian government feared that, at least in the immediate future, the strict requirements for record keeping and other administrative work under the VAT system[7] would prove too much for its thousands of small shopkeepers, who were singularly ill-equipped to meet them and not exactly eager to cooperate with the authorities.[8] In December 1969, the Council of EEC Ministers granted Italy's request to postpone introduction of the value-added tax system until January 1, 1972,[9] but even so the switch was delayed for another full year.

VAT outside the EEC Area

In the meantime, several countries then outside the EEC orbit had placed value-added taxation on their statute books. Denmark, in fact, was the first European country to adopt an all-stage VAT system,

---

[6] For some examples, see the article, "Taxation Vexation," *Wall Street Journal*, September 21, 1972, p. 1.

[7] Under VAT, these requirements may well be higher than under any other sales tax system, including even the gross turnover tax. The reasons, and some European experiences with the administrative problems posed by VAT, will be discussed more extensively later on.

[8] Tait, *Value-Added Taxation*, p. 146.

[9] See International Monetary Fund, *International Financial News Survey*, vol. 22, no. 1 (January 9, 1970), p. 5.

effective July 3, 1967. Sweden followed in 1969, and Norway in 1970. In the three Scandinavian countries, VAT replaced single-stage sales tax systems. In each of them, one motive for the changeover seems to have been the possible application for admission to the EEC (Denmark was admitted in 1972), where newcomers would probably be required to make the changeover.[10] In the United Kingdom and Austria, which decided to change over to the value-added tax system in 1973, the decision was decisively influenced by the prospect of joining the EEC.

This sketchy survey of the recent VAT sweep in Europe clearly links it into the chain of events leading to the economic unification of Europe. So far the contribution of VAT to overall unification has been limited, even within the original EEC area. Owing to differences that thus far have not been overcome (differential tax rates both between and within countries, divergent rules about exemptions, and so forth), the spread of VAT has not contributed as much to unifying the area into a genuine common market as was perhaps expected when the Neumark Report was released. But neither can the contribution be slighted.

Effective and Nominal VAT Rates in Europe

Table 1 summarizes a few facts that characterize the present situation. The tabulation of the tax rates (most of which are higher than they were immediately after adoption of the VAT system) calls for a few words of comment. All rates shown are "effective" rates—that is, rates applicable to the tax base *exclusive* of the tax itself. In their own publications, France, Sweden, and Ireland report rates where the tax base *includes* the tax itself. These rates are, in this sense, "nominal."

To be analytically useful, a rate applicable to the tax base including the tax itself must first be converted into the equivalent effective rate—that is, into the rate that, if applied to the base exclusive of the tax itself, yields the same revenue. The appropriate conversion formula is:

$$r = \frac{\bar{r}}{1 - \bar{r}},$$

---

[10] That the changeover to VAT was partly motivated by those expectations in the Scandinavian countries has been confirmed by the Norwegian Ministry of Taxes and Customs in their publication, *A Survey of the Norwegian Tax System in 1970* (Oslo: Royal Ministry of Taxes and Customs, Tax Law Department, 1970), p. 100.

Table 1

SELECTED DATA ON VAT IN EUROPE

(as of July 1, 1973)

Country	Effective Date of Comprehensive VAT	Replaced Taxes	Effective VAT Rates, February 1973			
			Lowest	Intermediary	Standard	Highest
France	Jan. 1, 1968	Various indirect taxes	7.53%	17.63%	23.45%	33.33%
West Germany	Jan. 1, 1968	Gross turnover tax	5.5		11	
Netherlands	Jan. 1, 1969	Gross turnover tax	4		14	
Belgium	Jan. 1, 1971	Gross turnover tax	6	14	18	25
Luxembourg	Jan. 1, 1970	Gross turnover tax	4		8	
Ireland	Nov. 1, 1972	Purchase tax, retail sales tax	5.26		16.37	30.26
Denmark	July 3, 1967	Wholesale sales tax			15	
Sweden	Jan. 1, 1969	Retail sales tax	(3.09) a	(9.89) a	17.65	
Norway	Jan. 1, 1970	Retail sales tax			20	
United Kingdom	April 1, 1973	Purchase tax, selective employment tax			10	
Italy	Jan. 1, 1973	Gross turnover tax, various minor indirect taxes	3	6	12	18
Austria	Jan. 1, 1973	Gross turnover tax	8		16	

a Rates on reduced base. See discussion in text.

Source: Data compiled by author from various original sources.

where $\bar{r}$ (in decimals) is some nominal rate, and r (in decimals) is the equivalent effective rate.[11] The conversion is simple enough, but it is hard to think of any other than cosmetic reasons for the detour. A nominal rate is, of course, always lower than its equivalent effective rate and (as demonstrated in Appendix A) a rate increase, when expressed in nominal rates, is always smaller, in percentage points as well as in percentages, than its equivalent increase in effective rates. Thus, on January 1, 1971, Sweden increased her standard (nominal) VAT rate from 10 percent to 15 percent. This increase (5 percentage points, 50 percent) looked more moderate than it would have had it been stated in equivalent effective rates—from 11.11 percent to 17.65 percent, an increase of 6.54 percentage points, or 58.87 percent.

To the nominal-rates detour, Sweden added still another, probably likewise for cosmetic purposes only. In point of form, Sweden has only one VAT rate—at present, 15 percent nominal, or 17.65 percent effective. However, the taxable value to which this rate applies is in certain cases reduced to 60 percent, and in certain other cases to 20 percent. This is the same thing as applying rates of 9 percent nominal (9.89 percent effective), or 3 percent nominal (3.09 percent effective) to the full taxable value. In Table 1 the two reduced rates have been put in parentheses to indicate that as a matter of official presentation only the standard rate applies.[12]

The table suggests that, notwithstanding the de facto rate differentiation in Sweden, there is somewhat more rate uniformity in Scandinavia than in the original EEC. This is noteworthy in view of the fact that the EEC countries have been under stronger pressure to make uniform their VAT rate buildup.

[11] The reader interested in the mathematical derivation of the formula is referred to Appendix A.

[12] The tabulation of European VAT rates in *The Economist*, March 25, 1971, p. 65, contains a few errors. Ever since July 1970, the Danish rate has been 15 percent, not 12.5 percent as indicated by *The Economist*. The two Swedish reduced (effective) rates are, as mentioned in the text and given in Table 1, 9.89 percent and 3.09 percent, not 10.59 percent and 3.53 percent. For the Netherlands, *The Economist* lists a "highest" rate of 32 percent. Such a rate has never been set.

2

THE STRUCTURE OF VAT:
SOME PROPERTIES,
RELATIONSHIPS AND EQUIVALENCES

VAT and GTT

The general properties of the value-added tax as *the* noncumulative, multistage turnover tax system have been described so often[1] that it might appear unnecessary to elaborate on them once more. Yet a comparison of the stage-by-stage buildups of the value-added taxation (VAT) system and the gross turnover tax (GTT) system in a special tabular and algebraic form might sharpen understanding of the European experience with VAT, especially in countries where it has recently supplanted GTT.[2]

In Table 2,

$V_1, V_2, V_3, \ldots, V_n$ = the values added at stages 1, 2, 3, $\ldots$, n

R = the effective tax rate (in decimals) in the VAT system

r = the effective tax rate (in decimals) in the GTT system.[3]

---

[1] See, for example, the authoritative analytical description in Carl S. Shoup, *Public Finance* (Chicago: Aldine Publishing Company, 1969), pp. 250-66; Tait, *Value-Added Taxation*, pp. 1-5; Charles E. McLure, Jr., and Norman B. Ture, *Value Added Tax: Two Views* (Washington, D. C.: American Enterprise Institute, 1972); and numerous articles in technical journals.

[2] Readers who are not interested in the algebra may skip Table 2 and turn to the final results (the expressions for sales values and tax contents set forth on page 13 in terms of the symbols explained in text) and to the discussion of their implications that follows.

[3] In most countries that have used the gross turnover tax system, the officially published rates have been nominal rates (applicable to the taxable value including the tax itself). For our purpose we need uniformity in this respect, and we assume therefore effective rates in both systems. For the relationship between nominal and equivalent effective rates, see above, p. 8.

The differentiation in the symbols for the tax rates (capital versus small letter) indicates that any given VAT rate is substantially higher than the GTT rate that yields equivalent revenue.

275

Table 2

COMPARISON OF THE VALUE-ADDED TAX AND THE GROSS TURNOVER TAX

Stage	Paid to Supplier[a] (1)	Sales Value before Tax[b] (2)	Tax Paid to Treasury (3)	Charged to Customer[c] (4)
A. Value-Added Tax				
1[d]	0	V_1	RV_1	$(1+R) V_1$
2	$(1+R) V_1$	$(1+R) V_1 + V_2$	RV_2	$(1+R) (V_1 + V_2)$
3	$(1+R) (V_1 + V_2)$	$(1+R) (V_1 + V_2) + V_3$	RV_3	$(1+R) (V_1 + V_2 + V_3)$
$\cdots$			$\cdots$	$\cdots$
n	$(1+R) (V_1 + V_2 + \ldots V_{n-1})$	$(1+R) (V_1 + V_2 + \ldots V_{n-1}) + V_n$	RV_n	$(1+R) (V_1 + V_2 + \ldots V_n)$
B. Gross Turnover Tax				
1[d]	0	V_1	rV_1	$(1+r) V_1$
2	$(1+r) V_1$	$(1+r) V_1 + V_2$	$r[(1+r) V_1 + V_2]$	$(1+r)^2 V_1 + (1+r) V_2$
3	$(1+r)^2 V_1 + (1+r) V_2$	$(1+r)^2 V_1 + (1+r) V_2 + V_3$	$r[(1+r)^2 V_1 (1+r) V_2 + V_3]$	$(1+r)^3 V_1 + (1+r)^2 V_2 + (1+r) V_3$
$\cdots$			$\cdots$	$\cdots$
n	$(1+r)^{n-1}V_1 + (1+r)^{n-2}V_2 + \ldots (1+r)^2 V_{n-2} + (1+r) V_{n-1}$	$(1+r)^{n-1}V_1 + (1+r)^{n-2}V_2 + \ldots (1+r)^2 V_{n-2}(1+r) + V_{n-1} + V_n$	$r[(1+r)^{n-1}V_1 + (1+r)^{n-2}V_2 + \ldots (1+r)V_{n-1} + V_n]$	$(1+r)^n V_1 + (1+r)^{n-1}V_2 + \ldots (1+r)^3 V_{n-2} + \ldots (1+r)^2 V_{n-1} + (1+r)V_n$

a Column (1) from preceding stage. b Column (1) plus value added at stage indicated. c Column (2) plus column (3). d The assumption of a first stage that pays nothing is unavoidable in any tabular analysis of the stage-by-stage buildup of a turnover tax whether algebraic or in assumed absolute figures. Strictly speaking, no first stage exists in this sense. The chain of stages has an end point but no starting point; in backward direction it is circular.

Source: Author's calculations.

Table 2 assumes that all stages of production and distribution up to and including n are taxable, whereas any stage after n is tax free. It is further assumed that the tax load is shifted forward fully from stage 1 to stage n.

In the VAT system the tax base (taxable value) at each stage is column 2 minus column 1. In the GTT system the tax base at each stage is column 2. The total sales value at stage n (the amount that the firm operating at that stage must recoup from its customer) is the entry in column 4 at stage n. The tax content of this value is the sum of all entries in column 3. If the customer of the firm operating at stage n is a final consumer (regardless of whether n represents the retail stage or some preretail stage—for example, a manufacturer selling directly to a consumer), then the consumer pays the sales value of stage n. If there are tax-free production or distribution stages between n and the consumer (as, for instance, in the French VAT, 1954-68, when retail trade, and in most cases even wholesale trade, was excluded), the sales price in either system in these post-n stages rises further, but only by values added. The tax content remains the same as at stage n.

For the rest, the table is self-explanatory. The sales value at stage n is available, for both systems, directly from column 4. The tax content for VAT (the simple summation of the entries in column 3) can be grasped at a glance; the cumulating process is more complicated for GTT.[4] The final results for stage n are embodied in the following expressions, where S — sales value, T — the tax content of this value, and VAT and GTT denote the two types of tax.

$$SVAT_n = (1+R)(V_1 + V_2 + \ldots + V_n) \tag{1}$$

$$TVAT_n = R(V_1 + V_2 + \ldots + V_n) \tag{2}$$

$$SGTT_n = (1+r)^n V_1 + (1+r)^{n-1} V_2 + \ldots + (1+r)^2 V_{n-1} + (1+r)V^n \tag{3}$$

$$TGTT_n = (1+r)^n V_1 + (1+r)^{n-1} V_2 + \ldots \ldots (1+r)^2 V_{n-1} + (1+r)V_n$$
$$- (V_1 + V_2 + \ldots \ldots + V_n). \tag{4}$$

In either system, the tax content at stage n equals the total sales value minus the sum of all values exclusive of tax that have been added up to and including stage n.

Relationships Defined by the Equations

Equations (1) through (4) tell a few familiar stories, though perhaps a bit more precisely than would purely verbal exposition.

---

[4] The reader interested in the steps involved is referred to Appendix B.

(1) Under VAT, the tax load embodied in the sales value of the product or service at stage n depends on the tax rate R and on the value accumulated at n exclusive of the tax $(V_1 + V_2 + \ldots + V_n)$. But the tax load is independent of n, the number of stages the product or service passed through, and also of the distribution of the values added at the successive stages. Since the tax rate R is known, and the aggregate value exclusive of the tax can be calculated simply by dividing the given sales value inclusive of the tax by $(1+R)$, the tax content of the sales value at n can be easily determined.

The fundamentally different situation under GTT is brought out strikingly by the two expressions relating to that system. Here, the tax load embodied in the sales value at n depends not only on the tax rate r and on the total accumulated value exclusive of the tax, but also on the number of stages (indicated by n)[5] and on the distribution of the values added at the successive stages.[6] Of these four variables, only the tax rate r is known. The number of stages the product or service has passed is not known at stage n to the taxpayer or to anybody else, nor is the time distribution of the values successively added up to that stage. Therefore the magnitude by which the given sales value inclusive of the tax must be reduced to yield the accumulated value exclusive of the tax cannot be determined. This is the root of the well-known impossibility, in the gross turnover tax system, of calculating the exact tax content of the sales value at any stage.

This impossibility was one of the main reasons why the Neumark Report and later EEC documents directed the member countries to change over to the VAT system, which, by contrast, makes feasible the proper computation of the tax rebates that, under the principle of taxation in the country of destination, must be allowed on exports.[7]

---

[5] The higher this value, the greater is the number of additive terms in the equations, and, moreover, the higher the power of the $(1+r)$ factor in each term. The fact that all $(1+r)$ factors except the last have powers reflects the cumulation, the "cascade" feature that characterizes the GTT system: the value added at any stage before stage n is repeated at all subsequent stages. See Shoup, *Public Finance*, pp. 223-24; also p. 215, note 14.

[6] The "weight" of the value added at any particular stage, measured by the power of the $(1+r)$ factor attached to it in these expressions, is greater than the "weight" of the value added at the next following stage (because the earlier a value has been added, the more often it is subsequently repeated; see previous note).

[7] Not all exporters welcomed the changeover from inaccurate to accurate calculation of the rebates. In Italy there was reason to think that the rebates on gross turnover taxes embodied in the values of goods destined for exportation were too high. So Italian exporters, who probably stood to lose by the switch to a tax system under which rebates could be computed precisely, opposed the switch,

(2) Another familiar advantage of VAT over GTT is its neutrality with respect to vertical integration. Under VAT, the tax content of any total sales value at stage n is independent of whether that sales value has been produced in two or twenty stages. Thus the degree of vertical integration in the production and distribution processes is immaterial. Of course, if the elimination of some stage in the process[8] entails internal or external economies, the sum of the values added up to and including n will be smaller, and so the tax content of the aggregate sales value will be smaller at this point. But that is not caused by the structure of the tax system.

In the case of the gross turnover tax, on the other hand, it is the structure of the system itself that precludes neutrality with respect to vertical integration. Even if the integration entails no economies, and thus leaves the sum of the added value (exclusive of tax) unchanged, the replacement of a taxable *inter*firm transfer with a non-taxable *intra*firm transfer is bound to diminish the cascade effect. When a taxable stage has been eliminated by vertical integration, each taxable added value (except the last one), as well as its taxation, is repeated on the way to stage n one time less than before,[9] and so the cumulated sales value of the product or service at n, as well as the cumulated tax load, is smaller than before the integration. In and of itself, this certainly benefits the final consumer or user, who cannot pass on his tax load to anybody. But there may be offsetting disadvantages, such as enhanced monopolistic market power of a

---

thus contributing to Italy's long delay in changing over to VAT. Tait, *Value-Added Taxation*, p. 147. By contrast, GTT tax rebates on German exports had probably been too low (see below, pp. 28-29).

[8] Through vertical integration or otherwise, as for example when a product that normally passes through the wholesale and retail stages is sold directly by the manufacturer to the consumer, thereby eliminating costs (including profit margins) of distribution.

[9] That this must be so can be seen by a glance at the stage-by-stage buildup in Table 2. In the algebraic expressions defining the situation under GTT at stage n, the reduced cumulation resulting from the elimination of a taxable stage would be reflected in a reduction by 1 of the power of each $(1 + r)$ factor except the last. To illustrate, suppose that some commodity is produced and distributed in four stages, involving, say, a raw material producer, a manufacturer, a wholesaler, and a retailer. The values added at each stage are, in this order, V_1, V_2, V_3, and V_4. Suppose that some day the wholesaler and the retailer merge, without any resulting reduction of either total costs or total profits. The equations reveal this situation strikingly.

Under VAT, the merger leaves the final sales value unchanged, for $(1+R)V_1 + (1+R)V_2 + (1+R)(V_3 + V_4)$ is equal to $(1+R)V_1 + (1+R)V_2 + (1+R)V_3 + (1+R)V_4$. Not so under GTT, however, for $(1+r)^3V_1 + (1+r)^2V_2 + (1+r)(V_3 + V_4)$ is smaller than $(1+r)^4V_1 + (1+r)^3V_2 + (1+r)^2V_3 + (1+r)V_4$.

firm as a result of the vertical integration. Since it is generally held that a sales tax system should affect market structure as little as possible, the neutrality of the VAT system with respect to vertical integration is regarded as one of its main virtues. Some empirical studies have found that under GTT, the cumulated tax burdens in integrated and nonintegrated sectors of an industry may differ substantially.[10] To the extent that such findings may be regarded as typical and traceable to the specific properties of the GTT system, there is prima facie evidence that the changeover to VAT in Europe has removed a powerful incentive to vertical integration.

Equivalence Problems in the Changeover to VAT

In each European country that has recently introduced a system of value-added tax, the tax has replaced some other system of sales taxation. Decisions about the new system's details—its tax rates, coverage, exemptions, and so on—depended on what the decision makers sought to achieve, and these decisions naturally were guided in many respects by the performance of the system to which the country had grown accustomed.[11] The aims varied greatly from country to country. In West Germany, the stated expectation was that VAT would not yield more revenue than the old GTT would have yielded under equal conditions.[12] Norway, on the other hand, wished the changeover to result in a substantially increased tax revenue and organized the new system accordingly. The aims with respect to the effects of VAT on prices also varied considerably. West Germany expected decisions about tax rates and other features of the VAT system to forestall any appreciable effect on the price level from the changeover. In other EEC countries, the conscious aim of policy makers for VAT systems was specified price increases.[13]

---

[10] W. Schubert, *Die Kumulativwirkung der deutschen Umsatzsteuer* (The Cumulative Effect of the German Turnover Tax) (1951) found that in the German bar steel industry the cumulated tax burden was 5.8 percent of the sales price in the highly integrated system and 11.3 percent in the nonintegrated system (quoted by John F. Due, *Sales Taxation* [London: Routledge & Kegan Paul, 1957], p. 62).

[11] In West Germany the gross turnover tax, introduced in 1918, had remained virtually unchanged for fifty years.

[12] *Jahresgutachten des Sachverstaendigenrates zur Begutachtung der gesamtwirtschaftlichen Entwickelung* (Annual Report of the Council of Economic Experts for the Examination of Aggregate Economic Development), *1967/68*, Ziff. 472, p. 222 (hereafter cited as *CEE Annual Report* for respective years). See below, p. 26.

[13] The proposition that a tax measure may affect the general price level raises some theoretical questions, which will be discussed in Chapter 3.

In any case, the formulation of purposes and plans presupposed at least some "feel" for the tax rates and other features of the proposed VAT system that would likely make it *equivalent* to the replaced system in terms of some target variable such as revenue yield or price level. In the United States, where VAT would not replace any existing (federal) sales tax system, no such question will arise.[14] But a few words may underscore the intricate difficulties that several European countries, especially those in the EEC, faced in deciding the details of their VAT systems.

Conditions of Equivalence between VAT and GTT. It is easy to demonstrate that any policy decision involving a comparison of VAT and GTT was largely a matter of hit or miss. Let us make the most favorable assumptions imaginable for defining an equivalence, couching it in terms of only one target variable, the revenue yielded by the tax (which may also measure the tax load placed on the final consumer or user). Let us further assume that everything except the basic structure is equal in the two systems—taxable stages, commodities and services covered, exemptions, and so on—and that in either system only one tax rate is used, the one employed in the GTT system being known. To determine, then, the tax rate for the prospective VAT system that will make it yield the same revenue obtained from the existing GTT system requires equating the expressions representing the aggregate tax loads at the same stage n under the two systems [equations (2) and (4) on page 13] and solving for R.

$$R = \frac{(1+r)^n V_1 + (1+r)^{n-1} V_2 + \ldots (1+r)^2 V_{n-1} + (1+r) V_n}{V_1 + V_2 + \ldots \ldots V_{n-1} + V_n} - 1, \quad (5)$$

where the symbols are defined as above.

But this operation suffices to show that even under these unrealistically simplified assumptions, exact solution of the equivalence problem is impracticable. Two of the variables that determine the solution, n and the distribution of the added values, are unknown, and the only certainty is that R must exceed r if it is to satisfy the equivalence condition. However, to give a more concrete idea of the equivalence as a function of the number of stages in the production and distribution process, let us play with one additional unrealistic simplification. If the values added at each stage are all equal ($V_1 = V_2 = V_3 \ldots = V_n$), then the above equation reduces to

---

[14] Quite complex equivalence questions may, in fact, arise should a federal VAT partially supplant the federal corporate income tax. However, the substitution of indirect for direct taxes can be touched on only cursorily in this essay.

$$R = \frac{(1+r)\,[(1+r)^n - 1]}{nr} - 1, \tag{6}$$

and the equivalent R can be determined without difficulty for any assumed r and n. Table 3 displays the VAT rates equivalent to a gross turnover tax rate of 4 percent.

The table suggests that the difference between a gross turnover tax rate and the equivalent value-added tax rate is substantial even when the number of stages is not very high. This fact may not have been fully clear to some people in some of the countries that recently switched to VAT. According to some reports, a widespread feeling existed that the switch was *bound* to mean a woeful increase in the tax burden on the consumer. To the extent that this belief was really held, was it rooted in part in hazy knowledge about the structural difference between the two tax systems? Did people believe that the difference between the VAT and GTT rates in and of itself represented a heavy increase in sales taxation? [15]

Table 3
VAT RATES EQUIVALENT TO GTT TAX OF 4 PERCENT, SELECTED NUMBER OF STAGES

Number of Stages (n)	VAT Rate Equivalent to GTT Rate of 4 Percent (R in percent)	Number of Stages (n)	VAT Rate Equivalent to GTT Rate of 4 Percent (R in percent)
1	4.00	6	14.97
2	6.08	7	17.34
3	8.21	8	19.78
4	10.41	9	22.29
5	12.66	10	24.86

Source: Author's calculations.

[15] Careless statements in which GTT and VAT rates are quoted side by side in a manner suggesting direct comparability between them could generate such misunderstandings. A misleading statement of this kind can be found in *Value-Added Tax: A Report by the National Economic Development Office* (London: Her Majesty's Stationery Office, 1971). Discussing the price effects of VAT in Germany and referring to certain goods and services that showed particularly large price increases, the report says: "Formerly taxed at 4 percent, they now had to pay eleven per cent" (p. 44). This sounds as if the huge price increases were to be explained, wholly or partly, by a heavy increase in sales taxation, measurable by the difference between a current tax rate of 11 percent and a previous rate of 4 percent. The reader of the report is not warned that the percentage figures are totally noncomparable, nor that the nominal GTT rate of 4 percent (an effective 4.17 percent) quite possibly represented taxation as heavy as the VAT rate of 11 percent.

Conditions of Equivalence between VAT and RST. Such questions must have been in the minds of policy makers in Sweden and Norway when their retail sales tax systems (RST) were to be replaced with value-added taxation. The equivalence problem here is much simpler than the one involving GTT, for the basic structure poses no problem at all. But this topic has its proper place in Chapter 4, where the issue of VAT versus RST will be taken up in a wider setting.

3

PRICE EFFECTS OF
VAT IN EUROPE

The purpose of this chapter is to examine the impact of the value-added tax on prices in selected European countries for which worthwhile information could be obtained. The analysis is prefaced by a brief discussion of some general questions that have a direct bearing on the interpretation of empirical results.

Sales Taxes and Price Levels

Obviously, any change in the tax structure of an economy may lead to changes in *relative* prices. The question here, however, is whether and to what extent observed movements in certain *general* consumer price indices were caused by the switch from another indirect tax to VAT, or by an increase in VAT rates. Does not such an inquiry implicitly contradict one of the few noncontroversial propositions in the theory of inflation—that a sustained rise in the general price level never takes place without an accompanying increase in the quantity of money?[1] A tax measure does not by itself alter the quantity of money; it merely redistributes the money flows. Thus, when a government increases its tax revenue by introducing a new sales tax, or by raising the rates or widening the coverage of an existing tax, it channels some money flow away from the private sector and into the public sector, leaving the total quantity of money unchanged. How, then, can there be a causal connection between

---

[1] The validity of the proposition is not impaired by the fact that a change in the velocity of circulation of money occasionally causes mild and temporary changes in the general price level. See Gottfried Haberler, *Inflation: Its Causes and Cures*, rev. ed. (Washington, D. C.: American Enterprise Institute, 1966), p. 61 ff.

such an action and the movement of an index purporting to measure the overall level of consumer prices?

Part of the answer lies in the word "sustained" in the proposition referred to above. The price effects to be examined in this chapter are short-run phenomena. Suppose the tax burden on consumers is suddenly increased by a new general sales tax, or by new higher rates on an existing tax. Then, if the new tax burden is being passed on all the way[2] and if the tax is really general, leaving consumers no option to shift their demand to tax-free items, the primary effect may well be a noticeable rise in the average price level. But some counteracting forces will come into play in due course. An all-round rise in consumer prices not accompanied by an increase in money incomes will force consumers to restrict their demand for some goods or services, and this will tend to bring prices down to their previous level. This secondary effect takes time to work itself out, however, whereas the primary price-raising effect, as we shall see, often follows promptly upon the tax measure that triggered it.

Moreover, even the most comprehensive price index does not encompass everything that is relevant to interpreting the theoretical statement of the tie between a rise in the general price level and an increase in the supply of money. A general consumer price index covers the prices (inclusive of sales taxes) of the goods and services that the consumers buy *directly*. A comprehensive rise in these prices caused by an increase in their sales tax content (and not accompanied by rising money incomes) obviously reduces the possibilities consumers have of satisfying their needs for such goods and services. But this reduction is partly or wholly offset, although usually with a lag, by the new ability of the government, through the increased taxation, to raise transfer payments or to expand or improve public services, without separate levies to cover their full costs. In other words, one set of consumer needs is now being served, through taxes, at the cost of another set, whose satisfaction was curtailed by the price rise of the goods and services for which consumers were paying directly. But these countervailing benefits remain outside the scope of any consumer price index, although they may be regarded quite properly as equivalent to reductions in consumer prices. If they were somehow integrated in the structure of the index, making it an indicator of the price (money cost) of meeting *all* consumer needs that are actually satisfied in modern economies, and if all primary and secondary effects (including those

---

[2] On this point, see below, p. 23 ff.

countervailing consumer benefits) originating in an increase in sales taxes took place without any leads or lags, then the increase could never be regarded as the cause of an observed upturn of the index. But no such all-embracing consumer price index has ever been constructed, nor can those leads and lags be removed.

The primary price-raising effect of an increase in sales taxes may stimulate demands for higher money incomes which, if granted, may set off an inflationary spiral or intensify an ongoing inflation. But that is a different story. The price rises induced by such a sequence of events *would* be accompanied by increases in the quantity of money.

The Question of Forward Shifting

In Table 2 above, the derivation of expressions for consumer prices and their tax content under VAT and GTT was based on the assumption that under both systems the tax burden is being shifted forward from stage to stage all the way. For the purely expository purpose of illustrating in tabular form the stage-by-stage buildup of sales values and tax burdens, such an assumption is obviously necessary, regardless of whether the tabulation is in algebraic terms, as in the table, or in assumed absolute figures.[3]

This does not, of course, settle the question of how realistic the assumption is. The usual characterization of VAT as a tax on consumption implies that normally the assumption is realistic. But the question remains: how much weight should be given to special situations of highly depressed markets that force taxpayers at some preconsumption stage to absorb part of the tax to avoid curtailing demand on the part of their customers? The issue is still highly controversial.[4] Although the question of forward shifting of sales taxes is beyond the scope of this essay, there follows a brief survey

---

[3] For instance, Charles E. McLure, Jr., "The Tax on Value Added: Pros and Cons," in *Value Added Tax: Two Views*, pp. 12, 14, 15; C. Lowell Harriss, "Value-Added Taxation," *Columbia Journal of World Business*, vol. 6, no. 4 (July/August 1971), p. 79.

[4] With respect to VAT, see the partly contrasting views of the two contributors to the recent AEI publication, *Value Added Tax: Two Views*: McLure, "Tax on Value Added," p. 33, and Norman B. Ture, "Economics of the Value Added Tax," pp. 77-89. Doubts have also been expressed about the "passing on" of the tax burden in the buildup of other turnover taxes. Thus, Shoup, in discussing the gross turnover tax and its results, calls "unrealistic" the assumption that forward shifting of the tax has been complete (*Public Finance*, p. 211).

of the views on the question that were expressed or implied in European studies on the probable effects of a value-added tax.[5]

Most of these studies start from the premise that, in general, it is reasonable to expect full passing on. Thus, in Britain, the Richardson committee expressed the opinion that in all probability a value-added tax that yielded revenue equivalent to the purchase tax and selective employment tax would be fully passed on in higher prices.[6] Full forward shifting is also implied in the general characterization of an all-stage VAT given by one of the EEC study groups that, after publication of the Neumark Report, analyzed plans and prospects of tax reform in EEC countries.[7] Likewise, one of the releases in which the French government clarified issues raised by the tax reform of January 1, 1968, implied full forward shifting of the prospective generalized VAT. It stated that one of the characteristics of a value-added tax was that, after all stages had been passed, the sum of the tax amounts collected on a commodity or service should equal the tax charged to the final consumer in the sales price.[8] In the Netherlands, calculations made by the Central Planning Board (CPB) and the Ministry of Finance before the switch to VAT, explicitly assumed full forward shifting[9] and the CPB now holds that the four years of experience with VAT in the Netherlands by and large support this view.[10]

---

[5] It seems advisable to avoid, in this connection, the term "incidence," because even the assumption of full forward shifting of a sales tax to the final consumer does not answer the question of the incidence in its full scope. If the imposition of the tax is combined with, say, a widening of social benefits (by transfer payments or otherwise) that would be impossible in the absence of the tax, these countervailing benefits to consumers must be taken into account.

[6] Committee on Turnover Taxation, *Report*, Cmd. 2300 (London: Her Majesty's Stationery Office, March 1964), p. 105. Cf. Tait, *Value-Added Taxation*, pp. 78, 84, 105. While discussing alternative possibilities, Tait agrees that the assumption of the Richardson committee is the most plausible one (ibid., pp. 83-84).

[7] "Thus, the T.V.A. [taxe sur la valeur ajoutée]—although the levying is spread over all stages—bears only once on the final price of a product, and therefore has the same effect as a single-phase tax levied at the final stage." *The EEC Report on Tax Harmonization* (Amsterdam: International Bureau of Fiscal Documentation, 1963), Report of Subgroup C, p. 60. The study groups had been appointed in 1962 by the Commission for the EEC.

[8] Ministère de l'Economie et des Finances, *Les Remboursements des Crédits de T.V.A.* (1972), p. 2.

[9] "These calculations are made on the assumption that any tax changes, whether increases or reductions, will be reflected entirely in prices" (*Calculation of Effect on Prices of the Introduction of the Value-Added Tax*, mimeographed, p. 1).

[10] This was stated in a letter in which Mr. J. Weitenberg of the Central Planning Board kindly answered a few questions this writer had asked.

On the basis of these statements, a working hypothesis can be formulated for interpreting price movements in the case of a turnover tax that is really general, leaving consumers no freedom to shift their demand to nontaxable substitutes. If the introduction of the tax, or an increase in the tax rates, raises government revenue by an amount equal to r percent of total consumer expenditure, *and* if the tax burden is fully shifted forward, consumer prices will likewise increase by roughly r percent—allowing, however, for possible price-raising effects of increased costs of administration that enterprises may incur after the tax has been introduced.[11] So, if an increase in consumer prices can be traced with some confidence to the introduction of such a tax, or to an increase in tax rates, and the rise is in the proportion just indicated (or somewhat steeper), it may be concluded that the tax has been fully passed on.

Some Problems of Empirical Analysis

The price effects produced by the introduction of a sales tax, or by a change in the rates, need not occur immediately, but may be spread over an extended period. On the other hand, the announcement of a plan to introduce such a tax, or to raise rates of an existing tax, may trigger speculative purchases with ensuing price increases in the interim. Uncertainties about these lead and lag phenomena make the interpretation of observed price movements difficult, although there are some cases, discussed below, where the effect of anticipations is fairly clear.

The empirical analysis will be concerned only with overall price effects as reflected in general indices of consumer prices. The main problem in this approach is the difficulty of isolating the price effects of a single factor (here, a particular tax) from those of a host of other influences on these comprehensive price indices. This problem may be more tractable in an analysis of particular groups of commodities or services. In Europe, where the value-added tax in every case supplanted some other sales tax, it placed a tax liability on some goods and services that formerly had been tax free, and exempted

---

[11] An article, "VAT Went Right," in *The Economist*, March 25, 1972, p. 88, pointed out that in the United Kingdom the adoption of a value-added tax, replacing the purchase tax and selective employment tax, would increase revenue by an amount equal to 0.3 percent of consumer spending, and that there was therefore no reason why prices should rise by more than that amount. This conclusion makes use of the working hypothesis set out above, but disregards (perhaps rightly) price-raising effects of increased costs of business administration that the changeover to VAT may entail.

some that had been subject to tax. Differentiations within the new system (exemptions, varying rates) further raised the number and significance of relative price shifts. European studies have discussed relative price changes to be expected from, or retrospectively to be attributed to, introduction of VAT.[12] However, given the great number and complexity of these relative price movements in all countries that would have to be covered, it is impossible to tackle the subject without extending this essay far beyond its intended scope.

We now turn to individual countries.

West Germany. The act providing for the changeover from the gross turnover tax to a value-added tax in West Germany was promulgated on June 2, 1967, and became effective on January 1, 1968. There is no evidence that the announcement led to speculative purchases of major proportions in the intervening months. The new tax was expected to yield, at first, revenues at most equal to those of the old GTT under the same conditions,[13] and though it is far from easy to find the VAT tax rate or rates that establish this equivalence, West Germany seems to have hit its target.

The Council of Economic Experts (CEE) pointed out that this equivalence did not necessarily ensure unchanged consumer prices, mainly because the correction of the border tax adjustments that was expected as a by-product of the tax reform would probably affect German prices in the same way as a mild devaluation of the German currency.[14] Some expected that the increased costs of accounting and record keeping imposed by VAT would inflate prices somewhat.[15] As it turned out, however, the changeover caused only a ripple in the general level of German consumer prices. In part, this may be attributable to the cyclical recession of the German economy at that time. The subsequent changes in the two VAT tax rates on July 1, 1968—from 10 percent to 11 percent, and from 5 percent to 5½ per-

---

[12] For a preview on price shifts expected from the impending introduction of VAT in Britain, see "VAT Went Right," p. 88.

[13] CEE Annual Report 1967/68, p. 222. On the Council of Experts, see my Incomes Policies Abroad, Part II (Washington, D. C.: American Enterprise Institute, 1972), pp. 17-18.

[14] According to the council, both the tax rebates on German exports and the tax equalization charges on German imports had probably been too low under the GTT regime. So the corrections to be effected after the switch to VAT would tend to make exports cheaper and imports more expensive. See CEE Annual Report 1967/68, pp. 219-33.

[15] Hans Kuntze, Einfuehrung in die Mehrwertsteuer (An Introduction to the Value-Added Tax) (Stuttgart: Deutscher Sparkassenverlag [Publication Service of the German Savings Banks], no date), p. 17.

Table 4

CHANGE IN THE COST OF LIVING INDEX AND ITS MAJOR COMPONENTS, WEST GERMANY, OCTOBER 1967 TO OCTOBER 1968 [a]

(in percent)

Index and Component	Actual Change (1)	Switch to VAT & subsequent increase of VAT rates [b] (2)	Other factors [c] (3)
Total cost of living	+ 2.0	0.0	+ 2.0
Foodstuffs	− 1.0	− 2.2	+ 1.2
Other consumer goods	+ 1.4	+ 0.9	+ 0.5
Services	+ 5.9	+ 3.5	+ 2.4
Dwellings	+ 8.5	0.0	+ 8.5

a Comparison with the corresponding month of the previous year eliminates distorting seasonal influences.
b CEE estimates, based on calculations of the "Ifo," Institut fuer Wirtschaftsforschung (Institute for Economic Research), Munich.
c Column (1) minus column (2).
Source: *CEE Annual Report 1968/69, p. 8.*

cent—are estimated to have raised the prices of goods for private consumption by 0.8 percent on the average.[16] There has been no change in the German VAT rates since then. Apparently convinced that the tax reform of January 1968 and the rate increases of July 1968 had had their full price effects by October 1968, CEE summarized the results, which are reproduced in Table 4.

If, as it seems, the intention was to minimize the effect of the changeover to VAT on overall costs of living, the table indicates that it was achieved. The switch and the subsequent increase in rates tended to reduce food prices and to raise the prices of other consumer goods and of services in such a way as to leave unchanged the weighted comprehensive index of the cost of living. However, the council qualified the interpretation in some respects. Column 3 shows the estimated changes in costs of living in the absence of the switch to VAT and of the subsequent rise in its rates. To obtain these hypothetical changes, the actual changes, column 1, were adjusted by subtracting estimates of the tax burden created by VAT from January to October 1968, and adding estimates of the tax burdens

16 *CEE Annual Report 1969/70, p. 52.*

the old GTT would have created during the same period. The balances are shown in column 2. However, the adjustments were inadequate: On the day before VAT went in effect, the values of the existing stocks at all stages of production, as well as the net values of the producers' durable goods then in place, were still burdened with the gross turnover tax that had been part of their acquisition costs. Hence, subsequent transfers of their values carried forward elements of accumulated GTT. This was true both of the values of goods sold from the stocks after December 31, 1967, and of the values that were being transferred, invisibly and gradually (pro rata of depreciation allowances), from the durable producers' goods to the products or services they helped to create. So the book values, as of December 31, 1967, of the stocks and of the producers' durables should have been cleared of the GTT burden still embodied in them.

This clearance could have been effected only by a tax rebate to the owners of those assets equal to the GTT burden. Here the impossibility of precisely determining the cascade effect accumulated under GTT at any given time, which was discussed in a previous chapter, made itself strongly felt. Besides, the rebates involved a heavy sacrifice on the part of the Treasury. While the government was agreeable in principle to a tax rebate on the stocks, the amount was a subject of hot debate in the government and in parliament. The compromise between fiscal and business interests that eventually became law is estimated to have cleared the stocks of only about 70 percent of their GTT burden, and no rebate at all was granted on producers' durables. To the extent that some GTT content had to be left in the values of stocks and in the net values[17] of the producers' durables in place on December 31, 1967, subsequent transactions involving transfers of these values were burdened by some double taxation that could not be reliably accounted for in attempts to measure the price effects of VAT alone.

And there is still another complication. Generally, under the "consumption-type" VAT that was adopted, a firm may deduct from its tax liability the VAT charged to it by a seller of durable capital goods, a practice not permitted under GTT. Hence an abrupt switch from GTT to a full-fledged consumption-type VAT would have meant a sudden substantial loss of government revenue and, perhaps, a

---

[17] Acquisition costs minus depreciation accrued up to December 31, 1967. Pro rata of the depreciation allowances charged *before* January 1, 1968, the GTT content accumulated in these assets had already been worked off at that date and had, on the whole, exercised its effects on prices at some earlier time.

temporary overstimulation of investment demand. To cushion these effects, all European countries that replaced GTT with VAT have provided that in the first few years after the switch, new investments would be taxable at gradually diminishing rates. Obviously, so long as consumer prices are affected by this transitional extra taxation, they differ from the prices that would be recorded under a "pure" consumption-type VAT. But it proved impossible to estimate what the difference was in the case of the German consumer prices of October 1968.[18]

While these transition problems would not arise in the United States, they plagued the European countries that switched from GTT to VAT. Moreover, they bedeviled attempts to measure the net price effects that the adoption of VAT had.

The Netherlands. Like West Germany, the Netherlands attempted to set an initial rate structure for VAT so that the new system would yield, in its initial phase, about the same revenue that might have been expected from the GTT system.[19] This equivalence, however, was not expected to allow consumer prices to behave after the switch as they otherwise would have done. The tax reform came on January 1, 1969, at a time when Dutch business was booming. In the year that followed, prices of goods for private consumption rose by 6.5 percent, exceeding the forecast of the Central Planning Board by 1.5 percentage points. Experts agreed that the changeover to VAT would, in some way or other, reinforce the cyclical upward pressure on consumer prices. Prices, indeed, did rise, leading to price control and a temporary price freeze. The issue was how much of the uptrend should be attributed to the tax reform. The Central Planning Board, assuming full forward shifting of the VAT, had predicted that the changeover would make private consumption in 1969 1.4 percent more expensive than it would otherwise have been;[20] in the event, the board has seen no reason to alter this

---

[18] See the analyses of the Council of Economic Experts in several *CEE Annual Reports: 1967/68*, pp. 219-25; *1968/69*, p. 8; *1969/70*, p. 52. Also Kuntze, *Introduction to the Value-Added Tax*, pp. 50-54; *Einfuehrung in die Mehrwertsteuer* (An Introduction to the Value-Added Tax) (Frankfurt a.M.: Frankfurter Bank), p. 19 ff.

[19] *Revision of Turnover Tax System in the Netherlands* (essay published by Allgemeene Bank Nederland N.V., 1969), p. 4.

[20] In a Memorandum, *Economische Consequenties van de Invoering van de Belasting op Toegevoegde Waarde* (Economic Consequences of the Introduction of the Tax on Value Added), submitted to Parliament in the course of the debates on reform of turnover taxation (p. 11).

estimate,[21] attributing the excess to some unforeseeable opportunities to widen profit margins. Measures were, in fact, taken in 1969 to prevent "unjustified" upward revisions of prices in connection with the switch to VAT.[22] But in March 1970, De Moor estimated that the switch directly or indirectly caused a 3 percent increase in consumer prices in the previous year.[23] These differences over the price effects of the switch were rooted in differences about the impact of certain measures of transition.[24]

Since 1969, there has been one change in VAT rates: the "general" rate was raised in 1971 from 12 to 14 percent. The CPB estimated at the time that the change would result in a price increase of 0.6 percent, and it has not revised this estimate, although the actual price movements in 1971 did not seem to be quite in line with it. The CPB again surmises that the divergence between expected and actual price movements can be traced to unpredictable increases in industrial profit margins.[25]

Belgium. In 1969 Belgium was still expected to meet the January 1, 1970, deadline that had been set for countries of the European Economic Community to effect the switch to VAT. Knowledge that the government intended to fix the VAT rates so as to yield a surplus over the revenue obtained under the GTT, and observation of the Dutch experience since the beginning of 1969, led the Belgian public to expect that the changeover would intensify the current inflation. These expectations induced a wave of speculative purchases of con-

---

[21] Information supplied by the board to the author.

[22] OECD Economic Survey of the Netherlands, 1970 (Paris: Organisation for Economic Co-operation and Development, 1971), p. 31.

[23] A. E. De Moor, Het Mysterie van de Prijsstijging (The Mystery of the Price Increase) (published in pamphlet form by N. Samson N.V., Alphen, 1970). In a paper by H. den Hertog (Mystificatie van de Prijsstijging, 1970, mimeographed), De Moor's estimate was sharply criticized.

[24] Basically, these measures were similar to those adopted in West Germany: a transitional extra levy, at tapering-down rates, on new investments; a tax rebate on stocks to clear them of GTT embodied in their book values of December 31, 1968; no corresponding rebate on producers' durables in place on that day. Like the German CEE, De Moor pointed out (Mystery of the Price Increase, p. 19) that the failure to clear the net values of the producers' durables of their GTT content, in conjunction with VAT levied on subsequent value transfers from these durables pari passu with depreciation allowances charged on them, involved double taxation. In den Hertog's essay of the same name (pp. 3, 7 ff.), this was denied with arguments that do not seem quite convincing.

[25] For 1973, another raise of the general VAT rate (to 16 percent) has been announced. There was also a plan to increase the special rate from 4 percent to 5 percent, but the trade unions opposed it and it was dropped.

sumer durables in 1969, especially automobiles, which indeed rein-
forced the inflationary trend.

Wishing to profit from the sharply contrasting German and
Dutch lessons, the Belgian government obtained the permission of
the Council of Ministers of the European Economic Community to
postpone the changeover to VAT until January 1, 1971. The postponement had its intended sobering effect on some Belgian markets.
Sales of motor cars, for example, were 12 percent lower in the first
nine months of 1970 than they had been in the same period of 1969.
But the move did not allay inflationary fears entirely. The initials
T.V.A., which stand for "taxe sur la valeur ajoutée," were jokingly
read, "tout va augumenter" ("everything is going to go up").

The complex rate structure and the strict price controls during
the initial phase of the VAT regime have complicated estimation of
the price effect of the switch to VAT. In its annual report for 1971
the National Bank of Belgium implied its belief that there was some
price-raising impact. It pointed out that, notwithstanding the introduction of the value-added tax, the 5.6 percent increase in consumer
prices during 1971 was milder than those that had occurred in the
Netherlands and in the United Kingdom, and about the same as
those in West Germany and Italy, though steeper than that in the
United States.[26] At any rate, the prevailing opinion seems to be that
Belgium chose a better time for the switch than the Netherlands
had done.

Sweden. In Sweden and Denmark, the analysis of the price effects
of VAT is helped by the availability of a special statistic. For a number
of years the two countries have been publishing side by side with a
comprehensive consumer price index, a "net" index which eliminates
the influence of indirect taxes by subtracting them from the consumer
expenditures used in computing the index. In Sweden, the net index
has been further adjusted by adding subsidies to the expenditures,
thus eliminating their price-reducing influence.[27] A marked *difference*
in the behavior of the two indices following some tax policy measure
involving VAT (adoption of the tax or a change in its rates) allows
a more precise allocation of the responsibility for an observed
change in consumer prices between the VAT measure and such

---

[26] National Bank of Belgium, *Report 1971*, pp. 41-42.

[27] For our purposes the difference between the two indices would be more useful
if it consisted solely of the inclusion or exclusion of general sales taxes (which
means VAT since January 1969 in Sweden and since July 1967 in Denmark).
Moreover, in Sweden the net index is published only every third month.

factors as monetary and credit policy, wage push, cyclical conditions, long-term trends, erratic influences, and so on.

Chart 1 depicts the behavior of the two consumer price indices in Sweden from 1965 to mid-1972.[28] Separate vertical scales are used for the two indices, but they are spaced equally, so that their absolute short-run and longer-term changes are comparable with each other.

The behavior of the two indices around the changeover date, January 1, 1969, verifies the thesis that VAT and RST have about the same effect on consumer prices, provided the coverage and the rates are approximately the same.[29] From mid-1968 to mid-1969, the trend of the comprehensive index is straight up without any break. The range of upward and downward deviations from the trend is equally small before and after the switch. There is thus no statistical evidence of any upward pressure on consumer prices resulting either from speculative purchases before the switch or from the switch itself. This impression is supported by the fact that during the period indicated, the trend growth rate of the net index was not smaller than that of the unadjusted index; in relative terms, it was even slightly higher. It is also worth noting that the uptrend of the net index was a little steeper in the first half-year after the switch than in the half-year immediately before. The comprehensive index shows no comparable kink in its gradient between mid-1968 and mid-1969. Had the switch to VAT been responsible for part of the price increase after January 1, 1969, the two indices presumably would have diverged in the opposite way.[30]

In February 1970, the VAT rate on passenger automobiles, boats, and television sets was raised from 11.11 percent (effective, corresponding to 10 percent nominal) to 16.28 percent (effective, corresponding to 14 percent nominal). In May 1970, the parliament adopted a resolution providing that on January 1, 1971, the standard VAT rate, which applies to the great majority of goods and services,

---

[28] The figure has been extended back to 1965 in order to show price developments under the former retail sales tax alongside those under the value-added tax.

[29] The Swedish VAT was introduced at a general (effective) rate of 11.11 percent. The RST had been levied since mid-1965 at the uniform rate of 10 percent (effective). The coverage of the VAT was comprehensive from its start, but the coverage of the abolished retail sales tax had also been quite complete.

[30] The chart also shows that the switch had definitely less impact on consumer prices than the raising of the retail sales tax from 6.4 percent to 10 percent in July 1965. From June to July 1965, the consumer price index rose by 2.66 percent (from 188 to 193—1949 = 100). From December 1968 to January 1969, the increase was only 0.46 percent (from 217 to 218).

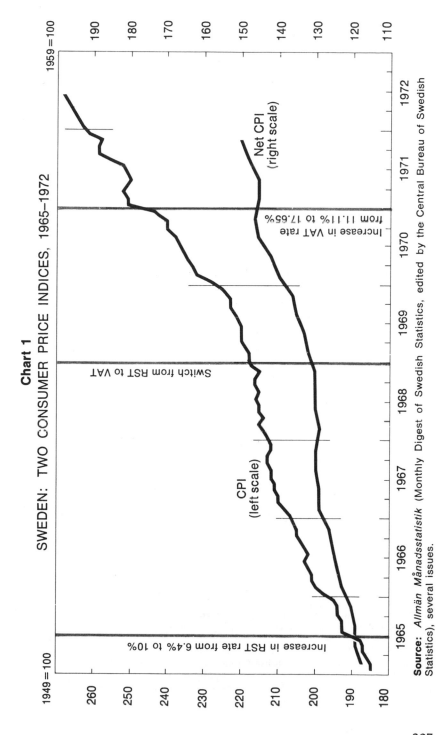

Chart 1

SWEDEN: TWO CONSUMER PRICE INDICES, 1965–1972

Net CPI (right scale)

CPI (left scale)

Switch from RST to VAT

Increase in VAT rate from 11.11% to 17.65%

Increase in RST rate from 6.4% to 10%

1959 = 100

1949 = 100

Source: *Allmän Månadsstatistik* (Monthly Digest of Swedish Statistics, edited by the Central Bureau of Swedish Statistics), several issues.

297

would be raised from 11.11 percent (effective) to 17.65 percent (effective, corresponding to 15 percent nominal).[31] The knowledge, eight months in advance, that the VAT content in the prices of nearly all goods and services was going to be augmented substantially led to large anticipatory purchases of consumer goods. The upward pressure on consumer prices that resulted should have affected both consumer price indices; the fact that during the first three quarters of 1970 the rise of the comprehensive CPI was distinctly steeper than that of the net CPI [32] probably means that the impact of the rate increase was spread over several months after it took effect.[33] Then, in October 1970, came the general price freeze. It is reflected in a temporary flattening out, starting in November, of the net CPI, while the unadjusted index continued its steep rise. One possible explanation for this divergence may be that the rise of VAT from 11.11 percent to 17.65 percent took effect for a number of household goods in November. From December 1970 to January 1971 (the month in which the increase to 17.65 percent became general), the comprehensive CPI rose from 243 to 251 (1949 = 100)—the sharpest month-to-month increase, in percentage points, during the whole period covered by the figure. The net CPI declined from 146 in November 1970 to 145 in February 1971 (1959 = 100). Here the impact of the change effected on January 1, 1971, shows strikingly. Although much of the impact had been anticipated in price increases during the preceding months, room remained for a marked further price effect immediately after the change.

This Swedish experience with undesirable anticipatory price increases leaves a plain message to all countries using a comprehensive general sales tax: a planned rise of the tax rates should not be announced too long in advance.[34]

---

[31] *The Swedish Value Added Tax—A Summary* (mimeographed release by the Swedish Ministry of Finance, November 1970), p. 1.

[32] The two trend gradients differed in relative as well as in absolute terms.

[33] In Sweden, according to observations made by the Association of Swedish Industries, prices generally do respond in full to rises in the rate of a general turnover tax. But frequently—especially when the rate increase is substantial—it takes time before the price adjustment is complete.

[34] As has already been mentioned, the Scandinavian nations, unlike the EEC countries, have so far refrained from adopting different turnover tax rates for "necessities" and "luxuries." The policy has been to neutralize the regressivity of the taxes in other ways, mainly by extending social services. In this respect, Sweden continues the policy followed under the retail sales tax. Since the increase in the standard VAT rate to 17.65 percent, there have been numerous proposals for lower rates on food, children's clothing, and some other items. So far the government has no plans in this direction.

In Sweden and Norway, as in the EEC countries surveyed, the price effect of VAT in its first few years, as reflected in the consumer price indices, must be assumed to be slightly distorted by certain aftereffects of the sales tax that previously had been in operation. Like the gross turnover tax in the EEC countries, the retail sales tax that had long been on the statute books in Sweden and Norway had applied to the sale of producers' durable goods. Purchasers of these goods had not been allowed any credit for the sales tax paid on them to their suppliers, nor were the book values of these assets cleared of their RST content by tax rebates at the time of the changeover to VAT. This content, to be sure, had become part of the purchasers' basis for calculating depreciation allowances on these durables, and so their owners could work off this residual tax burden piecemeal in proportion with the depreciation charges. But until the assets were completely written off, the prices of the goods and services that they had helped to produce were still burdened by some elements of RST. In many cases, this transitional phenomenon has presumably spilled over into the first few years of the VAT regime.

Furthermore, a transition problem was posed by the purchases of durables *after* the switch to VAT, that is, to a system where the purchaser *is* allowed a credit for the tax paid to the supplier. Here again, the problem paralleled that experienced by the EEC countries, but Sweden and Norway treated it quite differently. Sweden accepted the abruptness of the change, and did not provide any "cushioning" period during which these transactions would have been taxable at tapering-down rates.[35] Norway went to the opposite extreme. Along with the value-added tax, a special investment tax on purchases of capital equipment was introduced bearing about the same rate as the former general retail sales tax. No tapering down of the rate and no termination of the taxability has been provided for.

Denmark. Three major events have marked the history of the value-added tax in Denmark: its introduction on July 3, 1967, at 10 percent, replacing a wholesale sales tax, then at 12½ percent, that had existed since 1962; and two subsequent increases in the VAT rate, to 12½ per-

---

[35] The abruptness of the change was mitigated by the fact that the Swedish RST rates on capital equipment had been lower than the rates of the general retail sales tax. Even so, the new possibility of recouping at once a tax outlay that previously had been recoverable only over a number of years might have been expected to give a sudden impetus to capital expenditures. Investment in capital equipment did, in fact, boom in 1969. However, according to information obtained from the Swedish Association of Industries, experts in Sweden believe that the general cyclical business upswing of that year sufficiently explains the boom.

cent on April 1, 1968, and to 15 percent on June 29, 1970.[36] The price effects of these events have been analyzed in three studies prepared by the Monopoly Board in Copenhagen, which make it possible to carry the analysis of the topic surveyed in this chapter a few steps further for Denmark than for any other European country.[37]

Two factors make the Danish experience more relevant to the United States than that of any other country reviewed here. First, the wholesale sales tax that VAT replaced had not been levied on sales of producers' durable goods. Hence in Denmark, unlike Sweden, Norway, and the EEC countries, these goods embodied no residual elements of the old tax after the switch, and it may therefore be assumed that Danish consumer price indices reflect the impact of VAT with less distortion than is true of any other country surveyed in this section. In this respect, the conditions surrounding the Danish switch to VAT most closely resemble those under which the United States would adopt this tax. Second, while VAT was not the first national sales tax in Denmark, as it would be in the United States, its scope was so much wider than that of the abolished wholesale sales tax that the switch constituted a comparably drastic change.[38]

A few more words must be said about the two indices to be used for the analysis of Denmark's price developments under the impact of VAT. One, the general consumer price index, is an average of retail prices of consumer goods and services, weighted by expenditures of private households in general. The other, the "net" con-

---

[36] These were the standard rates, applicable to all nonexempt goods and services except certain imports, for which somewhat lower rates were set. There were only relatively few exemptions, rents on dwellings being the most important.

[37] The three studies, all in Danish, are *Direktoratets redogørelse for merverdiafgiftens virkninger på priserne* (Investigation of the Board of Chairmen on the Effects of the Value-Added Tax on Prices; hereinafter: "Investigation"), in *Meddelelser fra Monopoltilsynet* (Communications from the Monopoly Board), June 24, 1967, Nr. 6, pp. 133-37; *Analyse af Merverdiafgiftens Prisvirkninger*, 1967 (An Analysis of the Price Effects of the Value-Added Tax), a book-length study referred to hereinafter as "Analysis"; *Notat vedrørende monopoltilsynets undersøgelse af prisudviklingen i forbindelse med momsforhøjelsen i juni 1970* (Memorandum Concerning the Inquiry of the Monopoly Board on the Development of Prices in Connection with the Rate Increase of June 1970), a brief document hereinafter cited as "Memorandum," August 1970. Grateful acknowledgment is due to the Monopoly Board for providing the three documents to the writer.

[38] Services, most of which are liable to VAT, were of course tax free under the wholesale tax. Major commodity groups that came under a general sales tax for the first time when VAT was introduced in Denmark are foodstuffs and tobacco, solid fuels, mineral oil products, machinery and equipment used in production (including tractors and other implements used in agriculture and fishery). See "Analysis," pp. 5, 28-35.

sumer price index, is an average of prices of consumer goods and services, adjusted by subtracting the indirect taxes paid along with the prices, and weighted by expenditures of wage earners.[39] As in the case of Sweden, it is the *difference* in the movements of the two indices that is instructive. The net index, which is not affected by indirect taxes but does reflect all other factors influencing consumer prices, plays the role of a "test control indicator." [40]

---

[39] In contradistinction to the practice in Sweden, the net index is not adjusted further for subsidies. For our purpose this is an advantage. The smaller population basis of the net index reflects its purpose. The average of the net consumption index of the last three months is computed quarterly and published as a wage regulation index. On the basis of this index, cost-of-living adjustments are periodically made, in a manner prescribed by law, to wages and salaries paid to public employees, pensions, "social" payments of various kinds, and (by agreement between the negotiating parties) many wages in industry and trade. This practice has been followed since 1963.

[40] Because both indices are available on a monthly basis in Denmark, the differential analysis is one degree more informative than it is for Sweden. The difference in the population aggregates whose consumption expenditures are used in building up the two indices does not vitiate their usefulness for this analysis. The fact that VAT is not the only indirect tax that has been eliminated from our test control indicator undoubtedly introduces some uncertainty. While comparison of the movements of the two indices will isolate the price effects of VAT from those of all factors that affect both indices, it will not isolate them from possible coincidental price effects of other indirect taxes. But the bias, if any, can hardly be great. The table below shows that, from fiscal 1966/1967 to fiscal 1970/1971, the annual increments in government receipts were far larger, both absolutely and in percentages, from VAT than from all other indirect taxes taken together. This strongly suggests that a marked difference in the behavior of the two indices at or near the time of some major VAT event may be attributed with confidence to VAT and only in very minor degree, if at all, to coincidental developments in other indirect taxes.

	Fiscal Period (April 1–March 31)				
Source of Revenue	1966/67	1967/68	1968/69	1969/70	1970/71
General sales tax [a]					
Collection (mill. kr.) Increase from preceding period	2,230	3,302	5,298	6,786	8,316
Amount (mill. kr.)	—	1,072	1,996	1,488	1,530
Percent	—	48.1	60.4	28.1	29.9
Other indirect taxes (including customs duties)					
Collection Increase from preceding period	7,602	7,750	8,006	8,997	9,439
Amount (mill. kr.)	—	148	256	997	442
Percent	—	1.9	3.3	12.4	5.1

Chart 2 reveals the monthly movements of the two indices for the period 1967-71.[41] The movements of the two indices during 1967 reflect the impact of the introduction of VAT on July 3 in a striking fashion. Through June, both indices rose at about the same absolute rate. In July, the comprehensive index leaped up, while the net index exhibited little more than the previous months' changes. The comprehensive CPI resumed its pre-June growth rate in August, and moved about parallel with the net index for the rest of the year. The impact of the two subsequent increases in the VAT rate, in April 1968 and July 1970, is likewise clearly visible on the chart, although the differential behavior of the two indices is somewhat less striking. In none of the three cases do the figures in the months before the VAT event reveal any anticipatory upward pressure on consumer prices. During the years 1969 and 1971, in which no change was made in the value-added tax, the two indices ran fairly parallel, in general trend as well as in occasional steepenings or flattenings.

Table 5 supplements the long-term picture presented in the figure with the relative increases of the two indices at the time of the three critical points in VAT history—July 1967, April 1968, and July 1970 (columns 1 and 2). It also reports (columns 3 and 4) the monthly percentage increases of the two indices exclusive of rents or the monthly rental values of owner-occupied dwellings, also published by the Danish Statistical Office.

The table clearly reveals the effect of eliminating these tax-exempt expenditures on dwellings, an item of some weight in the cost of living. In all three critical phases (June-July 1967, March-April 1968, June-July 1970), the rise of the index inclusive of indirect taxes but exclusive of rents on dwellings (column 3) is steeper than

---

[a] Value-added tax since July 3, 1967.

Source: Statistisk Tiårsoversigt (Statistical Ten-Years Survey), 1972, p. 15 (Danmarks Statistik, the Danish Statistical Office).

For the rest, the two indices are sufficiently comparable for our purpose. Both are seasonally adjusted, both have fixed weights, and the grouping of the commodities and services used for the weighting is, on the whole, the same in both. The weighting systems are being revised from time to time, usually every fourth year; see *Indeksberegngen i Danmarks Statistik* (Calculation of Index Numbers in Denmark's Statistics), Danish Statistical Office and Economic Institute of Copenhagen University, 1971, p. 11.

The 1964 base used on Chart 2 is the original one for the comprehensive CPI. The net CPI is reported on a different base, but being of the Lespayre type, it can be converted to 1964 = 100 for convenient diagrammatical presentation.

[41] February 1967 is the first month for which the Danish source (Danish Statistical Office, *Statistiske Efterretninger*) gives the figure of the net consumer price index.

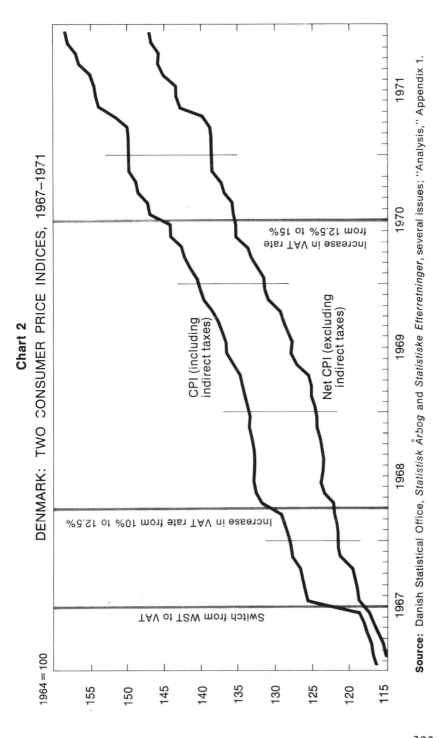

Chart 2

DENMARK: TWO CONSUMER PRICE INDICES, 1967–1971

Source: Danish Statistical Office, *Statistisk Årbog* and *Statistiske Efterretninger*, several issues; "Analysis," Appendix 1.

Table 5

CHANGE IN SEASONALLY ADJUSTED DANISH CONSUMER
PRICE INDICES, SELECTED MONTHS, 1967-70

(percentage increase from previous month)

Year and Month	Prices of Goods and Services, Including Dwellings		Prices of Goods and Services, Excluding Dwellings	
	Including indirect taxes (1)	Excluding indirect taxes (2)	Including indirect taxes (3)	Excluding indirect taxes (4)
1967				
May	0.34	0.41	0.34	0.41
June	0.76	0.49	0.85	0.66
July	5.72	1.06	6.23	1.14
August	0.80	0.24	0.32	0.32
September	0.24	0.32	0.32	0.32
1968				
February	0.23	0.24	0.23	0.24
March	0.54	0.31	0.62	0.40
April	1.86	0.08	2.09	0.08
May	0.76	1.01	0.30	0.39
June	0.30	0.31	0.30	0.31
1970				
May	0.91	1.14	0.64	0.73
June	0.07	0.71	0.07	0.07
July	2.02	0.21	2.31	0.22
August	0.20	0.70	0.21	0.14
September	0.88	0.91	0.89	1.01

Sources: Danish Statistical Office, *Statistisk Årbog* and *Statistiske Efterretninger*, several issues.

the rise of the index inclusive of both these items (column 1), and comes one step closer to reflecting the "pure" price effect of VAT.[42]

This comparison is what might be expected, but the approximation is still inadequate. From June to July 1967, the rise of the index excluding rents, while significantly steeper than the rise of its inclusive counterpart (6.23 percent versus 5.72 percent), was still substantially below the 10 percent rate at which VAT was introduced. This is largely because the index that excludes rents nevertheless

---

[42] For the rest, the percent increases shown in the table confirm the findings on the absolute increases shown in the figure. Before and after the three critical points, the increases of all four indices are of the same small order of magnitude; at the three critical points, the increases of the two indices inclusive of indirect taxes (columns 1 and 3) are significantly greater than the increases of the two exclusive indices (columns 2 and 4).

includes a few other, if minor, tax-exempt items, and commodities that *are* liable to VAT but also were subject to the wholesale sales tax before July 1967. Obviously, the "pure" price effect of VAT can be obtained only by confining the analysis to goods and services that were newly subjected to tax when VAT was introduced. In Table 6 the comparison of the indices inclusive and exclusive of indirect taxes has been done for a few of the numerous groups and subgroups specified in the Danish CPI statistics that fall in this category.[43] On the basis of the admittedly slender evidence furnished by the table, it seems that the price increases from June to July 1967 on goods for which VAT was the first general sales tax kept fairly close to the rate of 10 percent at which the tax was introduced. For the group "tobacco products" and the two subgroups "bread, flour, and grain" and "coke," this is the finding if the increases in the all-inclusive index and in the "test control indicator" are read together. The price increase in the relatively comprehensive "foodstuffs" group was smaller, but only slightly so. To the extent that the fragmentary information conveyed by the table supports a tentative generalization, it seems to bear out the expectation of the Monopoly Board that the newly introduced VAT would be fully shifted forward and that, accordingly, the prices of goods that had not been subject to the wholesale tax would generally increase up to 10 percent.[44]

An interesting feature, already touched upon and evidenced by Figure 2 as well as by Tables 5 and 6, is the concentration in time of the price effects of VAT. In contradistinction to the Swedish experience, consumer prices in Denmark do not seem to have sustained any appreciable upward pressure from speculative purchases in anticipation of impending price increases, either before VAT took effect or before the subsequent rate increases—this despite the fact that each of the three events had long been expected (although none so long as the rate increase in Sweden). Nor is there any indication of appreciable lags or protractions of VAT-caused price effects. In all three instances, the monthly index numbers suggest that the event spent most of its force in the month immediately after it occurred. These observations should certainly be interpreted with caution, but the case of Denmark shows that things at least *can* develop in this way.

---

[43] Selection of the groups to be analyzed was guided by the desirability of using those whose titles in the Danish tabulations of the two index series are identical (not simply roughly the same) so that their coverage may be assumed to be the same.

[44] "Investigation," pp. 134, 135; "Analysis," p. 10 ff.

Table 6

PERCENT CHANGES OF TWO DANISH CONSUMER PRICE INDICES FOR GROUPS AND SUBGROUPS OF COMMODITIES FIRST SUBJECT TO SALES TAX WITH VAT, 1967

Index Weight and Change	Groups				Subgroups			
	Foodstuffs		Tobacco products		Bread, flour, grain		Coke	
	Including indirect taxes	Excluding indirect taxes	Including indirect taxes	Excluding indirect taxes	Including indirect taxes	Excluding indirect taxes	Including indirect taxes	Excluding indirect taxes
Weight of group in total index at time of adoption of VAT[a]	22.0	28.6	6.0	2.3[b]	3.3	4.3	0.6	1.1
Change in index from previous month								
May	0	+0.16	0	0	0	−0.23	+0.93	+0.33
June	+1.72	+0.98	0	0	0	+0.24	0	−0.08
July	+9.32	+1.29	+10.74	+1.56	+11.48	+1.88	+11.01	+0.82
August	0	0	0	0	+0.74	+0.46	−0.83	−0.33
September	0	+0.16	0	0	+0.73	+0.38	+0.83	+0.73

a Instituted July 3, 1967.

b The far smaller weight of this commodity group in the net consumer price index, as compared with the comprehensive index, may be because the former reflects consumption expenditures of wage earners, and the latter consumption expenditures of the general population. Wage earners spend relatively less on tobacco products.

Sources: "Analysis," Appendix 1a, b; *Statistisk Årbog*, 1968, pp. 326-37.

4

VAT VERSUS RST:
THE ARGUMENT IN EUROPE
AND CANADA

Should the United States ever decide to adopt a federal sales tax, one of the first questions will be whether it should take the form of a value-added tax (VAT) or a retail sales tax (RST).[1] So it may be appropriate to conclude this essay with a brief survey of the influences on European tax reformers in their choice between the two alternatives. What were the main objections to RST in the reports and directives that paved the way for VAT in the European Economic Community? Why did Sweden and Norway choose to replace their long-established RST systems by value-added taxes?[2] What motives (besides the prospect of later joining the EEC) made Denmark discard the RST bill that had already been prepared and adopt the alternative?

A side glance at Canada helps to bring the arguments and counterarguments into sharper focus. In 1966-67 the Canadian Royal Commission on Taxation (called the Carter Commission, after its chairman) published a report on taxation in six volumes that may well be the most extensive of its kind ever to appear.[3] The report recommended abolition of the manufacturers' sales tax, discussed the relative merits of VAT and RST as candidates for replacing the existing system, and, unlike the Europeans, decided in favor of RST—although not quite unconditionally, as will be shown below. The commission's

---

[1] The issue of VAT versus RST has already been the subject of lively debate in this country. Besides many other, more extended, analyses, see Dan Throop Smith, "Value-Added Tax: The Case For," and Stanley S. Surrey, "Value-Added Tax: The Case Against," *Harvard Business Review*, vol. 48 (November/December 1970), pp. 77-85 and pp. 86-94, respectively.

[2] In Norway, the retail sales tax had been in effect for thirty years at the time of the switch to VAT. In Sweden, the switch came after nine years of RST.

[3] *Report of the Royal Commission on Taxation* (Ottawa: Queen's Printer and Controller of Stationery, 1966-67); hereinafter cited as the *Carter Report*.

recommendation has so far not led to any action: a white paper on tax reform published by the federal government in 1969 bypassed the question of whether and how to alter the sales tax system.[4] The reform bill that eventually was presented to Parliament in 1971, and the act that took effect on January 1, 1972, dealt with direct taxation, and no plan for replacing the manufacturers' sales tax has as yet been submitted to Parliament. But, for purposes of this essay, the Carter Report had pertinent things to say, and offers forceful counter-arguments to the views of European experts and policy makers in the 1960s.

As background to the discussion of the issues involved in making a choice between the retail sales tax and the all-stage value-added tax, Table 7 sets out the stage-by-stage buildup of the two systems in algebraic terms, in a manner exactly paralleling Table 2; stage n represents here the retail sale to the final consumer. The table demonstrates formally that when they have the same tax rate, the same coverage, and full forward shifting of the tax to the final consumer, the two systems yield the same revenue. and place the same tax burden on consumers.

Tax Evasion

One of the most crucial issues in formulating a tax program is the matter of evasion. Under the retail sales tax system, the government collects from the retailer much more tax than it does under an equivalent all-stage value-added tax system. Hence, when a government wants high revenues from a new sales tax, and therefore sets high rates, the strain imposed by concentration of tax collection at the retail level might invite evasion. Under VAT, evasion gains taxpayers less than it does under RST. And if evasion does occur at some stage (the retail stage is in any case the most vulnerable in this respect), the government has at least collected taxes from previous stages. Under the type of VAT that has gained acceptance in Europe (the "credit" method of tax deduction), the risk of evasion is further reduced by a self-policing property of the system: The supplier at each stage is supposed to indicate on the invoice to his customer the VAT he himself has paid and wants to recoup from the customer (who, in turn, may deduct it from his tax liability to the government). If he has actually paid less, then the discrepancy—

---

[4] Hon. E. J. Benton, *Prospects for Tax Reform* (Ottawa, 1969). See Martin Bukovetsky and Richard M. Bird, "Tax Reform in Canada: A Progress Report," *National Tax Journal*, vol. 25 (March 1972), pp. 15-43.

Table 7

COMPARISON OF THE RETAIL SALES TAX AND THE VALUE-ADDED TAX

Stage	Paid to Supplier[a] (1)	Sales Value before Tax[b] (2)	Tax Paid to Treasury (3)	Charged to Customer[c] (4)
A. Value-Added Tax[d]				
1	0	V_1	RV_1	$(1+R)V_1$
2	$(1+R)V_1$	$(1+R)V_1+V_2$	RV_2	$(1+R)(V_1+V_2)$
3	$(1+R)(V_1+V_2)$	$(1+R)(V_1+V_2)+V_3$	RV_3	$(1+R)(V_1+V_2+V_3)$
...	...	...	...	...
n	$(1+R)(V_1+V_2+\ldots V_{n-1})$	$(1+R)(V_1+V_2+\ldots V_{n-1})+V_n$	RV_n	$(1+R)(V_1+V_2+\ldots V_n)$
B. Retail Sales Tax				
1	0	V_1	0	V_1
2	V_1	V_1+V_2	0	V_1+V_2
3	V_1+V_2	$V_1+V_2+V_3$	0	$V_1+V_2+V_3$
...	...	...	...	...
n	$V_1+V_2+\ldots V_{n-1}$	$V_1+V_2+\ldots V_{n-1}+V_n$	$R(V_1+V_2+\ldots V_n)$	$(1+R)(V_1+V_2+\ldots V_n)$

[a] Column (4) from preceding stage. [b] Column (1) plus value added at stage indicated. [c] Column (2) plus column (3). [d] Transcribed from Table 2.

Source: Author's calculations.

his tax evasion—can be discovered by matching his tax return with the invoice.

These considerations carried great weight in the EEC countries, for the gross turnover tax had yielded high revenues,[5] and the governments did not want to replace it with a tax system that would yield appreciably less. This argument has obviously convinced the Neumark Committee that, in the EEC area, the retail sales tax would not be the right substitute for GTT.[6] In fact the Neumark Report went so far as to say that for a long time to come[7] a tax at the retail stage would be "impracticable" as the sole form of general sales tax.[8]

In the debate that eventually led to the adoption of VAT in the United Kingdom, the chancellor of the exchequer used similar reasoning. He expressed his conviction that an RST could be successful only if the rates were low and that, on the scale required to permit abolition of the purchase and selective employment taxes, it would saddle retailers with a tax liability that "would present very serious difficulties of collection and control." Such a tax, he told Parliament, "is now widely regarded as impossible."[9]

In Sweden the retail sales tax had on the whole worked well.[10] Immediately before its abolition it had provided more than 20 percent of the central government's revenue, and the rate of tax evasion had not been alarming. But around 1967, policy makers began to believe that increasing reliance would have to be put on indirect taxes. Such reliance inevitably meant higher rates on the general sales tax in the near future—and too great a risk of evasion if a tax significantly above the current rate of 10 percent were to be collected entirely at the retail stage.

In Norway the reform plans approved by parliament in June 1969 called for a great expansion of government revenue from indirect taxes, partly to offset the loss that was bound to result from

---

[5] In 1966, the German turnover tax accounted for about 42 percent of total federal tax revenues. See Henry J. Gumpel, *Taxation in the Federal Republic of Germany*, 2nd ed. (Cambridge: Harvard Law School, World Tax Series, 1968), pp. 4203-04.

[6] *Neumark Report*, pp. 122, 124, 126 (English text).

[7] Not "over the long term," as the semi-official English translation incorrectly renders the original German, "noch auf lange Zeit hinaus."

[8] *Neumark Report*, p. 124.

[9] *Value-Added Tax*, presented to Parliament by the chancellor of the exchequer, Cmd. 4621 (London: Her Majesty's Stationery Office, March 1971), p. 4.

[10] The following observations draw heavily on the article by Martin Norr and Nils G. Hornhammar, "The Value-Added Tax in Sweden," *Columbia Law Review*, vol. 70 (March 1970), p. 388 ff.

the planned reduction of income tax rates, partly to finance the planned widening of social services. Largely because of the same difficulties of control that had weighed so heavily in Sweden's decision shortly before, it was deemed impracticable to raise the rate of the existing retail sales tax (then 13.64 percent) as drastically as necessary to meet the new revenue requirements. So Norway switched to VAT, for which a rate of 20 percent right from the start was held to be practicable.[11]

In Denmark, the national tax office had, in fact, prepared a retail sales tax bill, but in the end did not recommend it. They had the same misgivings about RST that were expressed in the Neumark Report and later by the British chancellor of the exchequer—doubts about the wisdom of relying entirely on the retail stage for collecting a heavy sales tax.[12]

In discussing the relative merits of VAT and RST for Canada, the 1966 Report of the Royal Commission very explicitly stressed the criterion that weighed so heavily in Europe—the level of the rates deemed necessary. The report emphasized that "a retail tax in excess of 14 percent might result in a significant evasion problem. Should that occur, the case for a value-added form would be strengthened."[13] However, the commission was of the opinion that, for a Canadian federal retail sales tax, a rate of 7 or 8 percent would be sufficient. At such a rate, the commission argued, "it would be unrealistic to consider instituting a value-added tax rather than a federal retail tax . . . for in our opinion such a rate would not be high enough to encourage a significant evasion of a retail tax."[14] The report did not overlook the possibility that the provinces might continue to levy retail sales taxes, and that federal and provincial rates combined might total or exceed 14 percent. If, in this case, significant evasion occurred, "a federal value-added tax should be considered up to, and including, the retail level."[15] This situation was regarded by the commission to be "the only one in which a value-added form of collection could

---

[11] See, for example, Royal Ministry of Taxes and Customs, *A Survey of the Norwegian Tax System in 1970*, p. 98 ff.; Bank of Norway, *Economic Bulletin*, vol. 40 (1969), pp. 58-59.

[12] ". . . it was judged too risky to count on the small retailer for the entire tax one levied at a rate of 10 percent or more, if only because he might go bankrupt through carelessness under this heavy fiscal obligation." Carl S. Shoup, "Experience with the Value-Added Tax in Denmark, and Prospects in Sweden," in *Finanzarchiv*, Neue Folge, vol. 28, no. 2 (March 1969), p. 241.

[13] *Carter Report*, vol. 5, part A, p. 50.

[14] Ibid.

[15] Ibid.

be justified for Canada." [16] So the commission recommended that the federal government should impose a single-stage sales tax at the retail level in place of the manufacturers' sales tax. "Only if the problem of administrative control of a single-stage retail tax becomes too great, should a value-added tax be adopted." [17]

Border Tax Adjustments

Another important issue concerning the form of taxation is how it lends itself to the adjustments required in international trade. Under the value-added tax, as has been pointed out earlier, border tax adjustments can be effected with the necessary precision. Under the retail sales tax, sales of capital goods for use in production may present a problem. If these sales are taxable, as they generally were in Sweden during the RST era (the purchasing manufacturer was regarded as a "consumer" of these goods), then the goods or services produced with their help are burdened with some RST levied at a previous stage. Hence, when these goods are being exported, precise calculation of the required tax rebate may be difficult.

There are ways to get around this difficulty. If the RST system could be organized in such manner that only durable goods sold to consumers for nonbusiness purposes were taxable, then the tax treatment of export transactions would not be more difficult than it is under VAT. In fact, it would be simpler, because no border tax adjustments would be required at all. Producers' goods would leave the country tax free and unburdened by any RST from previous stages. Goods sold at retail to final consumers for nonbusiness use are not usually destined for exportation anyway, and those that occasionally are would not be carrying any previously generated tax burden when they left the country. All that would be required would be to exempt their sale to a foreign consumer from retail tax at home.

But it is not easy to organize a retail sales tax system in this way. Many durable goods are used by consumers as well as by business. To exempt them altogether would therefore exempt many sales that ought to be taxed. The device of exempting durables only when sold to business firms (on the assumption that private persons nearly always buy such goods for nonbusiness purposes) is not a satisfactory solution either. It would require many enterprises to divide their sales of otherwise identical commodities into taxable and tax-

---

[16] Ibid.
[17] Ibid., p. 53.

exempt transactions—an onerous addition to record keeping and accounting. In Sweden, awareness of these difficulties was a decisive factor in the choice of VAT over an attempt to reform the existing RST system.[18]

The report of the Canadian Royal Commission recognized that, under a retail sales tax system that extended to producers' durables, a "capricious tax element" would be embodied in the selling prices of goods produced with the help of such tax-paid producers' durables, and that "it would be impossible to remove all such built-in sales tax elements from the prices of goods exported." [19] The report recommends, therefore, that the proposed Canadian retail sales tax should be applied to consumer goods (including consumer durables), but not to equipment and construction materials used in production.[20] The difficulties of applying this distinction are not discussed. The authors of the report were undoubtedly aware of them, but, unlike those who made the final decision in Sweden, they obviously thought that they could be overcome.

Paperwork

Still another criterion for selecting a tax system is the relative burdens of record keeping that the alternatives impose. Under VAT, firms must keep tax records with respect to their purchases (in connection with the deductibility of the VAT charged by their suppliers) as well as with respect to their sales. This means much more paperwork than under RST, where only the sales side is involved.[21] Here again, retail trade poses the main question mark. As has been pointed out in an earlier chapter, the basic EEC reports and directives, while expressing the conviction that the fiscal needs of the member countries made it too risky to rely on an RST as the sole general sales tax, did permit member countries temporarily to exempt the retail stage from VAT, and to place it under a separate tax. The Royal Commission in Canada strongly emphasized the disadvantage of heavier

---

18 On the whole problem, see McLure, "Tax on Value Added," pp. 24-26. Specifically with respect to Sweden, see Norr and Hornhammar, "Value-Added Tax in Sweden," pp. 391-97.

19 *Carter Report*, p. 8.

20 Ibid.

21 As already noted, with respect to administrative costs and work load, even the gross turnover tax, for all its defects, has an advantage over the value-added tax, for business as well as government.

record-keeping requirements under the value-added tax.[22] For Canada at least, the commission obviously gave more weight to this consideration than to the argument that the evasion problem is easier to cope with under VAT. So it recommended that a federal retail sales tax be given at least a trial.

In Europe, the views from business organizations and other nongovernmental quarters had some influence, especially in countries where the decision was made by the national government and not, as in the EEC area, by a supernational agency. In Denmark, when business groups were asked for their opinions, all of them expressed a preference for the value-added tax.[23] Swedish business organizations felt the same way,[24] and welcomed the switch from RST to VAT after it had taken place.

Some European Experiences

In no European country has VAT been in operation long enough to permit a final judgment as to whether the experience has justified the decision to adopt it rather than RST. In the countries where the system has operated for a few years, little regret has been expressed that the decision went in favor of VAT.[25] To be sure, VAT could be held responsible for some increases in consumer prices during the last few years—inasmuch as in some countries its tax rates were set at levels that, for reasons discussed earlier, could hardly have been ventured for a retail sales tax. But these price increases, some of which have been analyzed in the preceding chapter, were widely regarded as inevitable, given the apparently unalterable trend towards meeting increased fiscal needs by indirect taxes at high, and rising, rates.

Following are a few notes on European experiences with VAT that shed some light on the arguments discussed in the first part of this chapter.

---

[22] "Any consideration of its adoption must take into account the large number of taxpayers involved, the increased cost and complexity of administration, and the more onerous record-keeping burden placed on taxpayers, particularly on retailers" (*Carter Report*, p. 50).

[23] Shoup, "Experience in Denmark," p. 241.

[24] Norr and Hornhammar, "Value-Added Tax in Sweden," p. 408.

[25] Some government officials and business spokesmen in West Germany have expressed satisfaction with the working of the system. See "Europe's Value-Added Tax: Model for U.S.?" *U.S. News and World Report*, March 6, 1972, pp. 75-77.

The greater requirements for record keeping by business under VAT as compared with RST may have been a problem in some instances, but there is no evidence that it was insoluble. In Sweden, "the accounting burden of the TVA was worse in prospect than it proved to be in fact." [26] The Netherlands had the same experience. There, however, the absence of difficulties probably related to the fact that small-scale firms are exempt from the tax. [27] In most of the countries where small traders *are* liable to VAT, their record-keeping and return-filing problems have been alleviated by permitting them to pay the tax at intervals longer than the prescribed general tax payment period. [28]

The higher cost and greater complexity of government administration and control under VAT as compared with single-stage sales tax systems may have created some problems in the Scandinavian countries. [29] In Sweden, a significant increase in administrative personnel proved necessary. In some countries a brief transitional period passed before business adjusted to the new requirements sufficiently to ensure a smooth flow of tax collections. In Denmark, where the changeover to VAT involved a very substantial broadening of the scope of tax liability, owing particularly to the inclusion of retail trade, a few delays in tax payment occurred during the initial phase of the new system, and some respites had to be granted. In the Netherlands, too, there were some delays of this kind in the first year after the switch. Apart from such transitional difficulties, however, nothing turned up in Europe that threatened to obstruct the functioning of the VAT mechanism. [30]

Scant empirical evidence has developed from the European experience concerning the argument that, under VAT, high tax rates can be prescribed with less risk of inviting tax evasion than under RST,

---

[26] "By international standards, Sweden had already achieved a fairly high standard of bookkeeping, even in the retail field. To minimize bookkeeping difficulties, moreover, business groups and the tax authorities as well, spent millions of kronor before the TVA went into effect to educate taxpayers to its requirements. Once the tax became effective, the problems seemed to diminish rapidly" (Norr and Hornhammar, "Value-Added Tax in Sweden," p. 408).

[27] This is the view of the Central Planning Board, as communicated by letter to the author.

[28] The extent to which small traders have made use of this option varies greatly. In France, more than 90 percent of them have done so; in West Germany, less than 50 percent, despite the fact that the standard period for VAT tax payment is only one month. See Tait, *Value-Added Taxation*, p. 155.

[29] In the EEC countries, where VAT replaced another multistage turnover tax, there was less change in this respect.

[30] In Sweden, tax collections proceeded smoothly right from the start, without any delays in tax payment.

and with better means to detect it. Such evidence could be furnished only by a country that switched from RST to VAT *and* prescribed about the same (high) tax rate at least during the last few months before the switch and the first few months afterwards. Sweden is the only country where things developed in this way. But, according to communications from that country, it is hard to tell whether the new sales tax system engendered less tax evasion than the old one.

In the light of experience to date, have the main advantages of VAT over RST—its "self-policing" feature, its greater assurance that the government will harvest the full tax amount due—outweighed its main disadvantages—the higher administrative costs and heavier work load imposed on both taxpayers and tax authorities? The expert who replied on behalf of the Dutch Central Planning Board to this last summarizing question in the information-gathering correspondence that the writer conducted with agencies in some European countries did not venture any definitive opinion on the question. The answer given by an expert of the Association of Swedish Industries was a clear-cut "yes."

The following analysis holds for any type of turnover (sales) tax system (single-stage, multistage cumulative, multistage noncumulative).

Relationship between Effective and Nominal Tax Rates

With the "effective rate" defined as a tax rate applied to the tax base exclusive of the tax itself, and the "nominal rate" as a tax rate applied to the tax base inclusive of the tax itself, the equation spelling out the mathematical relationship between effective and nominal rates that are equivalent in terms of the tax yield (revenue) obtained can be derived as follows. We denote:

B = the tax base *before* the tax·itself

r = the effective tax rate (in decimals)

$\bar{r}$ = the nominal tax rate (in decimals)

Y = the yield obtained by applying the effective tax rate

$\bar{Y}$ = the yield obtained by applying the nominal tax rate.

The desired equivalence is found by expressing Y in terms of B and r, and $\bar{Y}$ in terms of B and $\bar{r}$, and equating the two expressions. For Y we have simply

$$Y = rB. \tag{1}$$

Derivation of the corresponding expression for $\bar{Y}$ is slightly more involved. Inclusion of the tax in the tax base does not make the base simply equal to $B + \bar{r}B$, or $B(1 + \bar{r})$. Rather, the inclusion

317

leads to an infinite regression by which the tax base becomes

$$B + \bar{r}\,[B + \bar{r}\,\{B + \bar{r}\,(B + \dots \text{et cetera ad infinitum})\}\,],$$

which is equal to

$$B\,(1 + \bar{r} + \bar{r}^2 + \bar{r}^3 + \dots \bar{r}^{\infty}).$$

Since $\bar{r} < 1$, the expression in brackets is an infinite declining geometric series with common ratio $\bar{r}$. It equals

$$\frac{1}{1 - \bar{r}},$$

and the tax base inclusive of the tax is therefore

$$\frac{B}{1 - \bar{r}}.$$

For the yield obtained by applying $\bar{r}$ to this base, thus

$$\overline{Y} = B\,\frac{\bar{r}}{1 - \bar{r}}. \tag{2}$$

Given equations (1) and (2), Y and $\overline{Y}$ are equal if

$$r = \frac{\bar{r}}{1 - \bar{r}}, \tag{3}$$

or if

$$\bar{r} = \frac{r}{1 + r}. \tag{4}$$

Relationship of Increases in Nominal and Effective Rates

This section derives a proof that a given increase of a nominal tax rate is always smaller, absolutely and relatively, than the equivalent increase of the equivalent effective rate.

Absolute Increases.[1] The effective rate equivalent to $(\bar{r} + a)$ is, by equation (3),

$$\frac{\bar{r} + a}{1 - (\bar{r} + a)},$$

where

a = amount by which a given nominal tax rate $\bar{r}$ (in decimals) is being increased.

---

[1] Percentage-point increases, if tax rates are expressed in percentages.

At the same time, this rate is, again by equation (3), equal to

$$\frac{\bar{r}}{1 - \bar{r}} + x,$$

where

    $x =$ amount by which the effective tax rate equivalent to $\bar{r}$ must be increased to give the effective rate equivalent to $(\bar{r} + a)$.

Thus,

$$\frac{\bar{r} + a}{1 - (\bar{r} + a)} = \frac{\bar{r}}{1 - \bar{r}} + x.$$

Solving for x, we obtain after simplification,

$$x = \frac{a}{(1 - \bar{r} - a)(1 - \bar{r})}. \tag{5}$$

Since the denominator is smaller than 1, the expression on the right-hand side of the equation is greater than a. Hence, $a < x$. Q.E.D.

Relative Increases.[2] The effective rate equivalent to $a\bar{r}$ is, by equation (3),

$$\frac{a\bar{r}}{1 - a\bar{r}},$$

where

    $a =$ the multiple by which a given nominal tax rate $\bar{r}$ (in decimals) is being increased $(a > 1)$.

At the same time this rate is, again by equation (3), equal to

$$\frac{x\bar{r}}{1 - \bar{r}},$$

where

    $x =$ the multiple by which the effective tax rate equivalent to $\bar{r}$ must be increased to give the effective rate equivalent to $a\bar{r}$.

Thus,

$$\frac{a\bar{r}}{1 - a\bar{r}} = \frac{x\bar{r}}{1 - \bar{r}}.$$

Solving for x,

$$x = \frac{1 - \bar{r}}{1 - a\bar{r}} \cdot a. \tag{6}$$

Since, by assumption, $a > 1$, the denominator in the expression on the right-hand side of the equation is smaller than the numerator, and the quotient is therefore greater than 1. Hence $a < x$. Q.E.D.

---

[2] Percent increases, if tax rates are expressed in percentages.

The sum of the entries in column 3 of Table 2 (section on the gross turnover tax) is

$$r\,V_1 + r\,[(1+r)\,V_1 + V_2] + r\,[(1+r)^2\,V_1 + (1+r)\,V_2 + V_3]$$
$$+ \ldots r\,[(1+r)^{n-1}\,V_1 + (1+r)^{n-2}\,V_2 + \ldots + (1+r)^2\,V_{n-2}$$
$$+ (1+r)\,V_{n-1} + V_n].$$

After the brackets are broken up, and the terms rearranged, this expression becomes:

$$
\begin{array}{llll}
r\,V_1 & + r\,V_2 & \ldots & + r\,V_{n-1} & + r\,V_n \\
+\,r\,V_1\,(1+r) & + r\,V_2\,(1+r) & \ldots & + r\,V_{n-1}\,(1+r) & \\
+\,r\,V_1\,(1+r)^2 & + r\,V_2\,(1+r)^2 & & &
\end{array}
$$

$$r\,V_2\,(1+r)^{n-2}$$

$$+\,rV_1\,(1+r)^{n-1}\,.$$

Factored again, this time vertically, the expression becomes:

$$r\,V_1\,[1 + (1+r) + (1+r)^2 + \ldots\ldots (1+r)^{n-1}]$$
$$+\,r\,V_2\,[1 + (1+r) + (1+r)^2 + \ldots\ldots (1+r)^{n-2}]$$
$$\ldots\ldots\ldots\ldots\ldots\ldots\ldots\ldots\ldots\ldots\ldots\ldots\ldots\ldots\ldots\ldots$$
$$+\,r\,V_{n-1}\,[1 + (1+r)]$$
$$+\,r\,V_n.$$

The serial expressions in the brackets are geometric progressions with common ratio $(1+r)$. Their nonserial equivalents are, in succession,

$$\frac{(1+r)^n - 1}{r}\,,\ \frac{(1+r)^{n-1} - 1}{r}\,,$$

and so forth.

320

After substitution, and clearing of fractions, the expression is

$$V_1 [(1 + r)^n - 1] + V_2 [(1 + r)^{n-1} - 1] + \ldots \ldots$$
$$+ V_{n-1} [(1 + r)^2 - 1] + V_n [(1 + r) - 1],$$

which can be rearranged as

$$(1 + r)^n V_1 + (1 + r)^{n-1} V_2 \ldots \ldots + (1 + r)^2 V_{n-1} + (1 + r) V_n$$
$$- (V_1 + V_2 \ldots \ldots + V_n).$$

RICHARD E. WAGNER is associate professor of Economics, Virginia Polytechnic Institute and State University, Blacksburg, Virginia. A specialist in public finance, he was formerly a senior research associate with the Urban Institute. Prior to joining the Urban Institute, he taught economics at Tulane University and the University of California at Irvine.

ROGER A. FREEMAN is a senior fellow at the Hoover Institution on War, Revolution and Peace at Stanford University. The author of numerous books and articles in the field of public finance, he has served as a special assistant to both President Nixon and President Eisenhower, as well as in other high governmental and nongovernmental posts.

CHARLES E. McLURE, JR., is professor of economics at Rice University.

NORMAN B. TURE is president of Norman B. Ture, Inc., an economic consulting firm in Washington, D.C.

ERIC SCHIFF, formerly resident economist of the Machinery and Allied Products Institute, is an economic consultant in Washington, D.C. He is the author of a two-part study published by the American Enterprise Institute: *Incomes Policies Abroad*, Part I: *United Kingdom, the Netherlands, Sweden and Canada (1971)*; Part II: *France, West Germany, Austria, and Denmark (1973)*.